The Challenge of Third World Development

6TH EDITION

THE CHALLENGE OF THIRD WORLD DEVELOPMENT

HOWARD HANDELMAN

Emeritus Professor, University of Wisconsin–Milwaukee

Longman

Boston   Columbus   Indianapolis   New York   San Francisco   Upper Saddle River
Amsterdam   Cape Town   Dubai   London   Madrid   Milan   Munich   Paris   Montreal   Toronto
Delhi   Mexico City   Sao Paulo   Sydney   Hong Kong   Seoul   Singapore   Taipei   Tokyo

Acquisitions Editor: Vikram Mukhija
Editorial Assistant: Toni Magyar
Marketing Manager: Lindsey Prudhomme
Production Manager: Kathy Sleys
**Project Coordination, Text Design, and Electronic
  Page Makeup:** Shiny Rajesh/Integra Software Services
Creative Director: Jayne Conte
Cover Designer: Mary Siener/Bruce Kenselaar
Cover Illustration/Photo: © Philippe Lissac/CORBIS All Rights Reserved
Printer/Binder/Cover Printer: Courier Companies

Library of Congress Cataloging-in-Publication Data

Handelman, Howard
  The challenge of third world development / Howard Handelman. — 6th ed.
    p. cm.
Includes bibliographical references and index.
ISBN-13: 978-0-205-79123-1 (alk. paper)
ISBN-10: 0-205-79123-9 (alk. paper)
  1. Developing countries—Economic conditions.   2. Developing
countries—Economic policy.   3. Developing countries—Politics and
government.   4. Economic development.   I. Title.
HC59.7.H299 2010
338.9009172'4—dc22

                                                    2009048541

2 3 4 5 6 7 8 9 10—CRS—14 13 12 11

Longman
is an imprint of

PEARSON   www.pearsonhighered.com   ISBN-13: 978-0-205-79123-1
                                                          ISBN-10:   0-205-79123-9

TO KRIS AND TO THE MEMORY OF RAJESH KALIYAMBATH

Brief Contents

CONTENTS

Chapter 5

Women and Development   133

PREFACE

W hile Westerners often find the politics of developing areas (Africa, Asia, the Caribbean, Latin America, and the Middle East) difficult to comprehend, events in those regions are an inescapable part of our lives. Asia's emergence as a global economic force (especially China, India, and South Korea), wars in Iraq and Afghanistan, Islamic fundamentalism and the war on terrorism, genocidal warfare in Sudan, and emigration from the developing world are but a few of the events that draw our attention. The purpose of this book is to better understand the dynamics and challenges of political and socioeconomic changes in these Third World nations, which account for most of the world's population.

For want of a better term, I refer to the more than 150 disparate, developing nations as the "Third World" (defined in Chapter 1). They include desperately poor countries such as Afghanistan and Ethiopia and rapidly developing industrial powers such as China, South Korea, and Taiwan. Some, like Trinidad and Costa Rica, are stable democracies; others, such as Myanmar and Syria, suffer under highly repressive dictatorships. All of them, however, share at least some of the aspects of political, economic, and social underdevelopment that this book analyzes.

NEW TO THIS EDITION

Since the publication of the fifth edition of this text, there have been a number of major developments that have merited new or extended discussion in this new edition.

- As the evidence of global warming has mounted, numerous scientists warn of an impending disaster if the world's largest producers of greenhouse gas do not take action very quickly. Other experts fear that it is already too late to avert some catastrophic consequences of global warming. This issue presents a special challenge to industrializing Third World nations, which are reluctant to take environmental measures that might slow economic growth and condemn many of their citizens to continued poverty.
- The current global economic crisis originated in the United States and spread to a number of European nations that were highly involved in the global financial bubble, including Ireland, Iceland, and several Balkan nations. But the resulting economic slowdown in all of the world's industrialized nations has had devastating spillover effects on much of the developing world as well.
- While the expansion of democracy to many less developed countries (LDCs) in recent decades (part of the Third Wave) has been impressive, the rate of democratization has slowed appreciably and there have been a number of reversions to authoritarianism. Chapter 2 presents analysis of one stumbling block that has apparently blocked democratization in a number of relatively more affluent Third World countries, the so-called "curse of oil wealth."
- The winding down of the U.S.-led coalition's military involvement in Iraq and the corresponding escalation of the war in Afghanistan have had continuing effects on

ethnic relations within those two countries and on the West's relationship with the Muslim world.

- While the war against terrorism and U.S. military involvement have focused on Iraq and, now, Afghanistan, only recently has the Western media's spotlight shined on Pakistan. As the home to Al Qaeda's top leadership and with its own powerful Taliban organization, Pakistan is a major terrorist target. The country's history of ethnic division, government corruption, and political instability makes it vulnerable. The possibility of a Taliban–Al Qaeda victory in Pakistan is particularly chilling because the country is a nuclear power. A number of chapters in this edition (on Democracy, Religion, Cultural Pluralism, Women and Development, and Soldiers and Politics) analyze aspects of Pakistani political and economic development.
- Barack Obama's election to the presidency of the world's major superpower has brought a number of policy changes that impact the developing countries and are discussed at various points in this edition. One of these areas more extensively discussed in this edition is the threat of global warming, particularly its relationship to the Third World.

FEATURES

No text is capable of fully examining the political and socioeconomic systems of so many highly diverse countries. Instead, we will look for common issues, problems, and potential solutions. We start in Chapter 1 by exploring the nature of political, social, and economic underdevelopment, and then analyze the leading theories attempting to explain underdevelopment and development. Besides updating information on social, economic, and political conditions in the LDCs, this edition introduces several contemporary approaches to the study of underdevelopment including postmodernism and antidevelopmentalism. Another new section briefly summarizes the developing world's economic, social, and political progress in recent decades, as well as its ongoing or worsening problems.

Chapter 2 discusses what has been arguably the most important political change in world politics during the late twentieth and early twenty-first centuries—the wave of democratic transitions that has swept over the developing nations of Africa, Asia, Latin America, and the Middle East (as well as southern Europe and the former Soviet bloc of nations). Because these often still-fragile transitions from authoritarian to democratic government are potentially so important, the chapters that follow discuss how democratization is likely to influence issues such as the level of ethnic conflict, the role of women in the political system, and the nature of economic development. This edition contains new information on contemporary attitudes toward democracy in the Third World. It also discusses the so-called "the curse of oil wealth" and the way in which petroleum-based economic growth has a counterintuitive effect on political development.

Chapters 3–5 on religion and politics, ethnic conflict, and women and development analyze religious, ethnic, and gender issues that have often divided developing nations, but also provide identities that can be helpful in the processes of political and economic development. This edition discusses recent events in Afghanistan, Iran, and Lebanon that affect ethnic relations within the Muslim world and influence the ongoing challenge of Islamic fundamentalism. Other new topics include the growth of European-based Islamic terrorism, but also the emergence of moderate Islamic alternatives in countries such as Indonesia and Singapore.

Chapters 6 and 7 on rural change and urbanization discuss the specific problems and challenges that LDCs face in those two sectors of society. This edition includes updated and expanded analysis of Third World urban growth, the advanced economic nations' millennium development goals to improve rural conditions in the developing world, and the expansion of integrated rural development.

Next, Chapters 8 and 9 on revolutionary change and on soldiers and politics consider the records of each of those regime types (such as, revolutionary governments in China and Cuba, as well as military regimes in Brazil and Indonesia) as alternative models of political and economic development. This edition includes updated data on military expenditures, analysis of attempts to improve civil–military relations, and discussion of the new efforts by the Organization of American States (OAS) and the African Union (AU) to curb military coups in Latin America and Africa.

Finally, Chapter 10, dealing with Third World political economies, compares alternative paths to economic development, and evaluates the relative effectiveness of each. This edition contains new discussion of the current global economic crisis, as well as expanded analysis of globalization and global warming.

It is easy to despair when considering the tremendous obstacles facing most developing nations and the failures of political leadership that so many of them have endured. Unfortunately, many inhabitants of the First World have suffered from "compassion fatigue" or have become cynical about cooperative efforts with Third World countries. The assaults on the World Trade Center and the Pentagon in 2001 and the subsequent wars in Afghanistan and Iraq have reinforced many people's perception of developing nations as poor beyond redemption, politically unstable, authoritarian, and prone to religious and political fanaticism. Yet the recent burgeoning of democracy, the decline in military rule, and the enormous economic growth that has taken place in parts of the Third World all provide new bases for hope. It is incumbent upon the West's next generation of citizens and leaders to renew efforts to understand the challenge of Third World development.

SUPPLEMENTS

For Instructors and Students

MyPoliSciKit Video Case Studies   This DVD series contains video clips featured on MyPoliSciKit for this and other Longman political science titles. Featuring video from major news sources and providing reporting and insight on recent world affairs, this DVD helps instructors integrate current events into their courses by letting them use the clips as lecture launchers or discussion starters.

For Students

MySearchLab (0-205-71936-8) Need help with a paper? MySearchLab saves time and improves results by offering start-to-finish guidance on the research/writing process and full-text access to academic journals and periodicals. Order MySearchLab with this book and receive a 15 percent discount.

Longman Atlas of World Issues (0-321-22465-5) Introduced and selected by Robert J. Art of Brandeis University and excerpted from the acclaimed Penguin Atlas Series, the *Longman Atlas of World Issues* is designed to help students understand the geography and major issues facing the world today, such as terrorism, debt, and HIV/AIDS. These thematic, full-color maps examine forces shaping politics today at a global level. Explanatory information accompanies each map to help students better grasp the concepts being shown and how they affect our world today. Available at no additional charge when packaged with this book.

ACKNOWLEDGMENTS

Because of the broad geographic and conceptual scope of any book on Third World politics, I am particularly indebted to others for their kind help and advice.

I would like to thank the many people at Prentice Hall and Longman who have worked with me through six editions of this book. I particularly appreciate Longman's Vikram Mukhija and Toni Magyar for their guidance and support on this edition. Also, my thanks to the project coordinator, Shiny Rajesh of Integra Software Services, who was a pleasure to work with.

My greatest debt is to the scholars who generously agreed to read portions of the manuscript of the first edition and whose insights continue to guide subsequent editions. They include Lourdes Benería (Cornell University), Josef Gugler (University of Connecticut), Stephan Haggard (University of California–San Diego), Kathleen Staudt (University of Texas–El Paso), Mark Tessler (University of Michigan), William Thiesenhusen (University of Wisconsin–Madison), and M. Crawford Young (University of Wisconsin–Madison). Thanks also to Longman's reviewers: Michael Fleet (Marquette University), Wendy Hunter (University of Texas–Austin), David Penna (Gallaudet University), and Susan Walcott (University of North Carolina–Greensboro). The quality of the manuscript benefited enormously from their many insights, suggestions, and corrections. The usual caveat, of course, applies: Any remaining errors of fact or interpretation are my own responsibility.

Howard Handelman
Professor Emeritus
University of Wisconsin–Milwaukee

CHAPTER 1

UNDERSTANDING UNDERDEVELOPMENT

Most Americans focus infrequently on the less developed countries (LDCs) of Africa, Asia, the Middle East, the Caribbean, and Latin America. Media coverage of these countries is sporadic and tends to concentrate on tragedies or disturbances of various magnitudes—a devastating earthquake in China, civil war in Sri Lanka, ethnic conflict in Darfur (Sudan) and Congo, and political repression in Syria. To almost any observer, the problems currently plaguing the developing world appear daunting. Warfare, internal violence, and massive human suffering beset the most troubled countries in these regions: insurgency and religious intolerance in Afghanistan; poverty and revolutionary conflict in Colombia; ethnically based massacres in Iraq and Nigeria; and political repression in Zimbabwe and Myanmar (Burma). Of course, many of those problems exist in industrialized democracies as well, though in a milder form. For example, in recent times, both Northern Ireland and the Basque region of Spain have experienced ethnic violence and terrorism. Portions of Washington, DC have higher infant mortality rates than do Cuba and Singapore. Nevertheless, it is the scope and persistence of the developing world's political, economic, and social challenges that ultimately draw our attention.

Understanding the nature and causes of underdevelopment is a complex task complicated by theoretical debates between scholars and a profusion of terminology. There is not even agreement on a collective name for the approximately 150 countries that constitute the developing world. At one time, it was common to call these countries *underdeveloped nations*. However, many found this title objectionable, suggesting, as it did, that those countries' political and economic systems were backward. Because of its pejorative connotations and implied inferiority, the adjective *underdeveloped* fell into disfavor. Instead, many political scientists prefer using the term *developing nations (areas)*. Though clearly more positive, this term unfortunately suffers from the opposite problem—excessive optimism about the prospects of many countries.

At various times during the 1970s and 1980s, most African and Latin American countries suffered from political and economic decay, and today many remain trapped in the worldwide recession, often laboring under repressive governments. Countries such as Congo, Haiti, and Cambodia still show few signs of forward progress in any dimension. In short, for many years, a number of so-called "developing countries" have experienced very little political or economic development. Hence, the United Nations and many other international organizations favor the label *less developed countries* (or LDCs), an expression that escapes the normative flaws of its competitors.

Many social scientists prefer the term *Third World countries* (or simply, *the Third World*), and this is the label most frequently employed in this book.[1] It has both the virtue and defect of being somewhat fuzzy. Simply put, Third World countries are the nations of Africa, Asia, the Middle East, Latin America, and the Caribbean that do not belong to the First World—Japan and the Western industrialized democracies that were the first countries to develop advanced industrial economies and liberal democracies.* Nor were they part of the now-defunct Second World—the bloc of former communist nations that included the Soviet Union and Eastern Europe.† Thus, "Third World" is essentially a residual category. Countries fall under its banner not because of any specific quality, but simply because they are not members of either the First or Second World. Like the previously discussed classifications, "Third World" glosses over the many political and socioeconomic differences among its members, placing all of them under one big tent. Of course, in reality they differ considerably. A few (including Taiwan and Kuwait) are relatively affluent, while many others (such as Afghanistan, Yemen, and Malawi) are desperately poor. Some (Barbados, Costa Rica, and India) are stable democracies. Many others, however, suffer from severe political instability, government repression, and other manifestations of political underdevelopment.

Therefore, like any residual category, the term *Third World* suffers from a degree of imprecision. Its virtue, however, is that unlike the terms *underdeveloped nations* and *developing nations*, it makes no value judgment or predictions. As one author writes, paraphrasing Winston Churchill's comments on democracy, "It is the worst term we have, except for all the others."[2] With some irony, Christopher Clapham has written, "I have chosen to use the term [Third World] because of its meaninglessness. Its alternatives all carry conceptual overtones which are even more misleading, in that they imply positive elements of commonality rather than a simply negative residual category."[3] Taking a less cynical position than Clapham, I maintain in the next section that, despite their many differences, there are enough commonalities among Third World countries to make the category useful. Of course, one may argue that the collapse of Soviet bloc Communism (the Second World) made the term *Third World* anachronistic. Nevertheless, I continue to use the term because I feel that it is conceptually useful and is still comprehensible to readers.

In order to avoid repetitious usage, throughout this book, I interchangeably use the terms *Third World*, *less developed countries* (or LDCs), *developing countries* (*nations*), and *developing world*.

THIRD WORLD COMMONALITIES:
THE NATURE OF UNDERDEVELOPMENT

Despite the substantial differences among them, Third World nations still share a number of common characteristics. All of them suffer from some aspects of political, economic, or social underdevelopment. Although some of East Asia's

---

* The term *liberal democracy* indicates that the political system not only enjoys freely contested elections but also respects civil liberties such as free speech, freedom of the press, and religious freedom. For more on different aspects of democracy, see Chapter 2.

† In this and other books, the Third World includes non-European communist nations such as China, Cuba, and Vietnam, which resemble other developing nations on many dimensions.

newly industrializing countries (NICs)—South Korea, Singapore, and Taiwan—are no longer *economically* underdeveloped, they still share a high vulnerability to global economic forces (as evidenced by today's global economic crisis) and continue to suffer from aspects of political underdevelopment. On the other hand, Costa Rica and Botswana are relatively well developed politically and socially, but manifest a number of the problems of economic underdevelopment. In short, while some Third World countries are underdeveloped in all major aspects of modernization, others are far more advanced in some aspects of development than in others. As we shall see, economic, social, and political underdevelopment are closely related to each other, but they are certainly not perfectly correlated. The basic disciplinary approach of this text is Political Science. However, the text will also draw on theories and research from Anthropology, Sociology, and, especially, Economics.

Economic Underdevelopment

Perhaps the most salient characteristic of most developing countries is their poverty. At the national level, this is manifested by some combination of low gross domestic product (GDP) per capita (an indirect measure of per-capita income), highly unequal income distribution, poor infrastructure (including communications and transportation), limited use of modern technology, and low consumption of energy.* At the grassroots level, economic underdevelopment connotes widespread scarcity, substantial unemployment, substandard housing, poor health conditions, and inadequate nutrition.

While Third World countries are generally much poorer than countries in Western Europe and North America, there is also considerable variation among them and between world regions. Table 1.1 compares per-capita incomes and economic growth rates of the developing world's major regions. As the second column indicates, the world's economically advanced nations have per-capita

TABLE 1.1   Economic Production and Growth (by Region)

Region	GDP per Capita (PPP)($)	Rate of Economic Growth: 1990–2005 (%)
Developed Nations	29,197	1.8
Developing Nations	5,282	3.1
Arab States	6,716	2.3
East Asia and the Pacific	6,604	5.8
Latin America and the Caribbean	8,407	1.2
South Asia	3,416	3.5
Sub-Saharan Africa	1,998	0.5

Source: United Nations Development Programme (UNDP), *Human Development Report 2007/2008*, Human Development Indicators, Table 14, http://hdr.undp.org/en/media/HDR_20072008_EN_Complete.pdf

---

* GDP is a measure similar to gross national product (GNP)—the indicator most frequently used in the United States—but it excludes "net factor income from abroad." Economists and international agencies generally use GDP, rather than GNP, for comparing the economies of various countries.

incomes that are more than five times as high as the LDCs as a whole, more than twice as high as Latin America, and nearly 15 times higher than sub-Saharan Africa. At the same time, however, between 1990 and 2005, Third World economies grew at an annual rate of 3.1 percent, almost three times faster than the highly industrialized nations. But rates of development varied considerably between regions. East Asian nations, led by China with steady double-digit growth, had by far the fastest rate of growth (5.8 percent). By contrast, while Latin America and the Caribbean retained the highest per-capita incomes of any Third World region, their rates of economic growth were very anemic (not even keeping up with population growth). Worse yet, sub-Saharan Africa not only is the poorest region, with a per-capita income less than one-third of East Asia's, but it experienced virtually no growth in that period, with a rate far lower than its population growth. Since the global recession began in 2008, the rates of economic growth in most of these regions have slowed considerably.

Table 1.2 moves from the economic performance of Third World regions to an examination of a sample of individual countries in each of those areas. It offers a more comprehensive vision of economic underdevelopment by examining several variables besides per-capita income. The cases selected compare economic conditions in two highly developed countries (United States and Iceland), one affluent Third World country (Singapore), three middle-income nations—two of them in Latin America (Mexico and Brazil) and one in Asia (China); two lower-middle-income countries—one in Asia (India) and one in the Middle East (Egypt); and two impoverished African countries (Ethiopia and Nigeria). The second column in the table *GDP per capita* (i.e., *per-capita income*) indicates the annual dollar value of goods and services produced per

TABLE 1.2   Measures of Economic Development (by Country)

Country	GDP ("Income") per Capita (PPP)($)	Probability at Birth of Not Surviving to the Age of 40 (%)	Population Living on Less Than $2 a Day (the Poverty Line) (%)	Income Ratio— Richest 20% to Poorest 20% of the Population
United States	41,890	NA	—a	8.4
Iceland	36,510	NA	—a	3.9
Singapore	29,663	1.8	—a	9.7
Mexico	10,751	5.8	20.4	12.8
Brazil	8,402	11.4	21.2	23.7
China	6,757	9.1	46.7	10.7
Egypt	4,337	7.5	43.9	5.1
India	3,452	16.6	79.9	4.9
Nigeria	1,128	39.0	92.4	9.7
Ethiopia	1,055	33.3	77.8	4.3

NA—no data available

aEither nonexistent or the percentage is too small to be counted.

Source: United Nations Development Programme (UNDP), *Human Development Report 2007/2008: Fighting Climate Change: Human Solidarity in a Divided World*, Human Development Indicators, Tables 1 and 3, http://hdr.undp.org/en/media/HDR_20072008_EN_Complete.pdf

person.* The data illustrate both the tremendous gap in living standards between most First and Third World countries and the considerable variation within the developing world. On the one hand, they indicate that the average American earns some *four to five* times as much as a typical Mexican or Brazilian. At the same time, however, Mexicans and Brazilians earn about *eight* times more than the average Nigerian or Ethiopian and per-capita incomes in a few developing nations, most notably Singapore and Hong Kong, nearly equal that of Britain, Germany, or Japan (which are not shown in the table).

While per-capita income is a useful indicator of a nation's living standard, it does not give us a complete picture because it fails to take into account how equitably that income is distributed. For example, hypothetically two nations may have the same per-capita incomes, say $20,000 annually. However, in country "A," 40 percent of the population is poor, with annual incomes lower than $7,000, while the wealthiest 25 percent of the populace has an average income of $55,000. In country "B," with the same overall average income, earnings are far more evenly distributed, with almost everyone making between $15,000 and $25,000 annually. Thus, while the countries have the same *average* incomes, country A has far more people who are poor.

The remaining columns in Table 1.2 better reveal the nature or income distribution and the extent of poverty in each country. In the least developed Third World countries, a significant proportion of the population dies of disease or malnutrition before reaching the age of five and many others die in the next 35 years. Column 3 indicates the percentage of the population that fails to live to the age of 40. Since people dying before that age are generally very poor, these figures are a good measure of the degree of severe deprivation in a particular country, but also reflect sanitary conditions (especially the availability of clean water), the quality of public health services, and the rate of death by AIDS or by war.[†] Not surprisingly, countries with higher per-capita incomes tend to have lower mortality rates. Furthermore, in about 10 less developed nations not shown in this table (mostly in sub-Saharan Africa), life expectancy has declined tragically in recent decades because of high rates of HIV/AIDS.

As expected, the percentage of the population dying young is highest among the poorest countries in the table. Thus, while less than 2 percent of Singapore's population and less than 6 percent of all Mexicans die before the age of 40, more than one-third of all Nigerians and Ethiopians (between 33 and 39 percent) die young. But other factors beyond income influence a nation's mortality. For example, Table 1.2 indicates that the average person in China earns significantly less (about $1,700 less) than the typical Brazilian (column 2). Furthermore, the percentage of Chinese living below the poverty line is more than twice as high as in Brazil (column 4). Yet, Brazilians have a higher proportion of early deaths. This seeming anomaly is at least partially explained by China's more extensive public health services—particularly for

---

* "Per-capita income" (column 2) refers to "real gross domestic product (GDP) per capita based on parity purchasing power (PPP)." This is a measure of economic production per person, statistically adjusted to each country's cost of living. PPP adjustments allow a more meaningful comparison of what per-capita incomes in different countries can actually purchase.

† Because the number of people that die before age 40 in affluent nations, such as the United States and Iceland, is negligible, those countries do not gather that statistic.

the poor—and its superior sanitary conditions (including greater access to clean drinking water). But Brazil's highly concentrated income distribution, one of the most unequal in the world, also contributes (column 5). Such inconsistencies also exist in comparisons with other developing nations not shown in Table 1.2. For example, Nigeria's per-capita income is only a bit below Senegal's. But its citizens are more than twice as likely to die before the age of 40. And, while Trinidad-Tobago's per-capita income is nearly three and one-half times as high as in Cuba's, its population is nearly three times as likely to die by the age of 40.

In 2008, the World Bank estimated that 3.14 billion people in the LDCs (over half the Third World's population) lived in poverty (recently redefined as living on less than $2.50 a day, rather than the previously used definition of $2 per day).[4] Not surprisingly, countries with the lowest per-capita incomes have the most pervasive poverty. So, for example, column 4 shows that practically no one fell below the poverty line in Singapore, while almost half the Chinese population (46.7 percent) and almost 80 percent of Ethiopians and Indians did. Once again, however, while per-capita income had a *negative correlation* with poverty, that correlation was not absolute.* For example, countries such as Nigeria and India have particularly pervasive poverty compared with countries with comparable average incomes (Ethiopia and Egypt). And, although Egypt's average income is far lower than China's, its poverty rate is slightly lower. Indeed, despite their impressive rates of economic growth in the past 30 years, China and India—Asia's two economic giants (and home to more than one-third of the world's population)—have almost one-half (China) to 80 percent (India) of their respective populations mired in poverty. Although rapid economic modernization has benefited many of those countries' city dwellers, it has so far only slightly improved the lives of rural villagers, who still account for some two-thirds of each nation's population.

As we have noted, a country's rate of poverty and mortality tends to reflect both its per-capita income *and* its degree of economic inequality. The last column in Table 1.2 offers a direct measure of how equally or unequally income is distributed in each country. These figures indicate the ratio of the average incomes of the richest 20 percent of the population ("the rich") to the poorest 20 percent ("the poor"). For example, the 8.4 figure for the United States indicates that the richest 20 percent of all Americans earn more than eight times as much as the poorest 20 percent do, one of the highest levels of inequality among highly industrialized nations. In Iceland, on the other hand, the income ratio is less than 4 to 1, one of the smallest income gaps in the world (a distinction also shared by the Nordic countries of Denmark, Finland, Norway, and Sweden).

It is widely believed that income is more equitably distributed in economically advanced nations than in LDCs (i.e., the gap between rich and poor is greater in the Third World). While that is generally true, there are many exceptions. For example, the poor in the United States surely are better off economically than their Third World counterparts in terms of income, diet,

---

* A positive correlation (or simply a correlation) between two measures means that as one factor goes up the other factor generally also does. A *negative* correlation means that as one factor (such as income) rises, the other one (e.g., poverty) declines.

education, health care, and housing. Yet Table 1.2 reveals that, contrary to stereotype, the income gaps between the rich and poor in Ethiopia, Egypt, and India are actually narrower than in the United States.* At the same time, once again there is considerable variation between different developing nations. While Egypt, Ethiopia, and India have relatively low degrees of income inequality, the income gaps within Brazil and other LDCs not shown here (such as South Africa and Colombia) are enormous.

If developing nations have greatly varying degrees of income inequality, does the same hold true for Third World regions? Looking at the World Bank's latest data, we can discover the share of each region's income that is earned by the richest 20 percent of the population and compare it to the share going to the poorest 20 percent. Latin America's income concentration is greatest with a ratio of almost 20:1 (i.e., the average income of a person in the richest 20 percent of the population is 19.7 times as high as somebody in the lowest 20 percent). Sub-Saharan Africa follows close behind with a ration of almost 17:1. On the other end of the spectrum, although South Asia (primarily made up of India, Pakistan, and Bangladesh) is one of the poorest regions in the world, it has by far the most equitable income distribution, with a ratio of less than 5:1 between the top and bottom quintiles of the population.[†] In fact, income is slightly more equitably distributed in South Asia than in the highly industrialized countries. East Asia and the Middle East fall in the middle with ratios of about 9:1.[5]

Turning back to Table 1.2, two of the countries, Brazil and Mexico (Latin America's most populated countries), have extremely highly concentrated income patterns, as do Colombia, Chile, Panama, and several other nations in that region. In part, Latin America's income concentration traces back to the Spanish conquest, when the colonial administrators transferred large amounts of land from the Native American population to large, Spanish-owned haciendas. By contrast, both South and East Asia's far more even distribution of farmland contributed to a general pattern of more equitable income distribution.

Social Underdevelopment

Third World poverty tends to correlate with poor social conditions such as high infant mortality and low literacy rates, which in turn narrow opportunities for human development in other areas. If LDCs are to modernize and develop economically, politically, and socially, they must extend and improve their educational systems. An educated workforce—from farmers who can read instruction manuals to trained professionals—contributes to higher labor productivity. Moreover, improved education also expands mass political participation and contributes to greater government accountability to the governed. Thus, not surprisingly, political scientists have found that countries with higher literacy rates are more likely to attain and maintain democratic government.[6]

---

* Even though the gap between rich and poor is greater in the United States than in India, the poor in the United States are clearly better off because their actual income level and standard of living are far higher than those of their counterparts in India. If we think of income distribution as shares of an economic pie, the poor in India get a larger share (percentage) of their country's pie, but the total Indian pie is far smaller than the American pie.

† A quintile is one-fifth (20 percent) of the population.

TABLE 1.3   Measures of Social Development (by Country)

Country	HDI (rank)	Life Expectancy at Birth	Adult Literacy (Percent Age 15 and Above)	Per-Capita GDP Rank minus HDI Rank
United States	.951 (8)	77.9	99.9	−10
Iceland	.968 (1)	81.5	99.9	4
Hong Kong	.937 (26)	81.9	94.6	−14
Cuba	.838 (51)	77.7	99.8	43
Mexico	.829 (52)	75.6	91.6	7
Brazil	.792 (70)	71.7	88.6	−3
China	.777 (81)	72.5	90.9	5
Turkey	.775 (84)	71.4	87.4	−18
Tunisia	.766 (91)	73.5	74.3	−23
India	.619 (128)	63.7	61.0	−11
Ghana	.553 (135)	59.1	57.9	−1
Nigeria	.470 (158)	46.5	69.1	4

Source: UNDP, *Human Development Report 2007/2008*, Human Development Indicators, Table 1, http://hdr.undp.org/en/media/HDR_20072008_EN_Complete.pdf.

Table 1.3 presents data on several important indicators of social development for two highly developed nations (the United States and Iceland) and a number of LDCs. The second column lists each country's Human Development Index (HDI), a composite measure of school enrollment, adult literacy, life expectancy, and per-capita income (GDP). Many development specialists consider the HDI to be the best single measure of a nation's quality of life. The highest possible HDI score a country may achieve is 1.000 and the lowest is .000 (though, in real life, no country is at either of those extremes). Next to each country's raw HDI score, column 2 also shows (in parenthesis) its HDI *ranking* relative to other countries in the world. For example, Iceland's HDI score of .968 is the highest in the world, while Nigeria's HDI of .470 ranks 158th of the 177 countries for which data exist. Some developing countries (such as Mexico, Cuba, and, especially, Hong Kong) have relatively high indices, placing them in the top third of *all* nations with available scores.* In fact, their scores are not far behind those of European nations such as Portugal, Lithuania, and Bulgaria (not shown in the table). On the other hand, many South Asian and African countries—such as India, Ghana, and Nigeria—have very low HDI scores, reflecting a combination of deprivation, poor health conditions, and inadequate educational systems.

The next two columns, life expectancy and adult literacy, present two of the factors used to calculate a country's HDI. Life expectancy is largely determined by a nation's rate of infant mortality and by the rate of infectious disease and malnutrition among adults. From the 1960s to the 1990s, life expectancy increased impressively in most LDCs following a number of

---

* Hong Kong is officially part of China and must follow Beijing's dictates. But it maintains its own capitalist economic system and reports its own economic statistics. Hence, we will call it a "country."

national and international campaigns against infectious diseases (such as malaria and smallpox), improved sanitary conditions (including broader access to clean drinking water), and other advances. But, progress slowed considerably or even reversed itself slightly since the 1990s, partly because many developing countries have already achieved substantial improvements in areas such as infant mortality, sanitation, inoculation against infectious diseases and had little room to move higher. More importantly, the AIDS pandemic has reduced life expectancy by as much as 20 years in the most severely affected countries. Any further longevity gains in those countries will require reducing the HIV/AIDS rate, improving nutritional levels and providing better medical care.

As Table 1.3 reveals, some developing countries—most notably Cuba, Mexico, and especially Hong Kong—now have achieved life expectancies that are almost as long as or even longer than the United States. However, others, such as India, Ghana, and especially Nigeria, lag far behind. In some impoverished, AIDS-ravished countries such as Botswana, Malawi, Zambia, and Zimbabwe (not shown in the table), life expectancy has plunged below 40 years. For most LDCs, not as highly affected by AIDS, future increases in life expectancy will require further progress in reducing infant mortality rates. Despite many advances in this regard, some 12–13 million children under the age of 5 years still die annually in the developing world.[7]

Column 4 indicates each country's adult literacy rates. These too have improved impressively in recent years in most of the Third World. Indeed, the table shows that countries such as China, Hong Kong, Mexico, and especially Cuba have adult literacy levels (all of them over 90 percent) that approach those of developed nations such as the Britain and the United States. At the same time, however, a number of countries in Africa, the Middle East, and South Asia (such as India and Ghana) have literacy levels near or below 60 percent. Life expectancy and literacy are particularly valuable indicators of development because, unlike per-capita income, they are not distorted by highly skewed distributions.

Finally, although economic development usually improves social indicators, government policies significantly affect the extent to which economic growth produces social development. In other words, two countries with equivalent levels of wealth and economic growth may have very different records in education and health care because one country's government is more effective than the other in collecting taxes, avoiding corruption, and allocating a larger share of its public spending to health care, sanitation, and education. Column 5 compares a country's worldwide ranking for per-capita "real income" (income adjusted for cost of living) with its rank for HDI. For example, Iceland has only the world's 5th highest per-capita income yet enjoys the world's highest HDI (again, a composite index of income, education, and life expectancy). Subtracting its HDI ranking from its income ranking, it receives a score of 4 ($5 - 1 = 4$) as shown in the last column. Countries with substantial positive scores in that column are "overachievers" in the sense that their HDI ranks are higher than we would have predicted based solely on their income rankings. Overachievers in Table 1.3 include Nigeria (4), China (5), Mexico (7), and especially Cuba (43). On the other hand, countries whose HDI rankings are significantly lower than their per-capita income ranks would be "underachievers"—with negative scores—having scored more poorly on their HDI ranking than their per-capita income would predict. These include the United States (−10), Hong Kong (−14), Turkey (−18), and Tunisia (−23). The governments of "overachievers" presumably have a special commitment to education and public health. Conversely, a negative score indicates a nation's failure to fully translate available economic resources into an improved quality of life. Cuba's score (+43) makes it the world's greatest "overachiever." The world's greatest underachievers currently are the countries whose life expectancy has been drastically reduced by AIDS, including Botswana (−70), South Africa (−65), and Namibia (−47). Among nations with low rates of AIDS, major underachievers include Tunisia (−23), Iran (−23), Algeria (−22), and Saudi Arabia (−19). All of these, along with several other major underachievers, are Muslim countries whose HDI scores were probably below expectations because they offered lower educational opportunities to women. Countries whose economies depend heavily on oil exports—including Algeria, Iran, and Saudi Arabia as well as several non-Muslim nations—also tend to be HDI underachievers.

Despite economic declines in Africa and Latin America during the 1980s and early 1990s, in East Asia in the late 1990s, and most LDCs since 2008, the Third World has enjoyed considerable social development in the past 40–50 years. For example, adult illiteracy is almost two-thirds below its 1965 rate, falling from 59 to about 21 percent. Improved health care and sanitation have helped reduce infant mortality rates by 60 percent. This, in turn, helped raise life expectancy from 53.4 years in 1960 to some 65 years today.* In 1950, people living in economically advanced countries could expect to live 25 years longer than Third World inhabitants. By 2008, however, that gap had been halved to about 12 years. Of course, life expectancy increased in both developed and developing nations, but advances were more dramatic in the LDCs.

At the same time, the United Nations Development Program (UNDP) estimates that the level of Third World poverty fell faster in the last half of the twentieth century than it had in the previous 500 years combined. However, despite these gains, many in the Third World still face a bleak future. As we have noted, the World Bank estimates that 3.14 billion people currently live in poverty (using the recently revised poverty line of $2.50 daily). Almost half of them—1.4 billion people—live in "absolute poverty" (also recently adjusted to $1.25 per day). About 60 percent of those in poverty failed to consume the minimum recommended number of calories daily. In addition, 28,000 Third World children under the age of 5 years are still dying each day. Currently, life expectancy in 17 countries worldwide is less than 50 years. Of those, all but one (Afghanistan) are in sub-Saharan Africa (again, partially because of the high incidents of AIDS).[8] Furthermore, the current worldwide economic crisis has hit many LDCs particularly hard, though Third World giants, China and India, had resumed vigorous growth by mid-2009, far more quickly than the world's wealthiest nations.

---

* All life expectancy gains occurred between 1960 and 1990. Since that time, the AIDS pandemic has reduced life expectancy in a number of sub-Saharan nations and in parts of Asia. As a result, life expectancy is now only 50 years in sub-Saharan Africa, compared to 73 in Latin America and 77 in developed nations. Population Reference Bureau, *2009 World Population Data Sheet*, http://www.prb.org/pdf08/08WPDS_Eng.pdf.

TABLE 1.4   Quality of Life/Social Indicators (by Region)

Region	Life Expectancy		Child Malnutrition: Percent of Children Under Age Five	Child Mortality: Deaths per 1,000 of Children Under Age Five	Percent of Children Who Complete Primary School
	Male	*Female*			
East Asia and the Pacific	69	73	13.3	29	98
Latin America and the Caribbean	70	76	5.1	26	100
Middle East and North Africa	68	72	NA	42	90
South Asia	63	66	41.3	83	80
Sub-Saharan Africa	49	52	26.8	157	60

NA—no data available

Source: World Bank, *World Development Report 2009*: *Reshaping Economic Geography*, Select World Development Indicators, Tables 1 and 2, http://econ.worldbank.org/WBSITE/EXTERNAL/ . . .

Table 1.4 reveals the substantial socioeconomic differences between Third World *regions*. Despite relatively slow economic growth since the 1980s (about 2.5 percent annually) and several sharp economic downturns during that period, Latin America still leads the developing world for all of the indicators in the table, from life expectancy to completion of primary education. However, East Asia, the world's fastest-growing regional economy (about 7 percent annually since the 1980s), has closed the gap considerably and will probably soon match or pass Latin America in all of the categories except child malnutrition. In recent decades, economic growth has accelerated dramatically in South Asia (over 5 percent annually), but the region's social and economic indicators still lag well behind Latin America's and East Asia's, with child mortality rates approximately three times theirs and the world's highest rate of child malnutrition (over 41 percent) some eight times higher than in Latin America. Finally, although sub-Saharan economies have been growing by some 5 percent annually from 2003 until the 2008 economic crisis (after decades of decline), the region's socioeconomic indicators continue to trail the rest of the developing world, most dramatically in life expectancy (column 2). And, while its recorded level of child malnutrition is well below South Asia's, its child mortality rate is well above any other region (about twice as high as South Asia and more than five times greater than East Asia and Latin America).

Political Underdevelopment

When Western political scientists began to study the Third World systematically, they soon recognized that evaluating political systems in cultural and socioeconomic settings very different from their own was extremely challenging. While many modernization theorists believed that Third World governments should model themselves after Western industrialized democracies, they were also mindful of important differences between the regions that limited that possibility.

For example, recognizing that most Western European countries did not fully democratize until they were well along the path to industrial development, scholars were often reluctant to criticize authoritarian governments in countries still at the early stages of economic development. A number of African social scientists added to the debate by arguing that their continent had extensive village- and tribal-based democracy that adequately substituted for competitive elections at the national level. Others feared that, in the ethnically divided countries of Africa and Asia, multiparty systems would inevitably develop along ethnic lines, further contributing to national disintegration.

Conscious of such land mines, many political scientists suggested political standards that they felt were free of ideological and cultural biases. Political development, they suggested, involves the creation of specialized and differentiated government institutions that effectively carry out necessary functions, such as collecting tax revenues, defending national borders, maintaining political stability, stimulating economic development, improving the quality of human life, and communicating with the citizenry. In addition, they argued, developed governments must be responsive to a broad segment of society and respect the population's fundamental freedoms and civil rights. Presumably, any government satisfying these standards would enjoy a reasonable level of *legitimacy* (i.e., its own citizens would endorse its right to govern), encouraging individuals and groups to pursue their political objectives peacefully through established political institutions rather than through violent or illegal channels.

But while analysts agreed that governments should be responsive, representative, and nonrepressive, many of them also believed that a political system could be considered developed even if it was not democratic, at least as that term has been defined in the West. Accepted definitions of full democracy generally encompass the following basic components: honest and competitive elections in which opposition parties have a realistic chance of winning; universal or nearly universal adult suffrage; widespread opportunities for political participation; free and open mass media; and government respect for human rights, including minority rights.[9] As we have seen, many political scientists initially felt that it was unrealistic and perhaps culturally biased to expect democracy to quickly flourish in developing countries. Similarly, others argued that many developing nations were not ready for democracy. Concerned about the high levels of violence and instability in those political systems, they claimed that the LDCs' first priority had to be political stability, even if that might initially require military rule or other forms of authoritarian government.[10]

More recently, however, troubled by extensive government repression in the developing world and the obvious failures of most authoritarian regimes, political scientists have begun to insist that democracy and some degree of socioeconomic equality must be understood as integral parts of political development.[11] The collapse of communist regimes in the Soviet Union and Eastern Europe reinforced previous criticisms of authoritarian government. Beyond its obvious ethical attractions, democracy also has pragmatic appeal. For example, governments whose citizens hold them accountable through competitive elections are more likely to be efficient and honest (although the disappointing records of democratic governments in countries such as Brazil and the Philippines demonstrate that there are no guarantees). Similarly, free and independent forms of mass media also help keep governments accountable. The disintegration of the Soviet bloc and the fall of many dictatorships throughout the Third World in recent decades suggest that authoritarian regimes are often stable in the short run, but fragile in the long term. Thus, there is not necessarily a trade-off between democracy and political stability, as many had imagined. In fact, democracies are generally immune to revolutionary insurrection and less susceptible to other forms of mass violence.

Only a restricted, but growing, number of developing countries have fully met the standards of political development and democracy just listed—for example, the Bahamas, Uruguay, and Costa Rica. Others—such as Argentina, India, South Korea, and Taiwan—currently satisfy most of the criteria. Even a cursory review of the developing world, however, reveals that most governments still fall short. At one extreme—in nations such as Somalia and Sierra Leone—warlords have divided control over their country and have so deeply undermined their national governments that political scientists label them "failed states." Elsewhere in the Third World, many governments respond disproportionately to the demands of an affluent minority. Self-perpetuating and self-serving elites rule many Middle Eastern and North African nations, while some sub-Saharan African governments serve the interests of dominant ethnic groups. Political corruption, bureaucratic inefficiency, and police repression are all endemic to much of the developing world.

In the past, class-based revolutionary movements erupted in various Asian and Latin American nations, and a number of African countries have been torn apart by ethnic civil wars (with some countries still torn by such conflicts). Thus, until recently most LDCs were not democratic, stable, or legitimate. In recent decades, however, democracy (and with it, government legitimacy) has advanced in much of the developing world, most notably in Latin America and East Asia (see Chapter 2).[12]

Some Relationships between the Components of Development

It is logical to assume that political, economic, and social underdevelopment are interrelated. More economically advanced countries can better educate their populations and provide them with superior health care. An educated citizenry, in turn, contributes to further economic growth and participates in politics more responsibly. Responsive and legitimate governments, constrained by competitive elections, are more likely to educate their citizens and to make informed economic decisions. Indeed, these logical intuitions are supported by empirical evidence. Wealthier countries tend to have greater life expectancies, higher literacy rates, and more stable and democratic governments.

However, these correlations are not unqualified. For example, a country's literacy and infant mortality rates depend not only on its economic resources but also on government policies in the areas of education, public health, and welfare. Thus, as we saw earlier (Table 1.3), elitist government policies in some countries have contributed to social indicators (HDIs) that are far lower than are those of other nations with comparable economic resources. This would include many petroleum-rich states (such as Saudi Arabia) as well as other "underachievers," such as the Dominican Republic and Tunisia.* On the other hand, governments in Cuba, Uruguay, and Vietnam—with strong commitments to social welfare programs—have generated higher life expectancy rates and educational levels than their economic resources alone would lead us to predict ("overachievers").

Both economic and social development tend to correlate with political development. Wealthier, more educated countries such as Barbados, Botswana, Costa Rica, and Taiwan tend to have more politically stable, responsive, and democratic governments than poor nations such as Mozambique, Haiti, and Cambodia. Indeed, Third World countries are not likely to become democracies or to maintain democracy unless they have reached a minimal threshold of socioeconomic development.[13] However, as countries become more economically developed, there is often no smooth progression toward greater political stability or democracy. To the contrary, Samuel Huntington has observed that while the most affluent countries in the world (e.g., Switzerland and Canada) are politically stable and the poorest countries (such as Afghanistan, Congo, and Nepal) are generally politically unstable, countries that are in the mid-stages of economic development often become more unstable as their economies develop.[14] Thus, for example, some of Latin America's most economically advanced countries (Argentina, Brazil, Chile, and Uruguay) experienced internal conflicts and political unrest in the 1960s and 1970s, resulting in the collapse of their democratic governments and the emergence of highly repressive military dictatorships. In 2001–2002, nearly two decades after the restoration of democratic government, Argentina experienced an economic crisis, urban rioting, and political instability that produced five presidents in the space of less than a month. Huntington explained this political instability in mid-level developing nations (i.e., those that are more developed than, say, Peru, but less developed than, say, Poland) by suggesting that as countries modernize, the spread of urbanization, education, and mass media consumption produces an increasingly politically aware and mobilized society, whose citizens make greater demands on the government. All too often, however, political institutions, particularly political parties, are not strengthened quickly enough to channel and respond to this rising tide of demands. Or the government may lack the economic resources to address all these demands. As a result, he maintained, the system becomes overloaded and unstable.

Guillermo O'Donnell posited another theory explaining the rise of extremely repressive dictatorships in South America's more economically advanced nations during the 1960s and 1970s. He suggested that as those countries moved toward a higher stage of industrial growth, they required extensive new investment that they could secure only by attracting foreign capital. Such foreign investment, in turn, would materialize only if the government controlled labor unions and kept down workers' wage demands. In order to achieve those goals, the nations' business leaders and technocrats turned to repressive military rule through what he called "bureaucratic-authoritarian states."[15]

Similarly, some scholars have argued than an authoritarian government might be helpful in the early to middle stages of industrialization in order to

---

* Eighty-six members of the United Nations have been ranked on both economic resources (per-capita GNPs) and socioeconomic indicators of living standards (HDIs).

control labor unions and workers' wages, thereby increasing company profits and attracting new external investment (see Chapter 10). They point out that the Asian countries that enjoyed the most spectacular economic growth from the 1970s to the mid-1990s—Indonesia, Malaysia, Thailand, Singapore, Taiwan, and South Korea—were all governed by authoritarian regimes during their economic takeoffs. Although these theories have since been challenged, they indicate that the relationships between political, economic, and social development are complex. While, at least in the long run, the three generally go hand in hand, they need not progress at the same rate. Moreover, for some periods of time, they may even move in different directions.

THE CAUSES OF UNDERDEVELOPMENT

Our initial discussion suggested that there is some debate concerning the very *definitions* of political and socioeconomic underdevelopment. Social scientists disagree even more intensely over the underlying *causes* of underdevelopment and the most desirable pathways to change. How, for example, do we account for constant military intervention in Pakistani politics, political turmoil in Somalia, government repression in Syria, and a financial crises in Argentina? Do these problems originate from internal factors such as authoritarian cultural values, weak political parties, or misguided economic planning? Or, did foreign domination—stretching from the colonial era to today's age of multinational corporations (MNCs) and the International Monetary Fund (IMF)—cause many of these difficulties?

Questions about the origins of underdevelopment and the pathways to development elicit very different responses from scholarly analysts. Frequently, their evaluations reflect their personal background, country of origin, or ideology. Thus, for example, theories that attribute Third World political unrest or economic backwardness to traditional cultural values generally have emanated from the United States or other developed nations. On the other hand, approaches such as dependency theory and world systems theory, which view Western exploitation as the root cause of Third World underdevelopment, have been particularly popular among Latin American and African analysts. Similarly, liberal, conservative, and Marxist analysts are each drawn to different explanations.

For years, two competing paradigms shaped scholarly analyses of Third World politics and economic change. The first, *modernization theory*, emerged in the early 1960s as American political science's leading interpretation of underdevelopment. The second, *dependency theory*, originated in Latin America in the 1970s and offered a more radical perspective on development, one particularly popular among Third World scholars.

Modernization Theory and the Importance of Cultural Values

During the 1950s and 1960s, as the demise of European colonialism produced a host of newly independent nations in Africa, Asia, and the Middle East, Western social scientists began to study Third World politics and economics more intensively. That interest produced a complex conceptual model of under-development and development known as modernization theory. Its proponents included some of the most prominent figures in comparative politics: Gabriel Almond, James Coleman, Samuel Huntington, and Lucian Pye, among others.[16] For a decade or more, modernization theory reigned supreme in the study of political and economic development. Though later challenged, it has continued to influence our understanding of developing nations. While there have been variations and disagreement among modernization theorists, they generally share a number of underlying assumptions and perspectives.

Despite the tremendous array of problems facing the LDCs, moderniza-tion theorists were initially relatively optimistic about prospects for develop-ment. After all, Western industrialized democracies had also started out as underdeveloped countries. Most Third World nations, they argued, could—and should—follow a path of political and economic modernization parallel to the one first traveled by the advanced Western countries. To accomplish this, modernization theorists insisted, developing nations had to acquire modern cultural values and create modern political and economic institutions.

Transforming traditional cultures was considered the first and, by most accounts, most crucial step in the modernization process. Drawing on the theories of such eminent sociologists as Max Weber and Talcott Parsons, these analysts distinguished between "traditional" and "modern" values.[17] They saw many traditional political and economic values as somewhat irrational, or at least unscientific. For example, the Indian caste system assigned people, at birth, their rank in society, a rank that was difficult to change. Conversely modern men and women, they maintained, tend to do the following: to judge others by universalistic standards (i.e., to hire, vote for, or otherwise evaluate people based on their ability rather than caste, class, or ethnic origins); to believe in the possibility and desirability of change; to value science and technology; to think about issues outside the sphere of the family, neighborhood, or village; to believe that average citizens can—and should—try to influence the political system.[18] At its worst, the theory exhibited elements of ethnocentrism and con-descension, implying the inferiority of Third World cultures. Thus, one of the founders of Latin American studies in the United States argued,

> There is something in the quality of Latin American . . . culture which has made it difficult . . . to be truly modern . . . which has made this part of the Western world so prone to excesses of scoundrels, so politically irrational in seeking economic growth, and so ready to reach for gimmicks.[19]

But how can a traditional society make the transition to modernity? How does a culture modernize its values? Modernization theorists identified education, urban-ization, and the spread of mass media as the central agents of change. As peasants move to cities, the theory argued, as more children attend schools that teach modern values, and as more citizens access the mass media, cultural moderniza-tion will progress. Another critical component, it was suggested, was the diffusion of modern ideas from highly industrialized nations (especially the West) to the developing world and from city to countryside within the Third World. Foreign aid and institutions such as the Peace Corps could help to speed this process.

Gabriel Almond and G. Bingham Powell, depicting modernization as a rather inexorable force, contended that "the forces of technological change and cultural diffusion are driving political systems in certain directions, which seem discernible and susceptible to analysis in terms of increasing levels of development."[20] Others envisioned modernization as a process of getting developing nations to think and act "more like us" (i.e., the West). "As time goes on," Marion Levy predicted, "they and we will increasingly resemble one another. [The] more highly modernized societies become, the more they resemble one another."[21] Today, as the forces of modernization have spread McDonald's burgers and fries, computer technology, Hollywood movies, rock music, and democratic values around the world, that prophecy may seem accurate.

At the same time, the theory claimed, developing nations trying to modernize need to create more specialized and complex political and economic institutions to complement those cultural changes. For example, whereas a tribal culture might have a council of elders that carries out legislative, executive, and judicial activities, a modern society needs separate, specialized institutions for each of those tasks. Modernizing societies also need trained bureaucracies, which base professional advancement on merit rather than personal connections and make decisions according to uniform and consistent standards. Political parties have to channel citizens' demands and aspirations effectively to government policymakers. Eventually, it was argued, as these cultural and institutional changes progress, a modernizing society can lay the foundation for a more stable, effective, and responsive political system. During the decades after World War II, which featured the Cold War against Soviet Communism, modernization theory became far more than an academic perspective. Its assumptions dominated U.S. foreign policy toward the developing world, including foreign aid programs, the Peace Corps, and the tactics used during the war in Vietnam.[22]

In time, however, many of early modernization theory's assumptions had to be modified. To begin with, it had been too optimistic and too simplistic in its initial view of change. Its proponents generally expected developing countries to achieve economic growth, greater equality, democracy, political stability, and greater national autonomy simultaneously and smoothly. As Samuel Huntington noted, the theory erroneously assumed that "all good things go together."[23] In fact, economic growth proved to be no guarantee of democracy, stability, equality, or autonomy. As we have noted, in nations such as Brazil, Mexico, Singapore, and Taiwan, industrialization and economic development originated and advanced for many years under the direction of authoritarian governments.

Analysts were particularly disturbed to find that the very process of social and economic modernization often ushered in political instability and violence.[24] For example, in some of Latin America's most economically developed nations (Argentina, Brazil, Chile, and Uruguay), industrial growth and greater income inequality unleashed bitter class conflict, causing the collapse of democratic institutions and the rise of repressive military dictatorships.[25] Elsewhere, in much of Africa, Asia, and the Middle East, the hopes once inspired by decolonization gave way to ethnic conflict, military coups, and political repression.

Thus, the process of development often turned out to be more difficult and unpredictable than originally imagined. Modernization theory's initial optimism gave way to *conflict theory*. Developing nations, this new perspective argued, would have to make hard choices between seemingly irreconcilable development goals. Concerned about growing political turmoil in many developing nations, Samuel Huntington insisted that political stability was crucial, even if maintaining it sometimes necessitated authoritarian rule for a time. That is to say, democracy might have to take a back seat to stability, at least temporarily. At the same time, many economists and political scientists argued that the early stages of economic growth required wealth to be concentrated in a small number of hands, so that incipient capitalists could acquire sufficient capital for major investments.

More recently, the experiences of several countries in East Asia and Latin America have produced yet another new perspective. While certainly less naively optimistic than the earliest modernization theories, current analysis is also less pessimistic than conflict theory was. The *reconciliation approach*, offered by contemporary modernization theorists, maintains that, with the right policies, developing nations can simultaneously achieve goals previously thought to be incompatible.[26] Taiwan and South Korea, for example, have shown that it is possible to achieve rapid economic development together with equitable income distribution. Barbados and Costa Rica have managed to achieve democracy and stability simultaneously. Consequently, current research tries to analyze factors such as state policy, historical traditions, and cultural values that may contribute to successful development.

One of the major criticisms of modernization theory, at least as originally formulated, was that it was culturally biased, assuming the superiority of Western values. Explicitly or implicitly it suggested that the Western industrialized world was the source of modern (read "good") values and attitudes. Therefore, another modification of the theory addresses its initial view of cultural change. First, it recognized that all modern or modernizing cultures are not identical. Indeed, traditional values, which vary from society to society, may influence the nature of the modern culture that emerges positively or negatively. For example, in East Asian countries, such as Japan and South Korea, traditional Confucian and Shinto beliefs help explain why modern citizens of those countries tend to be less individualistic, more concerned with the good of the community or nation, and more family oriented than are Westerners.

Second, scholars now agree that the differences between traditional and modern cultures are not necessarily as stark or clear-cut as originally thought. For example, even though the United States is a highly modern society, many Americans have retained traditional values such as judging others by the color of their skin. Third, contrary to early modernization theory, it now appears that some traditional values not only are worth keeping but also contribute to political and economic development. For example, students of contemporary Japanese culture have argued that traditional religious values have strengthened that nation's work ethic.

Finally, while modern (Western) values have indeed swept across the Third World, they have not been universally welcomed. In Afghanistan, Iran, Saudi Arabia, and other parts of the Muslim world, for example, many people, including some with advanced educations, have rejected Westernization in favor of either peaceful or violent forms of Islamic fundamentalism. The September 11, 2001, attacks on New York and Washington and subsequent attacks elsewhere were extreme reflections of the distaste that many Muslims feel about Western values and lifestyles. Although extremists represent only a very small fraction of the Muslim world, many other nonviolent Muslims also reject Western culture, which they view as immoral—sullied, for example, by immodest dress, extramarital sex, and pornography.

Dependency Theory: The Core and the Periphery

During the 1960s and 1970s, social scientists in Latin America and the United States raised more fundamental objections to modernization theory, insisting that the modifications that we have just mentioned had failed to correct the theory's fundamental flaws. Under the banner of *dependency theory*, they challenged the modernizationists' most fundamental assumptions. A closely related approach was called world systems theory (or, more modestly, the world systems approach).[27] Like modernization theorists, dependency scholars differ among themselves, but agree on the theory's fundamental premises.

To begin with, *dependentistas* (as dependency theorists are known) rejected the contention that Third World countries can follow the same path to development as Western nations had, if only because the earliest industrialized nations changed the landscape for those that followed them. When Britain became the world's first industrialized nation, it faced no significant competition from other economic powers. Today, however, NICs must compete against well-established industrial giants such as the United States, Japan, and Germany. In addition, argued Brazil's Theotonio Dos Santos, developing countries need to borrow capital and purchase advanced technology from highly developed countries, thereby making them dependent on economic forces beyond their borders and beyond their control.[28]

As we have seen, modernization theory views Western influence over the Third World as beneficial, in that it spreads modern values, technology, and institutions. In contrast, dependency theorists maintain that Western colonialism and economic imperialism are precisely what first turned Africa, Asia, and Latin America into providers of cheap food and raw materials for the developed countries. Moreover, they charge, long after the LDCs had achieved political independence, many First World nations have continued to use their economic power to sustain dependent relationships that disadvantage the Third World. For the most part, the production and export of manufactured goods and technology—the most profitable economic activities—along with major control over world finance remained in the control of the *core*, the *dependentistas* label for the industrialized West (and Japan). Conversely, until recent decades, Third World nations, located in the *periphery*, were largely relegated to the production and export of agricultural goods and raw materials and were forced to trade for industrial imports on unfavorable terms.[29] That did not mean that the core developed nations controlled every aspect of Third World economic and political development (or misdevelopment), but rather:

> [Dependency is] . . . a historical condition which shapes a certain structure of the world economy such that it favors some countries to the detriment of others and limits the development possibilities of the subordinate economies . . . a situation in which the economy of a certain group of countries is conditioned by the development and expansion of another economy, to which their own is subjected.[30]

Finally, *dependentistas* contend that *economic* dependence also had brought about the LDCs' *political* dependence on the core. Within the periphery, the argument went, Third World political, military, and economic elites, backed by the might of the United States and other core nations, maintained a political system that benefited the powerful few at the expense of the many. Dependency theorists have noted, for example, how frequently France used to intervene militarily in its former African colonies to maintain corrupt and unrepresentative governments with which it was allied. Similarly, for many years, the United States has supported friendly, but repressive, regimes such as Saudi Arabia's.

As one might expect, many Third World scholars embraced dependency theory enthusiastically because it maintained that underdevelopment was not the developing world's "fault," but rather the result of foreign domination and exploitation. In time, dependency theory also challenged or displaced modernization theory in the United States and Europe as the major scholarly paradigm. As Omar Sánchez has observed, this "marks one of those rare instances in which ideas produced in the Third World come to influence the thinking of scholars in the developed world."[31]

However, just as early modernization theory had been overly optimistic about the prospects for simultaneous economic and political development, early dependency theory turned out to be excessively pessimistic about the likelihood of economic and political development. Analysts such as Andre Gunder Frank had warned that Third World nations—largely confined to production of crops, minerals, and other commodities—were ruled by unrepresentative elites and were doomed to continued backwardness. Some *dependentistas* believed that radical revolutions were the only solution.

Yet, despite the bleak prognosis of early dependency theorists, it was clear as early as the mid-1960s that nations such as Brazil and Mexico were undergoing substantial industrialization. Some two decades later, China emerged as one of the world's leading exporters of manufactured goods, and soon afterwards South Korea, Taiwan, India, Malaysia, and several other Asian nations began to enjoy rapid economic modernization and growth. In his far more sophisticated version of dependency theory, Brazil's Fernando Henrique Cardoso rejected the contention that all Third World countries were condemned to underdevelopment and precluded from significant industrialization.[32] Drawing heavily from the experiences of his own country, Cardoso noted that through the active intervention of the state and the linkage of domestic firms to MNCs, some developing countries had industrialized and experienced considerable economic growth. He referred to this process as *associated-dependent development*.

Cardoso radically altered dependency theory by arguing that countries such as Argentina, Brazil, Colombia, and Mexico could modernize and expand their economies while still remaining dependent on foreign banks and MNCs for loans, investment, and technology. Brazilian industrialization, he noted, had been stimulated largely by a sharp rise in foreign, corporate investment. Still, Cardoso and his colleagues considered associated-dependent development tainted in several important ways. MNCs were making critical economic decisions affecting LDCs, but were outside the developing nations' control. Furthermore, foreign corporations tended to invest in capital-intensive (highly mechanized) production that needed fewer workers than more traditional, labor-intensive firms did. And, these new industries tended to manufacture products for more affluent middle- and upper-class consumers. Hence, unlike many firms in the West, they had little incentive to raise wage levels in order to enhance working-class purchasing power. Rather than reduce poverty, *dependentistas* maintained, associated-dependent development had widened the income gap. At the same time, Peter Evans and others argued, the multinational corporations' alliances with Latin American economic, political, and military elites helped uphold the power of repressive regimes such as Brazil's military government.

Modernization and Dependency Theories Compared

The dependency approach offered useful corrections to modernization theory. Furthermore, it highlighted important influences over Third World societies that the earlier theory had largely neglected—international trade, finance, and investment. In fact, many political scientists now argue that a principal characteristic defining Third World countries is their dependence on the core. Consequently, these scholars still consider relatively wealthy nations such as Saudi Arabia as well as stable democracies such as Costa Rica to be part of the Third World because their economic and political systems are largely shaped by the developed world.

Regardless of how they view dependency theory, contemporary analysts of underdevelopment now recognize that political and economic modernization requires more than adopting new values or changing domestic political structures (i.e., more than modernization theory had postulated). Dependency theory shifted the focus of research from exclusively internal factors to international economic and political relationships. *Dependentistas* also helped redefine the concept of economic development. Whereas early mainstream research on economic development heavily stressed the goal of economic growth, dependency theorists also emphasized the importance of more equitable economic distribution and greater social justice. When rapid economic growth increases the concentration of wealth and income in the hands of a minority, as it frequently does, it offers limited benefits to the poor, or may even worsen their situation. Influenced by dependency theory and other leftist critiques, establishment pillars such as the World Bank reoriented their focus toward growth and redistribution.[33]

Despite its contributions, however, dependency theory suffered from serious failings. Just as early modernization theorists overemphasized the *internal* causes of underdevelopment, *dependentistas* erroneously attributed virtually all of the Third World's problems to *external* economic factors, including international trade, foreign investment and credit, as well as political alliances linking the core nations with the Third World's economic, political, and military elites.[34] Furthermore, many authors portrayed Third World nations as helpless pawns with no way out of their poverty. As Stephan Haggard charged, "countries are called 'dependent' by virtue of their characteristics and remain so regardless of their action."[35] To be sure, what is striking about much of that literature is its economic determinism and neglect of domestic social or political influences. Its proponents frequently have dismissed Third World governments as agents of the local economic elite who colluded with Western- or Japanese-based MNCs. Consequently, there is a disturbing similarity between many of their case studies. The details of Mexican, Nigerian, or Peruvian politics and economic development may differ in these works, but too often *dependentistas* offer identical explanations for the Third World's misdevelopment.

Cardoso refined dependency theory by insisting that the types of constraints imposed by core economies on the periphery varied from one developing nation to another. El Salvador may be extremely dependent—economically and politically—on the United States, while Argentina—a larger country more distant from North America—has been better equipped to guide its own course. Furthermore, the effects of external influences emanating from the core are mediated by conditions within each developing country. In other words, he argued, in varying degrees, developing nations have options within the limits imposed by their dependency. For example, a country's class structure and the influence of particular classes on government policy influence the type of associated-dependent development it experiences. As he and Enzo Faletto wrote, "We conceive the relationship between external and internal forces . . . as not [being] based on mere external forms of exploitation . . . but [as] rooted in coincidences of interests between local dominant classes and international ones."[36] In other words, decisions made by Third World governments and business leaders *do* matter, and some LDCs have enjoyed notable, if still flawed, economic growth. Combining Cardoso's ideas with elements of modernization theory, Argentine political scientist Guillermo O'Donnell offered a powerful explanation for the rise of authoritarian military governments in the most developed nations of South America.[37]

However, East Asia's "economic miracle" (its rapid and sustained economic growth) in recent decades—most notably in South Korea, Taiwan, Hong Kong, and Singapore—has confounded dependency theory. These countries have linked themselves very closely to the industrialized world through trade, credit, investments, and technology transfers. Contrary to what even the more sophisticated dependency scholars had predicted, however, they achieved spectacular economic growth coupled with comparatively equitable income distribution. Countries such as South Korea and Taiwan now have standards of living comparable to Portugal's and Hungary's, along with relatively high income equality. Hong Kong and Singapore have per-capita incomes slightly higher than Germany's or Italy's. Moreover, in a further blow to dependency theory, in recent years India, the world's second largest nation, has become one of the world's most dynamic economies by opening its doors to foreign trade and investment. Even Fernando Henrique Cardoso—dependency theory's most renowned exponent during his career as an academic scholar—later embraced foreign investment, trade, and technology in his second career as Brazil's finance minister and then two-term president.

Contemporary Perspectives

Many political scientists have statistically analyzed the competing theories of underdevelopment and development, drawing on contemporary economic and social data. For example, using regression analysis, they have examined whether there is a correlation between a country's level of economic development and its population's attitude toward science and technology—specifically, "Do societies with more positive attitudes toward science and technology tend to have higher per-capita incomes?" Similarly, others asked whether or not there is a relationship between a country's HDI and its dependence on foreign trade and foreign investment.

The results of this research have been mixed. Depending on which set of countries or what time period each scholar examined, his or her answers to such questions were sometimes quite different. In all, empirical research supports some modernization hypotheses, but not others. One study found that, in accordance with that theory and contrary to dependency theory, the diffusion of technology and communications from highly industrialized nations to developing nations appeared to raise HDI scores.[38] On the other hand, exploring the relationship between several modern attitudes and a country's standard of living, Maria Fernanda Trujillo-Mendoza found that when she used 1990 data there was a positive correlation, but in 1997 the relationship between them was not statistically significant (i.e., the correlation was not supported sufficiently to draw a conclusion). In all, her analysis indicated that modern values, such as "rational attitudes toward authority . . . [and] openness to ideas . . . do not reflect the underlying differences between developed and developing countries."[39] In other words, she found no evidence that countries with such modern values were more likely to undergo economic or political development.

However, when subjected to empirical testing, dependency theory fared worse. For example, contrary to that theory's predictions, the countries that have experienced the most impressive improvements in per-capita income and human development—including Singapore, South Korea, Taiwan, and Chile—tend to be the ones most closely linked to the global economy and its industrialized "core." Conversely, Third World countries that have the lowest levels of foreign investment and foreign trade tend to have the poorest record of economic development. Moreover, there is considerable evidence that those developing nations that reduce barriers to free trade, such as tariffs, tend to enjoy faster economic growth than countries that limit international trade.[40]

Similarly, a number of studies suggest that greater foreign investment tends to produce higher economic growth, in part because local firms often adopt technological innovations used by foreign-owned corporations. Using cross-national data over time to analyze the effects of several indicators of dependency—including levels of foreign trade and aid, foreign investment, and foreign debt—Brian Farmer found that there was no correlation between these factors and per-capita income, economic growth, income inequality, or HDI. Only one of the measures that he examined supported dependency theory. Countries that relied heavily on primary exports (such as agricultural products, minerals, and even oil) tended to do more poorly on measures of economic and social development.[41] Unfortunately, dependency theory literature rarely uses comparative data and statistical analysis to test its hypotheses. In fact, it often lacks any testable hypotheses that can be confirmed or disproved.

Today, few analysts accept either modernization or dependency theory in their entirety. In their original formulations, both approaches suffered from overgeneralizations that failed to recognize sufficiently the cultural, political, and economic differences between the LDCs. Subsequent theories and approaches, such as *bureaucratic authoritarianism* (which attempted to explain the rise of military dictatorships in some of the Third World's more economically developed nations) or *neoliberalism* (which offered a set of conservative economic prescriptions for less developed nations) have avoided global explanations of development and underdevelopment, focusing instead on more specific issues. Indeed, most contemporary analysts reject the very idea of a *single* theory of development. For one thing, the Third World is too diverse and the processes of political and socioeconomic development too complex to be explained by a single theory of change.

This does not mean, however, that the insights offered by dependency and modernization theories have not been useful. Our current understanding of development draws on the strengths of both approaches, while recognizing their limitations. Since the 1990s, several new approaches to the study of LDCs have emerged, but few claim to be explanatory theories. One intellectual approach, postmodernism, has influenced a number of disciplines (anthropology, geography, history, sociology, and literary criticism, among others). Postmodernists charge modernization theory with trying to impose its values on the Third World. Moreover, they reject the notion that the First World is "developed" and the Third World "underdeveloped." Further, they argue that *all* social science theories are subjective and that both modernization and dependency theories represent deterministic, Western interpretations of the Third World. Rejecting broad, explanatory theories of any kind ("meta-theory"), postmodernists stress local studies that give voice to people without power, most notably the poor and women. They favor "bottom-up" development based on the plans and desires of the underprivileged rather than "top-down" development projects designed by governments, outside agencies, or nongovernmental organizations (NGOs).[42]

Other analysts, who stress bottom-up development, reject modernization theory as an externally imposed, elitist ideology that has failed to serve the needs of most people in the LDCs. They refer to their own approach as "another development." Yet another group of scholars label themselves "anti-developmentalists." They reject the very idea that social, political, and economic development has been beneficial to the Third World. Instead, they argue that modernization, including its current most comprehensive form—globalization—has benefited only a small portion of the population and has further impoverished many others. At the same time, they maintain, development has taken political power (however limited it was in traditional society) from the rural villages and urban slums and transferred it to a centralized state dominated by the middle and upper classes. Political and economic reforms, they insist, need to respect and value the traditional beliefs and practices of the poor and must transfer state political power back to the grassroots.[43]

While these revisionist critiques of modernization theory (and, sometimes, of dependency theory) offer some useful insights and some needed modification of existing models of development, they have generally had little influence on political scientists or development specialists in other disciplines. Too often, their arguments are based on abstractions and redefinitions, rather than on empirical evidence. Their criticisms of modernization, globalization, and development itself frequently are based on isolated anecdotes rather than systematic, empirical evidence. Thus, despite the many challenges they raise to modernization theory, many of them quite legitimate, they have failed to emerge as workable alternatives.

HOW MUCH (OR HOW LITTLE) PROGRESS HAS BEEN MADE?

We have seen how "mainstream" political analysts (including most advocates of modernization theory) and leftist authors (including supporters of dependency theory) disagree on the causes of underdevelopment. Not surprisingly, they also differ in their assessments of how much or little Third World social, economic, and political conditions have improved in recent times. Mainstream observers—though well aware of the setbacks that many developing nations have suffered and the difficulties that lie ahead—point to a number of encouraging signs. They observe that the percentage of the Third World's population living in absolute poverty has been dropping steadily for a number of years.* Infant mortality has declined, life expectancy and literacy have increased, polio has almost been wiped out, a war on malaria is showing early signs of success, and treatment of AIDS, though still inadequate, has greatly expanded. China and India, which jointly account for some 43 percent of the developing world's total population, have enjoyed dramatic economic growth in recent times. And, as we will see in Chapter 2, improvements in social and economic conditions have contributed to the tremendous expansion of Third World democracy since the 1970s.

Dependency theorists and other left-of-center critics counter that some social and economic conditions have deteriorated and that, even where progress has been made, much remains to be done. They note that while the *percentage* of Third World inhabitants living in absolute poverty has declined, the *absolute* number has increased due to population growth. That is to say, that every year there are more people living in poverty (though their numbers have grown more slowly than the total population has). Further, they maintain that there is a widening income gap between developed and the developing nations, between urban and rural populations, and between the developing world's poor and the middle classes. Thus, for example, while India and China have enjoyed enormous economic growth, most of that growth has been confined to their urban areas and the total number of people living in poverty, ill-housed, and hungry remains enormous.

In many cases both sides are correct. Sometimes the division has been between those who call the glass half full and those who view it as half empty. For example, it is true that the disparity between rich and poor countries has widened in recent years if you measure growth in *absolute* terms. But if you measure the gap in *percentage* terms, it has narrowed. Imagine if you will that the per-capita income of rich country A has increased from $10,000 to $12,000 in the past 10 years, while poor country B's per-capita income has grown from $1,000 to $1,500 in the same time period. A modernization theorist might observe that per-capita income in the richer country, A, has increased by 20 percent, while country B's income has shot up by 50 percent. Furthermore, while 10 years ago people in country A made 10 times as much as the inhabitants of country B, today they only make 8 times as much. Clearly, they would note, the income gap has narrowed and, in fact, if both countries were to maintain their

---

* Technically that decline was temporarily reversed when the World Bank raised the poverty line from $2.00 to $2.50 per day. But the jump in poverty in 2008 was caused by a broader definition of poverty, not a real jump in the number of impoverished people.

current growth rates into the indefinite future, country B would eventually catch up. Critics of current economic policies would counter that whereas per-capita income 10 years ago in country A exceeded country B by $9,000, today that gap had widened to $10,500. Furthermore, they would insist, it is foolish to assume that each country will maintain their current growth rates indefinitely, allowing country B to catch up.

In short, each side presents a reasonable argument and each side backs it arguments with accurate statistics. The question is, "Which statistical interpretation [of the same data] is more valid?" For now, it appears that we can say that substantial progress has been made in Third World raising living standards, but an enormous amount remains to be done. Unfortunately, it is also likely that the current global economic crisis will worsen socioeconomic conditions in many parts of the developing world for years to come, especially in the world's poorest nations.

DISCUSSION QUESTIONS

1. If you wished to examine dependency theory's value in explaining the causes of underdevelopment, how would you design a test of that theory?
2. Pick one region of the Third World (Africa, Asia, Latin America and the Caribbean, or the Middle East) and discuss the relationship between social, economic, and political underdevelopment in that region.
3. What indicators do you believe are the most useful measures of political development?

NOTES

1. For a discussion of the strengths and many weaknesses of the term, see Allen H. Merriam, "What Does 'Third World' Mean?" in *The Third World: States of Mind and Being*, eds. Jim Norwine and Alfonso Gonzalez (Boston: Unwin Hyman, 1988), 15–22.

2. Merriam, "What Does 'Third World' Mean?" 20.

3. Christopher Clapham, *Third World Politics: An Introduction* (Madison: University of Wisconsin Press, 1985), 2.

4. Anup Shah, "Poverty Around the World," *Global Issues* (2008), www.globalissues.org/article/4/poverty-around-the-world.

5. World Bank, *World Development Indicators 2008*.

6. Axel Hadenius, *Democracy and Development* (London: Cambridge University Press, 1992).

7. *New York Times* (December 28, 2006).

8. CIA, *The 2008 World Factbook*, https://www.cia.gov/library/publications/the-world-factbook/

9. Hadenius, *Democracy and Development*; Robert A. Dahl, *Democracy and Its Critics* (New Haven, CT: Yale University Press, 1989.

10. Samuel P. Huntington, *Political Order in Changing Societies* (New Haven, CT: Yale University Press, 1968).

11. Guillermo O'Donnell and Philippe Schmitter, *Transitions from Authoritarian Rule: Tentative Conclusions about Uncertain Democracies* (Baltimore, MD: Johns Hopkins University Press, 1986); Dahl, *Democracy and Its Critics.*

12. Samuel P. Huntington, *The Third Wave: Democratization in the Late Twentieth Century* (Norman: University of Oklahoma Press, 1991).

13. Mitchell A. Seligson, "Democratization in Latin America: The Current Cycle," in *Authoritarians and Democrats: Regime Transition in Latin America*, eds. James M. Malloy and Mitchell A. Seligson (Pittsburgh: University of Pittsburgh Press, 1987).

14. Huntington, *Political Order.*

15. Guillermo O'Donnell, *Modernization and Bureaucratic-Authoritarianism: Studies in South American Politics* (Berkeley: University of California Press, 1973).

16. Within the extensive modernization literature, key works include Huntington, *Political Order* and Gabriel Almond and James Coleman,

eds. *The Politics of Developing Areas* (Princeton, NJ: Princeton University Press, 1960).

17. Max Weber, *The Protestant Ethic and the Spirit of Capitalism* (New York: Scribner, 1958); Talcott Parsons, *The Social System* (Glencoe, IL: Free Press, 1951).

18. Gabriel Almond and Sidney Verba, *The Civic Culture* (Princeton, NJ: Princeton University Press, 1963); Alex Inkeles and David Horton Smith, *Becoming Modern: Individual Change in Six Developing Countries* (Cambridge, MA: Harvard University Press, 1974).

19. Kalman H. Silvert, quoted in J. Samuel Valenzuela and Arturo Valenzuela, "Modernization and Dependency: Alternative Perspectives in the Study of Latin American Underdevelopment," *Comparative Politics*, vol. 10, no. 4 (July 1978), 542.

20. Gabriel A. Almond and G. Bingham Powell, *Comparative Politics: A Developmental Approach* (Boston: Little, Brown, 1966), 301.

21. Marion Levy Jr., "Social Patterns (Structures) and Problems of Modernization," in *Readings on Social Change*, eds. Wilbert Moore and Robert Cooke (Upper Saddle River, NJ: Prentice Hall, 1967), 207.

22. Michael E. Latham, *Modernization as Ideology: American Social Science and "Nation Building" in the Kennedy Era* (Chapel Hill: University of North Carolina Press, 2000).

23. Samuel P. Huntington, "The Goals of Development," in *Understanding Political Development*, eds. Myron Weiner and S. Huntington (Boston: Little Brown, 1987).

24. Huntington, *Political Order.*

25. See Juan Linz and Alfred Stepan, eds., *The Breakdown of Democratic Regimes: Latin America* (Baltimore, MD: Johns Hopkins University Press, 1978); David Collier, ed., *The New Authoritarianism in Latin America* (Princeton, NJ: Princeton University Press, 1979).

26. Huntington, "The Goals of Development."

27. Immanuel Wallerstein, *World-Systems Analysis: An Introduction* (Durham, NC: Duke University Press, 2004).

28. Theotonio Dos Santos, "The Structure of Dependence," *American Economic Review*, vol. 60, no. 2 (May 1970), 231–236.

29. Werner Baer, "The Economics of Prebisch and ECLA," in *Latin America: Problems in Economic Development*, ed. C.T. Nisbet (New York: Free Press, 1969).

30. Theotonio Dos Santos, "The Structure of Dependence," in *Readings in U.S. Imperialism*,

eds. K.T. Fann and Donald C. Hodges (Boston: Porter Sargent, 1971), 226.

31. Omar Sánchez, "The Rise and Fall of the Dependency Movement: Does It Inform Underdevelopment Today?" E.I.A.L. (Estudios Interdisciplinarios de América Latina y el Caribe), vol. 14, no. 2 (July–December, 2003), www.tau. ac.il/eial/XIV_2/sanchez.html.

32. The most influential work on this version of dependency theory is Fernando Henrique Cardoso and Enzo Faletto, *Dependency and Development in Latin America* (Berkeley: University of California Press, 1979). For a more readable work, see Peter Evans, *Dependent Development* (Princeton, NJ: Princeton University Press, 1979).

33. Hollis Chenery et al., *Redistribution with Growth* (London: Oxford University Press, 1974).

34. Barbara Stallings, "International Influence in Economic Policy," in *The Politics of Economic Adjustment: International Constraints, Distributive Conflicts and the State*, eds. Stephan Haggard and Robert Kaufman (Princeton, NJ: Princeton University Press, 1992).

35. Stephan Haggard, *Pathways from the Periphery: The Politics of Growth in Newly Industrializing Countries* (Ithaca, NY: Cornell University Press, 1990), 21–22.

36. Cardoso and Faletto, *Dependency and Development*, 26.

37. O'Donnell, *Modernization and Bureaucratic-Authoritarianism*.

38. Richard Labelle, *ICT Policy Formulation and e-Strategy Development* (New Delhi, India: Elsevier and the U.N. Asia-Pacific Development Information Programme, 2005).

39. Maria Fernanda Trujillo-Mendoza, "The Digital Divide: Exploring the Relation between Core National Computing and National Capacity and Progress in Human Development over the Last Decade" (New Orleans: Tulane University Doctoral Dissertation, 2001), Appendix G-p. 7.

40. Arvind Panagariya, "Think Again: International Trade," *Foreign Policy* (November/December, 2003), 20–28.

41. Brian R. Farmer, *The Question of Dependency and Economic Development* (Lanham, MD: Lexington Books, 1999).

42. Trevor Parfitt, *The End of Development: Modernity, Post-Modernity and Development* (Sterling, VA: Pluto Press, 2002).

43. Arturo Escobar, *Encountering Development* (Princeton, NJ: Princeton University Press, 1995).

CHAPTER 2

DEMOCRATIC CHANGE AND THE CHANGE TO DEMOCRACY

The first decade of the twenty-first century has been difficult for a number of former dictators and quasi-dictators. The deposed president of Yugoslavia, Slobodan Milošević, was arrested by Serbian authorities and put on trial at the United Nations International War Crimes Tribunal in The Hague (the Netherlands).* The father of Serbia's genocidal war against Bosnian Muslims and subsequent attacks on ethnic Albanians in the province of Kosovo, Milošević; became the first head of government since World War II to be tried on charges of human rights violations before an international court. Augusto Pinochet, Chile's military dictator for 16 years (1973–1990), fought to avoid a human rights trial in Chile after having returned from a humiliating house arrest in England. In 2006, Milošević; died in prison before a verdict was reached in his marathon trial. Pinochet died later that year as well while under confinement and facing numerous human rights charges. Indonesia's long-term dictator, General Suharto, also confronted possible detention after he was driven from office by mass demonstrations. Like Pinochet, this aged, once all-powerful leader hid behind a court plea that he was too physically weak and mentally incapacitated to stand trial. Former Peruvian president Alberto Fujimori—who had imposed authoritarian control after initially being elected democratically—was recently convicted of abuse of power, murder, crimes against humanity, and other offenses. And, most famously, United States and allied troops ousted Iraqi dictator Saddam Hussein. After months on the run, Saddam was captured and later handed over to the Iraqi authorities.† Found responsible for several civilian massacres, he was executed in 2006.

In 2002, the UN-affiliated International Criminal Court was established to prosecute individuals for war crimes, crimes against humanity, and genocide. The treaty establishing the court had been signed by 148 nations (but not the United States, China, India, or Russia) and has now been ratified by nearly 110. To date, the court has prosecuted warlords and other war criminals from four African nations and has recently issued an arrest warrant for Sudanese president Omar al-Bashir, charging him with war crimes and crimes against humanity in

---

* Serbia was the most powerful of six republics that had constituted the Yugoslav federation. Other republics had included Bosnia-Herzegovina, Slovenia, and Croatia. The federation fell apart as various republics seceded in defiance of Serbia's decades-old domination.

† Saddam Hussein did not use his family ("last") name, which was al-Majid. Saddam was his given ("first") name and Hussein was his father's first name. While some Western news sources call him Hussein for short, he is normally referred to as Saddam or Saddam Hussein, but not Hussein.

Darfur. And in 2009, the court placed Congo's former vice president on trial on charges that included torture and rape. Currently, deposed Liberian dictator Charles Taylor is on trial for war crimes (including murder, rape, enslavement, and the forced draft of child soldiers) before a UN-supported Special Court for Sierra Leone in The Hague, the first former African head of state to face such charges. In all, these trials and arrest warrants have established a new international standard of accountability for former dictators and, in the case of al-Bashir, even for a sitting head of state. They also capped three decades of transitions from authoritarian to democratic government throughout the world.

Since the 1974 military revolt that brought down Portugal's long-standing, fascist dictatorship, numerous authoritarian regimes, particularly in the Third World, have fallen in the face of democratic movements. Most Westerners considered the demise of Soviet and Eastern European Communism democracy's most renowned triumph in this era. But in the developing nations, equally dramatic events also deserve our attention. In early 1990, Nelson Mandela, the world's most revered political prisoner, left his cell in Pollsmoor Prison and was transported triumphantly to South Africa's capital, Pretoria, ending 27 years of incarceration. There, he and other freed Black leaders of the newly legalized political party, the African National Congress, eventually negotiated an end to White minority rule. President Mandela's triumph accelerated Africa's "second independence"—a wave of political liberalization (easing of repression) that has often led to either electoral or liberal democracy.*

In Asia, Corazon Aquino succeeded her assassinated husband as the leader of Filipino "people's power"—massive pro-democracy demonstrations by students, shopkeepers, professionals, businesspeople, and many others. Her supporters, backed by the nation's Catholic clergy, took to the streets day after day, peacefully challenging government troops. Ultimately, when the nation's dictator, Ferdinand Marcos, tried to deny Ms. Aquino her apparent victory in a hastily called "snap presidential election" (1986), the commander of the armed forces, General Fidel Ramos, along with Defense Minister Juan Ponce Enrile, joined the opposition, forcing Marcos to step down. Soon after, student-led demonstrations against South Korea's military regime (inspired, in part, by events in the Philippines) accelerated that country's transition to democracy. In 1998, "people's power" demonstrations in Indonesia toppled the 30-year dictatorship of President Suharto.

But the most sweeping democratic changes took place in Latin America (1978–1990), affecting almost every country in the region. Whereas all but a few countries (Colombia, Costa Rica, and Venezuela) had authoritarian or semiauthoritarian governments in the mid-1970s, 25 years later only Cuba and Haiti had failed to establish functioning electoral democracies. Unlike Asia and Africa, Latin America's democratization process generally lacked charismatic heroes in the mold of Mandela, Aquino, or Burmese opposition leader and Nobel Peace Prize winner, Aung San Suu Kyi. Nor did it typically feature mass demonstrations. Instead, democratic transitions often grew out of extended

---

* As discussed later in this chapter, electoral democracies are countries that have free and fair elections. However, some electoral democracies violate their citizens' civil rights and liberties and are, thus, not fully democratic. Liberal democracies are fully democratic political systems that enjoy *both* competitive elections and broad civil liberties.

negotiations between the outgoing authoritarian government and opposition leaders, often culminated by a relatively peaceful, gradual transfer of power.

Yet Latin America enjoyed two important advantages over Africa and Asia. First, prior to its wave of military takeovers in the 1960s and 1970s, the region had enjoyed the Third World's strongest democratic tradition, most notably in Chile, Costa Rica, and Uruguay. Furthermore, Latin American countries were among the first LDCs to achieve the levels of literacy and economic development that are generally associated with stable democratic government. Predictably, then, the region's recent democratic wave has been more sweeping and more successful than elsewhere in the developing world, ultimately affecting virtually every country in the hemisphere.

Of course, not all Third World democracy movements have been successful. In China, army tanks crushed student demonstrations in Beijing's Tiananmen Square (1989), putting that county's democracy movement in check ever since. More recently (2007), Myanmar's military dictatorship jailed thousands of Buddhist monks and Burmese students who had led large pro-democracy demonstrations, while probably killing over 100 protesters. And, in 2009, massive street demonstrations for democracy have so far failed to dislodge Iran's authoritarian government. Nor have transitions from authoritarian to democratic or semidemocratic regimes always endured. In recent years, countries such as Nigeria, Pakistan, and Thailand have swung back and forth several times between military rule and democratic or partly democratic civilian government. In other cases, presidents or prime ministers have been elected on democratic platforms but have turned authoritarian once in office.

Despite these setbacks, however, the upsurge of political freedom in the developing world since the 1970s, coupled with the breakdown of Communism in the Soviet bloc, has produced history's greatest democratic transition. By the end of the twentieth century, the surge of democratization had largely ended, but many of the new democracies have endured. If this progress can be sustained, it will likely influence many of the aspects of Third World politics discussed in this book. For example, by definition consolidation of democracy reduces military rule. It also lowers the likelihood of revolutionary movements. And, democracy generally contributes, at least eventually, to a better quality of political and economic life for women, peasants, and the urban poor.

DEMOCRACY DEFINED

Discussions of democratic transformations have frequently been complicated by disagreements over the *meaning* of democracy. Currently, most political scientists characterize democracy procedurally. That is, democracy is measured by the transparency and fairness of the essential procedures governing the election and behavior of government officials. The least-demanding definition focuses almost exclusively on elections. It simply defines democracy as a political system that holds fair, contested elections on a regular basis, with universal (or near universal) adult suffrage.[1] I will call countries that only meet that minimal standard "electoral democracies." Although this bare-bones definition seems reasonable (after all, most Americans think of democracy in terms of free and fair elections), it allows a number of rather questionable governments to be labeled democratic. For example, the current governments in Colombia, Turkey, and Sri Lanka meet this electoral standard, yet they have widely violated human rights while battling armed insurgencies. In all of those countries, government troops have periodically massacred villagers or tortured prisoners. At the same time, for much of the past two decades, Honduras and Bangladesh have met the standards of electoral democracy, yet both nations' armed forces have regularly intervened in politics, often overriding decisions made by elected officials.

As the norm of open elections became more universally accepted in recent decades, the number of electoral democracies worldwide tripled from 1974 to 2005. But many of these governments still manipulate the mass media and violate their citizens' civil liberties. In this chapter, I use the term *semidemocracies* to refer to those electoral democracies whose governments regularly repress civil liberties and breach the principles of a free society. Alternatively, they may be labeled *partly free*. Their elections may be relatively free and fair, but their societies are not. Such semidemocracies currently include Malaysia, Nigeria, and Venezuela. Finally, some semidemocracies have competitive elections but lack adequate mechanisms for holding the government accountable to its citizens between elections.

Consequently, a more stringent definition of "full" democracy (also known as *liberal* democracy) involves more than competitive elections. Instead, we define it as a political system that conforms to the following conditions: most of the country's leading government officials are elected;* there is universal or near universal suffrage; elections are largely free of fraud and outside manipulation; opposition-party candidates have a realistic chance of being elected to important national offices; and civil liberties—including minority rights—are respected, with guarantees of free speech, free assembly, free press (media), and freedom of religion. All these conditions help guarantee that democratic governments are accountable to their citizens in a way that authoritarian regimes are not.[2] Moreover, liberal democracy also includes the rule of law, civilian command over the armed forces and a vigorous **civil society**.† This definition suggests that competitive elections mean little if unelected individuals or groups who are not accountable to the public (such as military officers, organized crime bosses, business elites, or foreign powers) direct elected officials from behind the scenes. And, free elections do not bring full democracy if elected officials violate their citizens' civil liberties or arbitrarily arrest opposition leaders.

Finally, some scholars offer an even more demanding standard for democracy. They argue that any purely procedural definition of democracy, no matter

---

* Of course, even in some liberal democracies, high-ranking officeholders are appointed, not elected. In the United States, these include Supreme Court justices and cabinet members. But these positions are appointed by a popularly elected president and are subject to Congressional confirmation. Prior to the 1960s, the United States was not fully a liberal or even an electoral democracy because large numbers of southern Blacks were barred from voting. And, until the early twentieth century, women also were denied suffrage.

† Civil society is the array of voluntary organizations—including churches, unions, business groups, farmers' organizations, and women's groups—whose members often influence the political system, but are free of government control. Most authoritarian governments weaken civil society, so that it cannot generate a challenge to their rule. Consequently, rebuilding and strengthening civil society are essential tasks for establishing and consolidating democratic government.

how exacting, is incomplete. Instead, they insist, real democracy requires not only fair elections and proper government procedures (as just outlined), but also fair and just government policy outcomes ("substantive democracy"). For example, substantive democracy requires that citizens have relatively equal access to public schooling and health care regardless of their social class or ethnicity. Similarly, they insist, any procedural democracy—such as India or Brazil—that tolerates gross economic inequalities, ethnic prejudice, or other social injustices is not truly democratic.

These scholars make an important point. Procedural democracy alone does not guarantee a just society; it is merely a step in the right direction. But it is a far more important step than its critics acknowledge. Because governments in procedural democracies are accountable to the people, they are less vulnerable to revolution and other forms of civil unrest. They are also extremely unlikely to make war against other democracies (indeed, war between two liberal democracies is virtually unknown). Prodded by a free press and public opinion, they are more responsive to domestic crises such as famines (in fact, there has never been a prolonged famine in any procedural democracy), and while some (electoral) democracies have violated their critics' civil liberties, most respect their citizens' rights.

Mindful of the fact that democratic societies cannot correct all social injustices—the United States, for example, has long accepted racial discrimination, poverty, and a high degree of economic inequality—this book defines democracy strictly procedurally. Issues of substantive democracy (eradicating poverty, racism, sexism, and the like) are obviously important, but they are a separate matter.

DEMOCRATIC TRANSITION AND CONSOLIDATION

In the discussion that follows, the term *democratic transition* (or transition to democracy) means the process of moving from an authoritarian to a democratic regime. The transition period begins when an authoritarian government shows the first observable signs of collapsing or of negotiating its departure from power. It ends when the first freely elected government takes office. Thus, for example, in South Africa, the democratic transition began in 1990 when the White minority government of President Frederik de Klerk decided to free Nelson Mandela and open negotiations with his African National Congress party. It concluded 4 years later when Mandela was inaugurated as the country's first president to be elected through universal suffrage. Even after their transitions are completed, however, many new democracies remain fragile, with a real possibility that they will falter.

Only when democratic institutions, practices, and values have become deeply ingrained in society can we say that a country has experienced *democratic consolidation*. That consolidation is a process through which democratic norms ("rules of the game") become accepted by all politically influential groups in society—including business groups, labor unions, rural landlords, professionals, the church, and the military—and no important political actor contemplates a return to dictatorship. Or, as Juan Linz and Alfred Stepan have put it, democracy is consolidated when it becomes "the only game in town," even in the face of severe economic or political adversity.[3] Consolidation may begin only after the democratic transition ends and is completed only when democracy is securely entrenched.

Unfortunately, since 1960 fewer than half the transitions to democracy were subsequently consolidated. Many countries revert to dictatorship or remain mired in political disorder. Thus, Kapstein and Converse found that between 1960 and 2004, there were 123 cases in which countries changed from authoritarian to democratic government, 98 of which (nearly 80 percent) were in the Third World. A number of countries created democratic governments multiple times only to see most fail. For example, Pakistan established democracy four times in that 44-year time span, each of which failed (in 2008, it democratized once more, with a good chance it will fail to consolidate once again). Of the 98 democratic transitions in the Third World, fewer than half (46 percent) survived until 2004. Latin America had the highest success rate in the developing world (65 percent), whereas democratic change only succeeded 37 percent of the time in sub-Saharan Africa and 33 percent in Arab world (the Middle East and North Africa). In fact, one-fourth of the democratic governments created during that period collapsed within 2 years.[4] The authors identified several internal factors that increased the likelihood that a new democracy would fail, including ethnic divisions (a particular problem in sub-Saharan Africa and South Asia) and a failure to build strong political institutions, including institutional checks on the president's powers.[5]

In successfully consolidated (or reconsolidated) democracies—such as Taiwan, South Korea, Chile, and Uruguay—democratic *values* predominate among politically relevant individuals and groups. Even previously antidemocratic political parties and groups, such as the armed forces, former guerrilla groups, and far-right and far-left political parties—have come to accept democracy as the only game in town. That does not mean that consolidated democracies will *never* break down. "Never" is a long time, and in the past seemingly consolidated Third World democracies in countries such as the Philippines, Chile, and Uruguay weakened, and eventually fell to authoritarian forces. However, consolidated democracies are secure for the foreseeable future. They will probably endure unless some deep societal divide (such as class or ethnic conflict) emerges to tear them apart.

AUTHORITARIAN BEGINNINGS

With the surge in democratic transitions in recent decades, a global consensus has been emerging in support of democratic government. But that has not always been true. In the decades after World War II, as numerous African, Asian, and Middle Eastern countries achieved independence, many Third World leaders and foreign observers believed that these emerging nations were not ready for democratic government. Others argued that democracy was not even desirable at that stage of their socioeconomic development. To be sure, a number of newly independent countries—particularly former British colonies in the Caribbean, Asia, and Africa—established democratic political institutions modeled after their former colonial rulers, just as Latin American countries had patterned their political institutions on the U.S. model more than a century earlier. But only in a small number of cases (such as India, Costa Rica, and Jamaica) did democracy take a firm hold.

Since that time, Middle Eastern nations generally have been ruled by monarchs (e.g., Saudi Arabia, Morocco, and Jordan), all-powerful single parties (Egypt), or dictatorial strong men (Iraq under Saddam and Syria). Many new sub-Saharan nations created political systems dominated by a single party, including Kenya, Tanzania, and Guinea. Other African countries established military dictatorships (Nigeria and Ghana) or one-man rule (Uganda, Central African Republic).[6] Democracy fared somewhat better in Asia, but the military in that region frequently aborted the process (Myanmar, Pakistan, and Thailand). Communist revolutionaries toppled corrupt and inept governments in China, Vietnam, Cambodia, and Laos. Benefiting from greater socioeconomic development and more than a century of self-rule, Latin America had the most prior experience with democracy. Indeed, during the 1950s, relatively democratic governments predominated in that region. But the armed forces continued to meddle in national politics and in the 1960s and early 1970s, a new wave of military takeovers swept the region (including Argentina, Brazil, Chile, and Peru), often as a result of political and economic instability. It was not until the 1980s that democracy once again became the norm.

JUSTIFYING AUTHORITARIAN RULE

In the midst of democracy's recent broad advance, it seems hard to believe that not long ago, many analysts considered freely elected government unattainable or even undesirable in the LDCs. Some modernization theorists believed that the newly emerging African and Asian states were insufficiently developed, economically or socially, to sustain democracy.[7] And dependency theorists declared that democracy was unlikely to emerge because powerful industrialized nations and multinational corporations had allied with Third World elites to bolster unrepresentative governments.

At the same time, other scholars worried that levels of mass political participation in democratic or semidemocratic states were often exceeding their governments' capacity to accommodate all the new political demands. Unless Third World political institutions were strengthened, they warned, political unrest threatened to derail economic and political development.[8] Concerned about the dangers of substantial disorder, many analysts and Third World leaders justified authoritarian rule as a necessary stopgap. Only after LDCs experienced sufficient socioeconomic modernization, some argued, could they educate their citizens how to peacefully and effectively participate in politics. At the same time, modernizing societies needed to establish political institutions capable of accommodating the people's expanding demands. Until recently, developing countries were very unlikely to establish stable, democratic government unless they had raised their per-capita incomes and reached a literacy rate of at least 50 percent.[9] To be sure, in recent years, a number of countries have achieved liberal democracy without having reached that level (including Mali, with only 20 percent literacy, Benin, and Senegal), but they are few and far between. In addition to raising literacy, modernization also enlarges the size of the middle class and the organized (unionized) working class, both of whom are essential for a more stable and inclusive democracy.[10]

But, this left a troubling question. If socioeconomic modernization was necessary to establish democracy, what type of political system could bring about those necessary economic and social changes? Some social scientists believed that only a strong and stable authoritarian government—such as General Augusto Pinochet's dictatorship in Chile (1973–1990) or South Korea's military governments (1961–1987)—could jump-start modernization, economic growth, and industrialization. Authoritarian regimes alone, they noted, could limit workers' wages and control labor unrest in order to attract more multinational and domestic, private-sector investment. In East Asia, for example, several repressive governments that had produced significant economic growth (Indonesia, Singapore, South Korea, and Taiwan) insisted that dictatorial governments could better impose rational, long-term development plans. Thus, the father of Singapore's authoritarian political system and its spectacular economic growth, former president Lee Kuan Yew, stated, "I believe what a [developing] country needs to develop is discipline more than democracy . . . Democracy leads to indiscipline and disorderly conduct, which are inimical to development."[11] Only later, others said, when a country was "ready," would dictatorships give way to democracy.* Other analysts pointed to additional alleged obstacles to democratic government, for example: authoritarian or parochial traditional values and deep ethnic divisions. Consequently, they argue, only when nations developed a democratic political culture and modern social values could they hope to create stable democracies.[12]

Using some combination of these justifications, many Third World leaders insisted that democracy was inappropriate for countries in the early stage of social and economic development. In Africa, leaders in the struggle for independence often created single-party systems, banning or restricting opposition political parties. Some analysts warned that competitive elections in ethnically divided societies would only encourage candidates to organize along tribal lines, thereby further polarizing their country (see Chapter 4). In Africa and other LDCs, some founding fathers, influenced by Marxist-Leninist ideology, asserted that their nations needed an all-powerful state, led by a "vanguard party" (i.e., one that knew what was in the best interests of the masses) if they hoped to combat severe poverty, dependency, class tensions, or ethnic divisions. By 1964, roughly two-thirds of the independent African countries had become single-party states.[13] Subsequently, after many of these governments failed miserably, military dictators took their place, claiming that civilian rulers were too corrupt or too weak to govern effectively (Chapter 9). In the Middle East, similar justifications were used to defend one-party or military rule. More recently, Islamic fundamentalist governments in Iran, Sudan, and Afghanistan also have prohibited or restricted political opposition groups.

---

* Of course, even defenders of authoritarian governments had to concede that *most* dictatorships are *not* efficient modernizers. Far from it! The developing world has had more than its share of corrupt dictators who have stolen millions, ran their country's economy into the ground, and wrecked the nation's infrastructure and educational system. What they *do* claim, however, is that *efficient* dictatorships such as Taiwan's or Singapore's offered many countries the best hope for modernization. Similarly, supporters of revolutionary dictatorships (such as Cuba or China) believe they are necessary for greater social equality, as well as improved literacy and health care.

In contrast, many Latin American nations had enjoyed democratic or semidemocratic governments in the 1950s and 1960s. But, the 1970s and 1980s witnessed the rise of right-wing military dictatorships in most of the region. The new leaders justified their rule by pointing to perceived leftist threats and the need to reinvigorate the economy. Meanwhile, a number of authoritarian rulers in East Asia clung to power long after their countries had surpassed the thresholds of economic and social modernization normally associated with democratic transitions. In Singapore, South Korea, and Taiwan, the governments claimed that their dictatorships were needed to ward off external threats (from North Korea, China, or Indonesia). Others said that their Confucian cultures rejected political opposition groups as being disruptive to social harmony.

Thus, in the mid-1970s, only about 39 of the world's nations were functioning democracies and almost all of those were prosperous, industrialized countries in North America, Europe, and Australia–New Zealand. Indeed, in the 1960s and 1970s, democracy was in retreat in the developing world, as countries such as Argentina, Chile, Nigeria, and the Philippines succumbed to dictatorships. Thus, Larry Diamond observes,

> The mid-to-late 1970s seemed a low-water mark for democracy and the empirical trends were reified by intellectual fashions dismissing democracy as an artifice, a cultural construct of the West, or a "luxury" that poor states could not afford.[14]

THE THIRD WAVE AND ITS EFFECT ON THE THIRD WORLD

Since that time, however, developing countries have played a notable role in history's most sweeping transition from authoritarianism to democracy. Writing shortly before the 1991 dissolution of the Soviet Union, Samuel Huntington counted 29 countries throughout the world that had democratized in the previous 15 years alone. Of these, 20 were LDCs.[15] Although some of the countries on his list had weak democratic credentials (Romania, Peru, and Pakistan, for example) and some subsequently slid back to authoritarian rule, there can be no denying that the global trend toward democracy since the late 1970s has been palpable.

Huntington noted that the recent surge of democracy is actually the third such wave that the world has experienced since the early 1800s. In each case, democratic ideals and movements in key countries spread to other nations. The first democratic wave (1828–1926), by far the longest, began under the influence of the American and French revolutions (as well as the Industrial Revolution) and was brought to an end by the great economic depression of the 1920s. Democratization during that wave was largely confined to Europe and to former British colonies with primarily European populations (the United States, Canada, New Zealand, and Australia). The second, much shorter, wave (1943–1962) was precipitated by the struggle against fascism during World War II and the subsequent demise of European colonialism in Africa, Asia, and the Middle East. In that wave, democratic governments emerged in a number of LDCs, though most of these only met the standards of electoral democracy (competitive elections).

It is the Third Wave (roughly 1974–2000) that most draws our attention because of its pervasive and seemingly lasting reverberations in the Third

World. Of course most dramatic Third-Wave transitions were in the Eastern and Central European communist bloc, which brought the Cold War to an end. Pictures of young Germans breaking off pieces of the Berlin Wall and of Boris Yeltsin facing down a military coup in Moscow were among the most powerful political images of the late twentieth century. But in developing nations as diverse as South Africa, Mali, the Philippines, South Korea, Argentina, and Brazil, years of authoritarian or semiauthoritarian rule also ended. Huntington noted that the first two democratic waves were followed by periods of backsliding—*reverse waves*—during which a number of those countries reverted to authoritarian rule. Although there have been a number of democratic reversals since the 1990s, there have not been enough to label them a *reverse wave*. Still the pace of democratization in the twenty-first century has slowed sufficiently that analysts generally believe that the Third Wave is over.

For almost 40 years, perhaps the most widely used and respected evaluations of global democracy have been published annually by Freedom House, a nongovernmental research and advocacy group.* Each year, its panel of experts evaluates the world's nations on two dimensions of democracy: first, their level of political rights (including the extent of electoral competition and citizen participation); and, second, the quality of civil liberties (such as free speech and freedom of religion) and the prevalence of the rule of law. Based on their evaluations, Freedom House's annual reports classify all countries as Free, Partly Free, or Not Free.[†] As Table 2.1 indicates, in 1972, less than one-third of the world's 151 countries (29 percent) enjoyed fully democratic government and nearly one-half (46 percent) were not free. Since then, the Third Wave of democracy has swept over Latin America and other parts of the developing world, with the percentage of full democracies (free countries) increasing fairly steadily for the rest of the century. Some of the major advances came from the

TABLE 2.1   The Global Growth of Democracy: 1972–2008

Year	Free Countries (%)	Partly Free Countries (%)	Countries Not Free (%)	Number of Countries in the World
1972	29	25	46	151
1985	34	34	33	167
1998	46	28	26	191
2008	46	32	22	193

Sources: Larry Diamond, "Is the Third Wave Over?" *Journal of Democracy*, vol. 7, no. 3 (July 1996), 20–37; Freedom House, *Freedom in the World 2009*, http://www.freedomhouse.org/template.cfm?page=445

---

* Some critics have accused the organization of having a conservative bias. During the Cold War, it tended to evaluate communist regimes more harshly than repressive but pro-American dictatorships. But it also criticized right-wing dictatorships such as Chile and American allies such as Saudi Arabia. Its board of directors has included both prominent conservatives and leading liberals.

[†] The panel of experts rates each country's level of political rights and civil liberties on a scale of 1 (most free) to 7 (least free). Countries which had an *average* score of 1.0–2.5 for these two factors were categorized as Free. Those with average ratings of 3.0–5.0 were ranked as Partly Free. And those countries with ratings of 5.5–7.0 were labeled Not Free.

TABLE 2.2   Democracy by Region: 2008

Region	Free Countries (%)	Partly Free Countries (%)	Countries Not Free (%)
Latin America and the Caribbean	70	27	3
Asia and the Pacific	41	38	21
Sub-Saharan Africa	21	48	31
The Middle East and North Africa	6	33	61

Source: Freedom House, *Freedom in the World 2009*, http://www.freedomhouse.org./template. cfm?page=445

mid-1980s to the mid-1990s. These included the fall of the Soviet bloc and the overthrow of extended dictatorships in Chile and the Philippines. The proportion of free countries worldwide rose from 34 percent (1985) to 41 percent (1996, not shown in the table) and continued rising to 46 percent in 1998. However, during the most recent decade covered by Table 2.1 (1998–2008), the rate of democratization slowed considerably, with no change overall in the proportion of free countries (46 percent). But several important transitions still took place as two major developing countries, Indonesia and Mexico, moved from Not Free to Partly Free. Of course, Table 2.1 presents the percentage of free countries in the entire world, developed and developing alike. Obviously the LDCs had a lower percentage of free countries (see Table 2.2 for a breakdown of Third World regions). But it is precisely in the Third World that the Third Wave spread most rapidly.

Table 2.2, reveals that Third-Wave democratization has expanded at very different rates in the various regions of the developing world. Latin America and the Caribbean now have the highest percentage of free countries (70 percent), while Asia and the Pacific (41 percent) is well behind in second place. Only 21 percent of the nations in sub-Saharan Africa are currently free, but the region has seen a significant upsurge in partly free countries (48 percent). The Arab world (the Middle East and North Africa)—with a mere 6 percent free countries and 61 percent not free—lags far behind the other three regions.

INTERNATIONAL CAUSES AND CONSEQUENCES OF THE THIRD WAVE

Obviously, widespread political changes of this magnitude are inspired and influenced by broad currents that transcend the politics of particular nations. A number of factors contributed to the recent democratic transitions. For one thing, the economic crises that devastated so many LDCs in the 1980s revealed that most authoritarian regimes were no more effective and no less corrupt than the elected governments that they had contemptuously swept aside years before (indeed, they were frequently less efficient and more dishonest). Furthermore, because dictatorships lack the legitimacy that free elections bestow on democratic governments, their support depends much more heavily on satisfactory job performance. So when authoritarian governments in countries such as Argentina and Nigeria dragged their country into war, economic decay, or rampant corruption, their support rapidly eroded. In Africa, the gross mismanagement and dishonesty of both military and single-party regimes caused their already-poor economies to implode, as the continent's per-capita GNP declined by some 2 percent *annually* throughout the 1980s. Within Latin America, the economic record of military rulers was relatively strong in Chile and Brazil, but military regimes performed poorly elsewhere. By the 1980s, almost all of that region's authoritarian governments were undermined by a major foreign debt crisis.

By contrast, many East Asian dictatorships (most notably South Korea, Taiwan, Indonesia, and Singapore) enjoyed spectacular economic success from the 1960s through the late 1990s. However, rather than produce wider support for those governments, growth and modernization often generated a burgeoning middle class having both democratic aspirations and the political skills to pursue them. As the number of politically informed citizens grew, they increasingly resented government repression, state corruption, and the lack of meaningful political participation.

Throughout the world, no sooner had democratic upheavals occurred in one nation than they then spread quickly to neighboring countries. In Eastern Europe, Poland's Solidarity movement inspired democratic challenges in Hungary, East Germany, and Czechoslovakia. They, in turn, prompted protests in Bulgaria, Albania, and Romania. Students in South Korea watched television news coverage of antigovernment demonstrations in the Philippines and took the lessons of Philippine "people's power" to heart.

As the democratic tidal wave swept forward, some authoritarian leaders began to get the message. Generals in Ecuador and Paraguay watched neighboring military dictatorships fall and decided to abdicate while the going was still good. After more than 40 years of authoritarian rule by the Kuomintang Party and political domination by the mainland Chinese minority, Taiwan's government opened up to authentic electoral competition and political freedom. In Africa, a number of single-party states liberalized their political systems, allowing greater freedom and political space for opposition groups, while a smaller but growing number established liberal democracies (including Benin, Cape Verde, Ghana, Mali, and São Tomé & Principe).

As we noted earlier, the demise of communist regimes in Eastern Europe exposed more clearly the deficiencies of their ideology and behavior. As Marxism-Leninism was discredited, even among many of its once-fervent adherents, democracy assumed greater international legitimacy. The end of the Cold War also permitted the United States to be more consistent in its advocacy of political freedom. That is to say, the United States no longer had any reason to coddle allied Third World dictators whose friendship it had previously cultivated to thwart the spread of Communism. For example, the United States had supported corrupt and repressive dictators in countries such as Zaire, Iran, and the Philippines, because they were considered necessary allies in the Cold War. With the end of the Soviet challenge, there was no reason to stand by such regimes. There remain, however, notable exceptions, as the United States has retained close ties to several strategically important, but repressive regimes, such as Pakistan under General Musharraf and to oil-rich autocracies such as Saudi Arabia.

THE PREREQUISITES OF DEMOCRACY
IN INDIVIDUAL COUNTRIES

While international developments were catalysts, providing developing countries with incentives and opportunities to democratize, not all developing nations took advantage of those opportunities. More than 30 years after the start of the Third Wave, some LDCs remain mired in dictatorship, with still no openings in their political system. Others either have failed to complete their democratic transitions or have alternated between authoritarianism and weak democracy. Finally, some fortunate countries seem to have consolidated their democracies.*

What accounts for these differences? What determines whether or not a particular country embarks on the road toward democracy, whether it completes that voyage successfully, and whether it eventually consolidates democratic values, practices, and institutions? In other words, how do we know whether democracy will take root and survive in Brazil, Indonesia, or Madagascar? Finally, why has democracy advanced further in some regions, such as Latin America, than in other regions, such as the Middle East?

There are no simple answers. Scholars have debated these issues for decades and have identified a number of historical, structural, and cultural variables that help account for democracy's presence in, say, India and Uruguay, and its absence in countries such as Syria or Laos. But political scientists still disagree about the relative importance of those variables. In the discussion that follows, we examine a number of factors that have been widely identified as prerequisites for democracy.

Social and Economic Modernization

Over 40 years ago, Seymour Martin Lipset observed that democracy was far more prevalent in industrialized countries such as the United States and Sweden than in poorer nations—a finding congruent with modernization theory (Chapter 1).[16] Subsequent political science research has largely supported that claim. The reasoning behind this relationship was that

> industrialization leads to increases in wealth, education, communication and equality; these developments are associated with a more moderate lower and upper class and a larger middle class, which is by nature moderate; and this in turn increases the probability of stable democratic forms of politics.[17]

Over the years, social scientists have identified more precisely the particular aspects of modernization that promote democracy. Philips Cutright determined that when other factors are held constant, there is a strong correlation between the extent of a country's mass communications and its degree of democracy, stronger even than the correlation between economic development and democracy.[18] A free and active mass media and opportunities for

---

* Whether or not a particular country has consolidated its democracy (i.e., has made it "the only game in town") is a judgment call over which experts may disagree. Only the test of time ultimately determines whether a democratic government has endured.

citizens to exchange ideas promote a free society. Years later, Axel Hadenius, examining the influence of dozens of independent variables, found that democracy correlates most strongly with higher levels of literacy and education.[19] An educated population, it appears, is more likely to follow politics and to participate in that process. It is also more capable of defending its own interests. From roughly 1990 to 2004, the Third World adult literacy rate rose from 68 percent to 79 percent.[20] This bodes well for Third World democracy because, as we have noted, in the recent past countries whose populations are more than half literate are far more likely to sustain democracy than those that fall below that mark. Today, only about 20 countries (all in sub-Saharan Africa or South Asia) are less than half literate.

Various analysts have also shown that countries with higher per-capita incomes are more likely to be democratic than poorer ones, a finding congruent with Lipset's observation. Today, for example, most LDCs with per-capita incomes that exceed $2,500 are democracies of some sort, while those with incomes under $2,500 are not.

That does not mean that countries inevitably become more democratic as their economies develop. In fact, middle-income countries are frequently *less* stable and more prone to dictatorship.[21] For example, even though the World Bank ranked South America's most industrialized countries (Argentina, Brazil, Chile, and Uruguay) as upper-middle-income nations, their democratic governments all fell to repressive, military dictatorships in the 1960s and 1970s. On the other hand, India—still a very poor nation—has enjoyed one of the LDCs' strongest records of sustained democracy. But, while these exceptions are important, there is still generally a correlation between economic development and democracy. Although poor countries may be as likely as richer ones to make the transition to democracy, they are less likely to *sustain* democratic government. In recent decades, for example, East Asia's rapid economic growth, higher literacy, and expanding middle classes promoted democratic transitions in South Korea, Thailand, and Taiwan (though Thai democracy was suspended, at least temporarily, in 2006). In Latin America, where levels of modernization are high by Third World standards, the democratic wave since the close of the 1970s has seemingly established consolidated democracies in most of the region. Conversely, Africa, which is home to most of the world's poorest nations, has suffered a number of failed transitions.

However, as the Third Wave of democracy has spread to further reaches of the developing world, the correlation between economic development and democracy has weakened somewhat. In fact, a growing number of very poor countries has overcome the odds and established some level of liberal democracy. As of 2004, there were 38 countries with per-capita incomes of $3,500 or less that Freedom House rated as Free (liberal democracies), 15 of which had incomes of $1,500 or less.[22]

Class Structure

Some scholars contend that it is not economic growth per se that induces and sustains democracy but rather the way in which that growth affects a country's social structure. Specifically, they reason, economic development supports stable democracy only if it induces appropriate changes in the country's class structure.

Since the time of Aristotle, political theorists have linked democracy and political stability to the presence of a large and vibrant middle class. The middle class, they suggest, tends to be politically moderate and serves as a bridge between the upper and lower classes. Its members also have the political and organizational skills necessary to create political parties and other important democratic institutions. An independent and influential business class (bourgeoisie) also seems essential for developing democracy. So, in those countries where economic growth has failed to create a politically independent and influential middle class and bourgeoisie, modernization does not necessarily buttress democracy and may even weaken it. To be sure, the political independence and the influence of the emerging middle classes and bourgeoisie have varied among different world regions, depending on the historical period in which those areas industrialized. For example, industrialization and urbanization produced a larger, more powerful, and more independent middle class and bourgeoisie in Northern Europe than it did a century later in Latin America. In the latter case, wealth and income were more concentrated and the middle class correspondingly weaker and more dependent. Predictably, democracy did not take hold as readily in Latin America as it had in Northern Europe.

Barrington Moore Jr. in his widely acclaimed study of economic and political change, *The Social Origins of Dictatorship and Democracy*, identified three discrete paths to modernization, each shaped by the relative power of the state and the strength of the major social classes. In one path, typified by nineteenth- and early-twentieth-century Germany, modernization was led by a strong state allied with powerful and antidemocratic agricultural landowners and a bourgeoisie that was dependent on the state. In Germany and subsequently in Third World countries with similar political configurations, that combination ultimately resulted in the rise of fascist and far-right authoritarian regimes. A second path to modernization, found in countries such as China, was characterized by a highly centralized state, a repressive landowning class, a weak bourgeoisie, and a large and eventually rebellious peasantry. The end result of that alignment was a communist revolution fought by the peasantry.

Finally, Moore's third path, identified most closely with Britain, featured a weaker state and a strong bourgeoisie at odds with the rural landowning elite. Only this alignment of forces, distinguished by the bourgeoisie's powerful and independent political role, has led to liberal democracy. "No [strong and independent] bourgeoisie," Moore noted, "no democracy."[23] Similarly, in developing nations today, a vibrant middle class and an influential business class have been critical ingredients in the establishment and consolidation of democracy. It should come as no surprise, then, that in countries as diverse as Chile, Indonesia, the Philippines, South Korea, and, most recently, Iran, middle-class citizens, including university students, have been on the front lines in recent struggles for democracy.

Very poor countries, such as Afghanistan, Haiti, Kenya, and Nepal, whose middle classes are small and dependent on the state or on rural landlords, are far less likely to achieve or sustain democratic government. But it is also important to remember that even though a strong middle class and bourgeoisie are necessary for democracy, those sectors are not always democratically oriented. For example, in pre-Nazi (Weimar) Germany and in Argentina and Chile during the 1970s, when the middle class felt threatened by social unrest from below, many of its members supported fascist or other right-wing extremist dictatorships.

More recently, Rueschemeyer, Huber Stephens, and Stephens have focused attention on the role of organized labor in building democracy. They argue that while the bourgeoisie and the middle class generally fostered democracy in Western Europe, Latin America, and the Caribbean, those groups usually favored a restricted form of democratic government that enhanced their own political strength (vis-à-vis the upper class and the state) but also limited the political influence of the lower class. Consequently, countries achieve comprehensive democracy only when they also have a politically potent, unionized working class that has pushed for broader political representation and increased social justice.[24]

In summary, democracy tends to flourish best where economic modernization produces a politically influential and independent bourgeoisie/middle class and where labor unions effectively defend the interests of the working class. When any of those classes are small, weak, or politically dependent on authoritarian actors, such as rural landowners, democracy is less likely to emerge.

Political Culture

In the final analysis, neither a country's level of socioeconomic development nor its class structure can fully explain whether or not it has been able to create or sustain democracy. For example, during the early decades of the twentieth century, Argentina was one of the most affluent nations on earth (far wealthier than Italy or Japan, for example), with substantial middle and working classes. Yet the country failed to develop into a liberal democracy. Instead, it embarked on a half-century of recurring coups and military dictatorships. More recently, Singapore, South Korea, and Taiwan retained authoritarian governments for many years after they had reached the normal social and economic thresholds for democracy.[25] And, as we have just seen, economic wealth has not brought democracy to petroleum states such as Kuwait and Saudi. On the other hand, India has sustained democracy for decades despite its extensive poverty and low literacy rate. And, several African nations have become democratic in recent years despite having literacy rates well below 50 percent. The same holds true for a growing, though still small, number of low-income countries.

Many scholars have argued that, aside from its level of economic development and its class structure, a nation's democratic potential is also influenced by its political culture—that is, its cultural beliefs, norms, and values relating to politics. A country's constitution may call for contested elections, a free press, and the separation of powers, but unless the people, especially elites and political activists, value these objectives, constitutional protections are unlikely to have great weight. Some of the most important values needed to sustain democracy include a belief that the vote and other forms of individual and group political participation are important and potentially productive; trust in government institutions and in fellow citizens; tolerance of opposition and dissenting political opinions and beliefs, even when those views are very unpopular; accepting the outcome of free and fair elections as definitive, regardless of who wins; viewing politics as a process that requires compromise; rejection of violent political action or other circumvention of democratic institutions; and, commitment to democracy as the best form of government, regardless of how well or poorly a particular democratic administration performs. Obviously there are no countries in which every citizen subscribes to all of these values or beliefs, but democracy normally is sustainable only if a large portion of the population supports them.

The recent wave of successful democratic transitions has renewed interest in how a country's political culture affects consolidation of democracy. Survey research allows us to measure more precisely a society's political beliefs. For example, public opinion surveys conducted soon after the fall of Soviet Communism revealed that Russia had yet to develop a broadly based democratic political culture. Only one in eight Russians expressed confidence in the new postcommunist administration. A substantial minority, distressed by Russia's economic decline at that time, yearned for the security and stability of the communist era, and many citizens cared little about protecting civil liberties and minority rights. For example, in one major opinion survey conducted soon after the fall of Communism, almost one in three Russians supported the death penalty for homosexuals and for prostitutes.[26] While such extreme intolerance has declined since then, racist prejudice has grown against darker-skinned immigrants from Central Asia and non-Slavic Russians from the North Caucuses. Lacking a democratic political culture, most Russians have supported Vladimir Putin (as Prime Minister and as President) in spite of his authoritarian behavior.

Robert Dahl, a leading democratic theorist, observes that all political systems eventually confront major crises such as economic decline, ethnic violence, or political stalemate. At those times, many political leaders in unconsolidated democracies are tempted to seek authoritarian solutions such as imposing martial law or restricting civil liberties.* If, however, a broad segment of the population (including members of the political and economic elites) shares democratic values, democracy can survive the crisis intact. Dahl stresses two particularly important democratic values: first, that the armed forces and police must willingly submit to the command of democratically elected civilian authorities; second, government and society must tolerate and legally protect dissident political beliefs.

The first value (civilian control of the military) is taken for granted in industrialized democracies, but not in countries such as Guatemala, Bangladesh, and Turkey, where the armed forces have frequently exercised veto power over the policy decisions of elected officials and have sometimes ousted civilian government. Dahl's second cultural standard (tolerance of dissent) also presents a challenge to many developing countries, where even freely elected governments sometimes silence critics and muzzle opposition leaders. The crucial question, then, says Dahl, is, "How can robust democratic cultures be created in countries where they previously have been largely absent?"[27] He responds that there is no easy answer, but that developing a democratic culture is a gradual process in which socioeconomic modernization and political development need to reinforce each other.

Sometimes external forces may promote or even impose a democratic political culture on another country, as U.S. occupation forces did in Japan after World War II. Many African and Asian countries were first introduced to modern politics by the colonial powers that ruled them. Analysis of the LDCs

---

* Even in a deeply consolidated democracy such as the United States, civil libertarians charge that the terrorist threat has led to government infringements on civil liberties. These include parts of the Homeland Security Act and the treatment of prisoners at Guantanamo Bay.

reveals that one of the factors most closely related to democratic government is having previously been a British colony.[28] Of course, not all former British colonies became democracies; in fact, until recently, most of those in Africa have not been. However, in general, countries that experienced British colonial rule were significantly more likely to maintain democracy after independence than were those nations previously colonized by France, Belgium, the Netherlands, Spain, or Portugal. This pattern suggests that Britain more successfully inculcated democratic values in its colonies than other European powers did. However, apart from those cases, external intervention has had a mixed record of success. And, today, many analysts question whether the current U.S. interventions in Afghanistan and Iraq will help develop a democratic culture in those two nations.

A country's political culture influences its political system in a number of ways. For example, communities with high levels of mutual tolerance and a politically informed population are more hospitable to democracy than are less tolerant or less knowledgeable societies. But how fixed in a nation's psyche are such values? Is there something inherently more democratic or more authoritarian about Norwegian, French, or Chinese cultures? Are some religions or philosophies, such as Christianity, more conducive to democracy than, say, Confucianism? Here scholars disagree strongly. Cultural stereotypes are inherently controversial and often prejudiced. But is it possible that objective analysis could show that countries with certain religions or cultural traditions are more likely to support democratic values, while others are more prone to authoritarianism? In fact, the data clearly show that predominantly Christian nations, particularly Protestant ones, are the most likely to be democratic, even when other causal factors (such as economic development or literacy) are held constant. For example, Protestant nations are more likely to be democracies than are countries that have similar levels of economic development but different religious beliefs. "Protestantism is said to foster individual responsibility and is thereby also more skeptical and less fundamentalist in character."[29]

More recently, observers have noted the low level of democracy in Islamic countries, especially in the Middle East. Some maintain that Islamic beliefs do not readily support democratic institutions because they fail to separate religion and politics (i.e., church and state).[30] At the same time, when impressive economic growth and increased educational levels during the 1970s and early 1980s were slow to bring democracy to China, Singapore, South Korea, and Taiwan, some experts concluded that cultural (religious) beliefs must have been overriding the positive influences of economic modernization. They argued that Confucian culture promotes rigidly hierarchical societies and encourages excessive obedience to authority, values that are antithetical to democracy.[31]

Not surprisingly, cultural explanations such as these are highly controversial. They are difficult to prove and may simply reflect their proponents' prejudice and ethnocentrism. Catholics may feel uneasy with theories that contrast the traditional strength of democracy in the United States, Canada, and the English-speaking Caribbean with Latin America's authoritarian tradition, leading many analysts to conclude that Catholic values offer less support for democracy than Protestant norms.[32] Similarly, most Muslims and Confucians reject theories that depict their religions as authoritarian. But do the facts support these hypotheses, however unpleasant some people may find them?

Although Protestant nations are more likely to be democratic than are Buddhist countries and even though democracy has fared poorly in most Islamic nations, it is difficult to ascertain how much these disparities are the result of differing religious values and how much they result from innumerable other historical, economic, and cultural factors that are not easily statistically controlled. We know that several Islamic nations—including Turkey, Lebanon, and, most recently, Indonesia—have achieved some degree of democracy. Moreover, Alfred Stepan and Graeme Robertson have demonstrated that, while Arab countries, even wealthier ones, have rarely achieved electoral democracy, *non-Arab* Muslim nations are somewhat more likely to be democracies than a matched sample of non-Muslim countries with comparable levels of economic and social development.[33] A recent article by Graham Fuller, a Middle East specialist and former high-ranking CIA official, makes a similar argument contending that if Islam did not exist most Middle Eastern nations would still not be democratic.[34] Finally, if Islamic and Catholic cultures inherently promoted nondemocratic values, one would expect that American Catholics would be less democratically inclined than their Protestant counterparts are. In the same way, we would predict that Bosnian Muslims would be less committed to democracy than Bosnian Serbs (Christians) and Indian Muslims would be less democratic than Hindus. But there is no evidence to support any of those expectations.

Furthermore, even if it were true that certain religions are more likely to predispose their adherents toward democracy or toward authoritarianism, there is so much variation within most world religions (e.g., Unitarian and Southern Baptist branches of Protestantism, or Shi'a, Sunni, and Sufi sectors of Islam), each with its own political subculture, that it is misleading to suggest that there is a uniform Protestant, Muslim, or Buddhist political culture. Over the years, conservatives in France, Italy, Spain, and Latin America have invoked Catholic theology to support right-wing authoritarian movements or governments. On the other hand, leftist supporters of liberation theology (see Chapter 3) have drawn upon Catholic doctrine and practices to support antiauthoritarian movements in countries such as El Salvador and the Philippines.

Finally, we need to remember that religious beliefs and political cultures are capable of change and do not permanently mire a country or region in a particular value system. For example, during World War II, the Japanese and German political cultures were considered militarily bellicose and authoritarian. Today, however, these countries are highly consolidated democracies whose citizens are far less inclined to support armed interventions (such as in Iraq or Afghanistan) than Americans are. Not long ago, many analysts viewed Confucian values as obstacles to East Asian democratization. However, despite such pessimism, Confucianism has apparently not impeded South Korea's and Taiwan's democratic transitions. Nor did the fact that Catholic societies were less hospitable to democracy in the past hinder their democratic transitions during the closing decades of the twentieth century. Indeed, from Portugal and Spain to Argentina, Brazil, and Mexico, democracy has recently taken root in Catholic nations that not long ago were depicted as culturally authoritarian. Moreover, in recent decades, the Church hierarchy itself has been a pivotal voice for democratic change in Catholic countries such as Poland, the Philippines, Chile, and Brazil.[35]

In short, political cultures appear to be more malleable than previously recognized. "This does not mean that the prevalent attitudes . . . within a society have no consequences for the character of its democracy, only that we should not look to unchanging belief systems for their explanation."[36] As Larry Diamond notes, often "democratic culture is as much the product as the cause of effectively functioning democracy."[37] Just as democratic values support democratic consolidation, sustained democratic *institutions* and *behavior* help inculcate democratic values. Many first-time democracies *initially* lack a healthy democratic political culture. In countries such as Russia (where citizens largely accept Vladimir Putin's authoritarian leadership) this has helped cut short democracy in its infancy. But other nations have overcome this obstacle and the longer they continue democratic practices, the better are their chances of acquiring democratic values. Indeed, if a country can sustain democracy for two decades, it is relatively unlikely to ever collapse. For example, Robert Dahl's examination of 52 countries in which democracy had failed identified only two (Chile and Uruguay) that had enjoyed democracy for more than 20 years prior to that failure.[38] And even those two exceptions subsequently reinstituted democracy more successfully than did neighboring countries such as Bolivia and Peru, which lack comparable democratic traditions.

The Curse of Oil Wealth

Some developing nations—such as Brunei, Kuwait, and Saudi Arabia—have become comparatively wealthy through development of their sizable oil reserves. On first glance, extensive petroleum resources seem to offer the possibilities of quick and easy economic growth and, hopefully, political development. We would expect that if oil wealth brings economic growth it would also increase the probability of a transition to democracy. Instead, almost all countries whose exports and government revenues are dominated by petroleum have been woefully unable to democratize. Hence, many political scientists and economist have refered to the "curse of oil."[39] In a recently published book, Larry Diamond identifies 23 nations—21 of them in the developing world—that receive 60 percent or more of their export earnings from the petroleum sales.[40] Yet only two of those nations had ever enjoyed a period of liberal democracy in recent decades (Nigeria and Venezuela) and those two have regressed to being only Partly Free.

Why has oil wealth seemingly been an obstacle to democracy? Analysts such as Diamond have suggested a number of reasons. For one thing, currently the petroleum industry in most oil-rich, developing countries is owned or largely controlled by the government. Consequently, the new oil wealth strengthens the power of the state, providing funds for the military and police and funding large government bureaucracies that offer patronage jobs to government supporters. Furthermore, in countries such as Iran, Syria, and Venezuela, major, private-sector firms are heavily dependent on the state for credit, licenses, and the like. Thus, they do not produce the independent bourgeoisie that has historically been crucial for democracy. Similarly, the middle class—another bulwarks of liberal democracy— also fails to challenge state power because so many of its members depend on jobs in the government bureaucracy. And, with little industrialization, a large portion of the working class is employed in the oil industry, making them dependent on the state and, like the middle class and bourgeoisie, incapable of challenging state power.

Armed with substantial oil and gas revenues, these petroleum states can lower taxes and offer private companies and the general public inexpensive services and goods such as subsidized credit, food, and housing. Although this obviously has its attractions, its consequence is that "people become clients and not citizens," that is, wards of the state who are not active in the political system.[41] With low taxes and an array of government benefits, the average citizen has little incentive to question government corruption, mismanagement, or repression. To paraphrase a battle cry of the American Revolution, "without taxation they have no effective representation." Another curse of oil dependency is massive corruption. Expanding bureaucracies and state enterprises give politicians opportunities to sell jobs. Businessmen seeking subsedized financial credit from the government and those in the hunt for state contracts routinely bribe public officials. High-level government officials often plunder the national treasury. In the worst example, former military dictator, General Sani Abacha of Nigeria, is believed to have stolen some $3–4 billion of government funds prior to his death. Indeed, according to the watchdog organization Transparency International, Third World, oil-centered countries (most of them in the Middle East and Africa) have particularly high rates of government corruption.

All of these factors—heavy concentration of economic power in the hands of the state, clientelism, capitalist and middle-class dependency, and corruption—have effectively impeded the growth of democracy. The fact that only two of the more than 20 developing countries that depend heavily on oil for their export earnings have ever been full democracies clearly demonstrates its negative impact. However, several cautionary observations are in order. First, neither an oil boom nor having oil as a very large percentage of export revenue absolutely prevents a country from developing or maintaining democracy. For example, Norway only began North Sea petroleum extraction in the 1970s and has emerged as a major producer since the 1980s. As of 2009, oil accounted for almost half of the country's export revenues—not far below Diamond's 60 percent cutoff for classification as an oil-rich country—and about one-third of government revenues. It is currently the world's third largest oil exporters, well behind Saudi Arabia and Russia (and slightly ahead of Iran and Venezuela).[42] Yet because of its political culture, commitment to equality, and long tradition of government honesty, Norway has remained one of the world's strongest democracies. On the other hand, virtually all oil-dependent developing countries—including Angola, Algeria, Chad, Iran, Iraq, and Syria—were already authoritarian (and often corrupt) *before* their oil booms. Still, Diamond notes that two of the most important countries to democratize in recent years— Indonesia and Mexico—only completed that transition after oil fell from over 60 percent to less 33 percent of export revenue.

HOW DO DEMOCRACIES PERFORM?
PUBLIC POLICY COMPARED

Some of the benefits of democracy are obvious: protecting personal freedom and holding governments accountable to the governed, to name but two. Nonetheless, over the years, scholars have debated whether democratic governments also better provide for the economic and social welfare of their citizens. As we noted earlier, during the closing decades of the twentieth century, many international agencies, journalists, and scholars maintained that certain dictatorships—in countries such as Chile, China, Indonesia, Singapore,

South Korea, and Taiwan—had imposed the efficiency and discipline necessary to generate rapid economic growth.[43] The dramatic economic growth these authoritarian regimes produced into the 1990s was often compared to the less impressive performance of democratic governments in countries such as India and Uruguay.

But, the passage of time and a more complete examination of over 100 LDCs dispel such claims. Generally, those who have insisted that authoritarian rule is more suited for economic development base their argument on the accomplishments of a few impressive cases. But for every authoritarian star economic performer—including Chile, China, South Korea, Singapore, and Taiwan—there were far more authoritarian regimes with disastrous economic records—such as Myanmar, Tajikistan, and Zimbabwe. In fact, "between 1960 and 2000, 95 percent of the world's worst economic performances . . . were overseen by nondemocratic governments."[44] Furthermore, prior to its market-oriented reforms begun in the late 1980s, China's communist regime had a much more erratic record of economic growth. Chile's rate of growth was generally strong under its military dictatorship, but growth improved when the country restored democracy. Finally, during the past two decades, the once-stagnant economy of India—the world's largest democracy—has become one of the most dynamic in the world.

Analyzing annual economic growth data from more than 150 countries during each year from 1960 to 2001, Halperin, Siegle, and Weinstein compared the performance of democratic nations with those of autocracies (dictatorships). They found that in every one of the more than 40 years studied, the democratic nations as a group grew faster than the autocracies. Furthermore, "citizens of democracies live longer, healthier lives, on average, than those in autocracies [with comparable per capita incomes]."[45] To be sure, when they examined only the world's poorest nations, they observed no difference in the economic growth rate of democracies versus dictatorship. Still, even among the poorest countries, economic growth was less volatile in democracies than in autocracies (less subject to sharp ups and downs). Similarly, Dani Rodrik used regression analysis to examine data for more than 80 countries over a span of 24 years (1970–1994). He found that there was no appreciable difference between the long-term economic growth rates of democracies and authoritarian governments. But, democracies outperformed authoritarian regimes on several other important economic indicators. Their economies were less volatile, more predictable, paid better wages to workers, and could "handle adverse shocks [like the Asian financial crisis or severe jumps in oil prices] much better."[46] Finally, another recent study comparing democracies with nondemocracies found that democratic countries spent more on public education, had higher school enrollments, higher literacy rates, and greater public access to health care services.[47]

Democratic government is not necessarily superior in all areas of governance. In theory, freely elected government official should be less corrupt than authoritarian administrators because they are held accountable in the next election. But in countries that have simultaneously switched from command economies to capitalism, as well as in nations that have enormous sources of natural resource wealth (such as oil revenues) linked to the government, and in countries with a historical tradition of corruption, democratization may not improve government honesty and may actually make things worse. Thus, for example, Russia's transition to capitalism and to democracy in the 1990s opened up the floodgates for corruption. In Cambodia, the communist regime has been replaced by a government of competing "mafias."

Nigeria has both extensive petroleum reserves and a tradition of deep government corruption. The military governments that had ruled the country for 16 years were enormously dishonest, even by Third World standards, and turned their leaders into billionaires. But, the 1999 transition to democracy brought little improvement. The Nigerian government is still considered one of the most corrupt in the world. Governors of the country's 36 states "get a check each month that represents their state's cut of Nigeria's booming oil fortune, and have almost no one to answer to for how they spend that money."[48] Small wonder that some governors, when faced with serious electoral opposition in their bids for reelection, have threatened the lives of their opponents and, in some cases, have had them eliminated.

DEMOCRATIC CONSOLIDATION

It is important to recall that although the breadth of democratic transitions in the developing world has been impressive, political change can occur in both directions. Many countries that have achieved electoral or liberal democracy have seen their new governments fail, followed by a return to authoritarian rule. In 1994, a military coup in Gambia ended 28 years of democratic government. Recent examples of renewed authoritarianism include Russia, Pakistan, Bangladesh, and Thailand. Between 1980 and 2000, democracy collapsed in 26 countries, though a number of those (such as Ecuador and Turkey) subsequently resumed being free or partly-free.[49] What makes democracy endure or falter? Which of the Third World's new democracies have the qualities needed to consolidate democracy? To answer that question, Adam Przeworski and his associates analyzed data for 135 countries over a 40-year period.[50] Democracy, they found, is most fragile in poor countries (with per-capita incomes of less than $1,000), and it becomes more stable as national income rises:* "Above $6,000 [per-capita real income], democracies are impregnable and can be expected to live forever; no democratic system has ever fallen in a country where per-capita income exceeds $6,055 (Argentina's level in 1976)."[51] Several factors explain why richer democracies are more likely to last. For one thing, they normally have a crucial foundation for democratic government—high educational levels.† For another, class conflict over the distribution of economic rewards is typically less intense in more affluent societies.

Contrary to what many political scientists had believed, Przeworski et al. also found the faster a nation's economy grows, the more likely it is to sustain

---

* All dollar figures in the study were expressed in constant dollars, meaning that they are adjusted for inflation, so that per-capita "real incomes" of $1,000 in 1960 and in 1990 are equivalent.

† In other words, countries that are more economically advanced normally have higher literacy and education rates, and countries with higher literacy rates are more likely to be democratic. There are several petroleum-producing countries in the Middle East (such as Saudi Arabia and the United Arab Emirates) that, although wealthy, do not have particularly high literacy rates. None of those are democracies.

democracy. Conversely, democracy is less likely to survive in countries suffering economic decline, high inflation rates, or other forms of economic crises. However, important as domestic economic factors are, the authors discovered that international political conditions exert a more powerful influence on democratic survivability. Specifically, the more prevalent democratic government becomes in other nations, the more likely any particular Third World country is to sustain its own democracy, regardless of its per-capita income, literacy rate, or economic growth rate. In other words, as many scholars had suspected, democracy is contagious. Other analysts have noted that developing and maintaining effective political institutions—including representative and responsible political parties, a broad array of interest groups, a representative and influential legislature, a strong but not unlimited executive branch, an honest and independent judicial system—are absolutely critical for sustaining stable and effective democracy. Too often, Third World judicial systems lack independence from the executive branch, do not have adequate legal training, and are excessively corrupt. Consolidating democracies must strengthen their judiciary systems, so that they can stand up to power-hungry presidents or prime ministers and so that court decisions are respected by the electorate. A related problem in many new and reestablished democracies is executive-branch dominance over the national legislature. In Latin America, Russia, and elsewhere, democratically elected presidents have sometimes interpreted their electoral victories to mean that the voters had delegated absolute authority to them. For example, even though they were initially elected democratically, once in office, Presidents Carlos Menem (Argentina) and Alberto Fujimori (Peru) ran roughshod over their nation's congress and court system. That is perhaps one reason that Juan Linz and Arturo Valenzuela have found that democracy is more likely to fail in presidential systems than in countries with parliamentary forms of government.[52] Other political scientists, however, have challenged that claim.

Improving the Quality of Democracy

More than three decades after the start of the Third Wave, its reach has become far broader than the previous two waves, and, equally importantly, to date there has not been an extensive backlash. To be sure, a number of new democracies have not survived. In their most recent report, *Freedom in the World* 2009, the authors note that "global freedom suffered its third year of decline in 2008." Although the 3-year deterioration is the longest since Freedom House began its evaluations in 1972, it did not signal a reverse wave of recently democratized countries reverting to authoritarianism. Rather, it indicated increased repression by already-authoritarian regimes (e.g., Iran, Venezuela, and Russia) and the decline of several nations from partly free to not free (e.g., Afghanistan and Mauritania).[53] Indeed, as Table 2.1 indicates, the percentage of countries in the world rated as Free in 2008 was the same as it had been in 1998. The fact that democracy is now widely accepted as the best form of government is cause for satisfaction. At the same time, however, in many Third World countries (and former communist nations), democratic governments have failed to meet the needs of their citizens. While free and fair elections, improved civil liberties, and civilian command over the military are important achievements, too often democratic rule has not lived up to mass expectations. As a consequence, many political scientists have turned their attention from the consolidation of democracy (how and why democracy lasts) to improving the *quality* of democracy. Public opinion surveys in both advanced industrial democracies and Third World democracies have indicated that citizens are generally becoming more distrustful of government and suspicious of political parties and politicians. Frequently they consider government officials corrupt and self-serving. Consequently, any search for higher quality democratic government has two important objectives: first, it is a moral imperative (fair, effective, and honest government is itself desirable); second, more effective and honest democratic government normally increases support for democracy and, thereby, increases democracy's longevity. Slightly modifying Larry Diamond and Leonardo Morlino's model, we can evaluate the quality of democracy in terms of seven dimensions, which, in turn can be grouped into three broad categories:[54]

1. **Procedural Dimensions**: The procedures used to elect government officials and the procedures that public officials use to govern must be honest, fair, and equitable. These procedures can be divided into four categories:
   A. *Participation*: All adult citizens must have the right to vote as well as to participate in the political system in other ways. Powerful groups should not intimidate the poor or ethnic minorities from participating. A politically aware citizenry should not allow apathy to restrict their own participation.
   B. *Competition*: There should be free and fair elections between competing political parties, and the incumbent party should not have any built-in advantage in gaining access to state funds or to the media. The electoral system should not give certain parties automatic advantages.
   C. *Accountability*: A democratic electoral system must guarantee that government officials are fairly elected. But officials must also be held accountable for their actions between elections. Vertical accountability refers to procedures that allow citizens or independent groups to challenge or criticize a government official's behavior. Horizontal accountability refers to the ability of one government body to check the power of another branch, such as the Supreme Court overruling a decision by the president or the parliament removing a prime minister.
   D. *The Rule of Law*: The legal system must apply equally to all citizens and all laws must be publicly known and clear. The judiciary must be neutral and independent.
2. **Substantive Dimensions**: Beyond adhering to proper procedures, quality democracies must pursue policies that advance:
   A. *Respect for Civil Liberties and the Pursuit of Freedom*: This includes respect for individual liberty, security and privacy, freedom of information, expression, and religion, and due process.
   B. *Reductions in Political, Economic, and Social Inequalities*: In order to attain political equality, where there is substantial social and economic inequality, government needs to reduce income gaps. Scholars such as Terry Karl and Dietrich Rueschemeyer maintain that political equality and democracy have been difficult to achieve in the face of glaring income inequalities in Latin America and parts of Africa.[55] Different analysts, however, will disagree on how much equality is acceptable or perhaps even desirable.
3. **Result Dimensions**: This final category includes only a single dimension—*responsiveness*. A democratically responsive government is one in which "the democratic process induces the government to form and implement policies that the people want."[56] In order to achieve that, there needs to be a stable political party system, with parties that offer coherent and distinguishable programs.

CONCLUSION

Too frequently, democratic transitions have produced unfulfilled economic aspirations, corrupt government, and widespread dissatisfaction with government institutions. Hence, even though most Third World citizens have an abstract preference for democracy as a form of government, too many of them are cynical about the *performance* of democratic regimes. In 2004, the United Nations Development Program commissioned a survey of 18,643 citizens in 18 Latin American countries. Although Latin America has made the greatest progress toward democracy of any Third World region, the survey uncovered growing disillusionment regarding that system's ability to remedy poverty and economic stagnation. Thus, "while a broad majority (64 percent) of those interviewed said they agreed that democracy is the only system capable of achieving development, about half admitted they would not mind if an authoritarian regime came to power as long as it could solve their financial problems."[57] Indeed, 55 percent of all respondents said that they would favor a dictator over a democratically elected leader if that improved their economic conditions.[58] The 2006 survey by Latinobarómetro demonstrated a modest increase in support for the concept of democracy. Thus, 74 percent of the nearly 19,000 respondents agreed that "democracy may have its problems but it is the best form of government," up from 64 percent 3 years earlier. At the same time, however, their evaluations of the specific performances of their own democratic governments were far more negative. In 2005 and 2006 surveys, respondents were asked "Would you say that [your country] is governed for the benefit of a few powerful groups or is it governed for the good of all?" Some 70 percent chose "for the benefit of a few powerful groups," while only about 25 percent chose "for the good of all." Similarly, most Latin Americans had low opinions of fundamental democratic institutions such as their political parties and the national congress.[59]

Latinobarómetro's 2006–2007 results showed that a majority of citizens in every country surveyed (Cuba was not included) believed that democracy was the best form of government despite its faults, though the percentage of support varied from 82 percent in Uruguay (almost equal to the United States' 87 percent) down to only 53 percent in Panama. But when they were asked whether they were satisfied about how democratic governments had actually performed in their country, people were not nearly as positive. In 11 of the 20 countries (including regional powers such as Brazil and Mexico), the majority of citizens were dissatisfied with how democracy had worked in their country. Levels of trust in political parties and other political institutions are considerably lower in most Latin American nations than in the United States or Canada. Citizens in most of the region's countries were also less tolerant of opposition points of view than are Americans or Canadians.[60]

Afrobarometer's survey of 18 sub-Saharan African nations in 2005–2006 revealed that despite the checked history of elections in that continent, citizens had a surprisingly positive view of elections in *their own* country. Two-thirds (66 percent) believed that their most recent national election was completely or largely free and fair. Most Africans (62 percent) continued to agree that "democracy [as an ideal] is preferable to any other kind of government." But, like Latin Americans, many had become disillusioned with the performance of their new democratic governments. For example, even though 46 percent of the population believed that elections worked well or very well at ensuring that their parliament reflects the views of the voters, almost as many (40 percent) disagreed. Moreover, only one-third felt that their parliamentary representatives regularly listen to what their constituents have to say, while fully two-thirds felt that they never or only sometimes listened.[61] Most troubling, the number of respondents who were satisfied with democracy as it is practiced in their country declined from 58 percent in 2000 to 45 percent in 2005–2006.[62]

Finally, a somewhat different picture has emerged in Asia. Based on data from Asia Barometer and an earlier poll, East Asian Barometer, political scientists Chu, Diamond, Nathan, and Shin examined support for democracy in seven East Asian nations.* Support for the principle of democracy ("preferable to all other kinds of government") was significantly *lower* than in the other regions, with fewer than half the respondents in Hong Kong, Taiwan, and South Korea answering affirmatively. Surprisingly, the Chinese, despite more than a half century of communist rule and political socialization, had a slightly more positive view of democracy, with over half (54 percent) rating it as the preferred form of government. Only in Japan (67 percent)—a wealthy, established democracy— Thailand (83 percent), and the Philippines (64 percent) did a solid majority endorse democracy as the best form of government. Worse still, when asked, "If you had to choose between democracy and economic development, which would you say was more important?" the majority in every country but Thailand chose economic development, often by an overwhelming margin (Hong Kong, the Philippines, South Korea, and Taiwan). Even in Thailand only 51 percent chose democracy.[63] At the same time, however, East Asians were more satisfied with the *performance* of democratic governments than Latin Americans or Africans were, probably not surprising in light of how spectacularly those governments have expanded their economies in recent decades.

As the LDCs now struggle through what may be the worst global recession since World War II and as the living standards of much of the population decline in the coming years, dissatisfaction with the performance of democratic regimes seems sure to widen. In and of itself, increasingly negative popular assessments of democracy do not necessarily mean that democratic governments will crumble. As long as political, economic, and military elites continue to support it, democracy is likely to survive. Moreover, despite growing citizen discontent with democratic performance, in only a small number of cases have many people supported revolutionary or other authoritarian alternatives. In some areas, most notably Latin America, the failures of recent military governments caused the armed forces so much internal discord and loss of national prestige that their officers are reluctant to seize power again. Still, in many partial democracies, elite commitment to democracy is soft and if there were to be a considerable decline in mass support for it, there could be a reverse wave.

To date, it appears that even among the many Third World inhabitants who have been dissatisfied with their government's performance under democracy, most have tacitly accepted Winston Churchill's conclusion that "democracy is the worst form of government except for all the others that have been tried . . ." But, without future improvement in social and economic conditions, democratic

---

* They are China, Hong Kong, Japan, Mongolia, the Philippines, Taiwan, and Thailand. Again, Hong Kong is not really a country but is treated as such in many statistical comparisons.

governments may cease commanding widespread support. In Latin America, where income inequality is higher than in any region of the world, the gap between "haves" and "have-nots" has generally widened since its transition to democracy. Likewise, income inequality has soared in postcommunist Eastern Europe and the former Soviet Union. From Colombia to the Philippines and from Pakistan to Peru, the poor suffer from highly unequal land and income distribution, pervasive poverty, rising crime rates, inadequate public health service, and corrupt police and judicial systems. Until such injustices are addressed, democracy will remain incomplete and often precarious.

DISCUSSION QUESTIONS

1. Discuss the differences between electoral democracy, liberal democracy, and substantive democracy. In what way does each of these definitions provide a useful measure of democracy in a range of countries?
2. What is the evidence supporting the belief that some religions support democracy better than others? What is the contrary evidence? Discuss the hypothesis that, while a society's religion does not determine its level of democracy, some religions make it more difficult for a society to democratize.
3. Why do you think the Third Wave of democracy has not been followed so far by a reverse wave like those that followed the First and Second Waves? How likely is this to change in the future?

NOTES

1. For example, Samuel P. Huntington, *The Third Wave: Democratization in the Late Twentieth Century* (Norman: University of Oklahoma Press, 1991).

2. There has been a long, ongoing debate over what conditions, and how many of those conditions, a country must meet in order to be called a democracy. The definition offered here represents the current consensus and is drawn from the several sources, including Philippe C. Schmitter and Terry Lynn Karl, "What Democracy Is and Is Not," *Journal of Democracy*, vol. 2, no. 2 (Summer 1991), 75–88; Robert A. Dahl, *Polyarchy: Participation and Opposition* (New Haven, CT: Yale University Press, 1971); Robert A. Dahl, *Democracy and Its Critics* (New Haven, CT: Yale University Press, 1989); Huntington, *The Third Wave.*

3. Juan Linz and Alfred Stepan, "Toward Consolidated Democracies," in *Consolidating the Third Wave Democracies*, eds. Larry Diamond, Marc F. Plattner, Yun-han Chu, and Hung-mao Tien (Baltimore, MD: The Johns Hopkins University Press, 1997), 15. Linz and Stepan have credited Guiseppe di Palma with originating the phrase "the only game in town" in reference to democratic consolidation.

4. During that span, there were only three democratic transitions in Arab countries, two of which failed. All of the statistics cited here are drawn from Ethan B. Kapstein and Nathan Converse, *The Fate of Young Democracies* (New York: Cambridge University Press, 2008), 39–40. Kapstein and Converse's statistics were adjusted to remove European data.

5. Ibid., 47–48, 142–147.

6. For a recent discussion of the challenges to African democracy, including ethnic tensions, see, Shadrack Wnjala Nasong'o, ed. *The African Search for Stable Forms of Statehood* (Lewiston, NY: The Edwin Mellen Press, 2008).

7. Seymour Martin Lipset, *Political Man: The Social Basis of Politics*, expanded and updated (Baltimore, MD: The Johns Hopkins University Press, 1980). For a review of such research, see Dietrich Rueschemeyer, Evelyne Huber Stephens, and John D. Stephens, *Capitalist Development and Democracy* (Chicago: University of Chicago Press, 1992), chap. 2.

8. Samuel P. Huntington, *Political Order in Changing Societies* (New Haven, CT: Yale University Press, 1968).

9. Mitchell A. Seligson, "Democratization in Latin America: The Current Cycle," in *Authoritarians and Democrats: Regime Transition in Latin America*, eds. James M. Malloy and

Mitchell A. Seligson (Pittsburgh, PA: University of Pittsburgh Press, 1987), 7–9. Since the time that Seligson did his research, the mid-1980s, literacy rates have risen sharply and few countries now have rates below 50 percent.

10. It is generally agreed that the emergence of the middle class and business class (bourgeoisie) in Western Europe was associated with the growth of modern democracy. See, for example, Barrington Moore Jr., *The Social Origins of Dictatorship and Democracy* (Boston: Beacon Press, 1966). More recently, political scientists such as Rueschemeyer, Huber Stephens, and Stephens, *Capitalist Development*, have emphasized the contributions of organized labor.

11. Quoted in Morton H. Halperin, Joseph T. Siegle, and Michael M. Weinstein, *The Democracy Advantage* (New York: Routledge and the Council on Foreign Relations, 2005), 25.

12. The groundbreaking major study of political culture was Gabriel A. Almond and Sidney Verba, *The Civic Culture: Political Attitudes and Democracy in Five Nations* (Boston: Little, Brown and Company, 1965), which examined political culture in the United States, Britain, Germany, Italy, and Mexico.

13. "Introduction," in *Women in African Parliaments*, eds. Gretchen Bauer and Hannah E. Britton (Boulder: CO: Lynne Rienner Publishers, 2006), 10.

14. Larry Diamond, "Introduction: In Search of Consolidation," in *Consolidating the Third Wave Democracies*, xv. While Diamond suggests there were 39 democracies, Samuel Huntington counted only 30 at that time. Part of the reason for Huntington's lower total is that he excluded from his research any country with a population of less than 1 million.

15. Huntington, *The Third Wave*, 271.

16. Seymour Martin Lipset, *Political Man*, 1st ed. (Garden City, NY: Anchor Books, 1960).

17. Rueschemeyer, Huber Stephens, and Stephens, *Capitalist Development and Democracy*, 14.

18. Philips Cutright, "National Political Development: Measurement and Analysis," *American Sociological Review*, vol. 28, no. 2 (April 1963), 253–264.

19. Axel Hadenius, *Democracy and Development* (New York: Cambridge University Press, 1992).

20. UNESCO, "World Literacy Day: 2008," 2, http://www.unesco.org/education/literacyday_2008/ILD_factsheet_en.pdf

21. Huntington, *Political Order in Changing Societies*. On the rise of repressive authoritarian regimes in Latin America's most industrialized nations, see Guillermo O'Donnell, *Modernization*

and Bureaucratic Authoritarianism* (Berkeley, CA: Institute of International Studies, 1973).

22. Adrian Karatnycky, "National Income and Liberty," *Journal of Democracy*, vol. 15 (January 2004), 82–93.

23. Moore, *The Social Origins*, 418.

24. Rueschemeyer, Huber Stephens, and Stephens, *Capitalist Development and Democracy*.

25. South Korea and Taiwan have subsequently democratized, but Singapore still has not.

26. Stephen White, "Russia's Experiment with Democracy," *Current History*, vol. 91 (October 1992), 313.

27. Robert Dahl, "Development and Democratic Culture," in *Consolidating the Third Wave Democracies*, 34.

28. Kenneth A. Bollen and Robert Jackman, "Economic and Non-economic Determinants of Political Democracy in the 1960s," in *Research in Political Sociology*, ed. R. G. Braungart (Greenwich, CT: JAI Press, 1985).

29. Hadenius, *Democracy and Development*, 118–119. Of course there are many branches of the Protestant religion and some of them are quite fundamentalist.

30. Amr G. E. Sabet, *Islam and the Political* (Ann Arbor, MI: Pluto Press, 2008), 251–252. Yet, a number of other prominent scholars of Islamic politics maintain that the notion that church and state are more closely linked in Muslim countries than in Christian ones is a myth. See, for example, Mohammed Ayoob, *The Many Faces of Islam: Religion and Politics in the Muslim World* (Ann Arbor: The University of Michigan Press, 2008), 10–13.

31. Samuel P. Huntington, "Will More Countries Become Democratic?" *Political Science Quarterly*, vol. 99, no. 2 (Summer 1984), 193–218; Huntington, *The Clash of Civilizations and the Remaking of World Order* (New York: Simon & Schuster, 1996).

32. For an argument along those lines, see Dealy, *The Latin Americans, Spirit and Ethos* (Boulder, CO: Westview Press, 1992).

33. Alfred Stepan with Graeme B. Robertson, "An 'Arab' More than 'Muslim' Electoral Gap," *Journal of Democracy*, vol. 14, no. 3 (July 2003), 30–44.

34. Graham E. Fuller, "A World Without Islam," *Foreign Policy* (January/February 2008), 46–53.

35. Daniel Philpott, "The Catholic Wave," *Journal of Democracy*, vol. 15, no. 2 (April 2004), 32.

36. David Beetham, "Structural and Cultural Preconditions for Democracy," in *Democracy and Development*, ed. Bernard Berendsen (Amsterdam: KIT Publishers, 2008), 178.

37. Larry Diamond, "Three Paradoxes of Democracy," in *The Global Resurgence of Democracy*, eds. Larry Diamond and Marc F. Plattner (Baltimore, MD: The Johns Hopkins University Press, 1993), 104.

38. Robert A. Dahl, "The Newer Democracies: From the Time of Triumph to the Time of Troubles," in *After Authoritarianism: Democracy or Disorder?* ed. Daniel N. Nelson (Westport, CT: Greenwood Press, 1995), 7.

39. Michael Ross, "Does Oil Hinder Democracy," *World Politics*, vol. 53 (April 2001), 328–356; Terry Lynn Karl, *The Paradox of Plenty: Oil Booms and Petro-States* (Berkeley: University of California Press, 1997). Freedom House's *Freedom in the World 2008* (New York, 2009) argues that expanded oil revenues in several former Soviet republics Union—Russia, Kazakhstan, and Azerbaijan—weakened democratic institutions there as well.

40. Larry Diamond, *The Spirit of Democracy* (New York: Times Books, 2008), 74–79.

41. Ibid., 75

42. Central Intelligence Agency (CIS) *The World Fact Book* (April, 2009), http://www.cia.gov/library/publications/the-world-factbook/geos/no.html; Daniel Gross, "Avoiding the Oil Curse," *Slate* (October 29, 2004), http://www.slate.com/id/2108873/

43. See, for example, M. G. Quibria, *Growth and Poverty: Lessons from the Asian Economic Miracle* (Asian Development Bank, Working Paper No. 33, 2002); more broadly, Huntington's *Political Order* argues that countries in the early stages of development often need authoritarian government.

44. Halperin, Siegle, and Weinstein, *The Democracy Advantage*, 13.

45. Ibid., 35. See also, 29–43. Data were collected from the Polity IV project, an inter-university project which collects a wide range of data on all the world's nations with populations exceeding 500,000. Polity ranks each country on a scale of 1–10 based on its degree of democracy.

46. Dani Rodrik, "Democracy and Economic Performance" (Cambridge, MA: Unpublished Paper, Harvard University, December 14, 1997), 2.

47. Iñias Macías-Aymar, "Does Income Inequality Limit Democratic Quality?" in *An Unequal Democracy?* eds. Carlo Benetti and Fernando Carillo-Flórez (Washington: Inter-American Development Bank, 2005), 84–85.

48. *New York Times*, "Money and Violence Hobble Democracy in Nigeria" (November 24, 2006).

49. Halperin, Siegle, and Weinstein, *The Democracy Advantage*, 71.

50. Adam Przeworski et al. "What Makes Democracies Endure?" in *Consolidating The Third Wave Democracies*, 295–311.

51. Ibid., 297.

52. Juan Linz and Arturo Valenzuela, eds. *The Failure of Presidential Democracy* (Baltimore, MD: The Johns Hopkins University Press, 1994).

53. Arch Puddington, *Freedom in the World 2009: Setbacks and Resilience*, Overview Essay in Freedom in the World Survey Release, http://www.freedomhouse.org/template.cfm?page=445.

54. The ideas in this section are based on Larry Diamond and Leonardo Morlino, eds. *Assessing the Quality of Democracy* (Baltimore, MD: The Johns Hopkins University Press, 2005). My major adaptation from the book's introduction was to combine vertical and horizontal accountability into one category.

55. Terry Lynn Karl, "Economic Inequality and Democratic Instability," *Journal of Democracy*, vol. 11 (January 2000), 149–156; Dietrich Rueschemeyer, "Addressing Inequality," in *Assessing the Quality*.

56. G. Bingham Powell Jr., "The Chain of Responsiveness," in *Assessing the Quality*, 62.

57. Inter-American Development Bank News, "*Democracy and Wallets*" (April 1, 2004), http://www.iadb.org/news/articledetail.cfm?Language=EN&artid=2019&artType=WS.

58. *New York Times* (April 22, 2004 and June 24, 2004).

59. Corporación Latinobarómetro, *Latinobarómetro Report 2006: Online Data Bank*, http://www.latinobarometro.org/uploads/media/Latinobar_metro_Report_2006.pdf.

60. Orlando J. Pérez, "Measuring Democratic Political Culture in Latin America," in *Latin American Democracy: Emerging Reality or Endangered Species*," eds. Richard Millet, Jennifer S. Holmes, and Orlando J. Pérez (New York: Routledge, 2009), 21–41.

61. "Citizens and the State: New Results from Afrobarometer Round 3" (Afrobarometer, Working Paper Number 61, 2006), www.afrobarometer.org/papers/AfropaperNo61.pdf.

62. "Afrobarometer Media Briefing" (May 24, 2006) and "Afrobarometer Briefing Paper No. 40" (November, 2006), http://www.afrobarometer.org/papers/AfrobriefNo40.

63. Chu et al. "Asia's Challenged Democracies," *The Washington Quarterly*, vol. 32, no. 1 (January 2009), 143–157.

CHAPTER 3

RELIGION AND POLITICS

In his influential book *The Secular City* (1965), Harvey Cox, a Harvard theology professor and Baptist minister, discussed the privatization of religion in modern urban society, particularly the separation of religion and politics.[1] While that trend was not yet apparent in the Third World, many social scientists were convinced that as those societies modernized, the role of religion in politics (and of politics in religion) would diminish, just as it had in the West.

In Latin America, the Catholic Church no longer exercised nearly as much control over education or reproductive rights as it once did. Following independence, the government of India tried to ameliorate the injustices of the caste system, a cornerstone of Hindu religious practice. And in the Middle East, modernizing regimes in Egypt, Syria, and Turkey created more secular political systems. Accordingly, one leading authority, Donald Eugene Smith, observed, "Political development includes, as one of its basic processes, the secularization of politics, the progressive exclusion of religion from the political system."[2]

For the most part, early modernization theorists viewed organized religion as an impediment to political and economic development, while dependency theorists scarcely mentioned it in their writings (see Chapter 1). Yet, contrary to those expectations, Third World religions have been a resilient, growing political force that has withstood the onslaughts of modernization. In some instances, such as pre-revolutionary Iran, rapid and destabilizing modernization has even stimulated a militant religious backlash. As David Little has observed, "Modernization was supposed to mean the gradual decline and eventual disappearance of religion from public life, but, as we know, that hasn't happened. Religion is very much alive as a part of politics."[3] In fact, since the 1970s, much of the Third World has experienced a religious resurgence, which has intensified the role of religion in the political arena.[4] In the Middle East, "ironically, the technological tools of modernization have often served to reinforce traditional belief and practice as religious leaders who initially opposed modernization now use radio, television, audio-, and videotapes to preach and disseminate."[5]

Nowhere is the change more apparent than in the Middle East and parts of Africa and Asia, where a resurgence of Islamic fundamentalism (also called *Islamism*, the term preferred by many scholars) and, in some cases, deepened sectarian violence between Sunnis and Shi'as have destabilized countries such as Egypt, Iraq, Lebanon, Pakistan, Somalia, and Sudan. The 1979 seizure of American hostages in Iran, subsequent hostage-taking in Lebanon, the assassination of Egyptian president Anwar Sadat, a terrorist attack on a U.S. air force barracks in Saudi Arabia, the bombing of two U.S. embassies in East Africa, and, above all, the 9/11 attacks on the World Trade Center and the Pentagon all focused Western attention on "religion and politics." Subsequent Islamist (Islamic fundamentalist) terrorist attacks on mass transit systems in Madrid and London along with the bitter conflict between Shi'ites and Arab Sunnis in Iraq, the recent expansion of Islamism in Pakistan, and the widening war in Afghanistan have all deepened that focus. In fact, since the end of the Cold War, radical (militant) Islamic fundamentalism has supplanted Soviet Communism as the most widely perceived threat to American and European security. Well before the 1991 Gulf War, a Gallup poll survey revealed that 37 percent of British respondents expected a war in the 1990s between Muslims and Christians.[6] The American-led overthrow of Afghanistan's Taliban government in 2001, the Taliban's recent resurgence in Afghanistan and its spread to Pakistan, continuing religiously based violence in Iraq, and ongoing Al Qaeda-linked terrorism have fortified that perspective. While Western anxieties sometimes derive from prejudice and misunderstanding, this chapter's discussion of religious fundamentalism indicates that there are some sound reasons for concern.

THE MEETING OF CHURCH AND STATE

Many preconceptions about religion and politics emerge from serious misinterpretations, both of American politics and political systems elsewhere. Most Americans accept a constitutional separation between church and state as the normal state of affairs (though some wish to blur that line). That formal barrier, however, does not exist in many industrialized democracies and LDCs. Many Western European nations, though generally less religious and less churchgoing than the United States, have not built legal walls between religion and politics. In Britain, for example, the Anglican Church (or the Church of England) is the official state religion and the monarch serves as its "supreme governor" (a ceremonial position). Italy's Catholic Church was closely linked to the Christian Democratic Party, that nation's dominant political party for some 40 years after World War II. And Norway's government provides housing and financial support for Lutheran ministers. Moreover, even in the United States, religious organizations and beliefs continue to influence political behavior. Black Baptist churches, for example, were in the forefront of the American civil rights movement. Ministers from Martin Luther King, Jesse Jackson, and Jeremiah Wright—on the left—to Jerry Falwell and Pat Robertson—on the right—have been deeply involved in U.S. politics. Since the 1980s, the so-called "Christian right" has been an influential force within the Republican Party (represented most recently by Sarah Palin's 2008 vice presidential candidacy). In recent decades, conflicts over issues such as abortion, school prayer, and stem-cell research have led one expert to observe that "far from rendering religion largely irrelevant to politics the structure of [American] government may actually encourage a high degree of interaction."[7]

Religion is even more firmly embedded in many Third World cultures, and its impact on politics is correspondingly more pronounced. Indeed, it is so central to traditional values that we often identify national or regional cultures by their predominant religion: Buddhist culture in Myanmar and Thailand, Catholic culture in Latin America, Confucian culture in China and Korea, Hindu culture in much of India and Nepal, and Islamic culture in North Africa and the Middle East.[8]

The blending of religion and politics is most apparent in theocratic states (political systems dominated by religious leaders and institutions) such as Iran, where the Shi'a clergy have been the final arbiter of public policy since that country's 1979 Islamic revolution. Similarly, when the Taliban ruled Afghanistan (1996–2001), their government became a mere extension of the fundamentalist clergy. But it is also very significant in ostracized Islamist states like Sudan, and in some American allies such as Saudi Arabia. In such Latin American nations as Brazil and Nicaragua, the theology of liberation, espoused by radical Catholics, has motivated many priests and nuns to mobilize the poor in their struggle against economic and political injustices. And in India, the Bharatiya Janata Party (BJP), which led the country's governing coalition from 1998 to 2004, carries the torch of Hindu fundamentalism.

GREAT RELIGIONS OF THE THIRD WORLD

Four of the world's "great religions" are predominant in the Third World. Catholicism, the only major religion to have penetrated extensively into both industrialized democracies and the developing world, is preeminent in the Philippines and Latin America and also is the faith of significant portions of the population in a number of sub-Saharan African countries. Hinduism is the dominant religion in only India and neighboring Nepal. However, there are also Hindu populations exceeding 1 million persons in nearby Bangladesh, Indonesia, Sri Lanka, Pakistan, and Malaysia, as well as significant immigrant communities in South Africa and English-speaking Caribbean nations such as Trinidad-Tobago. Buddhism is a major religion in East Asia, Southeast Asia, and parts of South Asia. Finally, Islam, the world's second largest religion, predominates across a broad span of Asia, the Middle East, and Africa—from Indonesia in the east through Pakistan and Bangladesh in the Indian subcontinent, to the former Soviet republics of Central Asia, into the Middle East, and North Africa. It also represents about half the populations of Malaysia and Nigeria, as well as substantial minorities in countries as far-flung as the Philippines, Tanzania, and Trinidad-Tobago.

To be sure, not everyone in the developing world belongs to one of these major religions. Protestantism is the leading religion in the English-speaking islands of the Caribbean and represents important minorities in a number of other LDCs. Confucianism (perhaps more a philosophy and way of life than a religion) still influences Chinese society (even after its revolution), as well as Japan, South Korea, and Taiwan. Christian Orthodox minorities are significant in Lebanon and Egypt, while many Africans believe in local, traditional religions. The impact of these religions on politics, however, is more limited. Consequently, this chapter limits its analysis to the four global religions just discussed, particularly emphasizing Islam and Catholicism.

None of the Third World's major religions is monolithic, though the Catholic Church, with its doctrine of papal infallibility on matters of faith and its hierarchical structure, comes closest. Buddhism has two major schools, each basing its doctrines on different ancient texts. Theravada ("Way of Elders," Southern) Buddhism, practiced in Myanmar, Sri Lanka (Ceylon), Thailand, Laos, Cambodia, and parts of Vietnam, is an older form of Buddhism. Mahayana ("Great Vehicle," Northern), a later branch, emerged in China, Japan,

Korea, most of Vietnam, and Tibet.[9] Doctrinal differences in nonhierarchical religions, such as Buddhism, have rarely provoked political conflict or violence, but elsewhere, particularly in several Muslim countries, conflict has often been intense and violent.

The most important division within Islam is between its major branches, Sunnis and Shi'as. The split between them, dating to the decades following the death of the Prophet Muhammad (570–632 A.D.), centered on the issues of "who should succeed him and the nature of the successor's [spiritual and political] role[s]."[10] Today, the Shi'ites have a more hierarchical clergy than the Sunnis, and they revere their most prominent politico-religious leaders, particularly the Imam (the Guide), who must be a direct descendant of the Prophet Muhammad and his son-in-law, Ali. As one scholar notes, "Shi'ism makes a cult of death and martyrdom," including "pilgrimages to the tombs of the Imams and their descendants."[11] Religious practices and beliefs of the two branches differ somewhat, although the similarities in their beliefs far outweigh the differences. Yet, many Sunnis do not consider the Shi'a authentic Muslims, and many Shi'as resent political and economic domination by Sunnis. In Chapter 4, we will examine political conflicts in Iraq and Lebanon linked to these discrepancies.

Currently, 85–90 percent of the world's nearly 1.5 billion Muslims are Sunnis, while Shi'ites account for only 10–15 percent (there is also a small Sufi branch). Shi'ism is the majority faith only in Iran, Iraq, and the small nations of Azerbaijan, Oman, and Bahrain. But Shi'ites also constitute the largest of some eighteen religious denominations in Lebanon and are significant minorities (15–35 percent of the population) in Afghanistan, Kuwait, Pakistan, Saudi Arabia, Syria, Turkey, and Yemen. Countries such as Iraq, Lebanon, and Syria, with significant Sunni and Shi'a populations, have experienced sharp political and cultural tensions between the two.[12] In the countries in which both groups represent a sizable segment of the population, Sunnis usually have held greater political power and higher social status, even when they have constituted the minority. Consequently, Shi'ites see themselves as "champions of the downtrodden," and glorify suffering and self-flagellation.

Other religions that lack such formal divisions may still have competing theological or ideological perspectives. For example, even though they are united by a single church hierarchy, Latin American Catholics span the ideological spectrum from the ultra-conservative members of Opus Dei to leftist believers in liberation theology. In the name of God and anti-Communism, some Latin American Catholics have supported fascist movements, rightist death squads, and repressive military regimes. Conversely, in the name of God and social justice, other Catholic priests and nuns have supported the Sandinista revolution in Nicaragua, fought with Marxist guerrillas in Colombia, and organized the poor in the slums of Brazil and Peru.

RELIGION, MODERNITY, AND SECULARIZATION

We have already observed that social and economic modernization does not necessarily reduce religious observance, at least not in the short run. What about the reverse side of that relationship? That is, what is the impact of religion on modernity? Here again, most early analysts felt they were largely incompatible. "It is widely, and *correctly*, assumed that religion is in general an obstacle to modernization."[13] In the realm of politics, this interpretation suggested that the intrusion of religious institutions into government impedes the development of a modern state. Others associated traditional Catholic, Islamic, and Hindu beliefs with authoritarian values.

Subsequently, political scientists have developed a more nuanced understanding. Religious institutions may inhibit development in some respects, while encouraging it in others. For example, all of the great religions have legitimized the state's authority at some point in their history, a necessary step for state building. As nations modernize their political systems, religious authorities or groups may oppose important aspects of change (Hindu and Islamic fundamentalists, for example), or they may offer explicit or tacit support (Islamic leaders in Indonesia and the Catholic clergy in Chile). No longer facilely dismissing organized religion's contributions to development, many scholars now credit Confucianism with facilitating East Asia's rapid modernization in the second half of the twentieth century. Specifically, they credit the Confucian work ethic and its spirit of cooperation.

The argument that political modernization requires secularization has two bases—one empirical and the other normative. The *empirical* component notes that as Western societies modernized (i.e., became more literate, urban, institutionally organized, and industrialized), their political systems almost invariably became more secular. In effect, Western societies experienced a specialization of functions. Increasingly, the state controlled politics, while the church oversaw religion, and each has refrained from interfering in the other's realm. Political scientists anticipated that as the Third World modernized, it would experience the same division of responsibilities. The related *normative* argument holds that secularization is not only a common trend, but it is also desirable because it increases religious freedom, reduces the likelihood of state persecution of religious minorities, and permits the state to make more rational decisions free of religious bias.

We have already indicated the weakness of the first assumption. To be sure, modernization has induced political secularization in many developing countries, such as Turkey and Mexico. But elsewhere it has not altered church–state relations; in fact, modernization frequently has precipitated a religious backlash when pursued too rapidly. Saudi Arabia, India, and Iran illustrate three possible governmental approaches to managing the forces of modernization. In the most cautious approach, the Saudi royal family has introduced far-reaching socioeconomic changes but has carefully controlled the style of modernization in order to preserve a very traditional Islamic culture and maintain close links between Islam and the state. India represents an intermediate case, where the modernization of politics and constitutional secularization were widely accepted (at least until recently). Religious factors do affect the Indian government in some respects; thus, Hindus and Muslims are governed by distinct legal codes in areas such as family law. And while the prime minister's post has always been held by a Hindu (the majority religion), the largely ceremonial presidency has been reserved for a Muslim. Finally, Iran represents one of the most dramatic examples of religious backlash against modernization and a relinking of church and state. As we will see, the Shah (emperor) imposed rapid Western-style socioeconomic development (including "unveiling" women), which destabilized society and helped precipitate a radical Islamic revival.

At an individual level, many people in Africa, Asia, and the Middle East have defied the notion that more educated and professionally trained citizens will be less religiously orthodox. For example, Hindu and Islamic fundamentalist activists in India, Afghanistan, and Egypt are frequently professionals, not uneducated peasants.[14] Most of the terrorists who attacked the Pentagon and the World Trade Center in 2001 were relatively well educated and middle class. And, the Islamist terrorists who failed in their 2007 attempt to bomb downtown London and the Glasgow (Scotland) airport terminal were all health workers, mostly doctors. Church–state relationships are more varied and complex than early development theory had assumed. Clearly, some religious influences contradict accepted norms of modernity, as when they induce political leaders to violate the rights of religious minorities (or majorities). Iran's Islamic government, for example, has persecuted members of the Baha'i faith.[15] In Guatemala, the government of General Efraín Ríos Montt, a right-wing Evangelical, converted Catholic peasants to Protestantism at virtual gunpoint. Similarly, many religiously inspired restrictions on women—common in fundamentalist Muslim societies—are clearly antithetical to modernization.

But need there always be a strict wall between politics and religion or between clerics and politicians? Sometimes analysts offer contradictory answers prompted by their own political ideologies. The same people who lamented the political activities of leftist, Catholic priests in Nicaragua and Brazil, the protest marches by Buddhist monks in Sri Lanka, or the Taliban government in Afghanistan may have cheered political involvement by Dr. Martin Luther King Jr. or the Reverend Jerry Falwell in the United States.

Ultimately, most people's evaluations of religion's role in politics are influenced by how much that religious activity furthers the goals and policies that they (the observers) believe in. Perhaps this is as it should be. The recent histories of Iran and Tibet illustrate this point well. Iran has been a theocracy (a religiously driven political system) since its 1979 revolution, just as Tibet had been prior to its absorption by China in the 1950s. Each has had a political system "in which the political structures are clearly subordinate to the ecclesiastical establishment."[16] Yet most Westerners judged them quite differently.

Under the leadership of its Islamic mullahs (clerics), Iran became an international outcast because of its repression of civil liberties, persecution of religious minorities, support for international terrorism, its nuclear energy enrichment program, and, most recently, its apparently rigged presidential election. Until the late 1950s, Buddhist clerics also dominated Tibetan politics.[17] Viewed as divine by his people, the Dalai Lama had been the country's secular and spiritual leader. Buddhist monks held key posts in the government bureaucracy. Because of Tibetan Buddhism's record of pacifism and tolerance, however, theocratic rule aroused no foreign indignation. On the contrary, the world was appalled when China occupied Tibet and secularized the state. Since that time, the Dalai Lama's long struggle to free his people has won him worldwide admiration and the Nobel Peace Prize. Buddhist monks led Tibetan protests against Chinese occupation and cultural domination in advance of the 2008 Summer Olympics in Beijing. All of this suggests that the issue of separation of church and state may be less important to most outside observers than the way in which "the church" uses its political influence when it holds power.

STRUCTURAL AND THEOLOGICAL BASES OF CHURCH–STATE RELATIONS

The extents to which religions influence political attitudes and behavior as well as the degree of political involvement by different organized religions vary considerably from place to place. Just as the separation of church and state in Western Europe has historically been more pronounced in predominantly Protestant nations (e.g., Denmark and Britain) than in Catholic ones (such as Italy and Spain), the political impact of the Third World's four major religions also differs. Two factors help define a particular religion's political involvement: its theological views regarding the relationship between temporal and spiritual matters; and the degree to which its clergy are hierarchically organized and centrally controlled.

Donald Smith distinguishes two different types of religio-political systems: the *organic* and the *church*. In the organic system, there is a weak or nonexistent religious hierarchy. Hence, the clergy is insufficiently organized as an institution to influence or challenge the country's political leaders, although their religious beliefs may still influence politics. Examples of organic systems include Buddhism in most countries and Hinduism. Church religio-political systems, on the other hand, have a well-organized ecclesiastical structure, with a leader or leaders at the top who frequently exercise considerable political influence. For example, the Catholic Church and the Shi'a clergy often have formal links to the state.[18]

Islam

From its inception in seventh-century Arabia, Islam has been a "religio-political movement in which religion was integral to state and society."[19] That remains particularly true in Shi'a communities. More than any other world religion, traditional Islam has frequently erased the borderline between religion and politics. On the one hand, the Islamic faith and its clergy legitimized the state. At the same time, however, the political leadership recognized the supremacy of Islamic law, the Shariah (path of God). Because religious Muslims believe that God wants them to live in a community governed in accordance with the Koran—Islam's sacred scripture perceived as the word of God—the concept of separating church and state is alien to most Muslim nations. This does not mean that Islamic culture and theology were historically inhospitable to other religions. Perhaps because it accepted Jewish and Christian scriptures and drew from both of those religions, Islamic societies were often particularly tolerant of other faiths. From the eight to the eleventh centuries, for example, the large Jewish community in Muslim-controlled Spain enjoyed greater freedom and influence than it did in Christian Europe. But even there, ultimate political authority was restricted to Muslims.

Today, the bond between religion and politics remains strong in most Muslim societies, though there is considerable variation. John Esposito distinguishes three types of Islamic regimes: the *secular state*, the *Islamic state*, and the *Muslim state*.[20] Since its formation as a republic, Turkey has been the most notable secular state in the Islamic world. Starting in the 1920s, Mustafa Kemal Ataturk (the father of modern Turkey) ousted the sultan (the supreme political and religious official of the recently dissolved Ottoman empire), emancipated women, closed down Muslim seminaries, and established a firm wall between church and state. Turkey's current constitution still mandates compulsory state-supervised "instruction in religious culture . . . in the curricula of primary and secondary schools."[21] But, this mandate was not designed to strengthen Islam, but rather to establish state control over Muslim religious instruction and over Islamic institutions. In the words of one leading Middle East scholar, "the state [from Ataturk until the 1990s] aimed to end the power of organized Islam and break its hold on the minds and hearts of the Turkish people."[22] Moreover, the constitution offers Islam no special status in society and guarantees "freedom of . . . religious belief."

At the other end of the spectrum, *Islamic states* base their governing philosophies on the Koran and Islamic law. Afghanistan (when ruled by the Taliban), Iran, and Saudi Arabia are among the best-known examples, but Sudan, Pakistan, and Libya also fall in this category. These regimes can be quite distinct from each other. Whereas Iran subscribes to Shi'a Islam, the other countries in this group are dominated by Sunnis. Islamic regimes in Afghanistan (before U.S. intervention), Libya, Iran, and Sudan have pursued militantly anti-Western foreign policies and sometimes supported international terrorism. On the other hand, Saudi Arabia is quite conservative and closely allied to the West (though it has often tried to appease Al Qaeda and other extremist groups for strategic reasons). Thus, the term *Islamic state* (like the concept of fundamentalism) must be applied carefully to avoid artificial categorization that hides more than it reveals.

Finally, *Muslim states*, such as Egypt and Morocco, occupy an intermediate position on church–state relations and the role of religion. In contrast to secular states, they identify Islam as the official religion and require the head of state to be Muslim. However, the impact of religion on politics is far more limited than in Islamic states. For example, unlike Iran, Egypt's political leaders are not clerics, and some have not even been Muslims. For example, former Foreign Minister Boutros Boutros-Ghali, who later served as secretary general of the United Nations, is a Christian. So too is Iraq's Tariq Aziz, who served as Saddam Hussein's Deputy Prime Minister and Foreign Minister.

Catholicism

More than any other major religion, Catholicism has a well-defined and hierarchical ecclesiastical structure that enables it to have a considerable impact on the political system. At the Church's apex is the Pope, whose authority is unchallenged and whose official pronouncements on matters of faith and morals are accepted by believers as infallible. Consequently, papal declarations can carry considerable political importance. For example, many of the twentieth-century, Catholic reform movements in Latin America can be traced to Pope Leo XIII's 1891 encyclical, *Rerum Novarum*, which included an indictment of early capitalism's exploitation of the working class. Pope John Paul II was known for his strong stance against communist and other authoritarian regimes. More recently, Pope Benedict XVI, a religious conservative, has made very controversial statements regarding the Muslim religion and the worldwide campaign against AIDS. Within each country, the Church hierarchy is headed by bishops, who often have tremendous political influence in Latin America and other Catholic countries such as the Philippines.

Like Islam in the Middle East, Catholicism once was the state religion in many Latin American countries. Over the years, however, most nations in the region have either ceased having an official state religion or have rendered that link unimportant. Still, Church doctrine has generally supported the established political regime and helped legitimize it. "The ruling powers," said one encyclical, "are invested with a sacredness more than human. . . . Obedience [to political authority] is not the servitude of man to man, but submission to the will of God."[23]

That does not mean, however, that the Church has always supported the government. There have been periodic clashes between the two, most notably when the state challenged Church authority in areas such as education and human rights. Thus in the Philippines, Church support of Corazón Aquino's democratic reform movement helped topple the dictatorship of Ferdinand Marcos. Similarly, Catholic authorities opposed conservative military dictatorships in Brazil and Chile during the 1970s and 1980s. At the same time, Church relationships with Marxist regimes in Cuba and Nicaragua were often tense, though the first Sandinista cabinet included several radical Catholic priests. And, in the 1980s, Salvadorian Archbishop Oscar Romero spoke out forcefully against his government's human rights violations and urged his nation's soldiers not to obey orders that violated human rights. Soon afterwards, he was assassinated by a military "death squad."

Hinduism and Buddhism

Asia's organic religions, Hinduism and Buddhism, usually have been less directly involved in politics than Catholicism and Islam have. To be sure, India's BJP, led by Hindu fundamentalists, has recently governed that country. But the party has no linkage to the Hindu "clergy," and its ranks include a small number of non-Hindus. To be sure, Hindu social values, including the caste system, have significantly affected Indian and Nepalese politics. For example, prior to the recent termination of the monarchy, Nepal's king was considered an incarnation of the Hindu god Vishnu. But the religion is very diverse with no centralized, hierarchical structure. Consequently, it has no formal political voice.

Buddhism grew out of the Hindu religion in the sixth century B.C., emerging from the teachings of a Nepalese prince, Siddhartha Gautama, the Buddha (Enlightened One). Though greatly influenced by Hinduism, Buddhism rejects one of its basic tenets, the caste system. Indeed, as Buddhism spread through Asia, one of its great appeals was its egalitarian outlook. In recent decades, many of India's untouchables have left Hinduism for Buddhism, a religion far more hospitable to them.[24] Buddhism differs from Hinduism in that it has an organized ecclesiastical organization, namely the sangha (the monastic orders). And in some countries, such as Myanmar, each sangha has its own leader, providing a hierarchical structure. Still, when compared to the Roman Catholic

Church or the mullahs of Shi'ite Islam, Buddhism's religious structure is much less centralized and, thus, less able to impact the political system.

In addition to having less-hierarchically organized ecclesiastical orders, Eastern religions are less theologically inclined to political involvement than are Catholicism and Islam. Their otherworldly philosophy places less emphasis on such temporal matters as politics; hence, the remainder of this chapter focuses on the political impact of Islam and Catholicism in the Third World.

RELIGIOUS FUNDAMENTALISM AND ISLAMISM

No expression of religious influence on Third World politics has attracted more attention or inspired more fear and loathing than Islamic fundamentalism. In the 1980s and early 1990s, highly influential Washington columnists such as Morton Zuckerman (*U.S. News and World Report*) warned of Islamic "religious Stalinism" and a fanatical international movement orchestrated from Iran.[25] Nor are such concerns limited to Westerners. The leaders of moderate Muslim nations who find themselves under siege from militant Islamists frequently express them as well. Thus, for example, Tunisia's president, Zine el-Abidine Ben Ali, warned about the dangers of a "fundamentalist international [alliance]" financed by Iran and Sudan.[26]

The horrifying September 11, 2001, attacks on the World Trade Center and the Pentagon confirmed the world's worst nightmares about Islamic fundamentalist terrorism. However, experts on Islam insist that it is unfair to blame a major world religion, with more than 1 billion adherents, for the actions of a small minority. President George W. Bush and other leading U.S. public officials went out of their way to make that very point in the days after the attacks. Some people have noted that blaming the Islamic religion for Osama bin Laden's actions would be as misguided as holding Christianity responsible for violent actions taken in its name. For example, David Koresh, head of a religious cult called the Branch Davidians, claimed to be acting in the name of Christianity when he included underage girls in his large harem and when he later led the group into battle with U.S. federal agents, resulting in the death of most of his group. More recently, a number of "pro-life" religious extremists have bombed abortion clinics and assassinated doctors who perform those procedures.

Others point out that not even all Islamists (fundamentalist Muslims) support violence. Indeed, many scholars reject the very term *fundamentalism* to describe current militant revivals. The word, they charge, may falsely imply the existence of a unified threat to the West and, in the case of Islam, it lumps together groups and regimes that have little in common, such as conservative Saudi Arabia and radical Libya. Instead, these analysts prefer such terms as *revivalism, militancy* or *Islamist movements* rather than *Islamic fundamentalism*. One author observes "that the term 'Islamic Fundamentalism' . . . possesses Christian roots and carries considerable emotional baggage that makes it offensive to many Muslims."[27] Still, a number of leading authorities accept and even use the label *fundamentalism* in their writings. Fred Halliday notes that "there are some problems with applying the term fundamentalist to Muslim movements, but with the necessary caveats it can legitimately be so used."[28] In this chapter, I will use the term *fundamentalism* because of its common usage in contemporary political discourse. However, I also employ the terms *revivalism* (referring to its desire to revive the true faith) or *Islamism* to refer to Islamic fundamentalism. Finally, the term *Islamists* refers to believers in Islamism.

Semantic questions aside, experts such as John Esposito and Fred Halliday warn that whatever labels they use, Western writers often distort and exaggerate the nature of the so-called "Islamic threat."[29] Many of those people also seem unaware of the long tradition of liberal theology within Islam, which has advocated religious tolerance, progress for women, and democratic values.

> At the very core of this supposed [Islamic] challenge or conflict lie confusions: the mere fact of peoples being "Islamic" . . . [has been confused] with that of their adhering to beliefs and policies that are . . . "Islamist" or "fundamentalist." It has been assumed . . . that most Muslims seek to impose a political program supposedly derived from their religion. The fact that most Muslims are not supporters of Islamist movements is obscured.[30]

On the other hand, periodic Islamist terrorism in Israel, Western Europe, the United States, Indonesia, Morocco, and other parts of the world indicate that although it may be mistaken to speak of an *"Islamic* threat," it is surely reasonable to talk of an *"Islamist* threat." Hopefully, this chapter's discussion of Islamic fundamentalism conveys that distinction. In short, when this text discusses Islamic revivalism at some length—because of its obvious political importance—two caveats should be kept in mind: Most Muslims are not fundamentalists, and not all fundamentalists are repressive at home or violent abroad. Graham Fuller, a former CIA official and Middle East specialist, takes the argument one step further. He argues that although Islamism may facilitate terrorist ideology, Al Qaeda and other violent fundamentalist groups are primarily motivated by nationalist opposition to Western intervention in the region (from Israel to Afghanistan and Iraq), not by religion.[31]

Defining and Explaining Fundamentalism

> Fundamentalism is the . . . effort to define the fundamentals of a religious system and adhere to them. One of the cardinal tenets of Islamic fundamentalism is to protect the purity of Islamic precepts from the adulteration of speculative exercises. . . . Behind all this is a drive to purify Islam in order to release all its vital force.[32]

The precise meaning of fundamentalism varies somewhat from religion to religion. But its adherents do share certain points of view across religious lines. To begin with, they all wish to preserve their religion's traditional worldview and resist the efforts of religious liberals to reform it. They also want to revive the role of religion in private and public life, including politics, lifestyle, and dress.

In the developing world, fundamentalism often appeals particularly to people who are disgusted by the inequalities and injustices in their country's political and economic systems. This disgust reflects popular revulsion against unjust, local political and economic elites, against pervasive corruption, and against repression. In Lebanon, the radical Hezbollah (Party of God) grew out of Shi'a resentment against the economically powerful Christian community, as well as anger against Israel and the West. And in Algeria, Egypt, and the Sudan, militant fundamentalists expanded their support as a result of government repression directed against them. Mohammed Ayoob notes that Islamists seek "to re-create a future based on . . . a romanticized notion of a largely mythical golden age" of Islam (under the Prophet and his earliest successors).[33]

Radical fundamentalists also tend to be nationalistic or chauvinistic, rejecting "outside" influences that they feel challenge or pollute their culture and their true faith. Islamists view Western culture as particularly insidious, associating it with imperialism, immodest dress, and scandalous films and music that promote promiscuity and drugs. But they reject Western values for another reason as well. For years, government leaders, such as the Shah of Iran and Egypt's president Anwar Sadat, promoted Western-style modernization as the route to economic modernization. But, after decades of failed development in the Middle East, North Africa, and Asia, many people feel deceived and look elsewhere for answers to their problems.

Indeed, many analysts argue that the most powerful force behind radical Islamic fundamentalism, even more than religious faith, has been nationalism and resentment toward Western-backed dictatorships (in countries such as Egypt, Pakistan, Saudi Arabia, and pre-revolutionary Iran). Moreover, Ahmed Rashid argues that the most of the earliest volunteers for worldwide *jihad* (holy war) in the 1990s were primarily motivated by a desire for adventure. "The young men who trained in these [jihadist] camps were not educated in the Islamic schools called madrasas and they were inspired less by extremist Islamic ideology than by their desires to see the world, handle weapons, and have a youthful adventure."[34]

Fundamentalists: Radical and Conservative

Any analysis of revivalism must distinguish between radical and conservative fundamentalists. Radicals, inspired by a "sacred rage," feel that they are conducting a "holy war" against enemies that threaten to corrupt their fundamental religious values. As a Hezbollah manifesto declared, "We have risen to liberate our country, to drive the imperialists and the invaders out of it, and to take our fate in our own hands."[35] Indeed, contemporary Islamism first arose from resistance to nineteenth- and twentieth-century Western intrusions into the Muslim world. More recently, it has been nurtured by Muslim resentment against the American-led invasions of Iraq and Afghanistan. Islamist *mujahideen* ("holy warriors") in Afghanistan first waged jihad in the 1980s against that country's Marxist government and the occupying Soviet troops who supported it.[36] Iran's Ayatollah Khomeini and Al Qaeda's Osama bin Laden both declared jihads against the United States ("the great Satan"). Elsewhere, battles have been waged against domestic enemies as well. Having been denied an almost certain electoral victory in 1992, when the military canceled parliamentary elections, Algeria's fundamentalist movement, the Islamic Salvation Front (FIS), attacked the nation's armed forces, the police, secular politicians, and foreigners. Soon, more violent militant organizations, most notably the Armed Islamic Group (GIA), launched a war of terror against Algerian civilians, often mixing banditry with religious warfare. From 1992 through early 2001, the GIA, the Algerian military, and government-supported civilian militias massacred more than 100,000 Algerians between them. In recent years, Muslim extremists have killed innocent civilians in New York City, London, Madrid, Tel Aviv, Baghdad, Islamabad, and Mumbai. Hindu fundamentalists have periodically launched bloody mob attacks against India's Muslim minority as well (see Chapter 4).

Such radical militancy contrasts with the views and behavior of nonviolent fundamentalists, such as Hasidic Jews or the Saudi upper class, which do not see themselves in such a battle. To be sure, leaders of many nonviolent, fundamentalist groups also wish to shield their flocks from unwanted outside influences. But they do not view adherents of other religions or nonfundamentalist members of their own faith as enemies.*

In recent years, radical Islamic fundamentalists have been a major political force in Middle Eastern and North African countries such as Algeria, Lebanon, and Sudan as well as in Afghanistan and Pakistan. Afghanistan's Taliban regime was surely the world's most rigidly fundamentalist. For example, it prohibited girls and women from attending school or working outside the home. Similarly, the Ministry for the Prevention of Vice and Promotion of Virtue banned television, sports events, dancing, and secular music. The prohibition on female employment meant that the country's estimated 50,000 widows (the legacy of years of war) and their dependants—numbering several hundred thousand—were denied any legal means of support.[37] The Taliban also has sheltered Osama bin Laden and his Al Qaeda terrorist organization. Until the 1990s and the emergence of Al Qaeda's onto the world scene, however, Western observers viewed Iran's Islamist regime as the greatest threat to global stability. It is a concern that has revived of late as Iran seems to be developing a nuclear weapons capability.

The Iranian Revolution: Radical Islamism as a Reaction to Western-Style Modernization

The origins of the Iranian revolution can be traced to the early decades of the twentieth century, with the Muslim clergy's resistance to a government program of secular modernization imposed by the royal family.[38] Military, political, and economic intervention by a series of foreign powers—Czarist Russia, Britain, and the United States—turned the country into "a virtual protectorate" and made the ruling Shahs (emperors) appear to be tools of the great powers.[39] Years later, resentment against foreign domination became an important component of the Islamic revolution.

Starting with the reign of Shah Reza Pahlavi (1925–1941), the imperial government antagonized the Shi'a mullahs (clergy) with a series of modernizing reforms that included unveiling women, mandatory Western dress, and transferring control over various economic, educational, and political resources from the clergy to the state.[40] The Shah's son, Mohammed Reza Pahlavi, ruled from 1941 to 1979 as a close ally of the United States. His so-called "White

---

* However, a small minority of "ultra-orthodox," Israeli Jews *are* radical fundamentalists who have carried out violent attacks against Muslims and secular Jews.

Revolution" of the 1960s and 1970s expanded women's rights, extended general literacy, and promoted a land reform program that included the transfer of land from Islamic institutions to the peasants.

As a result of these programs, land was redistributed to some 3 million peasants, educational levels rose substantially, and oil wealth doubled the size of the middle class.[41] By 1976, Iran had the developing world's highest GNP per capita. On the other hand, the large gap between rich and poor widened, widespread government corruption alienated the population, and many suspected opponents of the government were brutally suppressed by the Shah's dreaded secret police, the Savak. Because of his close ties to the U.S. government (particularly the CIA), many Iranians saw the Shah as a tool of American neocolonialism. At the same time, the Islamic clergy and other devout Muslims objected to the secularization of society and the intrusion of Western values and customs. As tension between the government and the mullahs intensified, a revered religious leader, the Ayatollah Ruhollah Khomeini, emerged as one of the Shah's leading critics.* When Khomeini was briefly imprisoned in 1964, riots erupted in several Iranian cities, culminating in an army massacre of up to 10,000 demonstrators.[42] Khomeini was sent into exile for nearly 15 years. The effect was to turn him into a martyr in a Shi'a culture that greatly admires martyrdom, thereby greatly enhancing his influence over the masses. In January 1979, with much of Iran's urban population involved in strikes and demonstrations against the regime, the Shah went into exile. Khomeini returned home to a frenzied welcome shortly thereafter.

Three interrelated developments set the tone for the Islamic revolution. First was the merger of the country's religious and political leadership. The new "Islamic republic," declared the Grand Ayatollah, is "the government of God."[43] While nonclerical figures have since held many important government posts, including the present president, Mahmoud Ahmadinejad, ultimate power resides in the hands of the Supreme Leader (currently Ayatollah Ali Khamenei)—a cleric to whom the president and other government officals are beholden—and the Guardian Council (a body dominated by Islamist clerics), which must approve prospective candidates for political office and which has the power to overrule parliament.

The second important development was the revival of traditional Islamic observances. Women now must be veiled in public and are strongly encouraged to wear the chador, the shapeless shroud that conceals all parts of the body.† Highly intrusive Revolutionary Guards have penetrated all aspects of Iranian life, policing possible violations of "correct" Islamic behavior. In the first years of the revolution (into the early 1990s), the Guards joined with neighborhood vigilante committees to arrest or harass Iranians who violated the clerics' highly conservative Islamic standards. During the 1980s, in the Shi'a tradition of martyrdom, many thousands of young volunteers died in a holy

---

* The title of Ayatollah is bestowed on the highest and most respected Shi'ite religious authorities.

† But women are less repressed in Iran than in some Gulf States, such as Saudi Arabia. Also, unlike Afghanistan's Taliban government, which barred females from attending school at any level, Iran's Islamic government doubled the female literacy rate from 36 to 72 percent in its first two decades in office.

war against Iraq. Assuring their families that it was a privilege to die for the faith, the Ayatollah Khomeini proclaimed, "We should sacrifice all our loved ones for the sake of Islam. If we are killed, we have performed our duty."[44]

Finally, Iran's radical revivalism has embraced an aggressive foreign policy that has supported kindred Islamist groups abroad—such as Lebanon's Hezbollah—and has been highly antagonistic toward countries that it perceived as enemies—especially, Israel and the United States. Prior to the revolution, Khomeini had declared, "America is worse than Britain! Britain is worse than America! The Soviet Union is worse than both of them! They are all worse and more unclean than each other!"[45] The regime's hostility toward the outside world was best illustrated by two events.

First, on November 4, 1979, revolutionary students seized the U.S. embassy in Tehran, taking diplomats and embassy staff hostage in an extraordinary breach of diplomatic protocol and international law. It was not until 444 days later that the last of the 52 hostages were released. For five nights a week, over 14 months, ABC television covered developments in a late-night show entitled "America Held Hostage." That embassy seizure, Iran's later support for Middle Eastern terrorist groups, and, most recently, its nuclear program, have made it an international pariah.

In 1980, Iraqi president Saddam Hussein sent troops into Iran following a number of border disputes. Saddam was probably also motivated by Iranian support for Iraq's repressed Shi'a majority. Once the conflict began, "both sides . . . portrayed the war as a noble crusade: Iraq saw the conflict as a historic defense of Arab sovereignty. . . against the marauding Persians [Iranians]; Iran depicted it as a holy war against the [Iraqi] infidels."[46] Before the war finally ground to a halt 8 years later, with no victor, it had cost the two nations a combined total of some 1 million lives. Following the U.S. overthrow of Saddam Hussein's regime in 2003, Iraq's formerly repressed Shi'a majority gained primary political power. Many of the country's newly influential Shi'a clerics had found refuge in Iran after escaping Saddam's persecution. So, ironically, because of the religious bonds between these two Shi'a communities, the U.S. ouster of Saddam had the unintended consequence of substantially increasing Iranian influence in Iraq.

After Khomeini's death in 1989, the Islamic revolution moderated somewhat. The Revolutionary Guard relaxed its grip on daily life; fewer women wore the chador; students openly violated Muslim orthodoxy; in the secrecy of their homes, middle-class Iranians at private social gatherings danced to Western music while women shed their head coverings.[47] Mohammad Khatami, twice elected president of the country (1997–2005) with particular support from young voters and women, moderated the country's confrontational foreign policy and tried to introduce a number of democratic reforms. But, although his supporters achieved a parliamentary majority, the Guardian Council blocked the most far-reaching attempts at political liberalization.

In 2005, Iranian voters, disillusioned with the reformist faction's inability to bring about significant change, elected a militant conservative president, Mahmoud Ahmadinejad. His government has pursued a harder line at home and in its foreign policy, clashing with the West over Iran's nuclear program. The prospect of Iran having nuclear weapons is of great concern to the West and, especially, to Israel. At the same time, religious conservatives at home have cracked down on the press and rolled back many of the personal freedoms gained under Khatami.[48] Following the 2009 presidential election, tens of thousands took to the streets in major Iranian cities to protest Ahmadinejad's questionable victory over a more moderate opponent. It is important to understand, however, that the demonstrators and their candidate, Mir Hussein Moussavi, demanded a more restrained version of the Islamist revolution, not its demise. To demonstrate their religious commitment, thousands of Moussavi supporters took to the rooftops of their homes for many nights to cry out "Allahu Akbar" ("God is great").

Despite substantial evidence of fraud, both the Supreme Leader and the Guardian Council certified the election results. Unlike its predecessors, the Obama administration has expressed its willingness to sit down with the Iranian regime to discuss that country's nuclear program and other issues. Recently (October 2009), the United States and Iran (along with other major powers) held their first direct talks in 30 years to discuss Iran's nuclear program. While the Iranian delegation seemed to make some concessions, many Western analysts remain skeptical about that nation's future intentions.

Al Qaeda and Militant Islamism

Since the 9/11 attacks on New York and Washington, international attention on Islamic fundamentalism has largely focused on the Al Qaeda terrorist network. Although government intelligence agencies, the media, and scholars have revealed a great deal about that organization (and its leader, Osama bin Laden), many aspects of its objectives, religious beliefs, organization, and behavior remain unclear or misunderstood. Because of Al Qaeda's secretive nature and its links to a religious tradition little understood in the West, a number of analysts have waged heated debates about its nature.[49] Much of that controversy—particularly as it relates to the war on terrorism—lies outside the scope of this chapter. Instead, this section discusses the origin of the terrorist network, its relationship to Islamic religious beliefs, and its level of support within the Muslim world.

Defeating the Soviet Infidels in Afghanistan (1979–1989) Although officially founded in 1988, Al Qaeda's roots trace back to 1979, the year of the Iranian Islamic revolution and the Soviet invasion of Afghanistan. The victory of the Iranian mullahs heartened Islamic fundamentalists elsewhere, anxious to challenge Western-style modernization and to oust their national leaders, whom they perceived as corrupt and insufficiently devout. Subsequently Al Qaeda appears to have occasionally established links with Iran, but tensions between Shi'a Iran and Sunni Al Qaeda have kept the two at a distance. For the same reason, the Iranians have generally opposed Afghanistan's Taliban. Indeed, in late 2007, Hillary Mann Leverett, a former director for Iran and Persian Gulf affairs of the U.S. National Security Council under President Bush testified to Congress that Iran generally had cooperated tactically with the United States on Al Qaeda and, especially, Afghanistan.[50]

A more powerful influence on bin Laden and his associates was the Soviet Union's occupation of Afghanistan, aimed at shoring up that country's unpopular communist regime. When Afghan mujahideen resisted the Soviet occupation, they were joined by a growing number of foreign volunteers drawn primarily from the Middle East. Among the earliest arrivals was Osama bin Laden, the Saudi-born son of a self-made, construction tycoon. Bin Laden used his enormous wealth, international contacts, and magnetic personality to recruit large numbers of foreign volunteers. Ironically, because they were fighting the Soviet army, the mujahideen also received weapons and encouragement from their future enemies, the United States and Saudi Arabia (as well as Pakistan).

In 1984, bin Laden and a colleague established the Afghan Service Bureau (MAK)—later the foundation of Al Qaeda—which

> played a decisive role in the anti-Soviet resistance. . . . In addition to recruiting, indoctrinating, and training thousands of Arab and [other] Muslim youths from countries ranging from the U.S. to the Philippines, MAK distributed $200 million of [the Middle Eastern], American, and British, aid destined for the Afghan jihad. Osama also channeled substantial resources of his own to the cause, a gesture that resonated with his fighters [and increased] his own credibility.[51]

Eventually, the foreign mujahideen (primarily Saudis, Egyptians, Yemenis, and Algerians) numbered between 25,000 and 50,000 fighters, who helped their more than 200,000 Afghan colleagues to drive the Soviets from Afghanistan in 1989.[52] One year earlier, bin Laden together with Ayman Muhammad al-Zawahiri (an Egyptian physician who became bin Laden's chief ideologist) had created Al Qaeda, built largely out of MAK. Like other Islamist militant groups, one of its goals has been to topple their so-called "near enemy"— despised Arab national governments in countries such as Egypt and Lebanon, considered too pro-Western or too irreligious. But unlike the other groups, Al Qaeda also has far broader objectives. It seeks to destroy the "far enemy," the United States and its Western Allies, whom it detests for their support of Israel and of corrupt and unrepresentative governments in a number of Muslim nations.[53]

Fighting Another Superpower: The United States With the Soviets vanquished in Afghanistan and many of the "Arab Afghans" (as the Middle Eastern volunteers were known) returning home, bin Laden and al-Zawahiri looked for new worlds to conquer. They widened their original objective of defending Islamic nations against conquest by "infidels" (those who do not believe in Islam) to include toppling religiously "derelict" Islamic regimes (such as Indonesia and Egypt) and supporting the struggles of Muslims against non-Islamic governments in regions such as Chechnya (Russia), and Indian-controlled Kashmir. In addition, the mujahideens' underdog victory over the Soviets in Afghanistan convinced Al Qaeda's leaders that they were capable of defeating the world's remaining superpower, the United States.

A number of factors spurred Al Qaeda's hostility toward the United States. First was American support for Israel. Second, it blamed the United States for propping up corrupt and despotic regimes in Muslim nations such as Egypt. Third, like most Islamic fundamentalists, Al Qaeda despised the West's secular values and its perceived decadence.

Iraq's invasion of Kuwait and the ensuing Gulf War was a major turning point for Al Qaeda. Following the Iraqi invasion, bin Laden offered troops to Saudi Arabia's King Fahd—a close friend of bin Laden's father and a major supporter of the mujahideen in Afghanistan—to protect the kingdom and its Muslim holy sites against Saddam Hussein's armed forces (Saddam was a secular leader whom bin Laden scorned). When the king refused the offer and turned, instead, to the United States for protection, bin Laden was outraged. His rage deepened after the war when U.S. troops remained in Saudi Arabia in proximity to the Muslim sacred cities of Mecca and Medina. "The presence of infidels on Arabian sacred soil was too much for . . . bin Laden to bear."[54] By 1994, his relationship with his former supporter, the Saudi government, had deteriorated to the point where the Saudis revoked his citizenship.*

When Al Qaeda's relations with the Pakistani government also deteriorated, bin Laden took some 1,000 of his most radical and battle-trained supporters to Sudan. However, after 4 years, they were forced to return to Afghanistan. There they were protected by the Taliban government until the United States ousted that regime in 2001 in reaction to the 9/11 attacks. At that point, it appears that Al Qaeda's leaders fled into hiding in the mountainous, tribal area of neighboring Pakistan.

Western intelligence agencies had been slow to realize that Al Qaeda existed. And even today, experts differ sharply regarding the extent of its involvement in high-profile terrorist strikes and the degree of top-down control its leaders exerts over its tactical operations. There is general agreement, however, that bin Laden and Al Qaeda were directly or indirectly responsible for major terrorist acts that include the following: the 1993 truck-bombing of the World Trade Center in New York; an attack on the American military barracks in Saudi Arabia (1996); the nearly simultaneous bombing of the U.S. embassies in Tanzania and Kenya, which killed 258 people and wounded more than 5,000 (1998); an attack on the naval ship, USS *Cole* in the port of Aden (2000); the 9/11 assault (2001) on the World Trade Center and the Pentagon, which killed some 3,000 people; and, most likely, an intended attack on the White House or the Capitol by a fourth hijacked plane that crashed in Pennsylvania; the bloody bombing of a nightclub in Bali (Indonesia) (2002); bombings of commuter trains in Madrid (2004) that killed nearly 200 people; subway and bus bombings in London (2005); and a major share of the early suicide bombings in Iraq.

Still, many experts do not see it as a centrally controlled, tightly knit unit whose every move is controlled by bin Laden and al-Zawahiri. Rather, they argue that it is a loosely linked network of organizations, many of which operate independently as "terrorist entrepreneurs" who come to Al Qaeda (the name means "the base" or "base of operation") for financial or logistical support. In the words of one observer,

> Although bin Laden and his partners . . . create[d] a structure . . . that attracted new recruits and forged links among preexisting Islamic militant groups, they never created a coherent terrorist network. . . . Instead, Al Qaeda functioned like a venture capital firm—providing funding, contacts, and expert advice to many different militant groups and individuals from all over the Islamic world.[55]

---

* There is evidence, however, that some members of the Saudi royal family continued funding Al Qaeda until 2004.

The destruction of Al Qaeda's home base following the allied invasion of Afghanistan and the death or capture of many of its leaders since 2001 have contributed to further decentralization. Consequently, "some analysts have suggested that the word Al Qaeda is now used to refer to a variety of groups connected by little more than shared aims, ideals and methods." The most deadly terrorist attacks in Europe since 9/11—London and Madrid—were carried out by young, European-born Muslims inspired by Al Qaeda, but acting independently. In the eyes of many analysts, such as Britain's International Institute of Strategic Studies, this decentralization has made it even more elusive, "more insidious [than] and just as dangerous" as it was at the time of 9/11.[56]

Support for bin Laden Despite Al Qaeda's unbending theology and brutal attacks on civilians (often including Muslims, as in Iraq), opinion polls suggest that the organization and Osama bin Laden enjoy considerable support in the Islamic world. In fact, the mass media have described the popularity of Osama T-shirts in countries such as Jordan and Indonesia and have noted the many newborns named after him in Pakistan and other Islamic nations. To be sure, a Gallup opinion poll of nine Muslim countries, conducted one year after 9/11, found that, in eight of the nine, a majority of respondents condemned the attacks.[57] Yet, a Pew Center survey (in 2004) revealed that almost two-thirds of all Pakistanis (65 percent) and approximately half the populations of Jordan (55 percent) and Morocco (45 percent) viewed bin Laden favorably.[58]

It seems hard to reconcile the widespread condemnation of the 9/11 attacks with the substantial support for bin Laden. But the Gallup survey revealed that in five of the nine Islamic countries, a majority of respondents did not believe that Al Qaeda or any other Arab group was really behind the September 11 events. Instead, many claimed that the American or Israeli governments had staged the attacks in order to pin the blame on Al Qaeda and the Afghan government. Moreover, most Muslims—89 percent of Indonesians, 80 percent of Pakistanis, and 69 percent of Kuwaitis—believed that the U.S. invasion of Afghanistan in the wake of 9/11 was "morally unjustifiable."[59] Probing the viewpoint of Muslims on the use of terrorism, the Pew survey found that 86 percent of all Jordanians, 74 percent of Moroccans, and 47 percent of Pakistanis felt that suicide attacks on Israelis (including those that kill civilians) were justifiable.[60]

Those attitudes persist even though many leading Islamic clerics and scholars insist that the killing of innocent civilians is not moral or compatible with Islamic values. How well, then, do bin Laden's words and deeds correspond to traditional Islamic beliefs? Sohail H. Hashmi, a student of Islamic thought, suggests that there are two relevant questions to be asked here: first, "under what circumstances or for what ends are war justified?"—a question also much debated regarding the Western, Christo-Judaic concept of "just war." Second, "once war has begun, how may fighting be properly conducted?"[61] In this case, what means are acceptable to achieve legitimate jihadist goals?

In two important Al Qaeda policy statements (issued in 1996 and 1998), bin Laden and his associates declared a holy war against "the Zionist-Crusader alliance and their collaborators"—that is, Israel, Jews, Christians, and Muslim states such as Saudi Arabia, Egypt, Morocco, and Jordan that have ties to the

United States. The use of the term *Crusaders* to refer to Westerners was meant to evoke historical Islamic resentment against the Christian Crusades and contemporary opposition to the presence of American troops in Saudi Arabia, Islam's sacred soil. The 1996 declaration also expressed bitterness over Israel's occupation of Jerusalem. Hashmi argues that the stated goal of Al Qaeda's attacks on the West—protecting the Muslim world against the threat of U.S. and Israeli imperialism—is consistent with the long-established Islamic tradition of "defensive jihad" and, therefore, resonates with many mainstream Muslims and clerics. "By declaring that it is willing to take on the world's greatest power in order to redress widely felt injustices [in Saudi Arabia, Israel, and elsewhere]," wrote Hashmi, "Al Qaeda garners the support of many ordinary Muslims."[62] Other scholars also have noted that in mainstream Islamic doctrine, "Muslims are enjoined to take up arms against their oppressors, be they local despots or foreign occupiers. Jihad is one of the fundamental duties of a Muslim."[*][63]

But, Hashmi and others argue that where bin Laden and Al Qaeda clearly fail to adhere to Islamic standards of morality is in the means they have adopted to achieve their goals—a willingness to kill innocent civilians including women, children, and elderly men. Bin Laden has justified the killing of civilians by claiming that it is merely reciprocity for what the West has done to the Muslims. Thus, in an October 21, 2001, interview with the Arabic television network, al-Jazeera, he stated, "We will do as they do. If they kill our women and our innocent people, we will kill their women and their innocent people until they stop." But Hashmi draws on Koranic verse, the Prophet Muhammad, and "the vast majority of 'ulama' [orthodox Islamic scholars] who have condemned his terrorism" to insist that "the jihad tradition relaxes restrictions on the weapons or methods of warfare in the face of military necessity, but never [abandons] the principle that civilians are not to be directly targeted." These experts "cite well-known sayings of Prophet Mohammad that forbid killing the enemy's women and children or burning down their vegetation—what are today known as scorched earth tactics."[64] Similarly, suicide bombing, a major tactic of jihadis (holy warriors) in Iraq and now widely used in Afghanistan and Pakistan, violates the Koran's prohibition of suicide. While the Koran sanctions martyrdom "as the last resort of a cornered Muslim warrior," it does not condone it "as willfully planned [offensive] death."[65] In fact, suicide is considered *haram* (forbidden). For this and other reasons, Islamic scholar Ahmed Rashid argues that bin Laden's "tactics had hardly anything to do with religion and everything to do with gaining political power and influence."[66] During their years in power (1996–2001), Al Qaeda's ally, the Afghan Taliban, prohibited domestic consumption of opium (as well as alcohol and other intoxicants), in accordance with Islamic teaching. But while in power and subsequently as an insurgent group, it and the Pakistani Taliban have made huge profits from the opium trade to Europeans and Americans. Afghanistan currently provides about 90 percent of the world's opium supply (used to produce heroine and

---

* This does not mean that most Muslims specifically endorse a holy war against Israel and the West. It merely means that Al Qaeda's call for jihad is broadly consistent with mainstream Muslim theology.

morphine), which earns the Taliban about $300 million annually for its military operations.

Still, despite mainstream Islamic theological objections to terrorism, it will continue to attract considerable support within the Muslim world as long as its practitioners are a leading voice against corrupt and repressive Middle Eastern regimes, against American and Israeli military power, and against the perceived "sinful" aspects of Western culture. As the Obama administration began a buildup of American troops in Afghanistan (2009), the war against the Taliban and Al Qaeda had not going well in either Afghanistan or Pakistan. The United States faces a dilemma: without additional American troops, the Afghan army appears unable to stop the jihadis. However, sending in additional troops is likely to stir up anti-Western and antigovernment sentiment. The problem is exacerbated whenever a U.S. drone or airplane accidentally kills innocent civilians while bombing Taliban soldiers or leaders believed to be living in the local villages. Unfortunately, in any major air war, periodic mistakes such as these are inevitable. Moreover, there is considerable opposition in the United States and Europe to building their military forces in Afghanistan, an opposition that has been greatly exacerbated by the fraudulent vote count on behalf of President Hamid Karzai's reelection bid.

Islamist Terrorists in Western Europe: A New Frontier

Most Islamist terrorists live in the Middle East or other Muslim countries. However, in the first decade of the twentieth century, there has been an alarming rise in terrorist attacks in Western Europe, carried out wholly or in part by Muslim immigrants or their children. Swelled by a surge in immigration from the Arab world and Turkey from the 1940s to 1990s, family reunifications, and higher (but now declining) birth rates, the current Muslim population of Western Europe is approximately 17 million (over three times the number in the United States). In the decades after World War II, many European nations welcomed Third World immigrants as a source of unskilled, poorly paid labor. Today, France is home to the largest number of Muslims, with approximately 6 million (nearly 10 percent of that country's total population). In all, almost two-thirds of all Western European Muslims live in France, the United Kingdom, and Germany.

As with Muslims worldwide, the vast majority of these immigrants and their children reject violence. Many of them have become European citizens and have integrated into their new homes. However, a number of dramatic terrorist attacks carried out by immigrants or children of immigrants born on European soil have created security concerns and contributed to a backlash against the entire Muslim population. These have included the bloody bombings of Madrid commuter trains and mass transit in London, an attempted attack on the Glasgow (Scotland) airport, and the murder of Dutch filmmaker Theo van Gogh (a relative of the famed artist, Vincent van Gogh). Moreover, it was an Al Qaeda cell in Hamburg, Germany, that organized and helped carry out the 9/11 attacks on the United States.

What accounts for the "European jihadis," including terrorists born and raised in Europe? Among the millions of Muslims who flocked to Europe, particularly in the 1980s, most came for economic reasons. At the same time, however, some were political activists facing persecution in their homelands, who were granted political asylum under Western Europe's hospitable immigration laws. Many of those politicized immigrants were Muslim fundamentalists (some endorsing violence, others not) fleeing countries such as Egypt and Morocco, where Islamists were the leading challengers to entrenched authoritarian governments. These included a number of radical clerics, who established mosques, often supported by the private or government funds from Saudi Arabia and spread their Islamist beliefs in their new European homelands. Surpisingly, many of the future holy warriors were university students, who arrived in Europe without being especially devout or militant but were soon alienated by elements of Western culture (such as its very different role for women), felt culturally isolated, or were stung by real or perceived racial and religious sights. "Indeed, radical Islam in Europe . . . appears increasingly to have become an ideology of desperation, driven by frustration, helplessness and a sense of impotence."[67]

External events also contributed to their radicalization. As in the Muslim world itself, many young Muslim immigrants were radicalized in the 1980s by the Afghan resistance against Russian occupation, including some who fought there as volunteers. Then, in the early 1990s, other Western European Muslims resented the West's slowness to protect Bosnia's Muslim population against the brutal assaults by the Serbs and Croats (both Christians). Finally, the enormously brutal civil war in Algeria between armed jihadis and the Algerian military throughout the 1990s sent thousands of refugees, including many radicals, fleeing to France and other European nations.

Compared to the politically oppressive South Asian and Arab nations from which many of them had fled, Islamist immigrants found that Europe's civil liberties and open politics made it easy to organize and expand their movements. As one radical organizer told a British television reporter in 1997, "If I lived in Saudi Arabia [his native country], I could never get away with what I do here, ha, ha."[68] Indeed, prior to the 9/11 attacks—and in spite of prior Al Qaeda bombings of the U.S. embassies in Kenya and Tanzania as well as other assaults—European counterterrorism efforts were rather limited. Some of these small terrorist groups have had ties to Al Qaeda, but many of them—especially in recent years—have not. In the United Kingdom, many of the terrorists apprehended by the police were not initially suspect because they were second-generation Pakistanis who seem reasonably integrated into British society.

Turkey and Moderate Islamism

Before ending our discussion of Islamic fundamentalists, we should understand that Islamist political movements and parties are not all ultra-traditionalist, anti-modernization, or anti-Western. Recent political developments in Turkey offer an excellent example. As we have seen, soon after the founding of the Turkish Republic in 1923, its leader, Mustafa Kemal Ataturk, abolished the Ottoman Empire's link between church and state and introduced a series of secular reforms. Women were emancipated (up to a point), while the government westernized the alphabet, clothing, and the nation's legal code. In stark contrast with Saudi Arabia, Iran, and other orthodox Islamic countries, which require women to cover their hair, Turkey banned women from wearing headscarves in public high schools, universities, or any government building (the ban is often referred to as "unveiling women" although even religious Muslim women in Turkey do not wear actual veils). These changes, designed to modernize and westernize the country, are still supported by much of the urban middle class and are guaranteed by the politically powerful military, which considers itself to be the guardian of the nation's secular tradition. On the other hand, many devout Turks, especially within the rural population and the urban poor, resent aspects of secularization. For example, the law restricting the wearing of head scarves creates a dilemma for observant, young women wishing to teach, work in the judicial system, work in the government bureaucracy (a major employer), or merely attend university. They must either uncover their heads, in violation of their religious principles, or abandon their educational and career aspirations.

From the 1950s through the 1980s, as the Turkish regime became less autocratic, the state relaxed its control over religiously based political groups. As a result, the first Islamist political party was founded in 1970. Since that time, various parties have been organized by a newly emerging, fundamentalist sector of the middle class. In addition, Turkey's economic modernization has brought millions of religious villagers into the country's major cities, where most have settled in teeming urban slums. Influenced by the surge of revivalism elsewhere in the Muslim world and by the challenges of urban life, these migrants have been the backbone of the fundamentalist resurgence that has challenged the nation's secular tradition. Not surprisingly, the growing Islamist movement alarmed Turkey's secular establishment and much of the nation's urban, middle class. During the last decades of the twentieth century, a series of Islamist parties were created. One after another, they were banned by the courts or banished by the military, only to reorganize subsequently under a new name—the National Order Party, followed by the National Salvation Party, the Welfare Party, the Virtue Party, and, currently, the Justice and Development Party (known as the AK). In 1996, the Welfare Party briefly headed a coalition government, but was ousted by the military and banned as a party less than 18 months later. Sobered by that experience, more temperate Islamist leaders, with a more moderate party platform, established the AK in 2001. Led by Recep Tayyip Erdogan, who had earned a reputation for honesty and efficiency while serving as Mayor of Istanbul, the party swept to power in the 2002 national election, winning only one-third of the popular votes (still the most of any single party), but two-thirds of the seats in parliament. Interestingly, opinion surveys indicated that fewer than half of the AK's followers supported the party out of religious conviction. A greater number of voters favored it because of its record of honest and efficient government in a country plagued by corrupt and ineffective politicians.

After taking office, the AK government presided over unprecedented economic growth, widened civil liberties, supported close ties to Europe and the United States, and worked hard to secure eventual Turkish admission to the European Union. To be sure, the AK's quest to join the European Union has an important tactical component. Joining the Union would put the Turkish armed forces under EU constraints prohibiting both military coups and judicial prohibitions on legitimate political parties.[69] But it would also be a barrier to possible religious intolerance or militant Islam in Turkey. As evidence of its moderation, the AK government has maintained Turkey's longstanding economic and military ties to Israel. Both former president Bush and former

British prime minister Tony Blair cited Erdogan's government as proof that Islamic beliefs and democracy can be compatible. Earlier in his career, when serving as mayor of Istanbul, Erdogan used city funds to help renovate Christian churches and Jewish synagogues, as well as mosques. And he has indicated his respect for other faiths by declaring that "a person who is a genuine believer would not harm the community no matter what his religion is."[70] Finally, most Western scholars agree that the Erdogan government has modernized the country more effectively than previous administrations had. Examining surveys of public opinion, one scholar notes that, like other Turks, many voters for religious parties and many religious Muslims favor a secular state and share mainstream political values. Thus, "the [religious parties] are not parochial movements or reactionary reflections of the global surge of Islam. To the contrary, they have successfully positioned themselves as parties that link local, national, and global issues."[71]

Yet, despite its strong performance in office and its moderation to date, the AK has failed to earn the trust of Turkey's secular establishment—government bureaucrats, professionals, and, especially, the military. Their worries are based less on what the AK government has done, than on what its leaders have said in the past and what secularists fear the party may do in the future if it gains sufficient power. In other words, many secular Turks believe that the current government's restraint may only be a tactical smokescreen. These suspicions are understandable. While the AK's leaders now express moderate positions, the same men held more radical Islamist views a decade ago when they were activists in the AK's predecessor, the Welfare Party. But, even if Erdogan's moderation is sincere, his opponents fear that he may be succeeded by more militant fundamentalists in his party. To be sure, AK officials elected at the local level have sometimes violated Turkey's secular tradition by distributing religious literature in the public schools and by allowing religious study groups to meet in them. Many secular Turks, though themselves Muslims, fear that this is only the opening wedge toward a broader Islamist push in the future. While the Erdogan administration has generally not interjected its religious beliefs into government policy, more strident Islamists have often been appointed to midlevel posts in government.

Still, most objective observers of Turkish politics feel that the AK leadership has truly moderated its position, either out of pragmatism or conviction. To be sure, the Erdogan government has sometimes been guilty of human rights violations. Most significantly, it has continued its predecessor's repression of the Kurds (an important minority group, many of whom favor self-rule) and has periodically arrested journalists for "anti-Turkish" writings. The fact is, however, Turkey has a history of human rights violations that long preceded the current Islamist government. In fact, the AK's human rights record is superior to those of its secular predecessors. Amnesty International's (AI) 2005 report lamented Turkey's continuing human rights violations, but also noted that "the [Erdogan] government introduced further legal and other reforms with the aim of bringing Turkish law into line with international standards." Specifically, it observed that "international law was given precedence over domestic legislation. All references to the death penalty were removed from the Constitution and the Penal Code."[72] Subsequently, AI has not observed as much further progress as it had hoped for.

Symbolic issues, such as the country's restrictions on headscarves, have evoked emotional reactions. Indeed, headscarves have been the major lightening-rod in recent Turkish politics. Even though more than half of all Turkish women say they wear them—either for religious reasons or in deference to tradition—Turkish law prohibits teachers, professors, and students (in universities and public high schools) from wearing them in the classroom. Hundreds of university students have been expelled and some 300 school teachers have been fired for refusing to unveil.[73] Not surprisingly, many international human rights groups, such as Human Rights Watch, have condemned the ban. Earlier attempts by the AK government to end the headscarf regulations were beaten back by the president, the military, and the secular political parties. Indeed, because she wears a headscarf, Prime Minister Erdogan's wife could not attend state dinners hosted by former president Ahmet Necdet Sezer (2000–2007), a firm secularist who prohibited women from wearing scarves anywhere in the presidential palace. In fact, Prime Minister Erdogan did not take his wife to any official functions for that very reason.

Tensions between secular and fundamentalist Turks came to a head in 2007, when President Sezer's term drew to an end. Prime Minister Erdogan asked parliament, which selects the Turkish president, to elect his Foreign Minister and close ally, Abdullah Gul. Fearing that turning over the presidency to the AK, which already controlled parliament and the Prime Minister's office, would allow the Islamists to impose some hidden agenda, hundreds of thousands of secular, mostly middle-class, Turks took to the streets, with one anti-Gul rally in Istanbul drawing as many as a million participants. Many outside observers, however, believe that the protests were primarily a reflection of middle-class snobbery toward the lifestyle of AK's lower-class supporters. Ironically, Gul himself is a former economics professor with a Ph.D. in that field and 2 years of graduate study in Britain. With the Turkish military indicating that they might oust Prime Minister Erdogan and his cabinet—just as they had removed the first elected Islamist government a decade earlier—the country's constitutional court annulled Gul's election on procedural grounds. Thus, the subsequent (2007) parliamentary election became a national referendum on the presidential crisis. The AK's smashing victory (described below) strengthened its bargaining position. Still, in 2008, a government prosecutor argued before the nation's constitutional court that the AK should be disbanded and that Prime Minister Erdogan and President Gul should be barred from political activity for 5 years because of alleged Islamist activity. While earlier Islamic parties had been disbanded, a court ruling against the AK this time would have caused substantial political tensions and possible unrest. By the narrowest of margins (6-5), the court refused to impose a ban on the party or its leaders but decided to fine the party. Thus, relations between the country's powerful secular institutions (including the courts) and the Islamic ruling party remain tense.

While these events threatened Turkey's political stability, the conflict largely reflected the secular population's fears rather than the AK's behavior in office. As we have noted, the Erdogan government had pursued a very moderate course. In fact, some of their proposals—most notably, giving observant female students the right to wear headscarves in school—are accepted practice in countries such as the United States and Canada (though not in France). Ironically, while serving as Turkey's Foreign Minister, Abdullah Gul had carried out a pro-Western foreign policy, featuring vigorous efforts to join the European Union. To strengthen those efforts, the AK implemented a number of measures improving civil liberties and bringing the country more in line with Western European standards. In the 2007 parliamentary election, the AK raised its share of the national vote from 34 percent in the previous election to 47 percent, a clear indication that its moderate policies and strong economic record had won over many previously skeptical voters (though the AK slipped a bit in the 2009 local elections because of the global recession). Shortly thereafter, parliament again selected Gul as President, a decision that the military and the courts accepted this time.

The Strengthening of Moderate Islam

As we have noted, most Muslims and Muslim clerics, especially outside the Arab world, believe in a moderate, peaceful form of Islam. In some of those countries, those moderates are working with the national government to contain militant fundamentalism. For example, in Singapore, where about one-sixth of the total population is Muslim, the technologically oriented, national government has helped the Muslim clergy establish a madrasa (Islamic school) that offers first-rate secular instruction (including math and science) to both girls and boys (though classes are segregated) in addition to its religious studies. In contrast to fundamentalist schools elsewhere in the Muslim world, social science textbooks here speak positively of the United Nations and of globalization. The authorities hope it will serve as a model for other madrasas, both in Singapore and elsewhere in Southeast Asia. Two schools in Indonesia have already adopted its curriculum.

In Indonesia itself—the world's largest Muslim population—jihadis, though only a small percentage of the faithful, gained substantial notoriety following a tragic terrorist blast in Bali. In national elections held earlier in this decade, several Islamist parties drew a small but growing percentage of the vote. However, in the country's most recent parliamentary election (2009), fundamentalist parties suffered substantial setbacks.

THE PROGRESSIVE CATHOLIC CHURCH

At roughly the same time that many Muslims were becoming more conservative and traditional, important sectors of Latin America's Catholic Church were embarking on a progressive path. From the time of Spanish colonialism through the first half of the twentieth century, the Church had supported the political and economic status quo, thereby legitimizing Latin America's elite-dominated governments. In a region marked by a high concentration of land and wealth, the Church was a major landowner until late in the nineteenth century. Provoked by the anticlerical positions of European and Latin American liberals, the Catholic hierarchy allied with conservative political parties and factions.

In the decades after World War II, however, many Catholic clergy, particularly at the parish level, began to abandon the Church's erstwhile conservatism. That process accelerated in the 1960s, when Pope John XXIII moved the "Church universal" in a more liberal direction, placing greater emphasis on social concerns. "The Second Vatican Council [convened by Pope John between 1962 and 1965] moved international Catholicism from a generally conservative and even authoritarian position to one that supported democracy, human rights, and social justice."[74] Catholics were encouraged to address pressing social issues and to enter into political dialogue with liberals and leftists.

In 1968, the Latin American Bishops Conference (CELAM) met in Medellín, Colombia, to apply the lessons of Vatican II to their own region. Challenging the status quo, their ideas reflected the influences of reformist theologians from the so-called "progressive church" (those who followed the reformist orientation of Vatican II).[75] The themes of ending dependency and liberating Latin America's poor echoed through many of CELAM's pronouncements. The clergy, said the bishops, must heed the "deafening cry . . . from the throats of millions asking their pastors for a liberation that reaches them from nowhere else."[76] To do so, the Church must "effectively give preference to the poorest and the most needy sectors." In short, an institution historically allied with the region's power elite was now becoming, in many respects, the Church of the poor.

The CELAM conference must be understood in the broader context of political change that was shaking Latin America at the time. In 1959, the triumph of the Cuban revolution highlighted the poverty and oppression afflicting so many Latin Americans. Cuba's far-reaching educational, health, and land reforms impressed and radicalized many Catholics. Three years before CELAM, Colombian priest Camilo Torres had left the priesthood to join a guerrilla movement. He was subsequently killed by counterinsurgency forces, but became a hero to leftists throughout Latin America. Few other priests or nuns joined the armed struggle. Many, however, accepted elements of Marxist political and economic analysis, identified with the plight of their poor parishioners, and helped organize and politicize peasants and slum dwellers.

Though always a minority within the Church, leftist clergy had an important influence in Central America during the 1970s and 1980s, most notably in Nicaragua, El Salvador, and Guatemala. Many Nicaraguan priests and nuns supported the Marxist-leaning Sandinista revolution in the 1970s. When the Sandinistas came to power, Maryknoll priest Miguel D'Escoto was named foreign minister, Jesuit priest Xavier Gorostiaga was appointed head of national planning, Father Ernesto Cardenal served as minister of culture, and his brother, Father Fernando Cardenal, became director of the national adult literacy campaign and then minister of education. No government in Latin America has had nearly the number of priests in its cabinet as Nicaragua's leftist government did.

For most of Latin America, however, the 1970s and 1980s were not years of revolution. Instead, much of the region came under the control of right-wing military dictatorships. Reacting to a perceived radical threat, repressive military regimes replaced civilian democracies in Argentina, Brazil, Chile, and Uruguay. At the same time, military rule continued in much of Central America and the central Andes, where democratic traditions had never been strong. Ironically, right-wing repression spurred the growth of the progressive church more effectively than the Cuban or Nicaraguan revolutions had.

Many radical clergy and laity were outspoken in their criticism of the military regimes and, consequently, suffered severe reprisals. Dozens of priests and nuns were murdered and many more persecuted in countries such as

Brazil, El Salvador, and Guatemala. In El Salvador, for example, a far-right death squad called the White Warriors distributed handbills reading, "Be a Patriot, Kill a Priest."[77] But such repression only radicalized many moderate Catholics. "When committed Catholics were imprisoned, tortured, and even killed, bishops in a significant number of cases then denounced the state, setting off a spiral of greater repression against the Church, followed by new Church denunciations of authoritarianism."[78]

In Chile, Brazil, El Salvador, and Peru, the Church became a leading critic of government human rights violations.[79] The most celebrated example was El Salvador's Archbishop Oscar Romero, the nation's highest-ranking cleric, who had begun his tenure as a conservative. Increasingly appalled by the military's widespread human rights abuses, he gradually moved to the left. In 1980, Romero wrote President Carter asking him to terminate U.S. military aid to the ruling junta until human rights violations had ended. Subsequently, he broadcast a sermon calling on Salvadorian soldiers to disobey orders to kill innocent civilians. "No soldier is obliged to obey an order against God's law," he declared. "In the name of God and in the name of this suffering people, I implore you, I beg you, I order you—stop the repression."[80] The following day Archbishop Romero was assassinated as he said a requiem mass, murdered by a death squad linked to the military.

Like Romero, Latin America's progressive clergy have far more commonly been reformers rather than radicals. At times, their political rhetoric and analysis has found some common ground with the Left. For example, the progressive church shares the Marxists' indignation over the plight of the poor, and many of its clergy identify dependency and U.S. domination as root causes of Latin American underdevelopment. But almost all Catholic activists have rejected revolutionary violence and the Leninist state as solutions. Reform, not revolution, was also the proscription of CELAM's bishops when they suggested progressive Catholic theology as an alternative to both capitalism and Marxism.

A number of the bishops' pronouncements originated with a radical Peruvian priest, Gustavo Gutiérrez, the father of "liberation theology." Writings by Gutiérrez and other liberation theologians greatly influenced the progressive church in Latin America and other parts of the world. Liberation theology calls on Catholic laity and clergy to become politically active and to direct that activity toward the emancipation of the poor. Drawing on Marxist analysis, Gutiérrez accepted the notion of class struggle, but his form of struggle was nonviolent. The poor, liberation theologians argued, should organize themselves into Christian (Ecclesial) Base Communities (CEBs) where they can raise their social and political consciousness. In that way, they can recognize the need to transform society through their own mobilization.[81] CEBs spread through much of Latin America, most notably in Brazil, Chile, Peru, and Central America. While the number of base communities and even their precise definition are subject to debate, a CEB is essentially "any group that meets on a regular basis to deepen its members' knowledge of the gospel, stimulate reflection and action on community needs . . . and evangelize."[82] In part, the Church created CEBs—which allowed laymen to carry out some priestly functions—as a response to the serious shortage of priests in Latin America, particularly among the poor.

Typically composed of only 10–40 people, the individual Base Communities are primarily located in poor urban neighborhoods and, to a lesser degree, in rural villages. Estimates of how many have existed in Latin America vary widely, but one calculation placed the number at their peak in the 1980s at perhaps 200,000, with a total membership of several million people. Perhaps 40 percent of all communities were in Brazil, home of the world's largest Catholic population.[83] Most CEB members seemingly are not politically active and join for strictly religious purposes.[84] Still, many of these communities were the foundations for popular protests against oppression, most notably in Central America but also in Brazil, Chile, and Peru. In other cases, CEBs helped raise political awareness and sharpen political skills among the poor.

Since the early 1980s, the influence of Latin America's progressive church has diminished considerably.[85] One cause, ironically, has been the region's transition from military dictatorships to democracy. Absent massive human rights violations and open assaults against the poor, Catholic clergy have generally been less motivated to enter the political arena. Furthermore, without a common foe, moderate and radical priests no longer have a common cause. Finally, many political activists who had used the Church as a protective "umbrella" during the military dictatorships (since those regimes were less likely to persecute Church-affiliated radical groups) are now able to participate in politics through other political organizations.[86]

Perhaps more importantly, since the 1980s the Vatican has been unsympathetic to any type of political activism among priests and nuns, particularly when related to the CEBs and liberation theology. As progressive bishops and archbishops died or retired, they have been replaced by more conservative clerics. The Vatican's conservatism and its distaste for liberation theology since the 1980s have continued under Pope Benedict XVI (though more quietly than many critics had expected). Indeed, in his previous capacity as Cardinal Joseph Ratzinger, Benedict authored some of the Vatican's strongest criticisms of the progressive church. But, although liberation theology and the progressive church have lost much of their momentum, they remained important actors in the political mobilization of Latin America's poor. Moreover, many of today's activists in left-of-center political parties, such as Brazil's governing Workers' Party (PT), emerged in part from the Catholic left.[87]

THE FUTURE OF RELIGION AND POLITICS IN THE DEVELOPING WORLD

The hold of religion on the human heart and spirit, and its consequent impact on the political process, has been frequently misunderstood by Western scholars. As we have seen, the initial error of both modernization and dependency theorists was to undervalue the significance of religion. Several factors account for the unanticipated resurgence of fundamentalism and other forms of religiously based politics in recent decades. In many countries, rapid modernization has left people psychologically adrift, searching for their cultural identity. The breakdown of village life and the erosion of traditional customs and values often create an emotional void not filled by the material rewards of modern life. In the Middle East, the indignities of colonialism and neocolonialism, resentment against Israel and the West, and dismay over decades of failed development since independence have all contributed to the region's religious revival. However, contrary to Western stereotypes, the appeal of Islamic fundamentalism is by no means limited to the poor and uneducated, who are less familiar with modern ideas and lifestyles. For example, most of the 9/11 terrorists had university educations and had lived outside the Muslim world. A biographical study of 173 jailed jihadis—from nearly a dozen countries—found that most were middle or upper class, most had received secular educations in primary and secondary schools, nearly two-thirds had at least some college or university education, and more than 40 percent were professionals (including physicians, architects, teachers, and preachers).[88] And recently (2007), when British intelligence units averted terrorist car-bomb attacks in London and Glasgow, most of the arrested conspirators were doctors practicing in the United Kingdom. Further, many of the holy warriors operating in Europe (such as the London mass transit bombers) have been young men, raised in the West, who feel like outcasts, isolated from both European lifestyles and their own culture.

Turning to Latin America, the progressive church offered a shield against political repression and a voice for the poor. As vastly different as they are, Islamic revivalism and the progressive Catholic Church have a few similarities. For example, both were grounded in revulsion over poverty and over government repression and corruption. Thus, the resurgence of Third World religion often was linked to a yearning for social and political justice, even if that vision of justice is sometimes unpalatable to those outside the movement. Other religious movements, not discussed in this chapter, have different worldviews. For example, the most rapidly growing religious movement in Latin America today is Evangelical Christianity, particularly Pentecostalism. The number of Pentecostals and Charismatics in the region has exploded from under 13 million in 1970 to nearly 160 million today (28 percent of Latin America's population).[89] Unlike progressive Catholics, these converts generally are politically conservative and pursue different lifestyles.

Having previously underestimated the impact of religion on Third World politics, analysts now risk overstating its importance. To begin with, the political weight of the movements that have attracted the most attention—Islamic fundamentalism and progressive Catholicism—must be put into perspective. Influential as they have been, they are not representative of the religions from which they have sprung. This point requires particular emphasis in relation to Islam, because a militant minority has left many Westerners with an extremely negative image of the entire Muslim world. They consider Islam to be backward and intolerant when, actually, like all religions, it encompasses a range of outlooks, some reactionary, and some progressive. For example, the media sometimes suggest that all Muslim women are repressed and confined, yet there are many Islamic feminists and professional women in countries such as Egypt, Lebanon, and Malaysia. It is worth remembering that four Muslim nations—Bangladesh, Indonesia, Pakistan, and Turkey—have had female prime ministers or presidents, something the United States has yet to achieve. Similarly, contrary to stereotype, some Muslim countries, including fundamentalist Saudi Arabia, are on good terms with the West. Lastly, when fundamentalist parties

(Muslim or Hindu) have assumed power, no matter their original intentions, their behavior in office was often moderated by their need for parliamentary coalition partners, their desire to appeal to a wide range of voters in future elections, and the dangers of offending powerful secular actors, such as the Turkish military.

Finally, when evaluating the current religious revival, we cannot assume that current trends will continue long into the future. History reveals that "religious resurgence is a cyclical phenomenon."[90] Consequently, Jeff Haynes argues that "there is no reason to doubt that the current wave of religion-oriented political ideas and movements will in time give way . . . to [a] partial resurrection of secular ideologies."[91] For the foreseeable future, however, religion will continue to be an important influence in the politics of many developing nations.

CONCLUSION: RELIGION AND DEMOCRACY

The relationship between institutionalized religions and democracy has been complex and varied. Traditionally, the leaders of influential religions have tended to ally with their country's political and economic elites, becoming pillars of the status quo. Jeffrey Haynes's explanation of why most local Christian religious leaders, from the 1960s through the 1980s, failed to speak out against Africa's authoritarian rulers applies equally well to other religions in the Third World:

> Church and state developed mutually supportive relationships . . . [Frequently] it was in . . . the interests of both Church and state for there to be social and political stability, even if required authoritarian rule to achieve it.[92]

Speaking out against a dictator, at the very least, would cut off government financial support for the church and, at worst, would subject the clergy and perhaps their parishioners to persecution. Sometimes, church leaders actually held official positions in their ruling regimes. For example, for many years, the Catholic archbishop of Kigali (Rwanda's primary city) was a member of the central committee of the country's only legal party. The 32-year dictator of Zaire (now the Congo), President Mobutu Sese Seko, gave Cardinal Malula a mansion to live in and subsequently gave a Mercedes to every Catholic and Protestant bishop in the country.[93] While there were also some prominent clergymen who demanded social justice and criticized government repression and corruption, it was not until the 1990s that the Congolese church became a prominent voice for democracy.

In Latin America and southern Europe, the Catholic Church hierarchy also had supported authoritarian regimes. Historically, Latin American churches had close links with the landholding elite (and were themselves major landowners). Europe's Catholic Church frequently supported right-wing, antidemocratic parties and movements as well. But, as we have seen, many organized religions became more progressive in the closing decades of the twentieth century, supporting democratization and greater social and economic justice. Indeed, Samuel Huntington credits the Latin American Catholic Church with being a leading voice for democratic change during the Third Wave. The

Philippine Church and its leader, Cardinal Jaime Sin, also lent critical support to Corazon Aquino's "people's power" movement, which brought democracy to that country. In South Korea, social movements led by several Protestant churches as well as the smaller Catholic Church also played an important role in the country's transition to democracy. Looking beyond these cases, two important questions come to mind regarding the relationship between religion and democracy. First, Does liberal democracy require the separation of the church from a secular political system? Second, Are the cultural values of some religions more supportive than others of democracy?

In his classic work, *Democracy in America*, the French author Alexis de Tocqueville suggested that a linchpin of democracy in the United States was the separation of church and state.

> I learned with surprise that [the clergy] filled no public appointments . . . [and] I found that most of its members seemed to retire from their own accord from the exercise of power, and that they made it the pride of their profession to abstain from politics. . . . They saw that they must renounce their religious influence if they were to strive for political power.[94]

Today, many analysts still believe that maintaining the pluralist values and the tolerance underlying democracy requires limiting the influence of religion on politics. But others reject the notion that democracy can only exist under a strict separation of church and state. In their recent book, *Religion and Democracy*, David Marquand and Ronald Nettler insist,

> Even in the absence of a . . . bargain keeping church and state apart, religion and democracy can coexist. Communities of faith do not necessarily imperil the foundations of pluralist democracy by seeking to pursue essentially religious agendas through political action.[95]

But, they add, there is a necessary restriction if this intermingling of religious political action and democracy is to work. "A degree of mutual tolerance, or at least of mutual self-restraint, is indispensable. Religious groups have to accept the right of other religious groups—and . . . the right of the non-religious—to abide by their own values."[96] Many countries and religions uphold that tolerance, but in some fundamentalist religions—Islamic or otherwise—it is absent.

Our second question has been the subject of intense debate—whether certain religious cultures are more supportive than others of democratic values. We saw in Chapter 2 that empirical studies have shown that Protestant countries are significantly more likely to be democratic than are Catholic or Muslim nations.[97] In contrast, Islamic nations have had a rather poor record of democracy, leading some scholars to conclude that Islam has authoritarian underpinnings. For example, in the mid-1990s, Turkish sociologist Serif Mardin suggested that the values of democracy may be tied to broader Western cultural values—values the Islamic world does not accept.[98]

One problem with such arguments is that, while they may have an element of truth, they fail to take into account differences within religions. Not all religious Catholics or priests, for example, have the same political values. Militant Islamic fundamentalist cultures that have flourished in Afghanistan and Sudan are surely unacceptable environments for democracy. Yet, most analysts agree that Islamic values can be quite compatible with democracy in a more moderate Muslim setting such as Indonesia or Malaysia.[99] Indonesia, the largest Muslim country in the world, encompasses a range of Muslim believers, from Islamists (only a small portion of whom are active in terrorist groups) through very progressive clerics and laity. Traditionally, Indonesians have practiced a more moderate form of Islam than is normally found in Middle Eastern or North African countries. The streets of its cities feature many unaccompanied women on motor scooters, and women have been free to choose whether or not they wished to wear the *jilbab* (the Islamic headscarf), though in some areas pressure to wear it has mounted in recent years. Perhaps the country's most influential cleric in the years leading to the country's democratic transition (in 1998) was Abdurrahman Wahid, then head of Indonesia's largest Muslim organization, the Nahdlatul Ulama (NU). While religiously conservative, the NU preached tolerance toward Indonesia's Christian and Hindu minorities and was an important actor in the campaign against the Suharto dictatorship.[100] In Indonesia's first democratic presidential election (1999), Wahid was chosen by parliament to lead the country. In office, he continued to demonstrate the tolerance so essential to democracy. Criticizing the frequent local violence against Indonesia's Christian minority, he insisted that Christians were equal to Muslims in the eyes of God. Moreover, in a rather dramatic departure from most Islamic heads of state, he publicly and enthusiastically supported Zionism and one of his first presidential visits was to Israel.

Another important factor limiting generalizations about the compatibility of particular religions with democracy is that, like most institutions and value systems, religions change over time. At one time, there was solid empirical evidence that Protestant countries were most likely to sustain democracy and economic growth, while Catholic and Confucian nations were less supportive. Today, neither relationship (political or economic) seems to hold. Confucian East Asia and Catholic Southern Europe both enjoyed rapid economic growth in the second half of the twentieth century, faster growth than in many Protestant countries. And more recently, as democracy has spread to various Catholic and Confucian nations (including Spain, Portugal, Poland, Brazil, Mexico, Taiwan, and South Korea), the suggested linkage between religions and democratic norms has faded. That isn't to deny that some religions are more tolerant or more authoritarian than others. Rather, it does mean that we need to avoid sweeping generalizations and consider differences within religions as well as changes over time.

DISCUSSION QUESTIONS

1. What would you think are the major disadvantages of having a close link between church and state? What are possible advantages?
2. What factors caused the growth of the progressive church in Latin America, and what is distinct about its followers' beliefs? Why has the progressive church lost so much of its influence in recent times?
3. What factors have led to the resurgence of Islamic fundamentalism (or revivalism) in Afghanistan, Iran, and other parts of the Muslim world? Why do you think so many people in that part of the world admire Osama bin Laden?

NOTES

1. Harvey G. Cox, *The Secular City*, 25th ed. (New York: Collier Books, 1990).

2. Donald Eugene Smith, ed., *Religion and Modernization* (New Haven, CT: Yale University Press, 1974), 4.

3. Quoted in Timothy D. Sisk, *Islam and Democracy* (Washington, DC: United States Institute of Peace, 1992), 3.

4. Emile Sahliyeh, ed., *Religious Resurgence and Politics in the Contemporary World* (Albany, NY: SUNY Press, 1990), 1–16.

5. John L. Esposito, *Islam and Politics*, 4th ed. (Syracuse, NY: Syracuse University Press, 1998), 311. Of course, since that time, groups like Al Qaeda have added the Internet to that list.

6. Jeff Haynes, *Religion in Third World Politics* (Boulder, CO: Lynne Rienner Publishers, 1994), 3.

7. Kenneth D. Wald, "Social Change and Political Response: The Silent Religious Cleavage in North America," in *Politics and Religion in the Modern World*, ed. George Moyser (New York: Routledge and Kegan Paul, 1991), 240.

8. One of the most influential and controversial books using the framework of clashing, religiously based cultures is Samuel P. Huntington, *The Clash of Civilizations and the Remaking of World Order* (New York: Simon & Schuster, 1996); see also Bernard Lewis, "The Roots of Muslim Rage," *Atlantic Monthly*, vol. 226, no. 3 (September 1990). Leonard Binder, a leading Middle East specialist, criticizes such terminology, arguing that Islam is only one part of Middle Eastern culture; see *Islamic Liberalism* (Chicago: University of Chicago Press, 1988), 80–81.

9. Donald Eugene Smith, *Religion and Political Development* (Boston: Little, Brown, 1970), 40.

10. Latif Abul-Husn, *The Lebanese Conflict: Looking Inward* (Boulder, CO: Lynne Rienner Publishers, 1998), 35; see also Robin Wright, *Sacred Rage: The Crusade of Modern Islam* (London: Andre Deutsch, 1986), 63; Dilip Hiro, *Holy Wars: The Rise of Islamic Fundamentalism* (New York: Routledge and Kegan Paul, 1989), 5–26.

11. Yann Richard, *Shi'ite Islam: Polity, Ideology, and Creed* (Oxford, UK and Cambridge, USA: Blackwell, 1995), 7 and 11. For a very readable account, see Valid Nasr, *The Shia Revival* (New York: W.W. Norton and Company, 2007).

12. Akbar S. Ahmed, *Discovering Islam* (New York: Routledge and Kegan Paul, 1988), 55–61.

13. Smith, *Religion and Political Development*, xi. Italics added.

14. For discussions of religion as a positive force for development, see Jeffrey Haynes, *Religion and Development* (London: Palgrave Macmillan, 2007); John L. Esposito, *Islamic Revivalism* (Washington, DC: American Institute of Islamic Affairs, American University, 1985), 5–6.

15. John L. Esposito, *Islam and Politics*, 2nd ed. (Syracuse, NY: Syracuse University Press, 1987), 231.

16. Smith, *Religion and Political Development*, 70.

17. H. E. Richardson, *Tibet and Its History* (London: Oxford University Press, 1962).

18. Smith, *Religion and Political Development*, 57–84.

19. Esposito, *Islam and Politics*, 2nd ed., 1. As noted in Chapter 2, some scholars question whether the linkage of church and state is any closer in the Islamic world than in the West.

20. John L. Esposito, *The Islamic Threat: Myth or Reality?* (New York: Oxford University Press, 1992), 78–79.

21. Article 24 of the Turkish Constitution (as amended October 17, 2001). http://www.tbmm.gov.tr/anayasa/constitution.htm.

22. Bernard Lewis, *The Emergence of Modern Turkey* (London: Oxford University Press, 1976), 416, quoted in Yesim Arat, *Rethinking Islam and Liberal Democracy: Islamist Women in Turkish Politics* (Albany: SUNY Press, 2005), 4.

23. Smith, *Religion and Political Development*, 54.

24. Janet A. Contursi, "Militant Hindus and Buddhist Dalits: Hegemony and Resistance in an Indian Slum," *American Ethnologist*, vol. 16, no. 3 (August 1989), 441–457.

25. Morton Zuckerman, "Beware of Religious Stalinists," *U.S. News and World Report* (March 22, 1993), 80.

26. Esposito, *The Islamic Threat*, vii.

27. Joseph S. Szyliowicz, "Religion, Politics and Democracy in Turkey," in *The Secular and the Sacred*, ed. William Safran (London: Frank Cass, 2003), 190; for similar objections to the use of the term *Islamic fundamentalism*, see Esposito, *The Islamic Threat*, 7–24; Shireen T. Hunter, ed., *The Politics of Islamic Revivalism* (Bloomington: Indiana University Press, 1988).

28. Fred Halliday, *Islam and the Myth of Confrontation: Religion and Politics in the Middle East* (London: I. B. Tauris Publishers, 1996), 233, fn. 1.

29. Esposito, *The Islamic Threat*; Akbar S. Ahmed, *Discovering Islam* (New York: Routledge and Kegan Paul, 1988); Esposito, *Political Islam: Revolution, Radicalism or Reform* (Boulder, CO: Lynne Rienner Publishers,

1997); Halliday, *Islam and the Myth of Confrontation.*

30. Halliday, *Islam and the Myth,* 107.

31. Graham E. Fuller, "A World Without Islam," *Foreign Policy* (January/February 2008), 46–53.

32. Hiro, *Holy Wars,* 1–2.

33. Mohammed Ayoob, *The Many Faces of Islam: Religion and Politics in the Muslim World* (Ann Arbor: The University of Michigan Press, 2008), 2.

34. Ahmed Rashid, "Jihadi Suicide Bombers: The New Wave," *The New York Review of Books,* vol. 55, no. 10 (June 10, 2008), http://www.nybooks.com/articles/21473; For similar assessments, see Omar Nasiri, *Inside the Jihad: My Life with Al Qaeda, A Spy's Story* (New York: Basic Books, 2006).

35. Robin Wright, "Lebanon," in *The Politics of Islamic Revivalism,* 66.

36. Eden Naby, "The Changing Role of Islam as a Unifying Force in Afghanistan," in *The State, Religion, and Ethnic Politics,* ed. Ali Banuazizi and Myron Weiner (Syracuse, NY: Syracuse University Press, 1986), 124–154; Paul Overby, *Holy Blood: An Inside View of the Afghan War* (Westport, CT: Praeger, 1993).

37. Brian R. Farmer, *Understanding Radical Islam* (New York: Peter Lang, 2007), 115.

38. Useful sources on the origins and course of the revolution include Robin Wright, *In the Name of God: The Khomeini Decade* (New York: Simon & Schuster, 1989); Robin Wright, *The Last Great Revolution: Turmoil and Transformation in Iran* (New York: Vintage Books, 2001); Hiro, *Holy Wars,* chap. 6.

39. Hiro, *Holy Wars,* 151.

40. Ibid., 151–153; See also Shireen T. Hunter, *Iran after Khomeini* (New York: Praeger, 1992), 11–12.

41. Cheryl Bernard and Zalmay Khalilzad, *The Government of God: Iran's Islamic Republic* (New York: Columbia University Press, 1984), 12–13.

42. Hiro, *Holy Wars,* 160.

43. Wright, *In the Name of God,* 65.

44. Ibid., 87.

45. Quoted in Bernard and Khalilzad, *The Government of God,* 151–152.

46. Gary Sick, "Trial by Error: Reflections on the Iran-Iraq War," in *Iran's Revolution,* ed. R. K. Ramazani (Bloomington: Indiana University Press, 1990), 105.

47. Wright, *In the Name of God,* 191; Hunter, *Iran after Khomeini,* 32–41.

48. Nikki R. Keddie, *Modern Iran: Roots and Results of Revolution* (New Haven, CT: Yale University Press, 2006), 263–346, analyzes developments since the death of Khomeini.

49. Several works on Al Qaeda criticize alleged myths about it. See, for example, Jason Burke, "Think Again: Al Qaeda," *Foreign Policy* (May/June 2004) and Rohan Gunaratna, *Inside Al Qaeda: Global Network of Terror* (New York: Columbia University Press, 2002).

50. Greg Bruno and Lionel Beehner, "Iran and the Future of Afghanistan," *Backgrounder,* Council on Foreign Relations, http://www.cfr.org/publication/13578/iran_and_the_future_of_afghanistan.html.

51. Gunaratna, *Inside Al Qaeda,* 18–19.

52. Peter L. Bergen, *Inside the Secret World of Osama bin Laden* (London: Weidenfeld & Sicolson, 2001), 59–60.

53. Ayoob, *The Many Faces of Political Islam,* 112–151.

54. Marc Sageman, *Understanding Terror Networks* (Philadelphia: University of Pennsylvania Press, 2004), 38.

55. Jason Burke, "Think Again: Al Qaeda."

56. Both quotes are from a May 16, 2003, BBC report; see http://newsvote.bbc.co.uk/mpapps.

57. http://www.publicagenda.org/specials/terrorism, cited in Jeff Haynes, "Al-Qaeda: Ideology and Action" (Uppsala, Sweden: Paper prepared for the EPCR Joint Sections of Workshops, April 2004), 2.

58. The Pew Research Center for the People and the Press, "A Year After the Iraq War: Mistrust of America in Europe Even Higher, Muslims' Anger Persists" (March 16, 2004), 1. http://people-press.org/reports.

59. Haynes, "Al-Qaeda," 2.

60. Pew Research Center, "A Year After," 1.

61. Sohail H. Hashmi, "9/11 and the Jihad Tradition," in *Terror, Culture, Politics: 9/11 Reconsidered,* eds. Daniel J. Sherman and Terry Nardin (Bloomington: Indiana University Press, 2005).

62. Ibid.

63. "Analysis: Interpreting Islam," *BBC* (Friday, July 9, 2004), http://news.bbc.co.uk/1/h/world/middle_east/3880151.stm.

64. Ibid.

65. Rashid, "Jihadi Suicide Bombers."

66. Ibid.

67. Alison, Pargeter, *The Frontiers of Jihad: Radical Islam in Europe* (Philadelphia: University of Pennsylvania Press, 2008), viii. Pargeter's ideas greatly influenced this section.

68. Ibid., 32

69. Amr G. E. Sabet, *Islam and the Political* (Ann Arbor, MI: Pluto Press, 2008), 253.

70. Metin Heper, "The Justice and Development Party: Toward a Reconciliation of Islam and Democracy in Turkey?" (Tel Aviv University: The Annual Georges A. Kaller Lecture, 2003), 6.

71. Sultan Tepe, *Beyond Sacred and Secular: Politics of Religion in Israel and Turkey* (Stanford, CA: Stanford University Press, 2008), 342.

72. *Amnesty International Report 2005*, Turkey, http://web.amnesty.org/report2005/tursummary-eng.

73. Human Rights Watch, *Combating Restrictions on Headscarves*, http://www.hrw.org/reports/2000/turkey2/Turk009–05.htm.

74. Paul Sigmund, *Liberation Theology at the Crossroads* (New York: Oxford University Press, 1990), 19.

75. Scott Mainwaring and Alexander Wilde, eds. *The Progressive Church in Latin America* (Notre Dame, IN: University of Notre Dame Press, 1989).

76. Sigmund, *Liberation Theology at the Crossroads*, 29–30.

77. Jennifer Pearce, "Politics and Religion in Central America: A Case Study of El Salvador," in *Politics and Religion in the Modern World*, 234.

78. Mainwaring and Wilde, *The Progressive Church*, 13.

79. Scott Mainwaring, *The Catholic Church and Politics in Brazil* (Stanford, CA: Stanford University Press, 1986); Brian H. Smith, *The Church and Politics in Chile* (Princeton, NJ: Princeton University Press, 1982).

80. Philip Berryman, "El Salvador: From Evangelization to Insurrection," in *Religion and Political Conflict in Latin America*, ed. Daniel H. Levine (Chapel Hill: University of North Carolina Press, 1986), 58–78, 114.

81. Sigmund, *Liberation Theology at the Crossroads*, 28–39. These communities also are called Ecclesial Base Communities or Base Christian Communities.

82. W. E. Hewitt, *Base Christian Communities and Social Change in Brazil* (Lincoln: University of Nebraska Press, 1991), 6.

83. Hewitt, *Base Christian Communities*; Thomas C. Bruneau, "Brazil: The Catholic Church and Basic Christian Communities," in *Religion and Political Conflict in Latin America*, 106–123.

84. John Burdick, "The Progressive Catholic Church in Latin America," in *Latin American Research Review*, vol. 24, no. 1 (1994), 184–198.

85. Burdick, "The Progressive Catholic Church."

86. Thomas C. Bruneau, "The Role and Response of the Catholic Church in the Redemocratization of Brazil," in *The Politics of Religion and Social Change*, eds. Anson Shupe and Jeffrey K. Hadden (New York: Paragon House, 1986), 95–98.

87. José Ivo Fullman, "Progressive Catholicism and Left-Wing Politics in Brazil," in *The Church at the Grassroots in Latin America: Perspectives on Thirty Years of Activism*, eds. John Burdick and W.E. Hewitt (Westport, CT: Praeger, 2000), 53–68.

88. Sageman, *Understanding Terror Networks*, 74–78.

89. *The Pew Forum on Religion and Public Life: Surveys* (July 7, 2007), http://pewforum.org/surveys/pentecostal/latinamerica/.

90. Smith, "The Limits of Religious Resurgence," 34.

91. Haynes, *Religion in Third World Politics*, 155.

92. Jeff Haynes, "Religion and Democratization in Africa," in *Religion, Democracy and Democratization*, ed. John Anderson (New York: Routledge, 2006), 68.

93. Ibid., 69.

94. Alexis de Tocqueville, *Democracy in America*, ed. Alan Ryan (London: Everyman's Library, 1994), 309–312.

95. David Marquand and Ronald L. Nettler, "Forward," in *Religion and Democracy*, eds. David Marquand and Ronald L. Nettler (Oxford, England: Blackwell Publishers, 2000), 2–3.

96. Ibid., 3.

97. Axel Hadenius, *Democracy and Development* (New York: Cambridge University Press, 1992).

98. Quoted in Chris Hann, "Introduction: Political Society and Civil Anthropology," in *Civil Society: Challenging Western Models*, eds. Chris Hann and Elizabeth Dunn (London: Routledge, 1996), 1–26.

99. Robert W. Hefner, *Civil Islam: Muslims and Democratization in Indonesia* (Princeton, NJ: Princeton University Press, 2000).

100. Robert W. Hefner, "Muslim Democrats and Islamist Violence in Post-Soeharto Indonesia," in *Remaking Muslim Politics: Pluralism, Contestation, Democratization*, ed. Robert W. Hefner (Princeton, NJ: Princeton University Press, 2006), 273–301.

CHAPTER 4

THE POLITICS OF CULTURAL PLURALISM AND ETHNIC CONFLICT

In the early years of the twenty-first century, like the first decades of the twentieth century, much of the Third World suffered from ethnic, racial, and religious tensions periodically punctuated by outbreaks of brutality and carnage. Progress in one location was often followed by deterioration in another. For example, in 2005, the Sudanese government (led by Arab Muslims) signed a peace accord with the Sudan People's Liberation Movement/Army (SPLM/A)—a secessionist movement in the country's South, representing that region's predominantly Black (Christian and animist) population. The treaty, granting the South considerable autonomy (self-rule within Sudan), ended a 21-year civil war that had left about 2 million people dead (mostly Southerners killed or starved by the government). Soon after ending that conflict, however, the Sudanese government intensified its "ethnic cleansing" in the western region of Darfur, where government-supported Arab militias (called Janjaweed) killed many thousands of Muslim Blacks. The Janjaweed "raped women and destroyed villages, food stocks, and other [essential] supplies" and drove some 2.7 million people from their homes, many in refugee camps where they have often been victimized once again. To date, the United Nations estimates that approximately 300,000 people have been killed.[1] Other authoritative sources put the figure far higher, as high as 500,000 dead.

Such conflicts are not new. Nearly a century earlier (1915–1916), in the midst of World War I, Turkey's government massacred about 1.5 million Armenians within that country's borders. Thirty years after that, as Britain relinquished power over India, it divided that "jewel in the [imperial] crown," into two nations—largely Hindu India and overwhelmingly Muslim Pakistan. But the religious communities in each country then savagely turned on each other, with a resulting death toll of approximately 1 million. More recently, Hutus in the African nation of Rwanda massacred some 800,000 of their Tutsi countrymen, while in the former country of Yugoslavia, Serbian militias initiated "ethnic cleansing" of their Muslim and Croat neighbors, killing and raping untold thousands. During the twentieth century, religious conflicts (India and Lebanon), tribal animosities (Nigeria and Rwanda), racial prejudice (South Africa), and other forms of ethnic rancor frequently produced violent confrontations, civil wars, and genocidal brutality. Continuing ethnic tensions in the early years of the twenty-first century seem to confirm Mahabun ul Haq's prediction—that wars between "peoples" (ethnic, religious, racial, or cultural groups) will continue to far outnumber wars between nation-states.

> Classic accounts of modernization, particularly those influenced by Marx, predicted that the old basis for divisions, such as tribe and religion, would be swept aside. As hundreds of millions of people poured from rural to urban areas worldwide, during the nineteenth and twentieth centuries, it was expected that new alliances would be formed, based on social class in particular.[2]

But, significant as class conflict has been, no cleavage in modern times has more sharply, and oftentimes violently, polarized nations than ethnicity. "Cultural pluralism [i.e., ethnic diversity]," notes Crawford Young, "is a quintessentially modern phenomenon." It has been closely linked to the growth of the middle class and the emergence of politicians who articulated nationalist or other ethnic aspirations while mobilizing workers and peasants behind that ideal.[3] Scholars point out that fear of and hostility toward other ethnic groups are far older and often more entrenched than modern principles of tolerance or equality under the law. "No matter how we may wish for it otherwise, we did not leave violence against outsiders behind us as our nations became modern and democratic."[4]

To be sure, ethnic minorities have been victimized for hundreds of years. So such conflicts are not new. One needs only look to the nineteenth-century frontier wars between White settlers and Native Americans in the United States and Chile. And, contrary to common perceptions, the level of ethnic protests and rebellions within states actually diminished slightly since the early 1990s, after having grown steadily for the previous preceding 50 years.[5] Alarmist warnings notwithstanding, the world has not been crumbling into a cauldron of small ethnically based states.

Still, the level of ethnically based *internal* conflict remains far higher than in the decades prior to the 1990s, in marked contrast to the dramatic decline in wars *between* nations in the same period. Indeed, over the past 50 years, the most frequent settings for violent conflict have not been wars between sovereign states, but rather internal strife tied to cultural, tribal, religious, or other ethnic animosities. Between 1989 and 2004, there were 118 military conflicts in the world. Of those, only seven were between nation-states and the remaining 111 occurred within a single state, a large portion of which involved ethnic conflict.[6] According to another recent estimate, "nearly two-thirds of all [the world's] armed conflicts [at that time] included an ethnic component. [In fact], ethnic conflicts [were] four times more likely than interstate wars."[7] Another study claimed that 80 percent of "major conflicts" in the 1990s had an ethnic element.[8] Any listing of the world's most brutal wars in the past few decades would include ethnically based internal warfare or massacres in Rwanda, the Congo, Ethiopia, Sudan, Lebanon, and Indonesia (East Timor). In 1998, one authoritative study estimated that some 15 million people had died worldwide as a result of ethnic violence since 1945 (including war-related starvation and disease).[9] In the decade since, at least 5 million additional deaths resulted from ethnic conflict in the Congo alone, with hundreds of thousands more in Sudan, Ethiopia, Afghanistan, Iraq, and elsewhere. Since the end of the Cold War, the world's attention has focused increasingly on ethnic clashes. Some experts predict that poor, densely populated countries will experience increased ethnic conflict over scarce resources (such as farmland) in the coming decades.

Warfare between Serbs, Croats, Bosnian Muslims, and Kosovars in the former Yugoslavia, along with separatist movements by French-speaking Québécois, racially based riots in Los Angeles, Basque terrorism in Spain, and Protestant–Catholic clashes in Northern Ireland all demonstrate that interethnic friction and violence can erupt in both Western democracies and former European communist countries. But ethnic conflict has been particularly widespread and cruel in Africa, Asia, and other regions of the Third World—in part because LDCs tend to have more ethnically diverse populations, and in part because their political systems often lack the institutions or experience needed to resolve these tensions peacefully. A recent study determined that there are approximately 275 "minorities at risk" (i.e., ethnic groups facing actual or potential repression) throughout the world, with a total population exceeding 1 billion people (about one-sixth of the world's populations) scattered in 116 countries. Approximately 85 percent of that population at risk lives in the LDCs. Although Asia has the highest *absolute* population of ethnic minorities, sub-Saharan Africa has the highest *proportion* of its population at risk (about 36 percent), followed by North Africa and the Middle East (26 percent).[10]

The intensification of ethnic, racial, and cultural hostilities during the twentieth century undercut several assumptions of modernization theory; it also contradicted an influential social psychology theory known as the "contact hypothesis." That hypothesis predicted that as people of different races, religions, and ethnicities came into greater contact with each other, they better understand the other groups' common human qualities, causing prejudice to decline.[11] Although the contact hypothesis frequently predicts *individual* level attitudes and behavior (i.e., as individuals of different races or religions come to know each other better, their prejudices *often* diminish), increased interaction between different ethnic *groups*, occasioned by factors such as urban migration, frequently *intensifies* hostilities. Moreover, in some cases such as Rwanda and Bosnia, despite years of close interethnic contact and intermarriage, neighbors and even relatives by marriage viciously turned against each other once group violence had taken on a momentum of its own.[12] This is particularly true when the political and economic systems are biased in favor of one ethnic group or when ethnic leaders play on their followers' prejudices to advance their own political agendas. Neighboring ethnicities that lived peacefully, side-by-side for decades may also confront each other when new, valuable natural resources are discovered on their common lands. Thus, for example, in Nigeria, the upsurge of oil production in the Niger Delta sparked unrest by tribal minorities in the region, who protested that great wealth was being extracted from the delta while leaving the local population in poverty. Similar ethnic conflicts have arisen in the neighboring country of Niger after the discovery of substantial uranium deposits.

This chapter focuses on the most protracted and intense ethnic group conflicts in the developing world. In doing so, it runs the risk of conveying the mistaken notion that all LDCs are aflame with violent ethnic clashes. In truth, most ethnic tensions do not lead to systematic violence and many developing nations have been comparatively free of such conflict. Ethnic warfare is more pronounced in the Indian subcontinent, the Middle East, Southeast Asia, and much of Africa. It is less common in Latin America and the Far East. A number of developing countries—Uruguay and Korea, for example—are fairly ethnically homogeneous, eliminating the possibility of such conflict. Others have developed a fairly stable, if not necessarily just, relationship between ethnicities, including Venezuela, Ghana, and Taiwan. A number of Latin American countries are multiracial and have varying degrees of racial discrimination and tension. But rarely do those conflicts become violent any longer. So, although this chapter focuses on the difficult and brutal cases in order to illustrate the obstacles that ethnic conflicts may present to political and economic development, it does not imply that most LDCs are riddled with ethnic violence.

DEFINING ETHNICITY

Many scholars maintain that humans have a deeply rooted social and psychological need to identify themselves with a group that protects them from outsiders and gives them a sense of belonging (i.e., to create an "us" to protect oneself from "them"). Moreover, some argue that "conflict [between ethnic or cultural groups] is not extraordinary but instead grows out of the more [daily] practices and ordinary behaviors that characterize everyday life."[13] Although it is difficult to define ethnicity precisely, certain common qualities set ethnic groups apart. Most analysts agree that ethnic identity is usually a *social construction*—a way that certain groups have come to view themselves over time as distinct from others—rather than an inherent or primordial characteristic. Each ethnicity "share[s] a distinctive and enduring collective identity based on a belief in a common descent and on shared experiences and cultural traits."[14] While they frequently have some basis in fact, these identities and histories are typically created or embellished by entrepreneurial politicians, intellectuals, and journalists who gain some advantage by "playing the ethnic card." The real or imagined common history, tradition, and values not only unite the group, but distinguish it from neighboring ethnicities, sometimes giving rise to ethnic conflict.[15] Thus, J. E. Brown's cynical definition of a "nation" can be applied to ethnic identities generally: "A group of people united by a common error about their ancestry and a common dislike of their neighbors."[16] In times of great uncertainty or crisis, intellectuals and politicians are likely to create historical myths that give their ethnic group a sense of security in the face of perceived external challenges. In the words of Vesna Pesic, a Serbian peace activist, ethnic conflict is caused by the "fear of the future, lived through the past."[17]

Pakistanis and Indians in Uganda, Chinese in Malaysia, Hmong in Laos, and indigenous peoples (Indians) in Peru often form their own political organizations, business groups, or social clubs. However, ethnic groups are usually not socially homogeneous or politically united. Frequently, class, ideology, or religion divides them. For example, Sri Lanka's Tamil-speaking minority is divided between those who have lived in the country for centuries and those brought from India to work on plantations in the nineteenth century, with each group holding somewhat different political views. Each of those two subgroups is, in turn, divided by caste. Indian Muslims and Nigerian Ibos are internally divided by class. South Koreans may be Buddhist or Christian (or both). Still, the factors that bind these ethnic groups are more powerful than elements that divide them. Thus, Ibo peasants normally identify more closely with businesspeople from their own tribe than they do with fellow peasants from the Hausa or Yoruba communities. Indeed, Cynthia Enloe notes that "of all the groups that men [or women] attach themselves to, ethnic groups seem the most encompassing and enduring."[18]

At the same time, outside observers sometimes erroneously assert or assume that certain ethnic identities and ethnic conflicts are deeply rooted in history. For example, during the bloody civil war between Bosnian Muslims and Serbs (in the former Yugoslavia), many Western journalists and political leaders claimed that violence could be traced to centuries-old religious tensions and conflicts (dating to the Middle Ages) between Orthodox (Christian) Serbians, Muslim Bosnians, and Catholic Croatians. But actually, prior to the breakup of Yugoslavia in the early 1990s, the three groups had lived together in harmony for many years, and intermarriages were somewhat common. "In the 1970s, ethnicity played a minor and, compared to earlier realities, diminishing part [in Bosnian life]. The vast majority of Bosnians . . . were up to the 1990s determined to keep the significance of the ethnic factor to a minimum." Only after nationalist politicians [particularly Serbs] used ethnic appeals to replace the recent demise of Communism, "was every person forced to choose an ethnic identification."[19]

Some ethnic classifications were initially imposed by outsiders. In the Belgian Congo, White colonial administrators, missionaries, explorers, and anthropologists erroneously lumped together people of the upper Congo region into a nonexistent tribe (or ethnicity) called the Bangala. After a number of decades, the "myth of the Bangala" took on a life of its own, as migrants from the upper Congo settling in the city of Kinshasa joined together under the ethnic label that had been imposed on them by the Belgians. Similarly, the classification of "Coloured" (written here with its South African and British spelling), once used to denote racially mixed or Asian South Africans, was an artificial construct established by the White regime. And although few Mexicans feel much in common with Cubans, Ecuadorians, or Nicaraguans when they live in their home countries, all of these nationalities have become an ethnic group called "Latinos" or "Hispanics" after they immigrated to the United States—viewed as a homogeneous mass by their "Anglo" neighbors. Once individuals begin to accept the group label imposed on them, however, even artificially created ethnic classifications become politically relevant.[20]

Ethnic groups may have their own social clubs, soccer teams, schools, or cemeteries. For an insecure Peruvian Indian recently arrived in Lima from her rural village, or a Hausa migrant seeking a job in Lagos, ethnically based social clubs are invaluable for finding employment, housing, and friendships in an otherwise cold and inhospitable city. In the threatening environment associated with modernization and social change, "fear, anxiety, and insecurity at the individual level can be reduced within the womb of the ethnic collectivity."[21] At the same time, however, ethnic consciousness normally creates barriers *between* groups. Friends and neighbors often frown upon interreligious or interracial marriages, for example. Almost inevitably, when two or more ethnic groups live in close proximity to each other, there will be some tension or apprehension. But the way in which society handles these relationships varies considerably from place to place. Countries such as Canada, Malaysia, and Trinidad-Tobago have managed ethnic divisions fairly amicably and peacefully. More frequently, however, ethnic divisions lead to tensions or even conflict. In multiethnic countries such as Angola, India, Indonesia, and the United States, a common consciousness and culture unite certain religions, castes, tribes, or races, while generating distrust or even hostility toward other ethnicities.

ETHNIC AND STATE BOUNDARIES

If the world were composed of fairly homogenous countries such as Uruguay, South Korea, or Iceland, ethnically based wars might continue between nation-states, but there would be no ethnic tensions or strife *within* individual countries. In other words, the underlying cause of most internal ethnic conflict is that boundaries for *nations* (distinct cultural-linguistic groups such as Serbs, Russians, or Kurds) and other ethnicities frequently fail to coincide with boundaries for *states* (self-governing countries).[22] Indeed, the world's nearly 200 countries are home to approximately 5,000 ethnic groups. In the Middle East, 25–30 million Kurds have their own language, customs, and traditions, but not their own state. Consequently, they have struggled for decades to establish a state, which they call Kurdistan, carved out of the four countries in which most of them reside. Similarly, Sikh militants in the Indian state of Punjab have demanded the creation of a Sikh nation-state. When ethnic groups feel that they have been denied their fair share of political and economic rewards, they will frequently mobilize to demand their rights.

A recent study of 191 independent countries throughout the world revealed that 82 percent contain two or more ethnic groups.[23] Furthermore, earlier research indicated that in 30 percent of the world's countries, no single ethnic group accounts for even half of the total population.[24] This pattern is most striking in sub-Saharan Africa, where virtually every country is composed of several ethnic (tribal) groups. For example, it is estimated that Nigeria, the most populous sub-Saharan African state, has more than 200 linguistic (tribal) groups.[25]

Many Africans attribute their continent's legacy of tribal conflict to the European colonizers who divided the region into administrative units little connected with ethnic identities. In some cases, antagonistic groups were thrown together into a single colony, while elsewhere individual tribes were split between two future countries. In Africa, Asia, and the Middle East, colonial powers often exacerbated ethnic tensions by favoring certain groups over others and by using "divide and conquer" strategies to control the local population. Yet colonialism was but one of many factors contributing to ethnic discord. Given the enormous number of tribal groups in Africa, even if the European powers had shown greater ethnic sensibility, many multiethnic nations would have inevitably developed. The only alternative would have been the creation of hundreds of tiny states, which would not have been economically viable.

At the same time, however, the *breakdown* of European colonialism also led to a number of extremely unhappy ethnic marriages. When the Portuguese withdrew from the small Southeast Asian colony of East Timor in 1975, neighboring Indonesia annexed it against the local population's will. In its efforts to crush the organized Timorese opposition, the Indonesian military killed or starved approximately 150,000 people (about 25 percent of the region's population). Even after the Timorese was finally allowed to vote for independence in 1999, local militias tied to the Indonesian military slaughtered thousands more. Elsewhere, following years of Italian colonial rule and a brief British occupation, the East African colony of Eritrea was forcibly merged with Ethiopia in the early 1950s. The Eritrean people (who have different religions and cultures than the Ethiopians) generally resented the Ethiopian takeover and soon embarked on a long struggle for independence. Three decades of civil war resulted in thousands of deaths. The collapse of the Ethiopian military dictatorship in 1991 allowed Eritrea to finally achieve independence. But the two countries fought a bloody border war in 1998–2000 and are still on a war footing.

TYPES OF ETHNIC-CULTURAL DIVISIONS

In order to better grasp the range of ethnic tensions that currently pervade much of the developing world, I will classify all types of ethnicities into a set of somewhat overlapping categories: nationality, tribe, race, and religion.

Nationality

In ethnic analysis, the term *nation* takes on a specialized meaning distinct from its more common usage designating a sovereign country (as in the *United Nations*). It refers, instead, to a population with its own language, cultural traditions, historical aspirations, and, often, its own geographical home. Frequently, nationhood is associated with the belief that "the interests and values of this nation take priority over all other interests and values."[26] Unlike other types of ethnic groups, nationalities frequently claim sovereignty over a specific geographic area. But, as we have seen, these proposed *national* boundaries frequently do not coincide with those of *sovereign states* (independent countries). For example, India and Sri Lanka are both sovereign states that encompass several distinct *nationalities* (cultural identities). In each case, members of at least one of those nationalities—Kashmiris (India) and Tamils (Sri Lanka)—have waged long struggles for independence. On the other hand, the Chinese are a nationality that, through migration, has spilled over to several East Asian countries and to other parts of the world. The Kurds also reside in several countries, including Turkey, Iraq, Iran, and Syria. Unlike the Chinese, however, they are a nation without a state of their own.

As with many types of ethnicity, the political significance of national identity is related to a number of subjective factors. Nationality becomes politically important only when its members believe that their common history and destiny distinguish them from other ethnicities in their country. The most critical basis for national identification is the preservation of a distinct spoken language. Because French Canadians, Turkish Kurds, and Malaysian Chinese have maintained their "mother tongues," their national identities remain politically relevant. Chinese speakers in Southeast Asia have maintained their own cultural and political organizations and feel strong emotional ties to China. On the other hand, because most immigrants—including Chinese, Italians, and Germans—to countries such as the United States, Canada, and Australia have fully assimilated into their new language and culture, dropping their language of origin after one or two generations, their original national identity loses much of its political and social impact.

In their more limited manifestations, nationalist movements simply seek to preserve the group's cultural identity and promote its economic and political interests. For example, the large Lebanese community in Brazil, East Indians in Guyana, and Irish-Americans in the United States take pride in their distinctive cultures, but none has entertained visions of self-governance. On the other hand, nationalist movements become more provocative when they seek to create a separate nation-state of their own. Such separatist movements can arise when an ethnic minority is concentrated in a particular region of the country and represents a majority of the population in that area. Those conditions exist in Sri Lanka (formerly Ceylon), where the Tamil-speaking population is concentrated in the country's northern and eastern provinces, particularly the Jaffna Peninsula region in the far north. Even before the intrusion of European colonizers, the Tamils kept themselves apart from other ethnicities inhabiting Ceylon. The British conquest and colonization of the entire island produced a nationalist reaction among the majority Sinhalese (Sinhala-speaking) population, which, in turn, provoked friction between them and the Tamil minority.

Since Sri Lanka's independence in 1948, political power has been concentrated in the hands of the Sinhalese (who constitute some three-fourths of the country's population). As in most nationality-based ethnic clashes, language issues were at the heart of the conflict. Eight years after independence, Sinhala replaced English as the country's official language, giving the Sinhalese population a significant advantage in securing government jobs. As one Tamil political leader put it, "Not until 1956 did we really believe that we were second-class citizens. Until then all we engaged in were preventive measures, which we thought would hold."[27] From that point forward, however, the battle for Tamil self-rule intensified. Conversely, when Tamil acquired equal legal status in 1978, many Sinhalese felt victimized. Religious differences between the largely Hindu Tamils and the predominantly Buddhist Sinhalese augment their language and cultural divisions, though religious issues remained secondary.

As early as 1949, Tamil leaders (representing almost one-fifth of the country's population) demanded a federal system that would grant Tamil regions substantial autonomy (a high degree of self-rule within the Sri Lankan state). Sinhalese nationalists, in turn, tried to impose their language on the entire nation. In 1958, Sinhalese mobs attacked Tamils in various parts of the country, and in 1964, the Sri Lankan government signed an agreement with India calling for the eventual return to India of 525,000 Tamils whose families had migrated from that country. Faced with such threats, Tamil nationalism became increasingly strident and violent. Early calls for autonomy were superseded by demands for secession and the creation of a sovereign Tamil state. By the early 1980s, the most powerful force in the country's predominantly Tamil areas was the Liberation Tigers of Tamil

Eelam (also known as the Tamil Tigers or the LTTE), a secessionist force engaged in guerrilla warfare, terrorism, and ultimately conventional war.

In 1987, following a major national government offensive against the LTTE, India (concerned about demands for autonomy from its own Tamil minority) intervened militarily in Sri Lanka. The resulting Indo-Lanka Peace Accord called for a multiethnic, multilingual Sri Lankan state with increased regional autonomy for the Tamil areas. Though signed by the Indian and Sri Lankan governments, the accord was rejected by many Sinhalese, particularly the ultra-nationalist National Liberation Front (JVP). From 1987 to 1989, the JVP launched its own campaign of strikes, boycotts, and terrorism, resulting in thousands of deaths. A brutal government campaign eventually crushed the JVP, but the war against the Tamil Tigers continued. Although many Tamils welcomed the Indo-Lanka accord, the Tigers rejected it as inadequate. Instead, they expanded their bloody guerrilla war, first against India's 60,000-man occupation force and then, after the 1990 withdrawal of foreign troops, against the Sri Lankan government and moderate Tamils.

By the turn of the century, the LTTE allegedly was raising more than $60 million annually by smuggling illegal immigrants and drugs into Europe and the United States. In addition, it has received millions more in donations from the large, Tamil communities living in countries such as India, Britain, Canada, and the United States. The Tamil Tigers are generally considered the first group in the world to use suicide bombings widely as a tactic. They were responsible for the 1993 assassination of Sri Lankan President Ranasinghe Premadasa and more than 200 other suicide bombings. Human rights groups condemned the Tigers for using young girls as suicide bombers because they were more likely to get past police and army checkpoints with bombs strapped to their bodies. By 2000, about 62,000 people had been killed in the civil war, out of a total Sri Lankan population of 21 million. A cease-fire signed in 2002 restored relative peace to that devastated country for several years. But by late 2005, the truce had broken down as more militant factions of the Tamil Tigers emerged. The following year, the Sri Lankan armed forces launched a major offensive against the LTTE stronghold in the Northeast, progressively driving the rebels into a smaller and smaller area. Thousands of civilians died and many more fled the region as the Tigers regularly used the local population as human shields, while the government resisted UN calls for a cease-fire (to allow civilians to leave the conflict zone) and the armed forces shelled and bombed the enclave with little concern for civilian deaths. In May 2009, the rebels were forced to abandon their 25-year struggle and their legendary leader was killed. It is unclear, however, whether or not the insurgents will eventually continue their struggle through suicide bombings and small-scale guerrilla attacks.

Tribe

The very use of the category *tribe*—especially when applied to African cultures— is fairly controversial. Many anthropologists and political scientists find it arbitrary and unhelpful. They note that when cultural anthropologists first worked in Africa and South Asia, often they assumed that the social characteristics of the small groups of people they were studying could automatically be extended to larger units they called a *tribe*.[28] (See my earlier discussion of the Congo's "myth of the Bangala.") Critics also point out that the term *tribe* is sometimes used to describe African ethnic groups as large as the 15 million Yoruba (in Nigeria), a population that elsewhere in the world would be called a *nationality*. Hence, many scholars prefer to use the terms *ethnicity* or *ethno-linguistic group*. This text, however, still refers to *tribal groups* because that term is familiar to most readers and has long been used by some scholars of ethnic politics and by numerous political leaders in Africa and Asia. For example, in describing the problems of his own country, former Ugandan president Milton Obote lamented "the pull of the tribal force."[29] This chapter uses *tribe* to describe *sub*national groups that share a collective identity and language and believe themselves to hold a common lineage. The term is most often used in regard to African ethnicities and, to a lesser extent, Asia. In India, Vietnam, Burma, and other parts of Asia, tribe refers to hill peoples, such as the Laotian Hmong, who live traditional lifestyles in relative isolation from modern society. The term has also been used, of course, in discussions of North American Indians, as well as the lowland (Amazonian) Indians of South America. In none of these cases do we use the term pejoratively.

Recent survey data from 12 African nations indicate that tribal (or socio-linguistic) identifications tend to be the major determinant of support for political parties, though other variables—such as age, urban versus rural origin, and education—also play a role and sometimes reduce (though not eliminate) the influence of tribe.[30] Moreover, intertribal conflict has frequently sparked violence in sub-Saharan Africa, affecting more than half the countries in that region at one time or another. Nigeria, Ethiopia, Rwanda, Burundi, Uganda, Sudan, the Congo, and Ivory Coast, among others, have been torn apart by civil wars that were partially or primarily ethnically based. In Liberia, Angola, and Mozambique, conflicts begun about other issues were aggravated by tribal divisions. From the time of its independence, Nigeria witnessed antagonism between the Muslims in the North and the populations of the South and East. With 50 percent of the country's population, the Hausa-Fulani and other northern tribes were a dominant political force, resented by southerners and easterners such as the Ibo, who often considered northerners to be somewhat backward. Northerners, in turn, feared the influence of the more modern and commercially successful Ibo people. Each of the three major ethnic groups (Hausa-Fulani, Ibo, and Yoruba) prevailed in one region of the country, casting a shadow over smaller tribes in their area. Each major tribe, in turn, feared domination by the others.

Two military coups in 1966 intensified friction between officers of differing ethnic backgrounds and sparked violence against the many Ibos who had migrated to the North. As many as 30,000 Ibos may have been killed. In fear of their lives, 1–2 million more fled from northern Nigeria to their homeland. In May 1967, Colonel Chukwuemeka Ojukwu, an Ibo military leader, declared that eastern Nigeria was withdrawing from the country to become the independent nation of Biafra. But, backed by the Organization of African Unity (OAU), the Nigerian national government was determined to prevent Biafra's secession. In time, the armed forces surrounded Biafra and tightened their grip. Up to 1 million Ibo civilians died of starvation in a pattern of war-induced famine that later became tragically familiar in other parts of Africa. On the other hand, when Biafra finally did surrender in early 1970, the Nigerian military regime refrained from acts of vengeance. Since that time, the Ibos have been rather successfully reintegrated into Nigerian society, but intertribal tensions and periodic religious violence persist.

Unfortunately, the Nigerian conflict was but one of earliest ethnically based civil wars that were to plague the African continent over the next 40 years. Some of the most intense and prolonged tribal conflicts took place in the former Belgian colonies of Burundi and Rwanda in the Great Lakes region of eastern Africa. Burundi's ruling Tutsi minority has crushed a series of uprisings by the majority Hutus (about 85 percent of the population) since they gained power in the early 1970s, massacring perhaps 100,000 people in 1972 alone. In 1993, when a Tutsi soldier assassinated the country's first freely elected president, a Hutu, new bloodshed erupted. One year later, in the neighboring country of Rwanda, the Hutu president's death in a plane crash set off an orgy of violence. A government-directed massacre led by Hutu extremists was directed at the minority Tutsis and, to a lesser extent, moderate Hutus. During the next 100 days, local Hutu militia and allied villagers beat or hacked to death approximately 750,000 Tutsis and 50,000 Hutus. Eventually, a well-trained Tutsi revolutionary army, supported by neighboring Uganda, gained control of the country and jailed thousands of Hutus. Hundreds of thousands more fled to nearby Congo, where many of them starved to death or were massacred by the anti-Hutu regime of then-President Laurent Kabila.

In other conflicts, such as the Angolan and Mozambican civil wars (which had both ideological and ethnic origins), major world powers supported one side or the other, thereby intensifying the wars and adding to the bloodshed. For example, acting in consort with the Soviet Union, Cuba provided military assistance to the leftist governments of Ethiopia, Angola, and Mozambique. The United States armed UNITA, the Angolan rebel force, while the South African military supported Mozambique's RENAMO guerrillas. Belgium and France armed the Rwandan regime prior to its genocidal attacks on the Tutsi population. In each of those countries, hundreds of thousands perished from warfare or starvation. Although the end of the Cold War has reduced such inflammatory, superpower intervention, the recent brutal wars in the Congo, Liberia, Sierra Leone, and Ivory Coast indicate that tribally based violence will undoubtedly continue in the region for some time. More recently, Rwanda, Uganda, Zimbabwe, and Angola all intervened in the ethnically based civil war in the Congo.

Race

We have noted that cultural identity involves a common set of values and customs and a shared sense of history and destiny. Race, while normally the most visible of ethnic distinctions, is a more recent source of group identity. Only when people live in *multiracial* settings do individual racial groups use race to define themselves and distinguish themselves from "others." Indeed, Crawford Young indicates that "there was no common sense of being 'African,' 'European,' or 'Indian,' prior to the creation of multiracial communities by the population movements of the imperial age."[31] Slavery and other manifestations of Western imperialism in the Third World created an array of negative racial stereotypes about Asians, Africans, and (North and South) American

Indians. The subsequent migration of Asians to the plantations of East Africa and the Caribbean created further racial cleavages.

South Africa presented the most notorious example of race-based political conflict. From its colonization by the British until its 1994 transition to majority rule, the country was ruled by a White minority constituting only about 15 percent of the population. Meanwhile, Blacks, the majority population, were denied fundamental legal and economic rights, including the right to vote or hold political office.

Until the government renounced it in 1991, the legal centerpiece of South African racial policy was *apartheid* (separateness). That system rigidly segregated employment, public facilities, housing, marriage, and more, envisioning a day when most Blacks lived in eight allegedly self-ruling "homelands." In fact, these homelands, consisting of desolate rural territories, could not possibly support the country's Black population. Moreover, because important sectors of the South African economy, most notably its mines, were dependent on Black labor, the geographical segregation envisioned by apartheid was implausible even from the perspective of the White business community. Meanwhile, the millions of Blacks who lived outside the homelands were denied fundamental civil liberties, including the right to own property.

Apartheid officially created racial classifications for the entire population that defied international standards and often fell victim to their own logical contradictions. *Blacks*, by far the largest racial group, constituted 70–75 percent of the national population and were subjected to the greatest amount of legal discrimination. *Coloureds*—people of mixed race—totaled about 10 percent of the population, primarily concentrated in Cape Town and Cape Province. Asians (mostly Indians and Pakistanis) represented about 3 percent of the nation. Both Coloureds and Asians enjoyed a higher socioeconomic status and greater legal and political rights than Blacks did, but still ranked considerably below Whites. Finally, *Whites* (some 15 percent) held virtually all political and economic powers.

Despite international disapproval, South Africa's minority government seemed determined to maintain apartheid indefinitely. In time, however, the country came under intense domestic and international pressure to end that system of White domination. South Africa became an international outcast—particularly after several massacres of peaceful Black protestors—subject to diplomatic, economic, and cultural isolation. Though slow to take effect, these sanctions eventually impaired the country's economic growth. Growing protest and unrest in the Black townships (outlying urban slums) added to the country's international isolation. Finally, a growing number of powerful voices within the White economic, legal, and intellectual elites pressed the government for racial reform.

By the start of the 1990s, President F. W. de Klerk's government, recognizing that apartheid was no longer viable, legalized the African National Congress (ANC), the leading Black opposition group, along with two more radical organizations, after decades of banishment. The ANC's legendary leader, Nelson Mandela, the world's most celebrated political prisoner, was released from jail (after 27 years of imprisonment) along with hundreds of other political prisoners. These changes, coupled with the ANC's suspension of its armed struggle, opened the door to a new constitution enfranchising the Black majority and ending White minority rule.

In December 1991, the Convention for a Democratic South Africa (CODESA) brought together the government, the ANC, and 17 smaller groups for discussions of the new political order. Most Whites acknowledged that apartheid could no longer continue. In a 1992 national referendum called by de Klerk, nearly 70 percent of all White voters endorsed negotiations with the ANC and other Black groups. The following year, the government and the ANC agreed to the election of a constitutional assembly that would create a new political system with equal rights for all South Africans. Universal suffrage ensured a Black majority in the assembly and in 1994, the ANC parliamentary majority elected Nelson Mandela president of the new South Africa.

In the 15 years since that time, South Africa has established itself as perhaps the most democratic nation on the continent. However, significant challenges to democratic consolidation remain. Blacks have discovered that although majority rule has established greater social justice and human dignity, many of them remain mired in poverty. To be sure, government housing programs have benefited numerous urban slum dwellers and the Black middle class has swelled. On the other hand, with most farmland still owned by Whites and limited funds available for schools and clinics in the countryside, the Black rural population remains impoverished. Faced with high unemployment, soaring crime rates, and one of the world's highest incidences of AIDS, the urban poor also continue to struggle. Until now, at least, the government has pursued moderate economic policies to reassure the White business community. These policies have brought economic growth but have been slow to alleviate poverty. The ANC remains popular and still dominates all national elections. Over time, however, if Black living conditions do not improve and if there is not a sizable redistribution of economic resources, the ANC's Black constituency may demand more radical policies. Widespread demands for more extensive and redistributive economic reforms led the ANC to oust national President Thabo Mbeki as party leader and replace him with a more populist leader, Jacob Zuma, who subsequently succeeded Mbeki as the national president in 2009. But, Zuma's appeal to the urban poor may be eroding as the global economic decline increases already very high unemployment rates in the urban townships (slums). In mid-2009, only months after President Zuma took office, Johannesburg and other South African cities were rocked by riots over inadequate housing and poor urban services in a number of poor neighborhoods. The country's soaring crime rate, a reflection of widespread poverty and pervasive inequality, could also turn into wider political violence. Zuma has promised to better satisfy the needs of the poor. His election also widened the ethnic origins of the ruling party's leadership. He is the first ANC president and the first national president since the beginning of majority rule to come from the Zulu, rather than the Xhosa, ethnicity (tribe).

Religion

Because it involves deeply felt values, religion has frequently been the source of bitter "**communal strife**" (i.e., conflict between ethnic communities). In Chapter 3, we examined the influence of religious *beliefs* on political attitudes and behavior, particularly those of fundamentalists and others favoring close links between church and state. We saw that a group's religious orientation often shapes its political beliefs, including its ideas regarding a citizen's political rights and obligations as well as its understanding of the country's constitutional and legal systems.

In this chapter, we look at a related but distinct aspect of religion, namely the degree to which coreligionists identify strongly with each other and try to enhance their political and economic powers relative to other religious groups. In other words, we are concerned here, not with the political ramifications of religious beliefs (considered in Chapter 3), but with the potential tension or even conflict *between* religious groups (defined here as *ethnic communities*) living in the same country. Such discord may pit one religion against another or, particularly in the case of Islam, may involve conflict between two branches of the same religion. Two factors influence the likelihood of tensions between religious groups: first, the extent to which one religious community feels ill-treated by another; and, second, the degree to which any religion regards itself as the only true faith and totally rejects alternate theologies. Thus, Catholics and Protestants coexist rather harmoniously in the United States and Germany because neither of these conditions applies. On the other hand, in Northern Ireland, where Catholics have resented the Protestants' political and economic powers and Protestants have feared political domination by the larger Catholic community, paramilitary groups representing both sides engaged in a nearly 40-year armed struggle.

In 1992, thousands of Hindu fundamentalists destroyed a sixteenth-century Muslim mosque in the northern Indian town of Ayodhya. Like many such clashes, the incident grew out of centuries-old beliefs and hostilities. Many Hindus believe this to be the spot where the god Ram had been born ages before. To the Bharatiya Janata Party (BJP), the leading Hindu political party, and to the more militant World Hindu Council, the mosque was a symbol of Islamic domination during the 300 years of Mogul rule prior to the British colonial era. Within days of the 1992 assault, rioting in northern and central India left about 2,000 dead. Ten years later (2002), Hindu mobs in the village of Ahmedabad murdered over 1,000 Muslims, raping women, burning people alive, and occasionally cutting fetuses out of pregnant women. In neighboring Islamic countries, Pakistani crowds attacked Hindu temples and Bangladeshis assaulted Hindu-owned shops.

In fact, India and Pakistan were born of communal violence, and neither has been free of it since. Although both countries had been part of a single British colony, when negotiations for independence advanced in the late 1940s, the Muslim League insisted on the creation of a separate Muslim state. Using language that classically defines an ethnic group, League leader Mohammed Ali Jinnah declared, "We are a nation with our own distinctive culture and civilization, language and literature . . . customs . . . history and tradition."[32] In 1946, as independence approached, political conflict between the Muslim League and the dominant Congress Party (a nonreligious party led largely by secular Hindus) touched off communal violence that left thousands dead. Finally, the British reluctantly divided their most important colony into two countries: India, with roughly 300 million Hindus and 40 million Muslims at that time; and Pakistan, with approximately 60 million Muslims and 20 million Hindus. No sooner had independence been declared (August 15, 1947), when horrendous religious massacres began in both countries. Whole villages were destroyed, 12 million refugees of both faiths fled across the border in either direction, more than 75,000 women were abducted and raped, and somewhere between 500,000 and 1 million people were killed in one of the twentieth century's worst ethnic conflagrations. Two decades later, Pakistan itself split in two as geography, language, and cultural differences rather than religion divided its population. With support from India, the Bengali-speaking eastern region broke away from the dominant, primarily Urdu-speaking, West to form the country of Bangladesh.

Today, Muslim separatists in the Indian-controlled portion of Kashmir are waging guerrilla warfare aimed either at Kashmiri independence or unification with Pakistan. In 2001, Islamic fundamentalists attacked the Indian parliament, once again bringing India and Pakistan (both now nuclear powers) to the brink of war. Since early 2004, the two countries have engaged in a series of peace talks and confidence-building measures. But basic differences over Kashmir and engrained suspicions keep that region volatile as have recent terrorist attacks on India. In November 2008, an Islamist terrorists group named Lashkar-e-Taiba or LeT ("Army of the Pure") launched a deadly attack on the center of Mumbai (formerly Bombay, India's largest city and its financial center), killing nearly 200 people and wounding more than 300. Based in Pakistan, that group is committed to "liberating" the Indian-controlled portion of Kashmir. Like the Pakistani Taliban, the LeT and other Islamist groups have received assistance from their country's intelligence service in the past and may still be getting help from hard-line, anti-Indian segments of that service. Until recently, the Pakistani armed forces were reluctant to reorganize for counterinsurgency action against Islamist insurgents, preferring to train its soldiers instead for a possible conventional war against India. That may be changing, following the 2009 military's liberation of the Swat valley from the Taliban.

Lebanon, from 1975 to 1990 and again in 2006–2008 was also a battlefield for warring religious factions. Today, the specter of renewed violence continues to haunt the country. Among the 17 religious communities represented in the Lebanese political system, the most important have been Maronite Catholics, Shi'a Muslims, Sunni Muslims, and Druze (a religion that combines Muslim and other religious beliefs). Despite its religious heterogeneity, for its first 30 years after independence (1943) the country was considered a bastion of peace and economic prosperity in the midst of a troubled region. During that time, the dominant Maronite (Christian) and Sunni communities coexisted under the terms of a political power-sharing arrangement dating back to the 1920s, when Lebanon had limited home rule, and reinforced at the time of national independence.

But power sharing and peaceful coexistence broke down in the 1970s as the Muslim population, particularly the Shi'a community, perceived that the terms of the old agreement no longer reflected the relative sizes of the major religious groups. Although the faster-growing Muslim community currently accounts for perhaps 60–65 percent of the population (statistics vary widely depending on whose estimate one believes), through the 1972 election (the last before the civil war), they were allocated only 45 percents of the seats in the national parliament, with 55 percent going to the Christians. This division of seats reflected the country's religious affiliations in 1932, the last time a complete census was conducted. Since that time, the Muslim population had overtaken the Christians because of a higher birth rate and a lower rate of emigration. However, there was no new census and no reallocation of seats.

Religious, economic, and political differences also caused conflict *within* the Muslim community, between Shi'as and Sunnis. Despite outnumbering the Sunnis, the Shi'as had less political power, fewer allocated seats in parliament, and a lower standard of living than either the Sunnis or the Christians. Lebanon's two most powerful political offices—president and prime minister—were reserved, respectively, for a Maronite Christian and a Sunni.

External intervention further aggravated the nation's ethnic tensions. The influx of many Palestinian refugees (fleeing Jordan), including armed PLO (Palestine Liberation Organization) militia, radicalized Lebanon's political arena. Many poor Lebanese—particularly the Shi'as until the 1980s—were drawn to the Palestinians' revolutionary rhetoric. Christian militia leaders, who feared the threat to their power posed by the Shi'as and the Palestinians, responded by establishing a military alliance with Israel. At the same time, Syria, wishing to expand its power in the Middle East and create a buffer zone between itself and Israel, occupied much of Lebanon and dominated that country's politics for many years. By 1975, Lebanon's national government had become an ineffectual, hollow shell, as power shifted to a range of communal warlords. Conflicts between Christian, Sunni, Shi'a, and Palestinian militias engulfed Lebanon in a civil war that lasted 15 years and took perhaps 150,000 lives. The country's religious conflict had elements of a class struggle as well, pitting the more prosperous Christian community against the Shi'as, who saw themselves as the oppressed poor. Foreign forces, in the form of Palestinian militia, occupying Israeli forces in the South, and Syria all added to the bloodshed.

As Lebanese cities lay in ruins and Palestinian, Israeli, and Syrian forces threatened to destroy the nation's sovereignty, the multinational Arab League helped negotiate a treaty between the warring factions. The Taif Accord, signed in late 1989, raised the Muslims' percentage of parliamentary seats to 50 percent and established the basis for a "national pact" between the warring factions, finally bringing fighting to an end in 1990.[33] During the next 15 years, the Lebanese rebuilt their economy and maintained a fragile peace between religious factions, although Syrian troops and intelligence units continued their occupation and often dictated policy to the Lebanese government.

But even before the 1989 agreement was signed, there were further confrontations between the Sunnis and Shi'ites. In the early 1980s, Shi'a clergy founded Hezbollah (the "Party of God"), a combination political party, social-services provider, armed militia, and terrorist group. Its goals included driving the Israeli army out of southern Lebanon, promoting Shi'a fundamentalism, closer ties to Iran (the party's leading financial backer and arms supplier), and asserting Shi'a political power in the Middle East generally. The party gained widespread popularity within the Shi'a and Palestinian communities when it did help end Israel's 18-year occupation of southern Lebanon. Furthermore, it set up a parallel system of schools, health clinics, and other services that have operated far more effectively than the government's social services and have better served the Shi'a poor.

In 2006, after Hezbollah fighters crossed into Israel and captured two soldiers, Israeli troops invaded Lebanon and carried out saturation bombings of urban Hezbollah strongholds. Large portions of the country's southern cities were destroyed, about 1,150 Lebanese and 150 Israelis were killed, and the country's rebuilt economy once again lay in ruins. While many Christians and Sunnis blamed Hezbollah for foolishly provoking Israel, the movement's support intensified within the large Shi'a community as Hezbollah outperformed the Lebanese government in supplying emergency housing and services to the 400,000 civilians who had been forced from their homes during the 34-day war. By launching several thousand rockets (supplied by Syria and Iran) into northern Israel during the war, Hezbollah also enhanced its military reputation. Since that time, it has become the country's most powerful political party. In 2009, however, although the Hezbollah-led March 8 Alliance had been expected to gain a parliamentary plurality in national elections, it was rebuffed by Lebanese voters.

Elsewhere in the Middle East, the most well-known conflict between Sunnis and Shi'ites has been in Iraq. Like many of the Third World's ethnic clashes, its origins can be traced back to an earlier period. When Iraq received full independence in 1932, the outgoing British rulers transferred power to the Sunni Arab elite. For the next 70 years, the relatively small Arab Sunni community (about 15 percent of the total population) dominated both the Arab Shi'a majority (about 60 percent) and the Kurdish minority (20 percent). Although most Kurds are also Sunnis, they have long opposed Arab control, be it Sunni or Shi'a.* Upon taking full power, Saddam Hussein intensified persecution of the Shi'as, particularly after the United States defeated Iraq in the Gulf War (1990–1991). Believing that President George H. W. Bush's call to the Iraqi people to overthrow Saddam after that war meant that the United States would support an uprising, the Shi'a heartland in southern Iraq, like the Kurds in the Northeast, rose up. When U.S. assistance failed to materialize, both revolts were crushed. Towns across the South were razed and tens of thousands of Shi'as were massacred. Over time, thousands of Shi'ites migrated to the country's Sunni-dominated, central region. In greater Baghdad, neighborhoods such as Sadr City became home to huge Shi'ite enclaves, bringing them into closer contact with the Sunnis.[34]

Given Saddam's relentless persecution of the Shi'as, it was not surprising that they rejoiced in his overthrow. Indeed, when the United States first invaded Iraq, the Shi'ites most respected religious leader, the grand ayatollah Ali al-Husayni Sistani, instructed his followers not to resist the American forces. But, contrary to Washington's expectations, this did not mean that either Sistani or the Shi'a masses wished to ally with the United States. Once Sunni political domination was terminated—symbolized by the American program of "debathification," a purge of former members of Saddam's ruling Ba'ath party (mostly Sunnis) from government posts—Sistani opposed several U.S. proposals for a new Iraqi government, plans which he and his followers felt gave too much power to the Sunnis.

But despite their unhappiness with many American policies, Sistani and other Shi'a leaders favored peaceful negotiation with the occupation authorities. On the other hand, the Sunni community, unaccustomed to being out of power, were hostile toward American and allied occupation forces. Indeed, most Sunnis saw the American debathification of Iraq's military and security police officers as

---

* When the U.S. media refer to the Sunni community in Iraq (and Sunni–Shi'a conflict), they mean only the Arab Sunnis, not Kurdish Sunnis.

a de facto program of "de-Sunnification" of the government. Meanwhile, Shi'ites eagerly anticipated the dawn of a new state that they would dominate. Adding to long-standing theological differences between the two religious communities (Chapter 3), the Shi'as resented the persecution they had suffered at the hands of the Sunni-dominated, Saddam government. The Sunnis, for their part, viewed the Shi'as as agents of the Iranian government and its religious leaders. Iraq and Iran are among the few nations in the Middle East with majority Shi'a populations. But, they have been separated by language (most Iranians speak Farsi—Persian—while most Iraqis speak Arabic) and by each country's long-term aspirations for leadership in the Gulf region. As we have seen, during the 1980s the two had fought a brutal war. Yet many of Iraq's leading Shi'a clerics lived in exile in Iran while fleeing Saddam's persecution, adding to Sunni suspicions about their loyalty. Indeed, the grand ayatollah Sistani himself was born and raised in Iran and still speaks Arabic with a thick Persian accent. But, most of all, the Sunnis were afraid of losing political power to the Shi'as whom they had so long dominated and often mistreated.

Within a year of Saddam's fall, Sunni extremists were using their most lethal weapons—roadside bombs and suicide bombings—directed against police stations, outdoor markets, bus stations, religious shrines, and other crowded sites in Shi'a neighborhoods. Initially, foreigners carried out many of the suicide bombings, especially Saudis, Syrians, and Jordanians. In time, however, native Iraqis committed most terrorist acts. In April 2007, a suicide bomber penetrated the supposedly impregnable security of the parliament building in the American-controlled Green Zone, the most fortified area in Iraq. Although only one member of Parliament was killed, the attack sent a psychologically powerful message that no place in Iraq was safe from terrorism. From the start of the Sunni insurgency in 2003 through April 2007, there were more than 350 confirmed suicide bombings, killing thousands of Iraqis and many American soldiers. Of the bombers who have been identified posthumously, all have been Sunnis and almost all suicide attacks were directed at Shi'ites or foreigners. Bombs are delivered in cars, trucks, or, occasionally, on foot.

In May 2007, a leading American authority on these bombings noted, "Since our invasion, suicide terrorism has been essentially doubling in Iraq every year."[35] In fact, suicide bombings became so frequent that the mere rumor of a bomber can cause mass panic. For example, on August 31, 2005, 1 million Shi'a religious pilgrims converged on a holy shrine in Baghdad, their line stretching for miles. In the morning, a mortar attack on the worshippers killed 16 people. Later in that same day, a rumor spread in the massive crowd that a suicide bomber was in their midst. Panic produced a stampede in which more than one thousand people died—trampled or drowned in the nearby river—while trying to escape.

The 2007 surge in the number of U.S. troops sharply reduced the level of violence. At the same time, there have been important Sunni militia defections. Sunni military and terrorist organizations fall into two broad categories: first, religiously inspired groups (*jihadists*) who are often led by foreigners with ties to Al Qaeda; and, second, secular groups, led by Iraqis linked to the Ba'thist resistance. Of late, tensions between the two have been mounting. In 2007, some of the Sunni militias that had earlier battled U.S. troops formed alliances of convenience with the Americans in order to battle the jihadists. American arms and training seemingly have improved those militias ability to fight Al Qaeda, but they also risk strengthening Sunni extremists in the event of future religious conflict. Sunni terrorists' repeated attacks caused many Shi'ites to reject Ayatollah Sistani's admonitions against violence and civil war. Instead, a young cleric, Muqtada al-Sadr, emerged as the face of Shi'a militancy. In contrast to the aging Sistani, who rarely appears in public and issues most of his pronouncements through his aides, al-Sadr (age 36) has a charismatic personality. A fiery nationalist, he has demanded an immediate withdrawal of American troops from Iraq. Al-Sadr's support is most pronounced in Baghdad's huge Shi'a enclave, Sadr City—named after his father, a grand ayatollah who had been executed by the Saddam government—and, to a lesser extent, in Basra, Iraq's second largest city and the largest Shi'a stronghold. He and his followers have acted on two fronts: first, they formed a militia of several thousand men, called the Mahdi Army. For several years, they battled Sunni militias while also clashing with their chief Shi'a rivals and, occasionally, American troops. But its primary role has been to react to Sunni assaults on Shi'a neighborhoods, retaliating with kidnapping, torture, and execution of suspected Sunni militants. It has also provided medical and other services to Shi'a neighborhoods in the wake of Sunni bombings. Second, like Lebanon's Hezbollah, al-Sadr's faction has also created a political party that won several legislative seats in the 2005 national election. In 2007, the Mahdi Army declared a cease-fire in the face of the American troop surge and 1 year later it was weakened after U.S. troops and Iraq's strengthened security forces attacked Sadr City. Al-Sadr's political and military strength appear to have weakened considerably and in late 2009 his party chose to join Prime Minister Nouri al-Maliki's mostly moderate secular coalition in the coming parliamentary elections (see below).

The other major Shi'a militia is the Badr Brigade, the military wing of the Supreme Islamic Iraqi Council (SIIC).* The first Council was formed in 1982 and helped lead the Shi'a resistance to Saddam Hussein. Currently, its political party has one of the largest delegations in parliament. Though tied closely to Iran, SIIC has steered a comparatively moderate course—more militant than Sistani but less militant than al-Sadr—while fashioning a reasonable working relationship with the U.S military. As the Shi'ite government coalition's largest party, it wields considerable political influence. Furthermore, members of the Badr Brigade control important segments of the Iraqi government's security forces, where their history of reprisals against the Sunnis has included torture and extra-judicial killings. In 2006, the Badr Brigade and al-Sadr's Mahdi Army clashed on a number of occasions in a power struggle for control of the Shi'a community and its financial resources. Thus, like the Sunnis, Shi'a paramilitary groups are not united. Although SIIC was an important backer of al-Maliki's government, it plans to join an opposition bloc of Shi'a religious parties in the 2010 parliamentary elections.

The success of the American troop surge has lowered militia activity considerably. But, the country's political leaders have failed to resolve fundamental

---

* It was known prior to May 2007 as the Supreme Council for the Islamic Revolution in Iraq (SCIRI).

differences between the three ethnic communities. Starting in 2005, a number of Sunni, tribal militias in Anbar province (previously the center of insurgent attacks on American and Iraqi troops) agreed to switch sides and, in return for U.S. arms and supplies, turned their forces against Al Qaeda in Iraq. This movement—called The Awakening—spread to other provinces and was probably as important as the surge in reducing violence. But, now that the Sunni insurgency has diminished, the Shi'a-led government has reneged on its promises to pay Awakening soldiers and integrate them into the Iraqi military, raising concerns that these Sunni militias will resume their war against the government.

To date, most attempts to reconcile differences between the three ethnic communities at the highest levels of government have gone nowhere. However, in late 2009, Prime Minister al-Maliki announced the formation of a secular coalition that would team his own Shi'ite political party (Dawa) with a number of smaller, secular Sunni parties in parliamentary elections scheduled for early 2010. It remains to be seen whether there will be sufficient Shi'a and Sunni political cooperation to end the current stalemates in parliament and whether there will be a resurgence of sectarian violence as substantial numbers of American troops are withdrawn. Prime Minister al-Maliki has tried to create a governing coalition based on sectarian, nationalist aspirations. His level of success may well determine whether Iraq is capable of building a peaceful future.

DEPENDENCY, MODERNIZATION, AND ETHNIC CONFLICT

Western analysts once assumed that improved education and communications in the Third World would break down ethnic conflicts. Because of their country's experience as a "melting pot" for immigrant groups, Americans in particular have supposed that socioeconomic modernization enhances ethnic integration and harmony.* Yet in Africa and Asia, early modernization has frequently politicized and intensified ethnic antagonisms. In fact, Crawford Young observes that "cultural pluralism [and ethnic strife] as a political phenomenon" was not significant in traditional societies but, rather, emerged "from such social processes as urbanization, the revolution in communications and spread of modern education."[36] Early modernization theorists, who were quite optimistic about the positive effects of literacy, urbanization, and modern values, clearly underestimated the extent to which these factors might mobilize various ethnic groups and set them against each other. Dependency theorists, on the other hand, provided a rather superficial analysis of ethnic issues, tending to blame conflicts on colonialism or neocolonialism (the industrialized "core's" post-independence economics of the LDCs).

During the era of European colonialism, ethnic divisions in Africa and Asia were often kept in check by the struggle for independence, which

---

* Of course, America's image as a successful melting pot has been overstated. For example, prejudice, though much diminished, continues to divide Blacks and Whites. Furthermore, many Hispanic immigrants are barely integrated into society.

encouraged a common front against the colonial regime. After independence, however, previously submerged ethnic rivalries frequently rose to the surface. In the new political order, religious, racial, tribal, and nationality groups competed for state resources such as roads, schools, and civil service jobs. Subsequently, rural-to-urban migration has brought previously isolated ethnic groups into proximity with each other for the first time. Furthermore, urbanization, rising educational levels, and the spread of mass communications have politicized previously nonparticipating segments of the population. Because many of these newly mobilized citizens identify primarily with their own caste, religion, nationality, or tribe, their recently acquired political awareness often produces clashes with other ethnicities. The spread of higher education, rather than generating greater harmony, frequently produces a class of ethnically chauvinistic professionals and intellectuals, who become the ideologists of ethnic hostility. In time, as these groups come to know each other or as ethnic identities take on more conciliatory forms, these tensions may diminish. For now, however, ethnic conflict remains a potent phenomenon in the Third World.

Just as colonialism and modernization challenged traditional religious, national, and tribal identities, the economic and social forces of globalization may pose an even greater challenge. As international business conglomerates such as Nike, Coke, Wrangler, and McDonald's spread their brand names and associated cultural habits throughout the developing world, they bring a certain homogenization of world culture, which may undercut traditional ethnic practices and values. Western rock and blue jeans frequently replace distinct ethnic music and dress among young people.

Bhikhu Parekh notes that American films have driven out traditional, local films in many developing nations, not only because of their entertainment value but because U.S. studios can market their films at a lower price than local producers. Through the 1980s, Indonesia (the world's fourth most populous nation) protected the local film industry from foreign competition. While few of the Indonesian films—like American films—had outstanding artistic merit, they did reinforce national (or at least, Javanese) folktales and beliefs. In subsequent trade talks, Indonesia agreed to remove its barriers to foreign films, in return for which Washington lowered tariffs on Indonesian textile exports. By "1992, 66 out of 71 cinema houses in [Indonesia's] major cities showed only foreign, mainly US, films, and domestic gems such as *My Sky, My Home,* which won awards in France, Germany, and . . . the US, could not secure a domestic outlet."[37]

The long-term effects of the expanding "world culture" advanced by globalization are not entirely clear. On the one hand, it may be argued that the spread of Western world brands will eventually reduce or eliminate the differences of dress, food, and customs that currently separate different ethnic groups. For now, however, the prospect of globalized culture has often created a nationalistic or ethnic backlash and widened tensions between neighboring ethnic communities. To the extent that globalization economically benefits certain ethnic groups at the expense of others, it has the potential to sharpen ethnic conflict. If national governments can stop that from happening, ethnic relations may remain static or even improve.

LEVELS OF INTERETHNIC CONFLICT

Although most countries are ethnically heterogeneous, there are wide variations in how different ethnicities relate to each other. In some cases, different races or religions interact fairly amicably; in others, deep resentments inspire shocking atrocities. Having examined the various types of ethnic communities, we will now consider the *nature* and *intensity* of relations between them. In theory, these relationships can be measured by the frequency of interethnic friendships and marriages, by the degree to which political parties, trade unions, and other civic organizations are ethnically based, and by the extent to which ethnic divisions are reinforced by other social cleavages such as class. In any particular country, relations between ethnic communities may range from relative harmony (Brazil) to systematic violence (Sudan).

Relative Harmony

As we have seen, modernization often intensifies ethnic antagonisms in the short run, but usually ameliorates them in the longer term. Consequently, affluent democracies are more likely than LDCs to enjoy amicable ethnic relations. In Switzerland, for example, German-, French-, and Italian-speaking citizens have lived together peacefully for centuries. The United States and Canada also enjoy relative ethnic harmony, having successfully assimilated a large assortment of immigrant groups. In North Dakota or Saskatchewan, for example, few people are concerned when a person of Ukrainian-Orthodox or German-Catholic origin marries a Lutheran of Norwegian ancestry.

Relative ethnic harmony is less common in developing countries. However, in Brazil and the island nations of the Caribbean, relations between Blacks and Whites are generally more harmonious than in the United States. For instance, interracial dating and marriages are quite common, particularly among lower-income groups. Still, that harmony is relative, because even those countries have maintained a social hierarchy between races. Although there are many Blacks in the Dominican, Brazilian, and Panamanian middle classes, most Blacks in those countries remain mired in the lower class, and very few make it to the top of the political and economic orders.

In short, even the countries classified as harmonious are only categorized that way relative to other, more sharply divided societies. They continue to have some glaring examples of ethnic discrimination and tension. In Cuba, despite a long history of interracial marriage and more recent government efforts to promote racial equality, Blacks have yet to attain their share of leadership positions in government or the Communist Party. And Canada, in many ways a more successful melting pot than the United States, has not resolved the vexing problem of French separatism in Quebec. But such tensions are the exception, and conflict is rarely violent.

Uneasy Balance

In LDCs such as Trinidad-Tobago and Malaysia, relations between the principal ethnic groups are more strained than in the aforementioned cases of relative harmony. Although still generally peaceful, interethnic relations are in an *uneasy balance,* in which different groups predominate in specific areas of society. For example, in Malaysia the Muslim Malay majority dominates the political system, including parliament and the government bureaucracy, while the Chinese minority dominates the private sector. Race riots in 1969 led the Malaysian government to introduce a "New Economic Policy" designed, in part, to redistribute more of the country's wealth to the Malays. Fearful of Chinese domination, the Malays have benefited from a system of ethnic preferences in education and the civil service. Interethnic relations may soon be tested, however, as the Malaysian government has announced plans to sharply reduce these preferences.

The Caribbean nation of Trinidad and Tobago offers another example of uneasy balance.* During the second half of the nineteenth century, British colonial authorities encouraged the migration of indentured plantation workers from India who joined the Black majority and the small White elite. Contrary to the common Caribbean practice of extensive racial mixing, there was less interracial marriage between Blacks and East Indians (immigrants from India), at least until the twentieth century. Each group currently constitutes about 40 percent of the population, with the remaining 20 percent made up of Chinese, Whites, Arabs, and others. Following Trinidadian independence in 1962, ethnic frictions increased as Blacks and East Indians competed for state resources. Most of the important political, civil service, military, and police positions since that time have been held by Blacks, who predominate within the urban middle and working classes. Whites continue to predominate in the upper ranks of the business community. Traditionally, most East Indians have been either small to medium-sized businesspeople (with significant collective economic power) or poor farmers and farmworkers.

Trinidadian politics do not feature the same overt ethnic appeals that characterize many LDCs, but most of its political parties and unions represent one race primarily. During the first parliamentary elections after independence, each of the major parties received 80–90 percent of its votes from one ethnic group. For 24 years (1962–1986), the People's National Movement (PNM), the party that led the independence movement, headed the national government. While drawing votes from various races, the PNM's leadership and voter base have been primarily Black. For more than two decades, the opposition was led by various Indian-dominated parties, including the Democratic Labour Party (DLP) and the United Labour Front (ULF). Major labor unions also tended to be either predominantly Black or East Indian. Only in 1986 did the newly formed National Alliance for Reconstruction (NAR) finally dislodge the PNM from power by forging the first electoral alliance between the two dominant ethnic groups.

Black and Indian political and labor leaders cooperate periodically and in 1995 a party representing both races elected Trinidad's first prime minister of East Indian origin. At the same time, however, the two communities continued to maintain their social, political, and economic distance. In 1990, a radical Black Muslim movement, the Jamaat al Muslimeen, briefly captured the parliament

---

* Elsewhere in this text, I refer to Trinidad and Tobago as Trinidad-Tobago or simply Trinidad so that readers do not think that these are two countries.

building and held the prime minister and members of parliament hostage for 6 days while many poor Blacks rioted in the nation's capital. Jamaat's manifestos reflected the antagonism that many Black Trinidadians feel toward East Indians, but their violent behavior was an aberration in the nation's racial relations.

Enforced Hierarchy (Ethnic Dominance)

One important factor permitting ethnic balance in countries such as Malaysia and Trinidad-Tobago has been the division of political and economic powers between the different ethnicities. Typically, one ethnicity predominates in the political arena and the other is more influential in the economy. But, in *enforced hierarchies* both forms of power are concentrated in the hands of the ruling ethnic group. South African apartheid represented the most blatant example of such a relationship. Through the 1980s, Whites dominated both the private sector and the state, including the courts, police, and armed forces. Blacks were denied the most basic rights.

Latin American nations with large Indian (Native American) populations—including Guatemala, Bolivia, Ecuador, and Peru—have a less overt, but still significant, form of hierarchy. Since the Spanish conquest, most Indians in those countries have been poor peasants at the bottom of the social and political ladder. Even today, despite important recent gains in Indian rights, most positions of political and economic influence remain in the hands of Whites or Mestizos. At the same time, however, unlike the United States, racial classifications in Latin America tend to be culturally rather than biologically defined. Consequently, they are more flexible and open up opportunities for at least some people of color. If a young Indian villager moves to the city, adopts Western dress, and speaks Spanish, he or she becomes a Mestizo (or *Cholo*), a higher social status. And in the rural highlands of Ecuador and Peru, entire peasant communities that spoke Quechua a generation ago have switched to Spanish and changed to Western clothing in a process called *mestizaje* (becoming Mestizo). Consequently, over the years, the percentage of the population considered Mestizos has increased, with a corresponding decline in the number identified as indigenous (Indian). This, more flexible, cultural definition has obvious advantages, but an important disadvantage as well. Although it facilitates upward social mobility, traditionally Indians have only been able to enjoy that mobility by abandoning their own culture.

Since the 1980s, however, Indians have begun to assert their cultural rights and political influence in several South American countries through grassroots political movements and through the election of indigenous government officials, sometimes at the highest levels. In Bolivia, where 60 percent of the population is indigenous, new Indian social movements organized mass protests against the government's free-market (neoliberal) economic policies. Those protests brought down the nation's president and subsequently led to the 2006 election of Evo Morales, the country's first Indian president. Morales has placed several indigenous leaders in his cabinet and introduced laws to protect the rights of the country's Indian majority. In Ecuador, a national Indian federation (CONAIE) joined the military in a 2000 coup that briefly installed a ruling junta that included the CONAIE president. Founded in 1996, Pachakutik

("Awakening"), an Indian political party growing out of CONAIE, became an important political force. Peru elected a president of Indian descent in 2001. Finally, in the Mexican state of Chiapas, a group known as the Zapatistas staged a 1994 peasant rebellion in behalf of Indian rights. Though it never had a chance to seize national power (nor did it intend to), the group received a remarkable amount of national support from Mexicans of all ethnicities and social classes.

In all these cases of enforced hierarchy, racial and class distinctions are closely intertwined. Those higher up the social ladder tend to be lighter skinned; those at the lower ranks of society are generally darker. In Brazil, being Black is generally associated with being poor. Although upward mobility through the class–race hierarchy is possible, racial prejudice shapes social relationships and creates barriers to equality. Moreover, most Latin American Black families—like Indian families in the Andes—are too poor to provide their children with the education needed for significant upward social and economic mobility. Brazil prides itself in being a racial melting pot and in many ways it is. For example, there are numerous social and cultural bonds between Blacks, Mulattos, and Whites, including many interracial marriages, far more than in the United States. Yet, the most recent national census documented what most Brazilians already knew—people of color have less education and far lower incomes than Whites. Though Blacks and Mulattos constitute about 40 percent of the Brazilian population, they made up only 2–3 percent of university students. Furthermore, they are nearly twice as likely as Whites to earn below the official minimum wage. To rectify this situation, the current administration of President Luiz Inácio Lula da Silva has created affirmative action quotas that set aside university positions and government jobs for people of color. But, the program has been negatively received by the White middle and upper classes, which may weaken its implementation.

Unlike South Africa's old apartheid system, Latin America's racial hierarchy is enforced informally, not legally, and is far less repressive. Still, during nearly 40 years of revolutionary upheaval and intense government oppression, the Guatemalan armed forces viewed rural Indian communities as breeding grounds for Marxist guerrillas. Consequently, successive military regimes massacred tens of thousands of Indian peasants in a policy bordering on genocide. Fortunately, since the 1990s a peace treaty with the guerrillas has curtailed such violence.

Systematic Violence

In the worst-case scenario, deep ethnic resentments have sometimes led to mass violence or even civil war. As we have seen, in a number of Third World countries as well as in some European nations, *systematic violence* has resulted in thousands or hundreds of thousands of deaths and huge numbers of displaced refugees and rape victims—in Bosnia, Lebanon, India, Bangladesh, Ethiopia, Nigeria, Rwanda, and Sudan, among others. Often, as with enforced hierarchies, violence develops when ethnic divisions are reinforced by class antagonisms. Muslim antipathy toward Lebanon's Christian community has been fueled by Christian economic superiority. Similarly, in Nigeria, many Islamic northerners resent the economic success of the Christian Ibos.

Ethnic bloodshed sometimes occurs when one ethnicity seizes political power and then takes retribution for real or imagined past indignities. Thus, when General Idi Amin seized power in Uganda, he ordered the slaughter of Langi and Acholi soldiers who were identified with the regime of ousted President Milton Obote. In both Rwanda and Burundi, the deaths of Hutu presidents opened the floodgates to violence between Hutus and the long-dominant Tutsis.

OUTCOMES AND RESOLUTIONS

Whether ethnic antagonisms arise from competition over government resources, resentment over the division of political and economic powers, or an ethnic community's demands for greater autonomy, there are a number of possible results. Although some outcomes are peaceful, others may spawn intense violence. And while some resolutions are successful, others do not endure. In seeking a peaceful and lasting resolution, government and ethnic leaders are constrained by the history and intensity of their ethnic cleavages, by the degree of previous ethnic cooperation, and by the country's political culture. Nonetheless, within these constraints, the creativity and statecraft of national leaders and outside mediators can contribute to successful solutions. Of course, political elites may seek reasonable, negotiated solutions or they may choose to play on ethnic tensions for their own advantage.

Unfortunately, all too often self-serving, chauvinistic political leaders make a bad situation worse. For example, although Bosnian Serbs and Muslims had enjoyed rather amicable relationships for many years, after the breakup of Yugoslavia extremist leaders such as then-Serb-president Slobodan Milošević; promoted ethnic hatred and mass murder in order to build their own political power base. In the end, Milošević brought both Bosnia and Serbia to ruin. Similarly, the appalling 1994 massacres in Rwanda were orchestrated from above. Government officials induced Hutu villagers to attack their Tutsi neighbors with whom most of them had been living peacefully for many years.

When more responsible elites are willing to resolve bitter ethnic conflicts through negotiations, they may arrive at one of several types of resolutions. In the next section, we examine those possible outcomes and also look at several options that have been attempted when negotiations failed. Although the alternatives presented here are not exhaustive, they cover a wide range of Third World experiences.

Power Sharing: Federalism and Consociationalism

Power-sharing arrangements are designed to create stability by constitutionally dividing political power among major ethnic groups. These settlements generally follow protracted negotiations and constitutional debate. If power sharing is introduced into the constitution at the time of independence, it may head off ethnic conflict before it gets started. Unfortunately, however, such arrangements often break down.

Federalism, the primary form of power sharing, is "a system of government [that] emanates from the desire of people to form a union without necessarily losing their various identities."[38] It may involve the creation of autonomous or semiautonomous regions, each of which is governed by a particular ethnicity. It is only possible in situations where contending ethnic groups are concentrated in different regions of the country. For example, prior to its collapse, Yugoslavia consisted of six autonomous republics mostly governed by individual national-ities, including Serbs, Croats, and Slovenes. The constitution mandated power sharing between the various republics at the national level. But, that compro-mise began to unravel in the 1970s following the death of Marshal Joseph Broz Tito, the country's long-term strong man. It collapsed completely in the early 1990s when the Communist Party lost its grip on several republics.

Industrialized democracies have had greater success with ethnically based federalism. Each of Switzerland's 22 cantons is dominated by one of the country's three major language groups, with German-, French-, and Italian-speaking can-tons coexisting harmoniously. Canada's federalism, though not based on ethnic divisions, has allowed the primarily French-speaking province of Quebec a substantial amount of autonomy regarding language and other cultural matters. Although the country's constitutional arrangement has not satisfied many Québécois nationalists, it has accommodated many of their demands and, at least until now, has induced the province's voters to reject independence.

In the developing world, power sharing has been less successful. Following independence, Nigeria tried to accommodate its ethnic divisions through federalism. As we have seen, the country's North was dominated by the Hausa and Fulani, the East by the Ibos, and the West, to a lesser extent, by the Yoruba. That union came apart when the Ibos tried to secede. Although the Biafran war took a terrible toll, a new federal solution has subsequently taken hold. On the other hand, Pakistani federalism failed to overcome the antipathy between the country's more powerful western region (populated largely by Urdu speakers) and the Bengali-speaking East. In 1971, relations between the two regions broke down completely, resulting in the massacre of 500,000 Bengalis by western Pakistani troops. When India went to war with Pakistan, the eastern region was able to secede and form the new nation of Bangladesh.

Consociationalism offers another potential solution to ethnic conflict. It tends to be used where major ethnic groups reside in close proximity and have no particular "homelands." Like federalism, however, it has had a mixed record. Consociational democracy in plural (multiethnic) societies entails a careful division of political power designed to protect the rights of all partici-pants.* It involves the following components:

1. The leaders of all important ethnic groups must form a ruling coalition at the national level.
2. Each group has veto power over government policy, or at least over policies that affect them.
3. Government funds and public employment, such as the civil service, are divided between ethnicities, with each receiving a number of posts roughly proportional to its population.
4. Each ethnic group is afforded a high degree of autonomy over its own affairs.[39]

---

* Consociationalism can exist among conflicting groups other than ethnicities, but we confine this discussion to ethnically based consociationalism.

Thus, consociational democracy consciously rejects pure majority rule. Instead, it seeks to create a framework for stability and peace by guaranteeing minorities a share of political power—even veto power—to protect them against the majority. It has been tried in several developing nations, including Cyprus (where it failed) and Malaysia (where it has generally succeeded). Perhaps the most widely known effort has been in Lebanon. From independence in 1943 until civil war erupted in 1975, government positions and political authority were divided between the nation's various Muslim and Christian communities. As we saw, the system eventually broke down, in part because formulas for the proportional division of government posts were not adjusted to reflect population growth over the years among Shi'ites and other Muslims. Settlement of the country's 15-year civil war restored consociational rule, but with a division of government positions that more accurately reflected the Muslim share of the population. Still, ongoing confrontations between the national government and Shi'a Hezbollah demonstrate that ethnic tensions continue.

Some mutual trust and cooperation between the leaders of contending ethnic groups is the key to effective consociational arrangements. Sadly, trust is difficult to establish in times of ethnic hostility and becomes ever more problematic after that hostility has erupted into bloodshed. Iraq's current consociational arrangements involve the division of leadership posts (including prime minister, president, and speaker of the parliament) between the three major ethnic groups and the use of parliamentary election rules that indirectly guarantee a bloc of seats for the Kurds and Sunnis. But, continued mistrust between the three major ethnic groups has stalemated the national parliament.

Secession

When power sharing or other forms of compromise do not succeed, disgruntled ethnic minorities may attempt to secede (withdraw) from the country in order to form their own nation or join their ethnic brothers and sisters in a neighboring state. As one author put it, "Secession, like divorce, is an ultimate act of alienation."[40] It offers a potential way out of a "failed marriage" between ethnic groups within a nation-state. Unfortunately, however, like divorce, secession or the threat of secession frequently provoke bitterness and hostility.

Ralph Premdas indicates that these movements have several characteristics:

1. An ethnic group—defined by factors such as language, religion, culture, or race—claims the right of self-determination (independence).
2. The ethnic community has a defined territorial base that it claims as its homeland.
3. There is almost always some organized struggle.[41]

Given the large number of ethnically divided LDCs, we should not be surprised to find many secessionist movements. Central governments, faced with such breakaway efforts, almost always try to repress them because they are unwilling to part with some of their country's territory or resources, just as Abraham Lincoln was unwilling to part with the Confederate states. This chapter previously examined secessionist movements by Tamils in Sri Lanka, Ibos in Nigeria, Eritreans in Ethiopia, and Sikhs in northern India. Other secessionist movements have included, Blacks in southern Sudan, Karen in Myanmar, Moros in the Philippines, and Muslims in Kashmir.

Following the Gulf War, the world briefly focused its attention on Saddam Hussein's persecution of Iraq's Kurdish population. A decade later, Kurdish militia supported American-led coalition forces in the war to topple Saddam. But the Kurdish secessionist movement preceded Saddam's government and transcends Iraqi borders. Separatist efforts date to the collapse of the Ottoman Empire at the close of World War I. Residing in a mountainous region that they call Kurdistan, perhaps as many as 30 million Kurds live in adjacent regions of Turkey (home to about half of the region's Kurds), Iraq, and Iran, with a smaller community in Syria. Over the years, the Kurds have been persecuted in all of those countries, and today they still have little prospect of attaining the independent Kurdistan that so many of them desire (though they have achieved regional self-rule in northeastern Iraq). As a result of America's two wars with Iraq, Kurds have achieved virtual autonomy and currently exercise considerable influence in that country's national government.

Although many aggrieved Third World nationalities would like to secede, few have accomplished that goal. The Bangladeshi withdrawal from Pakistan is one of the few "successful" Third World cases, but it was only achieved at an enormous cost in human lives. Moreover, it could not have happened without India's military intervention. Eritrea attained independence from Ethiopia in 1993 after decades of struggle. But, more often than not, the most that secessionist movements can hope to attain is greater autonomy and government recognition of their group's rights.

Noting the spread of secessionist conflicts in the 1970s and 1980s and the breakup of the Soviet Union, Yugoslavia, and Czechoslovakia into many smaller, ethnically based states in the 1990s, many analysts predicted that Eastern Europe and portions of the developing world would see the disintegration of an ever-growing number of nation-states. Often they voiced alarm over the violence and disorder that this prospect suggested. For example, a widely cited book by noted sociologist and former U.S. Senator, Patrick Moynihan, predicted that the number of independent states in the world would increase from about 200 to 300 by the middle of the twenty-first century.[42] But, in fact, the number of secessionist wars has actually declined significantly since the start of the 1990s. From 1991 to 1999, 16 such wars were settled and 11 others were held in check by cease-fires or continuing negotiations. Thus, as this century began, only 18 secessionist wars continued worldwide, fewer than at any time since 1970.[43]

Outside Intervention

Because ethnic conflicts sometimes produces a considerable loss of life and other horrors—particularly when a conflict pits a government against a minority group—outside actors may face a moral and practical dilemma. On the one hand, they may feel morally compelled to somehow intervene on behalf of a victimized minority. Such intercession can span the gamut from simply agreeing to take in refugees all the way to armed intervention aimed at putting a stop to the bloodshed. At the same time, however, leaders of outside nations may be constrained from involvement by international law (concerning national sovereignty), international power alignments, lack of resources, or fear of alienating their own citizens. Even the nonaggressive act of offering refuge to the victims of ethnic strife and persecution may seem too costly, too risky, or too unpalatable to the home country's population. Indeed, the outside world stood by as millions died in ethnic massacres in such countries as Bosnia, the Congo, Rwanda, and Sudan.[44] Looking at the world's prolonged inaction regarding the Serbs' and Croats' bloody "ethnic cleansing" in Bosnia, military strategist Edward Luttwak asked, "If the Bosnian Muslims had been needle-nosed dolphins, would the world have allowed the Croats and Serbs to slaughter them by the tens of thousands?"[45] His blunt question raises important ethical and pragmatic questions about the world's obligations and limitations in such situations.

Unless outside forces are invited in by a country's own government (as when Sri Lanka asked India's armed forces to quell its civil war), external intervention normally violates the principle of national sovereignty. But, since most serious ethnic violence is perpetrated, encouraged, or condoned by these governments themselves, very rarely do they invite outside intervention. Consequently, most external intervention raises a number of difficult issues. At what point do other nations or international organizations (such as the United Nations, NATO, or the African Union) have the right to violate a country's sovereignty in order to save innocent lives? For example, should the United Nations or the West have sent troops into Rwanda or the Congo, with or without the permission of their governments, in order to stop the massacres of hundreds of thousands? Does the community of nations currently have any legal and moral obligations to protect the people of Darfur from genocide, even if that violates Sudanese sovereignty? Many Westerners would answer affirmatively. But if those interventions are justified, wouldn't the same moral principles have given United Nations the authority to send troops into Birmingham, Alabama, and rural Mississippi in the 1960s in order to protect the lives of Blacks who were being terrorized by the Ku Klux Klan and the local police? Who is to decide in which situations outside intervention is legitimate?

Furthermore, there are pragmatic questions regarding the likely effectiveness of a particular intervention. Under what circumstances does outside intervention (including military intervention) prevent ethnic persecution and impose a durable solution, and when are such efforts futile? Will countries such as the United States, France, India, or Nigeria be willing to commit their soldiers and economic resources on a sustained basis to support future peacekeeping operations? How many casualties among their own soldiers are peacekeeping nations prepared to accept?[46]

In the end, governments contemplating humanitarian interventions have to weigh their own national interests and the costs of intervention against their commitment to sustaining human rights abroad. Most nations are reluctant to risk their soldiers' lives for humanitarian purposes. A fairly small number of American soldiers (18) brutally killed in 1993 during a mission to restore order and distribute food in war-torn Somalia shocked U.S. public opinion and caused President Clinton to withdraw the remaining American troops. Only 1 year later, government leaders in Washington, Paris, and other Western capitals were warned that an ethnic massacre was likely to unfold in Rwanda. Sobered by the recently failed intervention in Somalia and unsure how well they could prevent genocide, they decided against interference. Some analysts insist that the United Nations or the United States or France could have saved many thousand lives if they had quickly sent a military force to quell the violence.[47] Others disagree, arguing that the Rwandan genocide took place so quickly (most of the deaths occurring within a few weeks) that intervention could not have arrived in time to save most of the victims.[48]

More recently, the United Nations, The African Union, and the Western powers have lamented the genocidal warfare unleashed against non-Arab minorities in Darfur (a western region of Sudan). Only after nearly 1–2 million people had fled Darfur to squalid and dangerous refugee camps and some 200,000 had died (largely of starvation) did the African Union send a small and ineffective military force, with the acquiescence of the Sudanese government. The United Nations has been even slower to take action. Several thousand U.N. peacekeeping troops were finally dispatched to Darfur in 2007 in a joint operation with African Union troops already on the ground. While some sources claim the level of violence has declined somewhat since 2007, other analysts insist that it has risen. What is fairly certain is that joint U.N. and AU peacekeeping force has been hampered by the Sudanese government and had been rather ineffective in protecting Darfur's population. More than a year after the Security Council authorized a nearly 20,000-person peacekeeping force, Sudan has only allowed in 12,000.

Even when world opinion has forced the host government to accept external intervention, such as United Nations intervention in East Timor (then a part of Indonesia) and Sudan, troops have normally been sent in only *after* the worst outrages had already been committed. To be sure, outside forces occasionally *have* imposed solutions on some seemingly intractable ethnic conflicts. In such cases, the intervening power is often a neighboring state that either has ties to one of the warring ethnic factions or has a strategic interest in the country it invades. Such was the case with India's intercession on behalf of the Bengalis in East Pakistan. Without that intervention, the nation of Bangladesh could not have been born. The Turkish invasion of Cyprus imposed an ethnic settlement by partitioning the island's Greek and Turkish communities. Recent examples of intervention by *non*neighboring nations include the U.S. and British protection of the Kurdish enclave in northern Iraq during the 1990s.

But international interventions frequently come too late and often end badly. While the Iraqi Kurds have benefited greatly from America's two wars against their oppressor, Saddam Hussein, a prior U.S. intrusion had devastating results. In 1974, the American CIA and Iran supported a Kurdish rebellion against the Iraqi government. But, for Washington, Kurdish interests were secondary to its own policy objective—supporting the Shah's government in Iran, which at that time was America's ally and Iraq's enemy. The following year, however, the Shah temporarily resolved his differences with Iraq and withdrew his support for the Kurdish insurrection. The CIA then also terminated its assistance to the rebels and the insurrection collapsed. Thousands of Iraqi Kurds were killed or driven from their homes.[49] Washington's behavior was not unique. Most countries—especially powerful ones with a broad international agenda—will only assist persecuted ethnic groups if that help does not conflict with their own national interests. Indeed, some outside interventions have intentionally intensified ethnic conflicts. For example, from the late 1990s to 2003, as many as nine African nations, particularly Rwanda and Uganda, intervened in the Congo's ethnic conflict, which pitted the Congolese government against Congolese Hutus and some 2 million Hutus who had recently fled Rwanda. In what some have called "Africa's World War," perhaps 5 million people have died (either from malnutrition, disease, or warfare) in a conflict that went largely unnoticed in the West and may now finally be winding down. While the loss of life would have been horrifying no matter what, the Ugandan and Rwandan interventions surely added to the death toll.

As we have seen, India's attempt to settle the Tamil–Sinhalese conflict in Sri Lanka ended disastrously. Not only did it fail to resolve the civil war, but it led subsequently to the assassination of India's prime minister Rajiv Gandhi by a Tamil Tiger suicide bomber. Foreign intervention did halt ethnic violence in the former Yugoslavia (Bosnia and Kosovo), but peacekeeping troops now face an indefinite stay. Finally, sometimes minority groups wishing to secede from their country receive help from neighboring countries with whom they share an ethnic identity. Somali rebels in the Ethiopian region of Ogaden have received help over the years from neighboring Somalia. In South Asia, the Pakistani military has aided Islamic secessionists in the Indian, predominantly Muslim, state of Kashmir.* In all these cases, outside intervention may merely have thrown gasoline on the fire of existing ethnic strife.

In short, outside interventions frequently fail to resolve ethnic conflicts. Furthermore, even when they are well intentioned, outside powers are often unwilling or unable to "stay the course." Thus, Glynne Evans notes,

> A half-hearted [outside] military response [to ethnic conflict] without any underlying political action is a poor option.... Conflicts with a high degree of ethnic mobilization last for generations rather than years, and are intense in their impact hellip;as neighbors turn on neighbors. An intervention for humanitarian purposes in such cases becomes a major military commitment, and one of long duration.[50]

Events in countries such as the Congo, Rwanda, and Sudan suggest that this is a commitment that outside powers are rarely prepared to make.

One of the most common types of outside intervention has come from a neighboring country that supports an ethnic rebellion, thereby enhancing the conflict rather than containing it. Idean Salehyan's recent study of ethnic rebellions involving violence found that nearly 80 percent involved ethnic groups located along an international border.[51] Put another way, ethnic groups (usually minorities) that reside along such borders are far more likely to rebel than living elsewhere. Why is this? If nothing else, proximity to a neighboring country often allows rebel soldiers and their supporters to take refuge from pursuing government troops. In many, if not most, of these cases the rebelling ethnic group lives on both sides of the border and can take refuge and gain support from their fellow tribesmen or nationals. Often, the neighboring government may also offer sanctuary or even military support. This chapter

---

* The Kashmir region, lying between India and Pakistan, is divided into two regions largely controlled by those two nations.

offers several examples. Kurdish rebels in Turkey are able to gain refuge and material support from the Kurdish-controlled regions of northern Iraq. Muslim rebels in Kashmir, as we have seen, have often been supported by the neighboring Pakistani armed forces and intelligence service. Rwanda's Tutsi-dominated government long supported Tutsi rebel forces in the Congo.

Outside Intervention in Iraq: The Effect of the U.S. Occupation on Kurdish Autonomy

While the purpose of the U.S. invasion of Iraq was surely not to resolve ethnic conflicts, the defeat of Saddam Hussein's Sunni-dominated dictatorship unleashed formerly repressed ethnic grievances. Having previously discussed the intense conflicts between Shi'as and Sunnis, we can now turn to the effects of foreign intervention on Kurdish national aspirations. Iraq is home to perhaps 5 million Kurds (the precise figure is in dispute), the world's third largest Kurdish community, after Turkey and Iran. Living primarily in the country's mountainous northeast, they are the majority population in three of Iraq's eighteen provinces. Under the Ottoman (Turkish) Empire, which governed much of Iraq and the Middle East from the sixteenth to the early twentieth centuries, ethnic minorities were treated reasonably fairly. Hence, Kurdish nationalism did not really blossom until Ottoman rule collapsed after World War I. At that time, Britain, France, and Italy signed the Treaty of Severes (1920), which promised the creation of an autonomous or independent Kurdistan. Yet, just 3 years later, the Treaty of Lausanne terminated that commitment. Because the newly created Turkish and Iraqi states viewed the Kurds as a threat, the Kurdish dream of autonomy or independence remained unfulfilled.

When the Iraqi monarchy was overthrown in 1958, the new government briefly allowed Kurdish culture to flourish. Soon, however, the republican regime initiated a 15-year campaign removing large numbers of Kurds from their homelands to other parts of the country, destroying Kurdish villages and moving Arabs into historically Kurdish regions. In 1980, only a year after Iran's Islamic revolution had toppled the Shah, Iraq and Iran entered into a brutal, decade-long war. Because Iraq's Kurds largely supported Iran, Saddam implemented a genocidal campaign against them (called *al-Anfal*) during the 1980s. During that operation, the Iraqi military was responsible for "the first documented instances of a government employing chemical weapons against its own civilian population."[52] In total, the Saddam dictatorship is believed to have killed over 300,000 Kurds, more than half of them during al-Anfal. Millions more were driven from their homes.

The Kurdish rebellion against Saddam following the Gulf War, like the Shi'a rebellion in the South, soon fizzled. As government forces recaptured the towns that had fallen to the rebels, more than a million Kurds fled toward or across Iraq's borders with Turkey and Iran. When Turkey refused to allow them in and numerous refugees died of exposure in the high mountains, the European Community and the United States endorsed the creation of a U.N.-protected, Kurdish enclave within Iraq. Under "Operation Provide Comfort," several Western nations placed troops on the ground and used their air power to establish a "no-fly zone" that prohibited Iraqi planes from flying north of the 36th parallel, thereby effectively creating the autonomous region that the Kurds had so long yearned for. Thousands of Kurdish families returned to the region and established democratic political institutions, including the election of a Kurdish National Assembly in 1992.

During the 2003 invasion of Iraq, U.S. forces received valuable military and intelligence support from Kurdish militias. The ouster of Saddam Hussein's regime raised the issue of the Kurdish role in postwar Iraq. In deference to U.S. pressure and Turkey's adamant opposition to a neighboring Kurdish state, the Kurdish political and military leadership provisionally forswore their ambitions for an independent Kurdistan, but demanded substantial autonomy in the new political order. Yet, Phebe Marr, a leading Middle East expert, notes that in her many interviews of Kurdish leaders during the past 15 years, all but one of them identified themselves as Kurds first and Iraqis second.[53] Iraq's interim constitution (2004), the electoral rules for the 2005 referendum on a new constitution, and the 2005 constitution itself all gave the Kurdish and Sunni minorities considerable power to block legislation if they believed it adversely affected them.

Currently, the future of the Iraqi Kurdish community remains uncertain. Once unified by their opposition to Saddam regime, Kurds and Shi'as each have a distinct vision for Iraq's political future. While Shi'ite leaders support the principle of majority rule, Kurdish representatives are more concerned with protecting minority rights. In sum, although foreign intervention—the Gulf War and the current war in Iraq—has benefited the Kurdish and Shi'a populations in many ways, it remains to be seen whether they can work out a way of living peacefully with each other and with their Sunni antagonists.

Settlement through Exhaustion

Finally, many ethnic conflicts have been resolved less through statecraft, constitutional arrangements, or external intervention than through the exhaustion of the warring parties. Although the Arab League helped negotiate an end to Lebanon's lengthy civil war, it was the weariness of the Lebanese, after the virtual destruction of Beirut that permitted a settlement (even though some 15 years later that may be unraveling). Similarly, although the Ugandan government continues to clash periodically with the Acholi and Langi tribes, conflict has been held in check because Ugandans do not want to return to the ethnically based bloodshed of the Amin and Obote eras. In Mozambique, Angola, Liberia, and Sierra Leone, exhaustion helped drive the warring factions toward United Nations-brokered peace treaties that halted their long and bitter civil wars. And, in Sudan, a similar process contributed to the end of a 21-year war between the Arab-dominated national government and the Black (non-Muslim) population of the South.

Toward a Peaceful Resolution of Conflict

If developing nations are to avoid the horrors of civil war, secession, and foreign intervention, they must arrive at legal, political, and economic solutions that can constrain ethnic tensions. That goal, though clearly reasonable, is more easily articulated than achieved. More difficult still is the task of repairing the damage done to plural societies that have been torn apart by bloody conflict (e.g., Rwanda, Iraq, Kashmir, and Lebanon) or by decades of prejudice and segregation (South Africa). Not long after South Africa's new, multiracial government was installed in 1994, President Mandela's administration created a Truth and Reconciliation Commission, before which perpetrators of racially based violence and injustices were invited to confess their crimes in return for amnesty. The goal of the Commission was to further unearth the crimes of apartheid and, more importantly, to allow the nation's races to live to together more harmoniously. Yet, as one observer of the Commission's hearings has suggested, in countries that have experienced systematic repression or extensive ethnic violence, reconciliation—the creation of harmony between formerly hostile parties—may be too much to hope for.[54] A more realistic goal, he suggests, may be establishing the basis for *coexistence* between these groups. Toward this end, governments or international agencies trying to assist countries previously devastated by ethnic violence need to create trauma centers for the survivors of atrocities, multicultural educational programs, contact programs that try to establish a dialogue between erstwhile perpetrators and victims of ethnic violence, and cross-ethnic economic development programs, all designed to help former antagonists live together peacefully. While, as we might expect, such efforts have had mixed records of success, they need to be tried.

CONCLUSION: ETHNIC PLURALISM AND DEMOCRACY

We have seen that, while modern plural societies (such as Belgium and Canada) are ultimately more capable of resolving ethnic tensions peacefully, in the shorter term early modernization has intensified such conflict in many LDCs. But, how has the spread of Third World democracy affected ethnic relations?

Crafting peaceful scenarios for multicultural societies remains one of the greatest challenges facing Third World leaders. Still, there is some basis for hope. The frequency and intensity of ethnic conflicts peaked during the late 1980s and early 1990s and have decreased modestly since that time. Although Africa has remained home to some of the world's most brutal conflicts (Sierra Leone, Sudan, Congo), it has also experienced the most progress of late in bringing ethno-warfare to a halt. In fact, most of the continent's remaining ethnic wars are conflicts that date back to the mid-1990s or earlier, as fewer new ones have emerged as of late. Realizing that their countries were being destroyed by ethnic hostilities and decades of the resulting economic decay, a number of governments and rebel groups in the region have become more accommodating.

During the 1970s and 1980s, increased ethnic violence in the developing world and the former communist states of Eastern Europe often coincided with the spread of democratic government. This raised two questions about the relationship between democracy and ethnic politics: First, "Are multiethnic countries less likely to maintain democracy than are culturally homogenous societies?" Second, "Do the growth of citizen participation and the creation of democratic government intensify conflict between ethnic communities?"

The first question can be answered quite easily. Democracy *is* clearly harder, though far from impossible, to establish and maintain in multiethnic countries. We have seen, for example, how Lebanon, long considered the most democratic

Arab country, was devastated by ethnic civil war. Looking at democracy's failure to take root in most of Africa and Asia from the 1960s to the 1980s, Alvin Rabushka and Kenneth Shepsle concluded that ethnic antagonisms had created important obstacles to democratization. Democracy, they argued, "is simply not viable in an environment of intense ethnic preference."[55] Here they referred to societies in which powerful ethnic groups receive special privileges, while others suffer discrimination.

An examination of both economically advanced and less developed nations reveals that democracy has fared best in countries that are most ethnically homogeneous (such as Botswana, Iceland, Uruguay, and Japan) and in countries of "new settlement" (including the United States, Canada, New Zealand, and Australia) populated primarily by immigrants and their descendants, who created a new common culture. In Africa, Asia, and the Middle East, where many countries labor with strong ethnic divides, the growth of democracy and mass political participation may unleash communal hostilities, sometimes intensified by opportunistic politicians who use group fears to build a political base.

Ethnic pluralism poses a particular obstacle to democracy in poorer countries, where various groups must contend for limited government resources (schools, roads, civil service jobs, etc.) in the "politics of scarcity." But although democracy is more difficult to achieve in plural societies, it is not impossible even in very poor nations. Despite its history of religiously based violence, India, one of the world's most ethnically diverse countries, has maintained democratic government for all but two of its 62 years of independence. Similarly, Trinidad-Tobago, a country divided by religion and race, is among the Third World's most democratic nations.

To be sure, the initial transition to democracy frequently intensifies existing ethnic animosities. Newly formed political parties often base their support in competing ethnic communities. Politicians, even those opposed to violence, are tempted to use ethnic appeals as a means of gaining public support. As public resources are distributed through more transparent legislative decisions, ethnically based interest groups and political parties fight for their fair share. Some analysts warn that "the opening of democratic space throws up many groups pulling in different directions, that it causes demand overload, systematic breakdown and even violent conflict," a danger particularly relevant in societies with deep ethnic tensions prior to their democratic transitions.[56] That danger is greatest in strict majoritarian democracies, where a single ethnic group or allied ethnicities can dominate parliamentary or presidential elections without affording constitutional or other institutional protections to minority groups. Thus, the Carnegie Commission on Preventing Deadly Conflict concluded that

> In societies with deep ethnic divisions and little experience with democratic government and the rule of law [a common phenomenon in Africa, Asia and the Middle East], strict majoritarian democracy can be self-defeating. Where ethnic identities are strong and national identity weak, populations may vote largely on ethnic lines. Domination by one ethnic group can lead to a tyranny of the majority.[57]

But this merely indicates the importance of limiting majority rule in democratic, multiethnic societies. It does not suggest that authoritarian government is preferable in such situations. Indeed, in the long run, the only way ethnicities can resolve their differences is through open discussion and bargaining in a reasonably democratic political arena, as long as majority rule is tempered by constitutional guarantees of human rights, consociational arrangements, or other institutional protections for minorities such as those previously discussed.

Although dictatorships in Yugoslavia and the Soviet Union were able to repress ethnic conflicts for many years, in the end they actually intensified these grievances by denying their existence, silencing them, and failing to deal with them. After the fall of Communism, long-repressed antagonisms in Croatia, Bosnia, Kosovo, and Chechnya burst to the surface, producing civil war or lesser forms of violence. Elsewhere, dictators such as Laurent Kabila (the Congo), Suharto (Indonesia), and Saddam Hussein (Iraq) presided over ethnic massacres that would have been unthinkable in a democracy monitored by public opinion and a free press.

Conversely, democratic politicians are open to interest-group pressure from ethnic minorities and, hence, are more likely to settle disputes peacefully before they degenerate into violence. Indeed, the recent study of "minorities at risk" throughout the world revealed that democratic regimes are more likely than dictatorships to negotiate peaceful settlements of ethnic warfare. And during the 1990s, political discrimination and, to a lesser degree, economic discrimination against ethnic minorities were more likely to decline in democracies than under authoritarian governments.[58] In short, to accommodate ethnic pluralism and resolve tensions, what is needed is democratic, mature, and enlightened political leadership, a spirit of compromise, and the implementation of politically negotiated solutions such as federalism and consociational democracy.

DISCUSSION QUESTIONS

1. What are the differences and similarities between ethnic tensions and conflict in the United States and ethnic divisions in the developing world?
2. Discuss the effect that modernization has had on ethnic identification and ethnic conflict.
3. What are some reasons that might explain why major civil strife related to ethnicity has declined in the last 10–15 years?

NOTES

1. UN estimates reported by Associated Press on the MSNBC Web site. http://www.msnbc.com/id/29494356 (updated on March 3, 2009). Because outside journalists and human rights workers have limited access to the conflict region, estimates of the number of dead and displaced vary widely and, of course, change over time.

2. Quoted in Yueh-Ting Lee, Fathali Moghaddam, Clark McCauley, and Stephen Worchel, "The Global Challenge of Ethnic and Cultural Conflict,"

in *The Psychology of Ethnic and Cultural Conflict*, eds. Y. Lee, C. McCauley, F. Moghaddam, and S. Worchel (Westport, CT: Praeger, 2004), 3.

3. Crawford Young, *The Politics of Cultural Pluralism* (Madison: University of Wisconsin Press, 1976), 23, see also, 23–26.

4. Patrick Inman and James Peacock, "Conclusion: Ethnic and Sectarian as Ideal Types," in *Identity Matters*, eds. James Peacock, Patricia Thornton, and Patrick Inman (New York: Berghahn Books, 2007), 208.

5. Ted Robert Gurr, "Preface" and "Long War, Short Peace: The Rise and Decline of Ethnopolitical Conflict at the End of the Cold War," in *Peoples versus States: Minorities at Risk in the New Century*, ed. Ted Gurr (Washington, DC: United States Institute of Peace Press, 2000), xiii and 27–56; Idean Salehyan, *Rebels Without Borders: Transnational Insurgencies in World Politics* (Ithaca, NY: Cornell University Press, 2009), 12–13; Frances Steward, *Horizontal Inequalities and Conflict* (New York: Palgrave MacMillan, 2007), 4–7.

6. Jennifer De Maio, *Confronting Ethnic Conflict* (Lanham, MD: Rowman & Littlefield Publishers, 2009), 23.

7. Monica Duffy Toft, *The Geography of Ethnic Violence: Identity, Interests, and the Indivisibility of Territory* (Princeton, NJ: Princeton University Press, 2003), 3; see also, Peter Wallensteen and Margareta Sollenberg, "Armed Conflicts, Conflict Termination, and Peace Agreements, 1989–1996," *Journal of Peace Research*, vol. 34, no. 3 (1997), 339–358.

8. David Bloomfield and Ben Reilly, eds. *Democracy and Deep-Rooted Conflict: Options for Negotiations* (Stockholm: International Institute for Democracy and Electoral Assistance, 1998), 4.

9. "By the Numbers: Ethnic Groups in the World," *Scientific American* (September 1998), http://www.sciamdigital.com/.

10. Gurr, *Peoples versus States*, 10–11.

11. G.W. Allport, *The Nature of Prejudice* (Cambridge, MA: Addison-Wesley Press, 1954).

12. Victoria M. Esses and Richard A. Vernon, eds. *Explaining the Breakdown of Ethnic Relations: Why Neighbors Kill* (Malden, MA: Blackwell Publishing, 2008).

13. Patricia M. Thornton, "Introduction: Identity Matters," in *Identity Matters*, 10.

14. Gurr, *Peoples versus States*, 5.

15. Donald Rothchild and Victor A. Olorunsola, "Managing Competing State and Ethnic Claims," in *State versus Ethnic Claims: African Policy Dilemmas*, eds. Rothchild and Olorunsola (Boulder, CO: Westview Press, 1983), 1.

16. Quoted in Francine Friedman, *The Bosnian Muslims: Denial of a Nation* (Boulder, CO: Westview Press, 1996), 1.

17. Quoted in David A. Lake and Donald Rothchild, "Spreading Fear: The Genesis of Transnational Ethnic Conflict," in *The International Spread of Ethnic Conflict*, eds. Lake and Rothchild (Princeton, NJ: Princeton University Press, 1998), 7.

18. Cynthia Enloe, *Ethnic Conflict and Political Development* (Boston: Little, Brown, 1973), 15.

19. Gunther Schlee, *How Enemies are Made: Towards a Theory of Ethnic and Religious Conflicts* (New York: Berghahn Books, 2008), 5.

20. Donald Horowitz, *A Democratic South Africa? Constitutional Engineering in a Divided Society* (Berkeley: University of California Press, 1991), 44–48.

21. Young, *Politics of Cultural Pluralism*, 20.

22. Uri Ra'anan, "Nation and State: Order Out of Chaos," in *State and Nation in Multi-ethnic Societies*, ed. Ra'anan et al. (Manchester, England, and New York: Manchester University Press, 1991), 4–7.

23. Toft, *The Geography of Ethnic Violence*, 17, 149–152.

24. Said and Simmons, *Ethnicity in an International Context*, 10.

25. Omo Omoruyi, "State Creation and Ethnicity in a Federal (Plural) System: Nigeria's Search for Parity," in *Ethnicity, Politics, and Development*, eds. Dennis L. Thompson and Dov Ronen (Boulder, CO: Lynne Rienner Publishers, 1986), 120.

26. John Breuilly, *Nationalism and the State* (Manchester, England: Manchester University Press, 1982), 3.

27. Appapillai Amirdhalingam, quoted in Jack David Eller, *From Culture to Ethnicity to Conflict* (Ann Arbor, University of Michigan Press, 1999), 123.

28. Aidan Southall, "The Illusion of Tribe," cited by Young, *Politics of Cultural Pluralism*, 19.

29. Milton Obote quoted in Donald Rothchild, "Hegemonial Exchange: An Alternative Model for Managing Conflict in Middle Africa," in *Ethnicity, Politics and Development*, eds. Dennis Thompson and Dov Ronen (Boulder, CO: Lynne Rienner, 1986), 77. Several scholars in that volume use the term *tribe* as does Cynthia Enloe's book, *Ethnic Conflict and Political Development.*

30. Pippa Norris and Robert Mates, "Does Ethnicity Determine Support for the Governing Party? The Structural and Attitudinal Basis of Partisan Identification in Twelve African Nations" (Cambridge, MA: Working Paper, Kennedy School of Government, Harvard University, 2003). The data analyzed came from the Afrobarometer surveys.

31. Charles W. Anderson, Fred R. von der Mehden, and Crawford Young, *Issues of Political Development*, 2nd ed. (Upper Saddle River, NJ: Prentice Hall, 1974), 21.

32. Cited in T. Walker Wallbank, *A Short History of India and Pakistan* (New York: Mentor, 1958), 196.

33. Latif Abul-Husn, *The Lebanese Conflict: Looking Inward* (Boulder, CO: Lynne Rienner

Publishers, 1998), 29–44; Carole H. Dagher, *Bringing Down the Walls: Lebanon's Postwar Challenge* (New York: St. Martin's Press, 2000).

34. Vali Nasr, *The Shi'a Revival: How Conflicts within Islam Will Shape the Future* (New York: W. W. Norton, 2006).

35. Robert Pape, Director of the University of Chicago's Project on Suicide Terrorism, quoted on "Spate of Suicide Bombings Threatens Iraq Surge," National Public Radio (NPR), *All Things Considered* (May 2, 2007). Sunni insurgents have also killed many American soldiers, but most of these have come from hidden roadside bombs, not suicide bombings.

36. Young, *Cultural Pluralism*, 65.

37. Bhikhu Parekh, *A New Politics of Identity* (New York: Palgrave, 2008), 199.

38. J. Isawa Elaigwu and Victor A. Olorunsola, "Federalism and the Politics of Compromise," in *State versus Ethnic Claims*, 282.

39. Arend Lijphart, *Democracy in Plural Societies* (New Haven, CT: Yale University Press, 1977), 25–40.

40. Ralph R. Premdas, "Secessionist Movements in Comparative Perspective," in *Secessionist Movements in Comparative Perspective*, eds. Ralph Premdas, S.W. R. de A. Samarasinghe and Alan B. Anderson (London: Pinter Publishers, 1990), 12.

41. Ibid., 14–16.

42. Daniel Patrick Moynihan, *Pandemonium: Ethnicity in International Politics* (Oxford, England and New York: Oxford University Press, 1993).

43. Gurr, *People versus States*, 276.

44. Samantha Power, "Bystander to Genocide," *The Atlantic Monthly*, vol. 288, no. 2 (September 2001), 84–108, www.theatlantic.com/doc/200109/power- genocide

45. Edward Luttwak, "If Bosnians Were Dolphins . . . ," *Commentary*, vol. 96 (October 1993), 27.

46. See, for example, Samantha Power, "Bystanders to Genocide"; Romeo Dallaire, *Shake Hands with the Devil: The Failure of Humanity in Rwanda* (Toronto: Random House Canada, 2003).

47. David Carment and Frank Harvey, *Using Force to Prevent Ethnic Violence* (Westport, CT: Praeger, 2001).

48. For example, Alan K. Kuperman, *The Limits of Humanitarian Intervention: Genocide in Rwanda*

(Washington, DC: Brookings Institution Press, 2001).

49. Nader Entessar, *Kurdish Ethnonationalism* (Boulder, CO: Lynne Rienner Publishers, 1992), 119–127. The Pike Commission of the U.S. House of Representatives revealed details of America's support for the abortive Kurdish revolt.

50. Glynne Evans, *Responding to Crises in the African Great Lakes* (New York: Oxford University Press, Adelphia Paper 33, 1997), 75.

51. Idean Salehyan, *Rebels Without Borders*, 86–87, 91. I took the total number of cases shown in Salehyan's Table and subtracted those "rebellions" that did not involve violence (over 70 percent of the 1,043 cases). This left 335 cases involving violence, 265 of which (79 percent) took place along an international border.

52. Human Rights Watch, *1993 Report on the Anfal*, http://hrw.org/reports/1993/iraqanfal/ANFAL1.htm, chap. 1, p. 3. Although the Geneva Protocol of 1925 banned chemical weapons, both sides used them in the Iraq–Iran war.

53. Phebe Marr, "Kurds and Arabs, Sunnis and Shiites: Can an Iraqi Identity be Salvaged?" in *Religion and Nationalism in Iraq*, eds. David Little and Donald K. Swearer (Cambridge, MA: Harvard University Press, 2006), 66.

54. Michael Ignatieff, "Afterward: Reflections on Coexistence," in *Imagine Coexistence: Restoring Humanity after Violent Ethnic Conflict*, eds. Antonia Chayes and Martha Minnow (San Francisco: Jossey-Bass, 2003), 325–333.

55. From *Politics in Plural Societies*, quoted in Larry Diamond and Marc F. Plattner, eds. *Nationalism, Ethnic Conflict, and Democracy* (Baltimore, MD: Johns Hopkins University Press, 1994), xix.

56. The quote comes from Claude Ake, "Why Humanitarian Emergencies Occur: Insights from the Interface of State, Democracy and Civil Society," *Research for Action*, vol. 31 (1997), 8.

57. Quoted in Robin Luckham, Anne Marie Goetz, and Mary Kaldor, "Democratic Institutions and Democratic Politics," in *Can Democracy Be Designed: The Politics of Institutional Choice in Conflict-Torn Societies*, eds. Sunil Bastian and Robin Luckham (London and New York: Zed Books, 2003), 43.

58. Gurr, *People versus States*, 152–163, 169, 204.

CHAPTER 5

WOMEN AND DEVELOPMENT

A Chinese adage observes that "Women hold up half the sky." Yet for many years, scholars, Third World governments, and Western development agencies appeared strangely oblivious to women's role in the modernization process. Most early studies of political and economic change in the LDCs said little or nothing about women's issues. In the past few decades, however, three factors have contributed to a new understanding of women in developing nations: the emergence of feminist or gender-related social science research; policy planners with heightened awareness of how women play a distinct and important role in political and economic development; and the growing political empowerment of women in many parts of the Third World. Like examinations of ethnicity and class, gender analysis provides a greater understanding of underdevelopment. Economic planners, for example, have found that women in the LDCs are concentrated in certain occupations and face barriers to entering others. Poorer women work primarily in agriculture, domestic service, or the semi-legal urban economy known as the "informal sector" (discussed below). Women who work in industry are disproportionately employed in labor-intensive, lower-wage industries such as apparel and electronics in the Far East and Southeast Asia or in assembly plants in Mexico and the Caribbean. Like their counterparts in developed nations, female professionals are overrepresented in such nurturing professions as nursing and teaching. A study of several major Asian and Latin American countries revealed that women made up roughly *half* of all professional and technical workers, but less than 20 percent of the administrative and managerial employees.[1] Distinctions between "women's work" and "men's work" have obvious economic and political implications, with women's jobs usually earning lower wages or salaries and wielding less power. At the same time, women are also greatly underrepresented in the political arena. Not only do they hold far fewer government posts than men do, but their share of those positions diminishes as one moves up the pyramid of power.

Although evidence of gender inequality and exploitation exists in most societies, the problems are more severe in many LDCs. In its most horrifying form, the list of injustices includes painful female genital mutilation (so-called "female circumcision") in parts of Africa; the sale of child brides for dowries in Bangladesh; wife beatings in Zambia and Peru; the murders of some 5,000 Indian women annually, committed by husbands who were dissatisfied with the size of their dowries; courts that condone "honor killings" of women suspected of extramarital relations; and economic deprivations that drive many women into prostitution, often involuntarily. Several years ago, a village tribal council in rural Pakistan found a 12-year-old boy guilty of having a sexual relationship with a higher-class woman (a relationship that government investigators later

133

concluded had never happened). As punishment for the boy's alleged behavior, the council ordered four of the woman's male relatives to gang-rape the boy's adult sister. Villagers did nothing to stop it. As it turned out, the trial was meant to intimidate and silence the young brother, who had been sodomized by members of the wealthy family. The event was so extreme that public pressure convinced the national government to pay the victim compensation of $8,200 and bring the perpetrators to trial.

More generally, however, ordinary rape, including gang rape, is widespread in Pakistan, especially in the province of Punjab where this incident took place, and is usually not reported to the authorities. Typically, a woman is raped every two hours in Pakistan (and gang-raped an average of once every four days in the state of Punjab), with only about a quarter of the cases reported to the police.[2] Until recently (2006), Pakistani law required a woman to produce four *male* witnesses to substantiate her claim of having been raped, an obviously impossible task in almost all situations. Worse yet, if she could not produce those witnesses, she could be charged with adultery. If convicted, she could be flogged, imprisoned, or, even, stoned to death. In one infamous case, 18-year-old Safia Bibi was raped by her employer. Because she was blind and unable to see or identify her rapist and because she was pregnant, she was convicted of adultery and sentenced to 30 lashes. Only after her case provoked international outrage did a Pakistani court acquit her.[3]

Although the West African nation of Guinea criminalized female circumcision in 1965, an act theoretically punishable by imprisonment for life or execution, not a single case came to trial for at least 40 years, and 99 percent of Guinean women continued to undergo this painful practice. Such nonenforcement is commonly the fate of women's rights legislation in Africa.[4] The persistence of such customs is complicated by the fact that so many women in these societies subscribe to these traditions. In Africa, the many older women who carry out those circumcisions support female genital mutilation. Despite the seemingly obvious, recurring repression of women in many Islamic societies (lower standing in the court system, less access to education, etc.), a Gallup poll of several thousand women in Pakistan and seven other Muslim nations in the Middle East and Asia revealed that the majority did not consider themselves oppressed and did not list gender discrimination among the most serious problems facing their country.[5]

Less chilling, but no less significant, examples of gender inequality in much of the developing world include divorce laws that greatly favor husbands; barriers to women seeking commercial credit for small businesses; the "double day" that working women typically face (coming home after a day's work and having to do most of the housework and child care); and restricted opportunities for women in government, the professions, and better-paid, blue-collar jobs.

But the study of women in the developing world is by no means confined to issues of inequality and victimization. After years of neglect, many international agencies and government planners have begun to recognize women's special status and particular needs in economic development projects. At the same time, increasing numbers of Third World women are refusing to be merely subjects who are victimized or "acted upon." Their political activity has ranged from the quiet subversion common to many oppressed groups to a more vigorous assertion of their political, economic, and social rights. A growing body of scholarly literature now focuses on women's *empowerment*. Throughout Latin America, for example, women have played a decisive role in independent, grassroots political organizations known as "new social movements (NSMs)," which have burst upon the scene since the 1970s. Focusing on gender issues, human rights, poverty, and a range of other concerns, NSMs have provided an important alternative to political parties, labor unions, and other mainstream political organizations that are typically dominated by men. Elsewhere, revolutionary movements in countries such as El Salvador, Nicaragua, and China have opened up opportunities for female activism and leadership that had not existed previously. In nations as diverse as Bangladesh, India, Nicaragua, Pakistan, Panama, and the Philippines, women have headed their national governments. And during the past 15 years, a growing number of developing countries have reserved seats for women in national, state, and local legislatures, while other nations have introduced gender quotas for those offices. Such measures have frequently increased the number of female political leaders dramatically. All of these aspects of female economic and political activity deserve our attention.

THE POLITICAL AND SOCIOECONOMIC STATUS OF THIRD WORLD WOMEN

One major problem in many LDCs is that women have far fewer educational opportunities and lower literacy rates than men. In the most extreme case, Afghanistan's Taliban government (1996–2001) prohibited females from attending school.* Because education and literacy significantly affect one's income, health, and political participation, an educational gender gap influences other important facets of political and economic life. We know, for example, that as average educational levels for women rise in a given LDC, birth rates and family size tend to decline.

Table 5.1 compares the literacy rates of men and women in the major regions of the Third World. Column 2 presents the overall adult literacy rate for each region. The next two columns indicate the literacy rate for each of the sexes, while the last column expresses the female literacy rate as a percentage of the male's. The larger the literacy differences between the sexes, the *lower* the percentage in the last column. That column reveals that countries in South and West Asia (including Afghanistan, Bangladesh, India, and Pakistan) have the greatest gender inequality in literacy, followed by the Arab states and sub-Saharan Africa.† In fact, in South and West Asia women are only 66 percent as likely as men to read and write. On the other hand, Latin America and the Caribbean have essentially eliminated this gender difference, while East Asia is only slightly behind them.

---

* Women also were prohibited from working outside the home even if the family had no male breadwinner.

† Note that the regions with the lowest literacy rates do not necessarily have the highest gender gap. For example, the Arab states have a higher literacy rate than sub-Saharan Africa, yet they have a larger gender gap.

TABLE 5.1   Women's Literacy Rates Compared to Men's (by Region)

Region	Adult Literacy Rate (%)	Female Adult Literacy Rate (%)	Male Adult Literacy Rate (%)	Female Literacy as a Percent of Male
Third World	79	70.2	83.6	84
Arab States	73	58.9	80.2	73
East Asia	91	88.1	95.2	93
Latin America and the Caribbean	90	89.5	91.1	98
South and West Asia	58	46.3	70.5	66
Sub-Saharan Africa	59	53.3	69.5	77

Source: World Bank, *World Development Report 2009*: *Reshaping Economic Geography*, Select World Development Indicators, Table 1, http://econ.worldbank.org.

Table 5.2 turns from regional literacy rates to a sample of countries representing those regions. In addition, for the sake of comparison, the table includes two developed nations, Australia and the United States. Both of those countries are nearly 100 percent literate and any gender inequality that may exist is negligible. What is more striking is how impressively some LDCs have narrowed the disparity between male and female literacy rates. In fact, as the last column indicates, South Korea and Argentina have achieved full equality between the sexes, while Mexico and China are not far behind. Even in Iran, a fundamentalist Islamic nation, the women's literacy rate has increased to 87 percent of the men's level. On the other hand, the literacy rate for women in Yemen is less than half the men's, and India and Nigeria also still have a substantial gender gap. These

TABLE 5.2   GDI and Comparative Gender Literacy Rates (by Country)

Country	GDI (Rank)	Female Adult Literacy Rate (%)	Male Adult Literacy Rate (%)	Female Literacy as a Percent of Male
Australia	.960 (2)	99.0	99.0	100[a]
United States	.937 (16)	99.0	99.0	100[a]
South Korea	.910 (26)	99.6	99.7	100
China	.776 (73)	86.5	91.1	95
India	.600 (113)	47.8	73.4	65
Argentina	.865 (36)	97.2	97.2	100
Mexico	.820 (51)	90.3	93.2	97
Nigeria	.456 (139)	60.1	78.2	77
Iran	.750 (84)	76.8	88.0	87
Yemen	.472 (136)	34.7	73.1	47

[a]Estimates

Source: UNDP, *Human Development Report 2007/2008*, Human Development Indicators, Table 28, http://hdr.undp.org/en/media/HDR_20072008_EN_Complete.pdf.

findings reinforce the data in Table 5.1, which show that Latin America has nearly achieved full gender equality in literacy, East Asia has a slightly larger disparity, while the Arab states, sub-Saharan Africa, and South Asia lag far behind.

Table 5.2 also presents each country's Gender Development Index (GDI), followed by its GDI world ranking in parenthesis. As we saw in Chapter 1, a country's Human Development Index (HDI) is a combined measure of its educational level, life expectancy, and income. As such, it is considered perhaps the best single indicator of a nation's quality of life. The GDI score in column 2 compares the *male* and *female HDIs* in each country. Like all indices of this kind, scores can theoretically range from .000 (absolute gender inequality) to 1.000 (total equality). The numbers in parenthesis indicate how that country's GDI compares to 138 other countries for which data is available. As column 2 reveals, Australia has the world's second highest GDI, the United States ranks 16th, and Nigeria 139th (the world's lowest known GDI). In other words, the difference between male and female living standards is relatively narrow in South Korea and Argentina, while it is quite broad in India and enormous in Yemen and Nigeria.

Finally, Table 5.3 offers data on women's economic and political power. The second column presents the Gender Empowerment Measure (GEM) for selected developed and less developed countries. The GEM is an index comparing women's income, share of professional, technical, managerial and administrative jobs, and share of parliamentary seats, relative to men. It is a widely used measure of women's influence and power in society. Again, the numbers in parentheses indicate how that country ranked in the world compared to other nations with GEM data. Note, however, that the U.N. was only able to collect the necessary data to construct a GEM for fewer than half of its members. Thus, Yemen's rank (93rd) put it last among countries for which there is data. As expected, more

TABLE 5.3   Measures of Gender Empowerment

Country	Gender Empowerment Measure (Rank)	Percentage of Members of Parliament (Lower House) who are Women	Average Women's Income as a Percent of Men's
Sweden	.906 (2)	47.0	81
United States	.762 (15)	17.0	63
Mexico	.589 (46)	23.2	39
Peru	.636 (32)	29.2	55
Namibia	.623 (36)	26.9	57
Rwanda	NA	56.3	74
South Korea	.510 (64)	13.7	40
Malaysia	.504 (65)	10.8	36
Saudi Arabia	.254 (92)	0.0	16
Yemen	.129 (93)	0.3	30

NA—no data available

Source: United Nations Development Programme (UNDP), *Human Development Report 2007/2008*, Human Development Indicators, Table 29, http//hdr.undp.org/en/media/HDR_20072008_EN_Complete.pdf; Inter-Parliamentary Union, *Women in National Parliaments* (2009), www.ipu.org.

modernized, economically advanced countries tend to have greater gender empowerment equality. Thus, as for almost any measure of women's status, Sweden, like the other Nordic countries (Denmark, Finland, Iceland, and Norway), has one of the world's highest scores. Its GEM of .906—second highest in the world—indicates that women are almost equally as empowered (economically and politically) as men are, a fact further supported by column 3, which shows that women have almost half the seats in parliament (47 percent). Yemen, on the other hand, has almost complete gender inequality (and virtually no female representation in parliament), while Saudi Arabia performed only a bit better. While these two countries are very different in many respects—Yemen is extremely poor and Saudi Arabia is far more affluent—both have traditional Muslim societies and rank at the bottom of the world's GEMs. Column 4 of Table 5.3 reveals that even in a highly egalitarian country such as Sweden, women earn only 81 percent as much as men do. The United States, where on average women earn only 63 percent as much as men, has greater income equality than most developing nations in the table, but less than Rwanda and only a bit ahead of Namibia and Peru.* In the most extreme income differential, Saudi women earn only about one-sixth (16 percent) as much as men do.

Some of the findings in Table 5.3 are particularly interesting or unexpected. Although American women rank well on measures of literacy and quality of life, their representation in Congress (column 3) remains low (17 percent) among developed nations and is much lower than several LDCs presented in the table—Mexico, Peru, Namibia, and, especially, Rwanda. In truth, of 190 countries in the world that presently have elected parliaments (or Congresses), the United States ranks only 72nd in the proportion of women's representation. Similarly, while South Korea has a high level of gender equality for literacy and human development (see Table 5.2), it fell to the bottom third of all countries that report a GEM (64th place). In short, while Korean women have achieved a high degree of equality in areas such as education, they are relatively excluded from positions of economic and political powers. Among the LDCs in the table, Saudi Arabia also underperforms. Although it has a rather high HDI (see Chapter 1) ranking in the top third of *all* nations, it still has the world's second lowest recorded GEM.

On the other hand, some of the least economically developed nations included in Table 5.3 are extreme *overachievers*. For example, Rwanda, a desperately poor country, has the world's highest percentage of women in parliament (56 percent). Similarly, Namibia, also a poor country, with a HDI in the bottom half of all nations, is almost in the top third of countries reporting GEMs.

Modernization and the Economic Status of Women

Modernization theory contrasts the egalitarian values of modern culture with the allegedly sexist perspectives of most traditional societies. Radical feminists, many of whom subscribe to dependency theory, counter that in many instances industrialization, urbanization, and the spread of world capitalism have

---

* Of course this only measures gender *equality*. Both American men and women obviously have far higher absolute incomes than Rwandans do.

widened the gender gap or otherwise disadvantaged women. Can we reconcile these opposing viewpoints? The evidence suggests that modernization positively affects women's status over the *long* run, but may be harmful in the short term. Without doubt, gender inequalities in education, literacy, income, and economic/ political influence tend to be less pronounced in developed nations than in the LDCs (see Tables 5.2–5.3). Economic growth eventually creates new opportunities for women. And expanded educational systems usually offer them additional opportunities while developing more egalitarian values and gender roles. For example, in seven of the eight fastest growing economies in East Asia, women have increased their share of the labor force, growing dramatically in four of them (Singapore, South Korea, Malaysia, and Indonesia). Elsewhere, high-growth LDCs have narrowed their gender disparities in education and literacy.

But the early stages of the transition to modernity often produce particular hardships for women. The discussion that follows focuses on the negative initial effects of economic growth, neoliberal economic reforms, and other elements of modernization. Policy makers and planners need to ameliorate these transition costs. However, that should not obscure the fact that, in the long term, modernization offers women the best hope for equality. The task, then, is to reduce the short-term pain and increase the likelihood of long-term gain.

Women in the Economy: Rural and Urban

It is in the comparatively more traditional countryside, rather than in more modern cities, where Third World women play the most vital economic role. The United Nations' Food and Agriculture Organization (FAO) has estimated that "women produce between 60 and 80 percent of the food in most developing countries."[6] Particularly in Africa, the percentage of farmers who are women has grown substantially in recent decades. In its article on "The Feminization of Agriculture," the FAO points out that "war, sickness and death from HIV/AIDS have reduced rural male populations (in that continent)." In both Asia and Africa, men are more likely than women to seek work for a period of time in urban centers or, in some cases, abroad.[7] But despite the predominance of female farming in most of the LDCs, Nici Nelson noted that for many years "too little attention ha[d] been given by researchers and administrators or planners to women and the roles they play in rural society." Even though male "heads of household" are increasingly employed off the family farm, leaving its cultiva- tion to their wives, government planners frequently cling to "the myth of the ever-present male head" while neglecting female farmers.[8]

In recent decades, however, international agencies and Third World governments have recognized women's role in rural development. For example, the United States Agency for International Development (USAID) established an office for Women in Development (WID) to better address women's needs in U.S. foreign aid projects. Many nongovernmental organizations (NGOs) are particularly involved in this issue. But, while development agencies have become more sensitive to the special problems of poor women in the LDCs, and while there have been many successful development projects that reflect this sensitivity, progress overall has been limited. The FAO laments the fact that "gender bias and gender blindness persist: farmers are still generally perceived as 'male' by policy makers, development planners, and agricultural service deliverers. For this reason, women find it more difficult than men to gain access to valuable resources such as land, credit and agricultural inputs, technology, extension, training and services that would enhance their production capacity."[9] And, one expert estimates that "two thirds of the poor in Asia [still] are women," with similar statistics in most of the developing world.[10]

During the past half-century in most developing countries, there has been an enormous population shift from the countryside to the cities (see Chapter 7). As we have noted, modernization theorists had expected that urbanization—often accompanied by increased industrialization, literacy, and exposure to the mass media—would offer women greater occupational and educational opportunities, thereby enhancing their status. In many Latin American nations, women have constituted the majority of the migrants to urban centers. But while many of them have benefited, a large portion has been left behind. Once arrived in the city, most women are only able to secure low-end jobs. Indeed, the most common type of employment among female migrants is domestic service, for which they generally earn the legal minimum wage or less. At one time, 25 percent of all women in the Mexican urban workforce were either maids in private homes or cleaning women in commercial establishments and hotels.[11] Another important source of employment is the so-called "informal sector"—including street vending, some small businesses, employment in "sweatshops," and doing "piece-work" at home for contractors. These activities are "unregulated by the institutions of society [most notably the state], in a legal and social environment in which similar activities are regulated" and taxed.* Of course, many men also work in this sector, but the majority of informal sector employees are women.[12] According to data compiled by the U.N.'s International Labor Organization (ILO), about two-thirds of the women in Third World cities work in the informal sector. They comprise some 30–90 percent of all street vendors (depending on the country) and 35–80 percent of all home-based workers.[13] Although some informal sector workers earn higher incomes than blue-collar laborers in the modern economy do, many others fall below the poverty line. Finally, in newly industrializing countries, women are often employed in low-wage manufacturing. Over time, as factories become more technologically sophisticated and as wages rise, the percentage of female employees in those firms tends to decline.[14]

East Asia's industrial boom since the 1980s has created many new jobs for women, particularly in labor-intensive industries such as apparel and electronics. Many of those firms prefer to hire young unmarried women for several reasons: the jobs frequently require manual dexterity, a skill that employers associate with women; because they are not the principal breadwinners in their families, young women are usually willing to work for lower wages; and, finally, Asian women are less likely to join unions or participate in strikes. During the late 1990s, Asia's economic crisis caused numerous plant closings and layoffs. Women were commonly the first fired because most employers believed that men needed their jobs in order to support their families. That crisis also forced

---

* That is, the informal sector engages in basically legal activities (not criminal operations) but evades tax collection, state labor and safety regulations, etc. In many LDCs, this sector includes 30–50 percent of the urban workforce (sometimes even more).

many poor and middle-class families to take their daughters out of school in order to save the costs of school uniforms, educational fees, and tuition. As a matter of fact, at the height of the crisis, Indonesian girls were six times more likely than boys to drop out of school before the fourth grade.[15] While the current, global economic crisis has so far impacted Asia less severely than the earlier crisis did, women and girls are again likely to be its greatest victims.

Because women in most developing regions tend to have fewer educational opportunities than men (see Table 5.1), their subsequent occupational opportunities are more limited as well. All too often, poverty and a lack of vocational skills force women into prostitution. Despite Thailand's economic boom since the mid-1960s, continuing rural poverty has driven many young female migrants into Bangkok's thriving "sex tourism" industry. One study of Manila (the Philippines) and Bangkok (Thailand) revealed that 7–9 percent of female employment in those two cities was "prostitution related."[16] Some desperately poor families in that region have sold young daughters to brothels or given them as collateral for loans. A study of Southeast Asia by the United Nations' ILO estimated that the number of sex workers in the mid-1990s was 140,000–230,000 in Indonesia, 43,000–142,000 in Malaysia, and 200,000–300,000 in Thailand, where the number of prostitutes grew from around 20,000 in the early 1970s to perhaps 200,000 in the 1980s. In the economically depressed Philippines, the situation was even worse as "the estimated 400,000–500,000 prostitutes in the country *approximated the number of its manufacturing workers* (italics added)." The situation worsened considerably during the Asian financial crisis of the late 1990s when many women employed in other areas of the economy needed to supplement their income: "the number of Southeast Asians earning a living directly or indirectly from prostitution—including waitresses, security guards, escort services, tour agencies—could easily [have] reached 'several millions.'"[17] Again, it is likely that prostitution has expanded once more during the current economic crisis. While some sex workers enter the trade voluntarily, others (including underage girls) do not. A 2001 State Department report on the status of women notes that a survey by a human rights NGO in Cambodia "found that 40 percent of women and girls who work as prostitutes do so voluntarily, while 60 percent have been forced to work as prostitutes or have been deceived into prostitution."[18] In the squatter settlements of Kenya's capital, Nairobi, impoverished women are rarely able to secure jobs in the economy's modern sector. Consequently, many of them have been employed in prostitution or the illegal brewing of beer.

While these studies document the severe problems that frequently accompany Third World modernization, it is important to recognize that long-term economic growth, most notably in East Asia, has improved the incomes of millions of other underprivileged women newly employed in the modern sector of the economy. This is particularly true in the countries where female educational opportunities also have improved. Among middle- and upper-class women, the advantages of higher-class status usually mitigate the educational and career disadvantages of being female. In Asia and Latin America, the number of woman professionals and businesswomen has increased rapidly in recent decades. At the university level as well, the gender gap has narrowed considerably. In Brazil, for example, the number of female university students has grown far more quickly than have the ranks of men.

And in some LDCs today—including, Muslim Kuwait—women university students outnumber men. Still, for now, "women [remain] vastly under-represented in government, business, political and social institutions."[19]

WOMEN AND POLITICS

Many of the same traditions and prejudices that have undermined women's social and economic positions have also disadvantaged them politically. In Latin America, for example, women won the right to vote substantially later than they did in industrialized democracies. Whereas the United States and most European democracies legalized female suffrage in the first two decades of the twentieth century, only 7 of 20 Latin American countries allowed women to vote before the close of World War II. Ecuador was the first nation in that region to extend the franchise (1929) and Paraguay the last (1961). In Africa and Asia, the situation was different. Because most of the countries in those regions did not become independent until the decades after World War II, when female suffrage was a universally accepted principle, women were normally enfranchised from the start of self-rule. However, Arab Gulf States such as Bahrain only enfranchised women in 2001, while Kuwait did it in 2005. Today, Third World women generally still vote at a lower rate than men, but that gender gap is narrowing.[20]

In many parts of Africa, Asia, and the Middle East, traditional cultural values have limited women's political participation and activism. Lower-income women generally have few educational opportunities, which effectively limit their level of political participation. Indeed, social class correlates particularly strongly with female political participation. In many LDCs, highly educated and westernized women, often born to elite families, are as likely to hold important political offices as are women in the West. For example, although the countries of the Indian subcontinent have some of the world's lowest levels of female literacy and empowerment, several of them—Bangladesh, India, Pakistan, and Sri Lanka have had women prime ministers. The first woman president of the United Nations General Assembly and the first female chair of the Security Council were both from Africa, rather than advanced, industrial countries.

Because the developing world encompasses so many cultural traditions, and because social change has impinged so differently on each nation's social classes and sectors, there are no simple generalizations about the way in which modernization has influenced women's political status. Modernization theory would lead us to expect that more socially and economically developed countries would be quicker to grant political rights to women. If we look at Latin America, however, we find little correlation between a country's literacy rate or per-capita income and the year in which it granted suffrage to women.[21] Thus, the spread of education alone does not guarantee women greater political equality. At the same time, governments of countries such as Rwanda, Mozambique, South Africa, Argentina, Costa Rica, and Cuba have made conscious efforts in recent times to change traditional values regarding gender. More recently, many countries have increased women's political representation by creating reserved seats and quotas for women in parliament (discussed below). This has given a number of developing countries a higher percentage of women MPs (members of Parliament) than many highly developed nations have. For example, the U.S. Congress has a lower proportion of women in its ranks than do the parliaments of 18 African countries and 16 nations in Latin America and the Caribbean.[22] Currently, eight countries have 40 percent or more female MPs, the world's highest share. Half of them are highly socioeconomically advanced nations (Sweden, Iceland, Finland, and the Netherlands), but four are LDCs (Rwanda, South Africa, Cuba, and Argentina).

Women's Political Activism at the Grass Roots

It may be that women exert the greatest influence on Third World politics when acting through grassroots organizations in their own neighborhoods and communities. Community-based groups afford them opportunities for participation and leadership normally absent at the national or regional level. For one thing, these organizations typically focus on issues that are of immediate importance to underprivileged women such as housing, health care, adequate diets, and education. Furthermore, neighborhood and village organizations are more accessible to poor women, who have no day care for their young children and usually cannot travel far from home. Hence, many women who have been excluded from mainstream political parties, interest groups, and government institutions are attracted to community groups because of their accessibility and their relevance to their own lives.

In recent decades, a range of grassroots organizations representing poor and middle-class women has emerged in much of the developing world. Some represent women exclusively, while others include members of both sexes but are led by women or contain women's wings. Jana Everett examined several Indian community organizations in urban and rural settings, finding important similarities and differences. Both urban and rural groups were initially led by politically experienced, middle-class women committed to organizing the poor. And in both locations, as low-income women became more involved in community activities, their political awareness, confidence, and assertiveness grew, stimulating, in turn, greater participation in the broader political system.[23]

But, the goals and tactics used by these groups varied. For example, Everett found that the rural, grassroots groups were more likely than urban organizations to stage demonstrations and other types of protest. They were also more prone to demand redistributive economic remedies such as land reform. In comparison, urban women's groups were generally more moderate in their goals and tactics. Armita Basu's study of female rural protests in the Indian state of Maharashtra also noted their militancy. In one case, when a woman villager complained that the local police had ignored her charges against a landlord who had beaten her severely, a crowd of 300 women and 150 men "smeared [the landlord's] face with cow dung . . . and paraded him through the surrounding villages."[24] The rural women's greater aggressiveness likely resulted from the more hostile political atmosphere they confronted. Because village political and economic elites are usually less willing than their urban counterparts to redress lower-class grievances through normal political channels, these women were forced to use more radical tactics.

Social movements often develop as a response to a specific crisis or danger. For example, the 1985 earthquake that destroyed large sections of Mexico City had a particularly devastating effect on the thousands of seamstresses in the city's apparel industry. The quake hit early in the morning when most residents had not yet left home for work. But seamstresses work longer hours, so many of them were already at their sewing machines when the earthquake occurred and were trapped under rubble at their places of employment. To their horror, some found that their employers were more interested in saving their sewing machines than in bringing out trapped workers. The clothing workers subsequently formed their own labor union led by women from their own ranks, independent of the government-affiliated federation to which most Mexican unions belong. With more honest leadership than is typically found in the Mexican labor movement, the new union not only has bargained with employers and the government for better working conditions but has also provided day care and related services for its members.

In Latin America, opposition to the authoritarian military governments that governed much of the region during the 1970s and 1980s was a major catalyst for grassroots political activity. In Argentina, Brazil, Chile, and Uruguay, military dictatorships suspended elections, banned leftist political parties and unions, and arrested, tortured, and killed many suspected "subversives." At the same time, a major debt crisis in the 1980s, coupled with harsh government economic remedies, produced the region's worst recession since the Great Depression of the 1930s and a precipitous decline in mass living standards. Women played an important role in antiauthoritarian social movements, which helped pave the way for the restoration of democracy in the 1980s and 1990s.

The women's movement incorporated three types of political organizations, all largely urban based. First were feminist groups, primarily consisting of middle-class women. They included many professionals who previously had been active in leftist political parties, but had become disillusioned by the left's disinterest in women's issues at that time. A second type, neighborhood organizations, represented women from the urban slums. In the face of the region's severe economic crisis, poor women organized self-help groups to run communal kitchens, infant nutrition centers, and other antipoverty activities. Though not initially highly politicized, many of these groups radicalized over time as they demanded more equitable distribution of state resources and the restoration of democracy. Finally, a third strand of the women's movement campaigned for human rights. Argentina's "Mothers of the Plaza de Mayo" regularly marched in defiance of government restrictions to demand an accounting of their missing children and grandchildren, who had disappeared at the hands of the police or armed forces. Responding to state-sponsored imprisonments, torture, and assassinations, women's groups in Brazil, Chile, and Uruguay also became a major component of the human rights movement. This was the most socially integrated branch of the women's movement, bringing together participants from the middle and working classes. In many cases, they also joined forces with other human rights activists in the Catholic Church and Christian Base Communities (Chapter 3).[25]

In the absence of democratic elections, grassroots movements such as tenants' associations offered the urban poor one of the only opportunities to pressure the government. In slums and shantytowns, radical priests, nuns, and parishioners—motivated by liberation theology—organized Christian Base Communities, which combined religious values with social activism. Leftist secular groups also helped to organize the poor. One study of neighborhood, grassroots organizations in Brazil's largest city, São Paulo, revealed that most members and leaders were women.[26] Typically, such organizations first focused on their rank-and-file's immediate economic needs—jobs, health care, and food—rather than feminist issues. Indeed, among their allies, many Church leaders were hostile to feminism and leftist groups were less concerned about gender issues than class conflict. In time, however, many poor women came to share "middle-class" feminist concerns regarding gender equality, domestic abuse, and aggressively macho behavior by male heads of households.

In the late 1970s, the third strand of the women's movement emerged: human rights groups protesting government repression. Progressive Catholic Church and political party activists often assumed leadership roles. Interestingly, this was one of the few instances in which women's organizations had an advantage over similar groups led by men. Because the military governments viewed women as inherently less political than men and, hence, less dangerous, they allowed women's human rights groups greater freedom than they gave other protest movements. Ironically, the restoration of democracy reduced the need for unity among the disparate wings of the women's movement. Furthermore, as female leaders and militants became increasingly involved in the restored democratic system, many of them lost their previously close ties to community groups representing the urban poor. Thus, ironically, the restoration of democracy demobilized many lower-income women and sometimes weakened their movements. More recently, however, the explosion of voluntary, nongovernmental organizations (NGOs) in developing areas worldwide has created new opportunities for women's grassroots political participation. As their name suggests, NGOs are issue-based organizations, independent of government control. Many try to influence public policy in areas such as democratization, human rights, women's rights, environmental protection, housing, health care, and education. Compared to the earlier social movements, NGOs are generally more specialized, more professionalized, better funded, and "more respectable." The best-known and financed groups operate internationally, including the Catholic Relief Services, Amnesty International, Greenpeace, and Oxfam. But most NGOs are limited to the local or, perhaps, national level, where many of them try to mobilize popular support and influence government policy. In India, for example, it is estimated that national or local NGOs number in the tens or likely hundreds of thousands. Throughout the Third World, NGOs have contributed enormously to the expansion of civil society, particularly in democratizing societies, where they often provide a political voice to otherwise powerless groups seeking reform. In countries such as Chile, Peru, India, and Thailand, they have helped expand women's political rights and economic opportunities.

Women as National Political Leaders

In political systems throughout the world (other than the Nordic nations), women are severely underrepresented in political leadership positions. The Third World is surely no exception. In the mid-1980s, for example, only 6 percent of Africa's national legislators and only 2 percent of its cabinet members were women. Despite dramatic gains since then, women remain greatly underrepresented in major government offices in most LDCs. Looking at the whole world a number of years ago, Elsa Chaney noted that "United Nations surveys repeatedly show that even in countries where women are active professionally, their level of responsibility as policy makers and planners [has usually been] low."[27] Furthermore, a disproportionate number of the women who *have* reached national leadership positions have been restricted to posts commonly associated with female qualities. For example, most of the African women who have held cabinet posts in the recent past served as ministers of education, women's affairs, health, or social welfare—areas traditionally believed to be suited for women's "nurturing role."[28]

An early study of Chilean and Peruvian female political leaders revealed a pattern common to much of Latin America. Female political leaders were forced to legitimize their activism outside the home by presenting themselves as *supermadres* ("supermothers") who were using their political position to nurture their constituents (their extended family). Argentina's legendary political leader, Eva Perón (Evita), had painted that image eloquently years earlier:

> In this great house of the Motherland [Argentina], I am just like any other woman in any other of the innumerable houses of my people. Just like all of them I rise early thinking about my husband and about my children . . . I so truly feel myself the mother of my people.[29]

Chaney's survey of 167 Chilean and Peruvian woman government officials showed that half of them felt that certain government posts (such as education and health) were more appropriate for women, while others should be held by men (finance and defense, for example). Only 13 percent of the women politicians interviewed believed that gender should be irrelevant.[30] Of course, it is not only in developing nations that women have generally been confined to political positions associated with gender stereotypes. Until the 1990s, female cabinet members in the United States usually presided over such departments as Labor, Education, and Health and Human Services. More recently, however, presidents Clinton, Bush, and Obama broke that mold by appointing (between the three of them) women as Attorney General, Secretary of State, Secretary of Homeland Security, and National Security Advisor, all previously male preserves. In the LDCs, a similarly groundbreaking appointment took place in 2002 when Michelle Bachelet was named Chile's Minister of Defense (she subsequently was elected Chile's first female president). Since that time, women have headed the defense ministry in several Latin American nations, including Argentina, Colombia, Uruguay, and a second time in Chile. Overall, in much of the developing world, the role of women in national politics has expanded tremendously in recent years, and their range of government positions has broadened.

Still, even today, female political leaders are constrained by a somewhat permeable "glass ceiling" that normally denies them the most important political posts. Thus, women are generally more likely to be elected to local or state legislatures than to the national parliament. In 1993, India passed a constitutional amendment reserving one-third of the seats in all local assemblies (village councils, etc.) for women. Since 1995, however, repeated efforts to extend that quota to the nation's parliament have failed.

At the same time, however, in Asia—especially South Asia—and to a much lesser extent in Latin America, a surprising number of women have risen to the top of the political ladder in recent decades. All three nations on the Indian subcontinent, as well as neighboring Sri Lanka, have been led by women prime ministers. The most prominent member of this group was Indira Gandhi, who served four terms as prime minister (1966–1977 and 1980–1984) and dominated Indian politics for 18 years, until her assassination in 1984, when she was succeeded by her son Rajiv. In 1998, Rajiv's widow (he was assassinated as well, in 1991), Sonia Gandhi, assumed the leadership of the Congress Party (the nation's most powerful party for most of the last 60 years). Six years later, she led the party back to power but declined the position of prime minister because of vehement opposition-party objections—objections unrelated to her being a woman, but rather to the fact that she was born and raised in Italy, still speaks Hindi somewhat haltingly, and is not a Hindu (she is Catholic).

In recent decades, women have served as prime ministers or presidents in Pakistan (Benazir Bhutto), Sri Lanka (Prime Minister Sirimavo Bandaranaike and her daughter, President Chandrika Kumaratunga), and Bangladesh (since 1991, two women, Begum Khaleda Zia and Sheikh Hasina Wajed, have alternated as prime minister for all but 3 years). Elsewhere in Asia, prominent female political leaders have included the Philippines' former president Corazón Aquino and its recently reelected president, Gloria Macapagal Arroyo; former Indonesian president Megawati Sukarnoputri; South Korean prime minister Han Myung Sook; and Burmese opposition leader Aung San Suu Kyi, winner of the 1991 Nobel Peace Prize.*

No other developing region matches Asia's array of women leaders, but Latin America and the Caribbean currently have three female, government heads—Argentine president Cristina Fernández de Kirchner, Chilean president Michelle Bachelet, and Haitian prime minister Michèle Pierre-Louis. Previous presidents in that region were Mireya Moscoso Rodríguez (Panama), Isabel Perón (Argentina), Violeta Chamorro (Nicaragua), Janet Jagan (Guyana), and Ertha Pascal-Trouillot (Haiti's provisional president). Other Western hemisphere nations with female prime ministers have included Bermuda, Bolivia, Dominica, Jamaica, and Peru.

In 2006, Ellen Johnson-Sirleaf became Africa's first popularly elected female president. Women have also briefly held the post of prime minister in Burundi, the Central African Republic, Rwanda, and Senegal. But they served as prime minister for 2 years or more in the Democratic Republic of São Tomé and Principe and in Mozambique. Yet, although several sub-Saharan African parliaments have among the highest percentage of women in the world (discussed below), that region has had far fewer woman heads of government or heads of state than either Asia or Latin America.

Several caveats must be raised regarding the political success of women leaders in Asia and Latin America. First, a number of them only served briefly

---

* San Suu Kyi rightfully should have been included in the list of Asian prime ministers because she led her party to a landslide victory in the 1990 national elections. But the results were annulled by the military and she has been under house arrest most of the time since then. For a constantly update list of women prime ministers worldwide, see "Women Prime Ministers," http://www.terra.es/personal2/monolith/00women3.htm.

as interim leaders. Second, most emerged from a tiny elite of highly educated, upper-class women in powerful families. Thus, they were not at all representative of women's societal status generally. For example, Pakistan's Benazir Bhutto and Burma's Aung San Suu Kyi were educated at Harvard and/or Oxford universities (Bhutto attended both). Corazón Aquino belonged to one of the Philippines' more powerful landowning families. Finally, many of the most influential women leaders, particularly in Asia, have been the widows, wives, or daughters of charismatic national leaders: Indira Gandhi was the daughter of India's legendary first prime minister, Jawaharlal Nehru; Aung San Suu Kyi's father was the founder of modern Burma (Myanmar); former Indonesian president Megawati Sukarnoputri is the daughter of President Sukarno, that country's first president and founding father; Filipino president Gloria Macapagal Arroyo's father had also been president; Benazir Bhutto's father preceded her as Pakistani prime minister. In Latin America and the Caribbean, government leaders Cristina Fernández de Kirchner (Argentina), Isabel Martínez de Perón (Argentina), Janet Jagan (Guyana), and Mireya Elisa Moscoso de Arias (Panama) were all the wives or widows of former presidents.

Indeed, a shocking number of female government leaders in the developing world, most notably in Asia, have been the widows (or daughters) of assassinated political leaders. Sri Lankan prime minister Sirimavo Bandaranaike was the widow of a slain prime minister, while that country's current president, Chandrika Kumaratunga, endured the political assassinations of both her father and her husband (30 years apart). Former president Corazón Aquino, hero of the Filipino democracy movement, was the widow of the assassinated opposition leader. Bangladesh's two long-standing female prime ministers are, respectively, the widow of a slain national president and the daughter of Bangladesh's founding father and first president. Benazir Bhutto's father, a former prime minister, was ousted by the Pakistani armed forces and then hung. In Myanmar, democracy leader Aung San Suu Kyi's father, General Aung San, was assassinated when she was a child. And in the Americas (Latin America and the Caribbean), former Nicaraguan president Violeta Chamorro was the widow of a famed newspaper editor whose assassination sparked the Nicaraguan Revolution.*

This does not imply that these women lacked political ability or leadership qualities. Indira Gandhi was recognized as one of the world's most accomplished political leaders, and Violeta Chamorro helped heal the wounds of her country's civil war. After Sri Lanka's Sirimavo Bandaranaike succeeded her assassinated husband as prime minister, she dominated that country's political system for the next three decades. Current Philippine president Gloria Macapagal Arroyo was an economics professor, finance minister, and vice president before becoming president.† Still, no matter how highly skilled they have been, most female

---

* Until the 1970s, the pattern for women in U.S. politics was actually somewhat similar. Prior to 1976, 73 percent of all female senators, 50 percent of the women ever to hold a seat in the House of Representatives, and almost all woman governors were the widows of men who had held those seats (though their husbands had not been assassinated). Since that time, that pattern has changed dramatically although at least one current U.S. Senator did succeed her husband after he died (Claire McCaskill of Missouri).

† On the other hand, some widows who succeed to leadership, such as Argentina's Isabel Perón, were far less capable.

political leaders in the LDCs, particularly in Asia, have been able to reach the top of their political system only as heirs to their fathers or husbands. For now, then, Third World women still find it difficult to gain influential political positions unless they were born into families of the political or economic elite.

Reserved Seats and Quotas: Female Representation in Parliament and the Cabinet

If we turn our attention from the most powerful political position (president or prime minister) to women's participation in Third World cabinets and national legislatures (hereafter referred to generically as "parliaments" even when they bear another name such as "congress"), we find a far more complex situation. Since women usually account for approximately half the national population, gender-neutral political systems would presumably produce a corresponding percentage of female representatives in these institutions. Yet today, despite years of impressive gains in many countries, women still constitute only about 18 percent of all MPs worldwide. As the second column in Table 5.4 indicates, only the five Nordic nations—where women hold more than 40 percent of the total parliamentary seats—comes close.* In less-developed regions, representation in the "lower house" of parliament (normally the most powerful chamber) varies. The Americas have the highest percentage of female representatives (21.8 percent), with sub-Saharan Africa and Asia close behind (both at about 18 percent). And the Arab states trail far behind with a mere 9.5 percent (Column 2).

We would expect women to hold a larger share of parliamentary seats in more modern and more educated countries. And to a certain extent, the

TABLE 5.4   The Proportion of Women in National Parliaments (Regional Averages)

Region	Single House or Lower House (%)	Upper House or Senate (%)	Both Houses Combined (%)
Nordic European[a] Countries	41.4	—	—
Europe excluding Nordic countries	19.3	19.4	19.3
The Americas[b]	21.8	20.2	21.5
Asia	18.0	16.5	17.8
Sub-Saharan Africa	18.1	21.4	18.5
Arab States	9.5	7.0	9.1

[a]The five Nordic countries have only a single chamber (House) in their parliaments.

[b]The IPU statistics on the Americas include the United States and Canada. I have removed data from those two countries in order to ascertain the statistics for Latin America and the Caribbean, which are the ones shown in this table.

Source: Inter-Parliamentary Union, *Women in National Parliaments* (February 28, 2009), www.ipu. org/.

---

* As noted previously, the Nordic countries are Denmark, Finland, Iceland, Norway, and Sweden.

statistics in this table confirm that belief. But, surprisingly, when we compare European nations *other than the Nordic countries* to sub-Saharan Africa and Asia (*excluding the Arab countries*), we find that percentages of women MPs are not that different. And national legislatures in the Americas have a slightly higher percentage of women than do non-Nordic, European parliaments. Furthermore, as we will see, since the early 1990s many Third World countries have equaled or surpassed highly developed nations through various affirmative action plans.

From 1996 to 2009, the number of women in parliament worldwide nearly doubled, from 10.1 to 18.4 percent. But despite this significant improvement, women remain severely underrepresented in most parts of the world. Several social, economic, and cultural factors help account for this. Pippa Norris and Joni Lovenduski argue that the number of women in elected office depends on various factors affecting "supply and demand."[31] Supply refers to the number of women who meet the typical socioeconomic standards of public officeholders in their country. Because Third World women in many LDCs have lower levels of education, lower status, and, most important, fewer economic resources—all factors closely related to political success—they are able to "supply" fewer viable candidates for office. In fact, Rae Lesser Blumberg's research in several regions of the world indicates that "the most important variable . . . affecting the level of [political] equality [or inequality] between men and women is economic power" as defined by their relative control over income and economic resources.[32] On the "demand" side (a measure of society's acceptance of female political leaders), widespread cultural prejudice in some regions against the empowerment of women, most notably in the Islamic world, has also restricted the number of women from holding public office.

In the past two decades, however, as women's educational levels have risen in most of the developing world, as they have entered the professions in greater numbers, and as cultural prejudices have diminished in many places, both the supply of and demand for women officeholders have increased. However, the most important change in recent years has come from the demand side—the introduction of gender-based quotas for parliament itself or for the lists of electoral candidates presented by competing political parties. Since 1991, the number of countries implementing such systems has skyrocketed and today about 100 countries, primarily in the Third World, have some form of quota system. While the alleged intent of all of those gender-based quotas is to enhance the number of women in parliament, we will see that some countries have made only token efforts and achieved few gains, while others have sharply increased the number of women in parliament. Latin America, though often associated with *machismo*, has been the world leader in effecting reform measures. Across that region, the number of female representatives has jumped from approximately 9 percent in 1997 to almost 22 percent in 2009 (a higher percentage than in Canada or the United States).

Legislated and voluntary attempts to raise the proportion of women in national parliaments have taken several forms. The most direct and certain method is to *reserve* a designated number of parliamentary seats for women. The basic justification for reserving seats is that because many cultures have deeply ingrained gender prejudices, the only way a significant number of women can gain office is by setting aside a bloc of seats for them. In fact, many of the reserved seats systems were introduced in Arab and other Muslim countries, where prejudices against women officeholders were generally strongest. However, at least initially, the number of seats reserved was small. Bangladesh's 1972 constitution only set aside some 5 percent of the seats in parliament exclusively for women. Jordan currently reserves less than 6 percent of the seats in its House of Deputies. In some cases, the number of reserved seats has been subsequently increased, sometimes more than once. Thus, for example, Bangladesh, which subsequently eliminated reserved seats for several years and then restored them, now sets aside 13 percent of parliamentary seats.

However, women's rights proponents have raised several objections to reserved seats. In many countries (though certainly not all), the number of reserved seats is very small. Although women are allowed to contest parliamentary seats beyond the number reserved for them, the use of reserved seats tends to signal voters that women have gotten their fair share and do not deserve to be elected beyond their guaranteed quota. Similarly, many political parties in more traditional societies have a similar attitude and see no need to include women in their regular slate of parliamentary candidates. In other words, in some cases, the number of reserved seats becomes a glass ceiling blocking further electoral gains. For example, in the 2007 Jordanian parliamentary election, only a single woman candidate won election to the country's 104 unreserved seats (she joined the 6 female MPs who had been allocated seats set aside for women).[33]

Second, initially in several countries, women were not elected to those reserved seats by the voters but rather were appointed. Since these appointments were determined by male-dominated institutions (such as political parties) or by a single male (the President of Kenya or the King of Jordan), they were not necessarily supported by women constituents. Appointed MPs also lacked the legitimacy and clout that electoral victories bring. Rarely do they become influential political leaders or effective advocates of women's causes.[34] Over time, however, a number of countries have switched from appointed reserve seats to elected ones. Furthermore, some countries, most notably in Africa, have set aside a substantial number of elected reserved seats for women, often with impressive results.

Finally in some countries women have been elected to a substantial number of seats beyond those set aside for them. Thus, in the East African nation of Rwanda, 30 percent of the seats (24 in all) in the Chamber of Deputies are reserved for women, who are elected directly by the voters. In the last parliamentary election (2008), women candidates were also elected to an additional 21 nondesignated seats—more than a quarter of the seats open to both male and female candidates. Together that gave women over 56 percent of all parliamentary seats, making it the world's only parliament in which women MPs are in the majority. In neighboring Uganda, 61 of 305 seats (20 percent) are set aside for women, while women also won 12 of the gender-neutral seats in the last parliamentary election (2006), bringing the total number of female MPs to 24 percent. Two of the most recent countries to introduce some form of gender quota are Afghanistan (an extremely conservative and religious Muslim country) and Iraq (also Muslim). In both cases, the United States had pressured the government to insert quota provisions in their new constitutions.

Another means of reducing gender underrepresentation is to establish quotas for the slates of parliamentary *candidates* in general elections. Quotas may take two forms. First, individual political parties may voluntarily guarantee that their slate of parliamentary candidates will contain a certain percentage of women. In Europe, for example, the first major gains in female parliamentary representation came in Scandinavia when that region's socialist parties (frequently the largest parties in their countries) agreed to gender quotas. In the Third World, the most successful example of voluntary quotas has been in South Africa's dominant party, the African National Congress (ANC).

The second type of candidate quota is legislated (or sometimes inserted into the national constitution) and is binding on all political parties. Both voluntary and legislated candidate quotas commit political parties to nominate a stipulated percentage of women candidates on their tickets. In most quota systems, parties must field a list of parliamentary candidates of whom a minimum of 30 percent must be women. That number reflects the "critical mass" of female MPs commonly needed to produce government policies friendly to women's interests. A dozen Latin American countries and a number of developing nations elsewhere passed some form of a gender candidate quota during the wave of democratic transitions in the 1990s.

The goal of quotas is purportedly to give women a greater opportunity to hold regularly elected seats rather than fill seats specially reserved for them. But candidate quotas, particularly when legislatively imposed, are frequently ineffective because their objective is easily circumvented if the major political parties end up nominating most of their women candidates for races that the party has little chance of winning. In electoral systems that choose a single legislative representative from each district (single-member districts or SMD—the method used to elect the U.S. House of Representatives and the British House of Commons), most electoral districts typically lean heavily toward one party or another. So political parties that want to satisfy the letter of the quota laws, but to circumvent their spirit, can simply nominate most of their women candidates in districts where they had little chance of winning. For example, imagine if the United States had a 30 percent gender quota for congressional candidates and if party leaders, rather than primary voters, selected candidates (primary elections exist in few countries outside the United States). If Democratic party chiefs (presumably mostly male) wanted to circumvent the goal of the quota law, they could nominate most of their 130 women congressional candidates (30 percent of the 435 House districts) in heavily Republican, "red states," such as Alabama or Utah, where they would almost always loose to their Republican opponents. Similarly, the Republicans could run almost exclusively male candidates in those states while fielding women candidates in Democratic strongholds such as Boston, New York, and San Francisco. While such a scenario would be totally unlikely in the United States, many of the major parties in France and Venezuela have made "end runs" on quota laws in the recent past.

While a number of Third World nations also elect their parliaments through an SMD electoral system—particularly former British colonies such as India, Jamaica, Nigeria, and Pakistan—others (like most Western European democracies) use an electoral system called proportional representation (PR). To understand how PR works, let us imagine a country with a 500-seat parliament divided into 25 electoral districts (assuming here that they have roughly equivalent populations), each of which elects 20 MPs. The national parties each nominate a "party list" of 20 candidates in each district, with candidates ranked from 1 through 20 (closed lists). Rather than select a single candidate, as American voters do when they cast their ballots for the House of Representatives, voters in PR elections choose an entire party list (i.e., the Christian Democratic Party list or the Socialist Party list of 20 candidates). Seats are then allocated in proportion to the percentage of votes that each list receives. Thus, if the Christian Democrats' list, for example, were to receive 40 percent of the votes in district 1, they would win 40 percent of the 20 seats in that district (i.e., eight seats). But which eight of that party's 20 listed candidates would go to parliament? It would be those who were ranked first through eight on the party's list prior to the election. If we further imagine that a quota law requires that at least 35 percent of each party's candidates be women (i.e., at least seven in each district), the number of women who actually are elected would still depend on where they had been *ranked* on the party list. Thus, even with the 35 percent quota requirement, all eight of that party's victorious candidates would still be men if all of the female candidates had been ranked in the bottom half of the party list.*

To put teeth into a legislated quota system and prevent dumping of women candidates into hopeless positions at the bottom of the party lists (in PR systems) or in districts (in SMD systems) that the party knows it cannot win, countries such as Argentina passed electoral laws requiring so-called *zipper-style quotas*. That means that each party must not only meet its quota of female candidates, but it must also alternate male and female candidates, according to that quota percentage from the top of the list downward. For example, if a country such as Argentina has a zipper-style gender quota of 33 percent, women candidates have to occupy every third position on the list from the top rank on down. So, if a party won 9 of the 30 seats in a PR multimember district, the 9 candidates becoming MPs would include 3 women.

In general, elections through zipper-style, proportional representation with closed lists (i.e., when voters cannot favor individual candidates on the list) benefit women candidates more than SMD elections do. Effective gender quotas are very difficult to enforce in a SMD system unless there are a large number of seats reserved for women.

Since 1991, the spread of legally mandated quotas, of whatever type, has been a major factor in the worldwide increase in female MPs. For example, in 10 Latin American countries that enacted quotas between 1991 and 1997, the number of women in parliament rose by an average of 8 percent in the very next national election.[35] However, results have been most impressive when electoral laws mandate zipper-style quotas or their equivalent. For example, when Costa Rica's Supreme Court strengthened that country's quota law by insisting that women be proportionally included in *competitive* races, the percentage of women in Congress rose from 19 percent in 1997 (already higher than in the U.S. Congress at that time) to 35 percent in 2002. Also, when the ANC took power in South Africa and voluntarily adopted a gender quota, the percentage of women MPs rose from 141st highest in the world in 1994 to 3rd highest in 2009.[†]

---

* Actually there are many varieties of PR elections. I have just described a simplified, generic version.

† The African National Congress is the only South African party to impose a gender quota. But since it holds some three-quarters of the seats in parliament, its quota obviously affects the nature of the entire legislature.

Ultimately, the issue of reserved seats and candidate quotas raises another fundamental question. How much difference does increased female representation have on government policy? The evidence suggests that legislatures with significantly higher female membership (in either LDCs or developed nations) are more prone to address issues such as gender bias, child care, education, and divorce law and are more likely to produce legislation in these areas that is beneficial to women. However, most analysts agree that even a substantial increase in female representation from a very low base—for example, tripling female representation in Arab parliaments from 3 percent (in 1997) to 9 percent (in 2007)—is ordinarily not enough to affect government policy on issues such as gender equality, rape, and children's health because there are still too few female MPs to influence policy. Indeed, when women hold fewer than 30 percent of parliamentary seats, they tend to be co-opted or are simply ineffective in pressing "women's issues." As female representation approaches that level, however, parliaments are more likely to pass "women-friendly" legislation. As of late 2009, there were 24 countries that had reached that threshold, 13 of them developing nations (7 in Africa, 5 in the Americas, and 1 in Asia).

While the percentage of women in parliament is a useful measure of their influence in national politics, their share of cabinet posts is perhaps more significant. Cabinet ministers normally operate at the center of political power and are among the nation's most influential government officials. Although women have held a relatively small percentage of ministerial posts in most countries (even lower than their share of parliamentary seats), their numbers have grown significantly over the past two decades. Between 1987 and 2004, the proportion of women ministers worldwide more than tripled, from a mere 3.4 to 11.3 percent.[36] That figure has continued to grow since that time, though women remain highly underrepresented in most national cabinets, especially in the LDCs. In general, European cabinets have greater female representation than their Third World counterparts, with three governments (Sweden, Spain, and France) recently fielding cabinets with equal numbers of women and men, without any quota system. However, from 2000 to 2006, the proportion of women ministers in Latin America grew from 14 to 21 percent, giving that region a level of female cabinet representation comparable to Western Europe and the United States. In fact, as of early 2007, women held 50 percent of the cabinet posts in Chile (appointed by a female president) and about 40 percent in Paraguay and Peru (a level also reached briefly in Colombia). Women are less well represented in Asian cabinets. For example, in Thailand, Pakistan, and Indonesia, they typically have held fewer than 5 percent of ministerial posts. And Arab nations trail far behind any other region, just as they did on GEMs, female literacy rates, and the proportion of women MPs.

Until recently, the types of cabinet posts occupied by women frequently conformed to gender stereotypes. In a 1999 study of 190 countries throughout the world, the Inter-Parliamentary Union found that women were Ministers of Women's Affairs in 25 percent of the countries. They also often headed the Ministries of Social Affairs (23 percent), Health (16 percent), Environment (15 percent), Family Affairs (14 percent), Labor (13 percent), Education, and Justice (both 12 percent)—mostly "nurturing positions." However, women held the following ministerial positions in fewer than 5 percent of the countries: Defense, Agriculture, and Science and Technology.[37] It appears that such gendering of cabinet positions has diminished somewhat since that time.

Earlier in this chapter, we noted the growing number of women prime ministers and presidents in the LDCs, most notably in South Asia. While we might assume that gains for women at the pinnacle of government would either reflect or cause broader political or socioeconomic advances for women generally—as they have, for example, in the Nordic countries—this has not necessarily been true in the LDCs. Sri Lanka and Bangladesh most glaringly demonstrate that point. Women have served for extended periods as Sri Lanka's president (11 years) and prime minister (18 years). Yet, they currently constitute less than six percent of that nation's MPs, one-third of the international average. Similarly, although Bangladesh has been led by a woman prime minister for 15 of the past 18 years, it still ranks in the bottom 20 percent of all nations with recorded GDI scores and in the bottom 15 percent of countries with recorded GEM scores.

Although electoral mechanisms such as quotas and reserved seats are the most important factors responsible for greater female representation in parliament, social, cultural, and historical forces also play a role. As a matter of fact, these factors help explain why a particular country introduces quotas or reserved seats in the first place. For example, in Scandinavia, the culture's strong emphasis on gender and class equality produced a very high number of female MPs even before the country's major parties adopted voluntary quotas. And it was that same societal commitment to gender equality that also led Norwegian and Swedish political parties to commit to such quotas. Denmark's parties abandoned gender quotas in 1996 (after enforcing them for nearly two decades), yet, even without the benefit of quotas, women currently hold 38 percent of their country's parliamentary seats, one of the world's highest percentages.

In Africa, many of the nations with parliamentary gender quotas are "post-conflict" states. That is to say, they are countries such as Mozambique, Namibia, and Rwanda, which had endured bloody civil wars. While South Africa did not have a civil war, it had experienced a long and difficult struggle for majority rule. All of those nations now have among the world's highest proportions of women MPs, ranging from 27 percent in Namibia to 56 percent in Rwanda. Although their past conflicts had produced enormous suffering and death, they also provided "new opportunities to articulate debate about gender politics as well as for individual women to live in a different way."[38] In countries such as South Africa, women played an important role in the liberation struggle, providing them greater access to the centers of political power. In countries such as Mozambique, Rwanda, and Uganda, where so many men had died in internal wars, women had to assume greater responsibilities at home and in their local villages and neighborhoods.

Women and Revolutionary Change

The political, economic, and social changes brought about by Third World revolutions often present women with rather unique opportunities. For one thing, revolutions tend to alter or destroy many of the traditional social structures and values that had previously held women back. When the communists came to power in China, for example, they eliminated the last vestiges of foot binding for young girls and prohibited the sale of women and girls as wives, concubines, or prostitutes. Elsewhere, many revolutionary armies and parties created new social structures that were more welcoming to women and offered them greater opportunities for upward mobility. For example, women held important military command positions in both the Nicaraguan Sandinista army and the Salvadorian FMLN during their guerrilla struggles. In South Africa and Namibia, many women now serving in parliament initially developed their political skills in their country's national liberation movement (respectively the ANC and SWAPO).

Because they need military recruits and are willing to put aside traditional gender roles, a number of revolutionary armed forces have included substantial numbers of female soldiers. For example, women constituted some 30 percent of the soldiers in the Eritrean People's Liberation Front (ELF), which engaged in a successful 30-year struggle for independence from Ethiopia.[39] Similarly, female guerilla fighters made up an estimated 20–30 percent of the Sandinista rebel forces in Nicaragua, perhaps 25 percent of Uruguay's Tupamaros, and a significant proportion of El Salvador's FMLN.[40] Because guerrilla armies usually assume a central political role when revolutionary parties take power, many female officers have moved into important political positions in the new government.

After the communist victory in China, Party Chairman Mao Zedong and the All-China Women's Federation assigned women an important role in rebuilding the nation's economy. Consequently, many Chinese women who previously had been confined to domestic roles entered the workforce, not because of any feminist agenda but because the government needed to reconstruct an economy devastated by almost four decades of war. But while women benefited from the opportunity to work outside the home, they generally were unable to attain the occupational equality that the government had promised. In both collective farms and urban industry, women tended to hold less-skilled, lower-paying jobs.

Radical regimes in countries such as China, Vietnam, and Cuba have tried to transform traditional cultural values through education and propaganda. Combating society's conventional restrictions on women has been a part of that process. But even revolutionary societies find it difficult to eradicate long-standing sexist attitudes. Although China's 1950 Marriage Law decreed that women could only wed of their own free will and also granted women equal rights within the family, enforcement of those provisions has been spotty, especially in rural areas. Since Mao's death (1976), the government's more pragmatic policies have stressed economic growth more than gender or social class equality. In recent years, as many state-owned factories have phased out guaranteed lifetime employment (the "iron rice bowl") in their search for higher productivity, women have most frequently been the first workers fired.

It is in the Chinese countryside, however, that one finds the most blatant remnants of sexist values as villagers have responded to stringent state policies aimed at controlling population growth in this nation of 1.4 billion people. Since the late 1970s, the government has limited most urban families to one child and rural families to two, denying them many government benefits if they exceed that number and sometimes requiring them to have abortions (though China has an overall abortion rate that is far lower than United States has because of rigorous family planning). Statistics on births indicate that the so-called "one-child policy" (again, two-thirds of the national population is rural and may have two children) has succeeded in lowering China's birth rate impressively, with the average fertility dropping from 2.9 children in 1979 (when the policy was introduced) to approximately 1.7 since 1995. But the policy has also had some disturbing unintended consequences. In 2007, the government announced that there were 119 registered male births the previous year for every 100 registered girls.[41] As the normal gender ratio worldwide is about 106 male births to 100 female, China's huge gender gap (the largest in the world) raises the question of what happened to "the missing girls."

Particularly in rural regions, where daughters are less valued than sons, many new-born girls are abandoned to orphanages, where they far exceed the number of boys. Because of the enormous overrepresentation of girls, more than 95 percent of Chinese children put up for foreign adoption are female. Since rural Chinese (and many urbanites) have a strong cultural and economic preference for sons, many parents opt for sex-selective abortions of female fetuses. And in some cases, newborn and young infant babies fall victim to infanticide, the murder of babies by parents who want their only child to be a boy (also called gendercide). It is impossible to know the frequency of gendercide and the topic has been the subject of heated debate. However, one recent, authoritative article indicates that the infanticide rate has dropped and the practice is now rare.[42] Although critics have blamed China's sex selection on its one-child policy and its authoritarian government, the evidence suggests that the main cause is a cultural preference for boys common to other Asian countries as well. Thus, Singapore, Taiwan, and Northern India—democracies or semidemocracies with no enforced limits on family size—all have almost the same sex ratio as China does. In recent years, the Chinese government has recognized the problems caused by the sex imbalance—including difficulties for young men hoping to get married and some kidnapping and trafficking of young women for marriage—and has taken steps to remedy it. These include a national propaganda campaign stressing the value of female children and a loosening of the family planning program. Cuba's revolutionary government has also tried to improve the status of women by changing traditional, sexist cultural values. In 1960, the Federation of Cuban Women (FMC) was created to mobilize women in support of the revolution and to give them a voice in the political process. Because Vilma Espín, the federation's leader from 1960 until her death in 2007, was married to President Fidel Castro's brother, Raúl (who assumed the presidency in 2008), the FMC had a direct line to the center of state power. Espín also had a distinguished career as a guerrilla officer in Cuba's revolutionary conflict. Officially representing 70 percent of Cuban women, the FMC encouraged its members to support the government and to enter the Cuban workforce. Thus, during the first decade of the revolutionary government, the proportion of women in the workforce rose from 17.8 to 30.9 percent, with even more impressive gains in the professions.[43] In the political arena, women have been particularly active in the neighborhood-based Committees for the Defense of the Revolution (CDRs). These Committees (to which some 80 percent of Cuban adults belong) promote revolutionary values, including gender equality. At their meetings, men who refuse to let their wives work or who do not put in their share of the housework sometimes find themselves criticized for machismo (perhaps by their own wives) and chastised by their peers for holding such unrevolutionary values. By the early 1980s, women represented half the local CDR leaders, 46 percent of the leaders of labor union locals, and 22 percent of the delegates to the National Assembly (the nation's congress).[44] Currently, 43 percent of congressional delegates are women, one of the highest rates in the world.

But revolutions are no panacea for women's problems. In many cases, radical rhetoric exceeds actual accomplishments. Like China, Cuba demonstrates that even egalitarian revolutions fail to achieve full gender equality. Thus, despite their prominence in local CDRs, labor unions, and the National Assembly, Cuban women have rarely penetrated the top ranks of national political leadership, such as the State Council (the equivalent of the national cabinet) or the Communist Party's Central Committee and Politburo. Because the National Assembly routinely passes all policy proposals from the Communist Party, it is in the party's leadership that real power lies. An analysis in the early 1980s showed that only 8.9 percent of Central Committee members were female.[45] Cuba's Family Code (the law governing family relations), passed decades ago, requires both spouses to contribute equally to domestic chores (child care, cooking, cleaning, etc.). While almost all Cuban men claim to subscribe to its regulations, most of them fail to contribute their fair share of housework. Change has been limited by ingrained male attitudes (*machismo*) and by most women's understandable reluctance to complain to their neighbors in the local CDR about their husband's noncompliance with the Code. As one observer noted, "It must take an extremely confident woman to bring her husband to public censure for failure to honor the code."[46] As in other revolutionary societies, traditional cultural values concerning gender roles have been hard to change.

THE STATUS OF WOMEN: THE ROLES OF MODERNIZATION, GLOBALIZATION, AND REGIME TYPE

Our discussion has revealed that the political and economic status of Third World women varies considerably from region to region and from country to country. Three factors are particularly influential: a country's dominant cultural values, its level of socioeconomic modernization, and its type of political system.

A nation's or region's culture—including its religious values—sets baseline boundaries for most women, affecting the opportunities available to them and the restrictions they face. This is most obvious in fundamentalist Islamist countries such as Afghanistan, Iran, Sudan, and Saudi Arabia. The Taliban government prohibited women from working or studying outside the household and largely confined them to their homes. These restrictions imposed particular hardships on the country's large number of war widows, who were not allowed to support their families even by begging. At the same time, these measures also deprived the country—one of the world's poorest—of badly needed teachers and health care workers. While educational and professional opportunities exist for the female elite in Saudi Arabia, most Saudi women are marginalized from the mainstream of political, social, and economic life. And, even women professionals in Saudi Arabia are barred from activities such as driving a car. Political leadership in all these fundamentalist countries is an exclusively male preserve. Cultural restraints are more subtle in East Asia, but even in modern societies such as Taiwan and South Korea women are underrepresented in the business world and in politics.

Yet, despite these religious and cultural restrictions, women have made some notable gains, sometimes in surprising places. In Algeria, where a 1992 military coup had headed off an expected Islamist election victory, the resulting civil war between fundamentalist militias and the armed forces (1992–2002) caused an estimated 100,000–150,000 deaths. Many Algerians (particularly men) migrated to Europe, leaving the country with serious labor shortages. Driven more by necessity and opportunity than by any government plan, women filled many of the openings. Today, women make up 70 percent of Algeria's lawyers, 60 percent of its university students, and most of the country's doctors. In all, they still represent only 20 percent of the nation's workforce, but that is twice as high as it was 20–25 years ago.[47]

Contrary to modernization theory, but true to radical feminist analysis, socioeconomic modernization has often adversely affected women in the LDCs in the short-to-medium term. In Africa, for example, the commercialization and mechanization of agriculture have benefited male cultivators disproportionately, frequently at the expense of women farmers. In East and Southeast Asia, rapid industrialization based on cheap labor has given many female laborers higher wages than they earned in their previous jobs, but has exploited many others. Yet, while modernization may initially harm many poor women, its longer-term effects are generally positive. A growing middle class, wider educational opportunities, and higher rates of literacy make women more aware of their rights and opportunities, while increasing their capacity to defend these gains. Socioeconomic development also tends to create more egalitarian values within society. It is not coincidental that the more modernized nations of Latin America—including Argentina, Chile, Mexico, and Uruguay—have the largest number of female political leaders and professionals, just as the most economically advanced nations of Europe generally have the greatest opportunities for women.

In recent decades, the feminist movement has spread from the world's economically advanced democracies into the Third World through the media and the demonstration effect. In many developing nations, women's rights movements have emerged where none had existed, or were even conceivable, a decade or two earlier. Educated women in more traditional countries, such as Bolivia and Jordan, are frequently influenced by the women's movements in more progressive, neighboring nations such as Chile and Lebanon. However, these new movements generally have taken on a distinct character, distinguishing them from Western feminism. The women's movement was born in the Western world only 40–50 years ago, and one can only speculate about its possible influence in the developing world three decades from now.

Finally, the status of women is shaped by the type of political regime and economic system prevailing in a country at a particular time. Women tend to fare more poorly under right-wing, authoritarian military regimes, such as those that dominated much of South America in the 1970s and early 1980s, and they seem to benefit most from revolutionary or democratic leftist regimes. Thus, for example, in countries such as Chile (like Sweden, Spain, and Norway), socialist and social democratic political parties have taken the lead in promoting increased female political representation. Many radical regimes—ideologically committed to equality in general—have championed women's rights. However, while revolutionary change in countries such as China, Vietnam, Cuba, and Nicaragua benefited women in many ways, significant gender inequalities have persisted. Sometimes, that inequality simply reflects the resiliency of deeply entrenched cultural values or continued male dominance of the political system. Frequently, it is also linked to the Marxist belief that all societal inequalities—whether related to gender, race, or religion—are derived from class divisions. That article of faith has caused regimes such as Cuba's to underestimate gender-related problems by erroneously assuming that the destruction of capitalism had, by itself, undermined gender discrimination.

Given that full gender equality does not exist even in the most advanced industrialized democracies (only small, mostly Nordic, northern European democracies come close), it seems unlikely that socioeconomic modernization or the spread of democratic norms will automatically bring gender equality to the developing world. Future economic development can be expected to produce both negative and positive consequences. In the short run, economic modernization, particularly in agriculture, will likely harm many low-income women. In countries suffering severe economic downturns, such as the current global financial crisis, or those experiencing civil conflict, women will doubtless continue to bear a disproportionate share of the burden. And the spread of Islamic fundamentalism in many parts of the Middle East and Africa does not bode well for women's rights in those nations. In the long term, however, economic modernization, higher educational levels, and modern values seem to offer Third World women their best hope.

CONCLUSION: DEMOCRACY AND THE ROLE OF WOMEN IN SOCIETY

Because democratic ideology endorses equal opportunity and equal rights for *all* citizens, we might expect the Third Wave of democracy to have advanced gender equity. Yet our discussion of revolutionary societies revealed that some nondemocratic governments have promoted women's rights more effectively than comparable democracies have. Many revolutionary regimes have established quotas for female participation in the national legislature, improved the legal status of women, banned oppressive traditional customs, and, to some degree, infused respect for women's rights into the new political culture. Consequently, there is much evidence that revolutionary governments in China, Cuba, and Mozambique advanced the cause of gender equality more successfully than the democratic governments of Brazil or India. It is also true that the Eastern European transition from Communism to democracy brought a precipitous drop in the percentage of women elected to parliament.[48] But most authoritarian governments are neither radical nor committed to women's rights. Women's right have fared poorly under both religious fundamentalist regimes and right-wing, military dictatorships.

How did women's groups influence the wave of democratization that swept through the developing world in the closing decades of the twentieth century, and how did the emergence of democracy affect women's economic and political standing? In a number of Asian and Latin American nations, women's social movements helped topple repressive regimes. For example, mass demonstrations by Indonesian women's groups in 1998 contributed to the fall of the Suharto dictatorship. As we have seen, women played an important role in the struggle for democracy in several Latin American countries. Often they were able to demonstrate for change in the streets when men could not.

Yet, the return to center stage of male-dominated political parties and interests groups during the subsequent democratic transitions tended to marginalize the grassroots political groups and NGOs in which women had played a major role. Thus, as Marta Htun has observed, the restoration of democracy had contradictory effects on women's political participation:

> The return to civilian rule and the consolidation of democratic governance created many more opportunities for women to be politically active, but also reduced the comparative advantage of gender-specific organizations as conduits for social demands. As a result, many women who had entered politics during the struggle against authoritarian rule left gender-specific organizations for political parties and other "traditional" organizations like labor unions.[49]

Bang-Soon L. Yoon has examined the effects of democratization on gender politics in South Korea. There, too, women had played an important role in the mass protests against the military government, working particularly through their labor unions. The transition to democracy in the late 1980s failed to raise the comparatively small percentage of women in the National Assembly, judiciary, and bureaucracy. But, on the other hand, spurred to action by emerging women's groups, the South Korean National Assembly enacted legislation on equal employment, child care, the prevention of family violence, and protection from domestic violence.

We have noted that some authoritarian regimes (such as Cuba) have made gender equality an important component of their domestic platform, while others have enforced a system of sexual inequality (Saudi Arabia). Similarly, some Third World democracies have a strong record regarding women's rights and equity (Argentina), while others have performed more poorly (Brazil). While the transition to democracy may not lead to immediate gains for women, and while there may even be some initial setbacks, in time democratic governments generally better advance women's rights and opportunities, particularly when democracy is coupled with social and economic development.

In order to systematically compare democratic and authoritarian governments in the Third World, we examine how each regime type performs on two important indices of gender equality—women's empowerment and women's living standards. The first indicator is the Gender Empowerment Measure (GEM). As discussed earlier in this chapter, this index compares women's economic and political empowerment with men's. The second indicator is the Gender-Related Development Index (GDI), which compares male and female school enrollment, literacy, life expectancy, and per-capita income.

Tables 5.5 and 5.6 examine the relationship between the degree of democracy in developing nations and their GEM and GDI rankings. The number of countries included in Table 5.5 is limited because GEM data is unavailable in so many LDCs, especially the poorest ones. We divided the 50 countries that had reported GEM scores into three groups of roughly the same size: those with the highest GEMs (18 cases in all), those with medium GEMs (16) and those with the lowest scores (16). They were also divided according to their degree of democracy, based on their Freedom House scores (see Chapter 2): 21 of them were Fully Free (liberal democracies), 17 were Partly Free, and 12 were Not Free

TABLE 5.5   Gender Empowerment: Democratic and Nondemocratic LDCs Compared

Degree of Women's Empowerment	Free (Liberal Democracies) Percent (Number of Cases)	Partly Free Percent (Number)	Not Free Percent (Number)
High GEM	48 (10)	29 (5)	25 (3)
Medium GEM	43 (9)	29 (5)	17 (2)
Low GEM	9 (2)	41 (7)	58 (7)

Source: Data are extrapolated from United Nations Development Programme (UNDP), *Human Development Report 2007/2008*, Human Development Indicators, Table 29, http://hdr.undp.org/en/media/HDR_20072008_EN_Complete.pdf; Freedom House, *Freedom in the World 2009*, http://www.freedomhouse.org./template.cfm?page=445

(authoritarian). The table reveals that the liberal democracies (Fully Free) had the highest share of countries with high GEMs (48 percent) and the lowest percentage of countries with low GEMs (9 percent). Conversely, the authoritarian nations (Not Free) had the poorest GEM performances—only 25 percent had high GEMs, while 58 percent fell into the lowest category. The partially free countries fell somewhere in between, but closer to the authoritarian cases.

The number of developing nations reporting GDI scores (96) was nearly twice as high. But like the GEM, democratic governments were clearly associated with higher GDI scores (Table 5.6), although the relationship was a bit less clear. Democracies were most likely to have high GDI scores (52 percent) and least likely to have a low GDI (only 6 percent). But, unlike the GEM cores in Table 5.5, authoritarian countries had higher GDI ratings than partly free nations did.

While they are insufficient to establish a causal relationship, both tables suggest that democracies promote gender equality more effectively than authoritarian regimes do. This seems logical since women's groups are able to mobilize politically, lobby government officials, and otherwise voice their concerns through democratic channels. At the same time, advocacy groups are more likely to be heard by a free press and by politicians who want to be reelected. To be sure, there are authoritarian regimes that have successfully put their

TABLE 5.6   Development Index: Democratic and Nondemocratic LDCs Compared

Degree of Gender Equality : Human Development	Free (Liberal Democracies) Percent (Number of Cases)	Partly Free Percent (Number)	Not Free Percent (Number)
High GDI	52 (16)	21 (9)	36 (8)
Medium GDI	42 (13)	28 (12)	36 (8)
Low GDI	6 (2)	51 (22)	28 (6)

Source: Data are extrapolated from United Nations Development Programme (UNDP), *Human Development Report 2007/2008*, Human Development Indicators, Table 28, http://hdr.undp.org/en/media/HDR_20072008_EN_Complete.pdf; Freedom House, *Freedom in the World 2009*, http://www.freedomhouse.org./template.cfm?page=445

power behind greater gender equality. The Cuban government has a good record of promoting women's rights and opportunities. For example, the number of women in the workforce has increased sharply since the revolution and, as we have seen, husbands are legally required to share domestic obligations equally with their wives. Yet in authoritarian governments, women's rights depend on the will of the (heavily male) political leadership. As the two tables indicate, in most authoritarian governments that will is lacking.

DISCUSSION QUESTIONS

1. Had Hillary Clinton been elected U.S. president in 2008, how much of an effect do you think that would have had on women's rights and opportunities in this country? Have Third World countries with women prime ministers or presidents made greater progress toward gender equality? What might explain why some governments headed by women made greater progress on "women's issues," while others did not?
2. Consulting with the UNDP Web site at http://www.undp.org enables you to compare a country's HDI score and its Gender Empowerment Measure (GEM) score. What relationship does there seem to be between those two scores? Identify several countries that have wide discrepancies (in either direction) between their HDI and GEM and offer your best explanation for these wide differences.
3. What are some of the reasons (hopefully including some not mentioned in the chapter) that democracy seems to contribute to greater gender equality? Under what circumstances might greater democracy ends up *diminishing* women's rights in some countries?

NOTES

1. United Nations Development Programme data cited in Jennifer L. Troutner and Peter H. Smith, "Empowering Women: Agency, Structure, and Comparative Perspective," in *Promises of Empowerment: Women in Asia and Latin America*, eds. Peter H. Smith, Jennifer L. Troutner, and Christine Hünefeldt (Lanham, MD: Rowman & Littlefield Publishers, 2004), 26.

2. *New York Times*, July 6 and July 17, 2002.

3. *New York Times*, "Vendetta Rapes Continues as Pakistan Resists Change" (October 14, 2006 and November 16, 2006); Human Rights Watch, "Discrimination under the Hudood Law," http://www.hrw.org/about/projects/womre/General-90.htm.

4. *New York Times*, "Women's Rights Laws and African Custom Clash" (December 20, 2005).

5. *New York Times*, "Muslim Women Don't See Themselves as Oppressed, Survey Shows" (June 8, 2006).

6. FAO, "Gender and Food Security: Agriculture," http://www.fao.org/Gender/en/agri-e.htm.

7. FAO, "The Feminization of Agriculture," http://www.fao.org/Gender/en/agrib2-e.htm.

LDCs with particularly high migration rates include Mexico, El Salvador, and Guatemala (migrating to the U.S.), as well as Algeria, Morocco, and Tunisia (migrating to Europe).

8. Nici Nelson, *Why Has Development Neglected Rural Women?* (Oxford, England: Pergamon Press, 1979), 4 and 45–47.

9. FAO, "Gender and Food Security."

10. Mandy Woodhouse, "Gender Mainstreaming into Poverty Reductions Strategies" (Siem Reap, Cambodia: Paper presented at a 2003 conference on Gender and Poverty Reduction Strategies).

11. Gloria González Salazar, "Participation of Women in the Mexican Labor Force," in *Sex and Class in Latin America*, eds. June Nash and Helen I. Safa (New York: J. F. Bergin Publishers, 1980), 187.

12. Manuel Castells and Alejandro Portes, "World Underneath: The Origins, Dynamics and Effects of the Informal Economy," in *The Informal Economy: Studies in Advanced and Developing Economies*, eds. Alejandro Portes, Manuel Castells, and Lauren A. Benton (Baltimore, MD: The Johns Hopkins University Press, 1989).

13. Ruth Pearson, "Reassessing Paid Work and Women's Employment: Lessons from the Global

Economy," in *Feminisms in Development*, ed. Andrea Cornwall, Elizabeth Harrison, and Ann Whitehead (London: Zed Books, 2007), 202–203.

14. Heleieth I. B. Saffioti, "Technological Change in Brazil: Its Effect on Men and Women in Two Firms," in *Women and Change in Latin America*, eds. June Nash and Helen I. Safa (South Hadley, MA: Bergin & Garvey Publishers, 1985), 110–111.

15. *New York Times*, June 11, 1998.

16. Cited in Alan Gilbert and Josef Gugler, *Cities, Poverty and Development: Urbanization in the Third World*, 2nd ed. (New York: Oxford University Press, 1992), 104, fn. 29.

17. Johanna Son, "South-east Asia: Sex Industry Thrives, But States Look Away," *InterPress News Service* (IPS) (August 19, 1998), which draws on the recent ILO study. http://www.aegis.com/news/ips/1998/IP980803.html.

18. *Women and Human Rights*—U.S. Department of State report (released by the Bureau of Democracy, Human Rights and Labor, U.S. Department of State, February 2001).

19. Sonia Nunes Jorge, "Gender-Aware Guidelines for Policy-Making and Regulatory Agencies" (Geneva: ITU Telecommunication Development Bureau Task Force on Gender Issues, 2001), 1.

20. World Bank, *Engendering Development*, 57.

21. Jaquette, "Female Political Participation," 223.

22. Unless otherwise cited, all of this chapter's statistics on the number of women in the world's parliaments come from two Web sites, which are frequently updated throughout the year: the Inter-Parliamentary Union, *Women in National Parliaments*, www.ipu.org; and IDEA (the International Institute for Democracy and Electoral Assistance), *Global Database of Quotas for Women*, http://www.quotaproject.org/.

23. Jana Everett, "Incorporation versus Conflict: Lower Class Women, Collective Action, and the State in India," in *Women, the State and Development*, eds. Sue Ellen M. Charlton, Jana Everett, and Kathleen Staudt (Albany: State University of New York Press, 1989), 163.

24. Armita Basu, *Two Faces of Protest: Contrasting Modes of Women's Activism* (Berkeley: University of California Press, 1992), 3.

25. Jane S. Jaquette, "Introduction," in *The Women's Movement in Latin America: Feminism and the Transition to Democracy*, ed. Jane S. Jaquette (Boston: Unwin Hyman, 1989), 6. This section draws heavily on Jaquette's book and Sonia Alvarez, *Engendering Democracy in Brazil* (Princeton, NJ: Princeton University Press, 1990).

26. Teresa Pires de Rio Caldeira, "Women, Daily Life and Politics," in *Women and Social Change in Latin America*, ed. Elizabeth Jelin (London: Zed Books, 1990), 47–79.

27. Elsa M. Chaney, *Supermadre: Women in Politics in Latin America* (Austin: University of Texas Press, 1979), 4.

28. Jane L. Parpart and Kathleen A. Staudt, "Women and the State in Africa," in *Women and the State in Africa*, eds. Parpart and Staudt (Boulder, CO: Lynne Rienner Publishers, 1989), 8.

29. Chaney, *Supermadre*, 21.

30. Ibid., 141.

31. Pippa Norris and Joni Lovenduski, *Political Recruitment: Gender, Race and Class in the British Parliament* (Cambridge, England: Cambridge University Press, 1994).

32. Rae Lesser Blumberg, "Climbing the Pyramids of Power: Alternative Routes to Women's Empowerment and Activism," in *Promises of Empowerment*, 60.

33. All of the data on reserved seats comes from the previously cited *Global Data Base of Quotas for Women*.

34. Pamela Marie Paxton and Melanie M. Hughes, *Women, Politics, and Power: A Global Perspective* (Los Angeles: Pine Forest Press, 2007), 161–162.

35. Mala Htun, "Women and Democracy," in *Constructing Democratic Governance in Latin America*, eds. Jorge L. Domínguez and Michael Shifter (Baltimore, MD: The Johns Hopkins University Press, 2003), 122.

36. 2004 Global Summit of Women Report: *Women in [sic!] Leaders Worldwide* (June 2004), http://www.globewomen.com/summit/2004/GSW2004Report.htm.

37. Cited in Maria Escobar-Lemmon and Michelle M. Taylor-Robinson, "Women Ministers in Latin American Government: When, Where, and Why" (paper presented at the conference on Pathways to Power: Political Recruitment and Democracy in Latin America, Clemson University, 2004), 2.

38. Donna Pankhurst, "Women and Politics in Africa: The Case of Uganda," in *Women, Politics, and Change*, ed. Karen Ross (Oxford, England: Oxford University Press, 2002), 127.

39. National Union of Eritrean Women, "Women and Revolution in Eritrea," in *Third World: Second Sex*, ed. Miranda Davis (London: Zed Press, 1983), 114.

40. *Envio* (Managua) 6, p. 78, quoted in Mary Stead, "Women, War and Underdevelopment in Nicaragua," *Women, Development and Survival*, 53; Vicky Randall, *Women and Politics: An International Perspective*, 2nd ed. (Chicago: University of Chicago Press, 1987), 61.

41. *New York Times* (January 12, 2007).

42. Therese Hesketh, Ph.D., Li Lu, M.D., and Zhu Wei Xing, "The Effect of China's One-Child Family Policy after 25 Years," *The New England Journal of Medicine*, vol. 353, no. 11 (September 12, 2005), 1171–1176, http://content.nejm.org/cgi/content/full/353/11/117.

43. Isabel Larguia and John Domoulin, "Women's Equality in the Cuban Revolution," in *Women and Change in Latin America*, 344, 363.

44. Ibid., 360. For two contrasting views on women in Cuba, see Lois M. Smith and Alfred Padula, "The Cuban Family in the 1980s," in *Transformation and Struggle: Cuba Faces the 1990s*, eds. Sandor Halebsky and John M. Kirk (New

York: Praeger, 1990), 176–188; and Julie Marie Bunck, "The Cuban Revolution and Women's Rights," in *Cuban Communism*, ed. Irving Louis Horowitz, 7th ed. (New Brunswick, NJ: Transaction Publishers, 1989), 443–465.

45. Randall, *Women and Politics*, 103.

46. Johnetta Cole, "Women in Cuba," in *Comparative Perspectives of Third World Women*, 176.

47. *New York Times*, "A Quiet Revolution in Algeria: Gains by Women" (May 26, 2007).

48. World Bank, *Engendering Development*, 58.

49. Htun, "Women and Democracy," 125.

CHAPTER 6

AGRARIAN REFORM AND THE POLITICS OF RURAL CHANGE

W hen we speak of "the people" of Africa and Asia, in large part we are talking about the peasantry—poor farmers living in a traditional culture. Despite substantial urbanization in recent decades, rural residents still constitute close to 60 percent of the Third World's population.[1] It is in the countryside where some of the worst aspects of political and economic underdevelopment prevail. In nations as distinct as China and Mexico, rural annual incomes are only 20–30 percent as high as urban earnings. Wide urban–rural gaps also persist in literacy, health care, and life expectancy. Rural villagers are less likely than their urban counterparts to have safe drinking water, electricity, or schools.

While the proportion of the Third World's population living in the countryside is substantially higher than in highly industrialized nations, that percentage varies greatly from country to country: from under 10 percent in Chile and Venezuela to over 80 percent in Cambodia, Ethiopia, and Nepal. Almost everywhere, the rural rate of poverty far exceeds the urban rate. Thus, for example, whereas the rural population constitutes some 60 percent of the LDCs population, it accounts for 75 percent of the 1.4 billion people living in absolute poverty.[2] These people suffer from inadequate housing, widespread illiteracy, malnutrition, and high rates of infant mortality. On average the rate of rural poverty is about 50 percent, but in the world's poorest nations (such as Nigeria, Cambodia, and Haiti) that figure rises to 70–80 percent.

In most of the developing world, political and economic powers are concentrated in the cities. Consequently, government policies—on issues ranging from social expenditures to agricultural pricing—have a predictable urban bias. As noted in Chapter 1, modernization theory argues that as countries develop, modern values and institutions will spread from the cities to the countryside, and the gap between the two will narrow. Conversely, dependency theorists maintain that the links between urban and rural areas replicate the exploitative international relationship between the industrialized core (the First World) and the periphery (the LDCs). What is certain is that resolving the political and economic tensions *between* urban and rural areas and reducing the vast inequalities *within* the countryside, the major subjects of this chapter, remain among the most difficult and important challenges facing most developing nations.

RURAL CLASS STRUCTURES

Within the countryside, there are generally substantial disparities in landownership. In many areas, agricultural property is concentrated in a relatively small number of hands. These inequalities have contributed to rural poverty and produced rigid class systems in countries such as El Salvador, Colombia, the Philippines, and parts of India. Many African nations—with notable exceptions such as South Africa, Morocco, and Kenya—have a somewhat more equitable pattern of land distribution, though they still suffer from sharp urban–rural gaps and intense rural poverty. East Asia (excepting the Philippines) has the most equitable distribution of farmland.

At the apex of the rural class system stand the large and powerful landowners, sometimes known as the *oligarchy*. Major Filipino sugar growers and Argentine cattle barons, for example, have historically exercised considerable political power in national politics. In El Salvador, the most influential coffee producers dominated the country's political system for most of the twentieth century. Land concentration has been most intense in Latin America, with its tradition of large estates (*latifundia*) dating back to the Spanish colonial era and the early years of independence. In the Philippines, Sri Lanka, Pakistan, and Bangladesh, along with parts of India, Indonesia, and Thailand, reactionary landed elites have also contributed to rural backwardness and poverty.

Since the middle of the twentieth century, the economic and political powers of rural landlords have declined considerably in many LDCs. In the most dramatic cases, radical revolutions in countries such as China and Vietnam stripped landlords of their property. Revolutionary governments sometimes killed many of the big landowners and sent others to prison camps for "political reeducation." Elsewhere, nonrevolutionary and relatively peaceful agrarian reforms undermined the rural elites of Peru and South Korea.* In industrializing nations such as Brazil and Thailand, the economic importance of agribusiness has diminished relative to the industrial and commercial sectors. Therefore, many wealthy landowning families have diversified into those economic sectors or have left agriculture entirely.

At the local and regional levels, however, landlords in Latin America and much of Asia continue to exercise considerable power. For example, upper-caste farmers in the Indian state of Bihar and large cattle ranchers in the Brazilian interior retain virtually unchallenged supremacy. At times, they have intimidated, or even murdered, peasant organizers and union leaders without fear of the legal consequences. Such was the fate of Chico Mendes, the celebrated Brazilian union leader who had organized Amazonian rubber-tree tappers against the powerful ranchers who were clearing the forest and destroying the local habitat. Despite Mendes's impressive international stature (the Turner broadcasting network and various U.S. senators had honored him, for example) and despite his links to influential American environmental groups, local landlords hired gunmen to assassinate him. Only after a sustained international outcry were his

---

* The terms *agrarian reform* and *land reform* are often used interchangeably. However, technically, *land reform* refers only to the redistribution of land to needy peasants or farm laborers. *Agrarian reform*, on the other hand, is a broader process also encompassing financial and technical aid, infrastructure, all of which must support land redistribution if it is to be effective.

murderers brought to trial. They were convicted, but after serving several years were able to walk out of prison and stay at large for 3 years. Hundreds of lesser-known Brazilians have been killed on orders from powerful landlords, crimes that often go unpunished.

On the rung beneath the landed elite, we find midsized landlords and more affluent peasants. The latter group (sometimes called *kulaks*) consists of peasants who, unlike small landlords, still work on the land themselves. However, unlike poorer peasants, *kulaks* can afford to hire additional peasant labor to work with them. While neither midsized landlords nor richer peasants belong to the national power elite, they usually exercise considerable political influence locally in countries such as India, Pakistan, and Brazil. Indeed, in much of Asia, where the biggest agricultural holdings are not nearly as large as those in Latin America, these two groups are a potent political force. Extended family networks typically magnify their influence.

Finally, at the bottom of the socioeconomic ladder, the rural poor—including peasants who own small plots of land, tenant farmers, and farmworkers—are generally the Third World's most impoverished and powerless occupational group. *Peasants* are defined as family farmers who work small plots and maintain a traditional lifestyle that is distinct from city dwellers. Because they are typically poor and poorly educated, many peasants lack the means to transport their crops to market themselves, lack ready access to credit, and lack the knowledge or resources to deal with the legal or bureaucratic proceedings that they periodically encounter. As a result, they depend on the services of merchants, moneylenders, lawyers, and government bureaucrats, all of whom frequently exploit them. Their links to the world—including the government, the military, the church, and the market economy—are largely dependent upon individuals and institutions outside the peasants' community.[3] Thus, as Eric Wolf has noted, "Peasant denotes an asymmetrical structural relationship between the producers of surplus [peasants] and controllers [including landlords, merchants, and tax collectors]."[4]

We may further subdivide poor peasants into two subgroups: those who own small amounts of land for family cultivation (smallholders) and those who are landless. The ranks of the landless, in turn, include tenant farmers (who enter into various types of rental arrangements with landlords) and farm wage laborers. However, these categories are not mutually exclusive. Smallholders, for example, may also supplement their incomes by working as farm laborers or renting additional land as tenants. Usually, it is the landless that constitute the poorest of the rural poor. While they represent a mere 10 percent of all agricultural families in countries such as Kenya and Sierra Leone, their numbers rise to 50–70 percent in India, Pakistan, the Philippines, and Brazil.[5] Not surprisingly, in Latin America and parts of Africa and Asia, where concentrated landownership and associated peasant landlessness have been particularly notable, the issue of land reform has often been at the center of rural politics.

PEASANT POLITICS

Despite their vast numbers, peasants often play a muted role in Third World politics. Because most LDCs did not have competitive national elections until recently and because, even where there have been elections, powerful groups have often controlled the peasant vote, the rural poor have not readily convert their numbers into political influence. The peasantry's political leverage is also limited by poverty, lack of education, dependence on outsiders, and physical isolation from the centers of national power and from peasants elsewhere in the country. Cultural values stressing caution and conservatism may further constrain peasant political behavior. Karl Marx's analysis of nineteenth-century European rural society questioned the peasants' capacity for political change or revolution. Writing on the French peasantry, he derided their alleged lack of solidarity and class consciousness, and disparagingly referred to them as a "sack of potatoes." Dismayed by their apparent conservatism, he dismissed peasants as "the class that represents the barbarism in civilization."[6] In the twentieth century, Robert Redfield's classic study of Third World peasants portrayed them somewhat similarly. "In every part of the world," he argued, "generally speaking, peasants have been a conservative factor in social change, a brake on revolution."[7]

Indeed, over the years, anthropological writings frequently have depicted peasant political culture as fatalistic and isolated. Hence, it was claimed, most of them doubt that collective political action can better their own fate. Discussing the reaction of Indian villagers to local government authorities, Phyllis Arora describes a sense of powerlessness resulting in political apathy. "Helplessness is . . . evoked by the presence of the district officer. The peasant tends to feel that all he [or she] can do before such authority. . . is petition for redress of grievances. . . . In the ultimate analysis, however . . . the peasant feels at the mercy of the whims of the [political] authorities."[8] Western journalists, visiting peasant communities in China after the massive urban protests demonstrations of 1989, noted how insulated the villagers were from those events and from the national political debate.

No doubt, peasants typically *are* wary of radical change and respectful of community traditions. To some extent, this conservatism reflects a suspicion of outside values—distrust frequently grounded in religious beliefs and other long-standing traditions. Indeed, the maintenance of a distinct peasant culture depends, to some extent, on the rejection of external influences. But peasant suspicion of social change is frequently understandable and rational. Struggling on the margins of economic survival, the rural poor have found that the commercialization and mechanization of agriculture, as well as other aspects of rural modernization, have often negatively impacted their lives. In rural Pakistan, for example, the introduction of tractors improved the output and income of the farmers who could afford them. As a consequence, however, many poorer tenant farmers who could no longer compete were forced off their plots, thereby concentrating land into fewer hands.[9] Political changes may also be threatening. For example, when outside activists have organized the rural poor to challenge local injustices, those peasants have often been ruthlessly repressed. Small wonder, then, that they may be suspicious of change, including any challenge to the power structure.

This does not mean, however, that they are incapable of standing up to landlords and government authorities who wrong them. Far from it! Examples of peasant resistance are commonplace, ranging from the most restrained to the most radical. James C. Scott has demonstrated that many peasants in Southeast Asia who appear to accept the established order actually engage in unobtrusive "everyday forms of resistance," such as theft and vandalism against their landlords, "foot dragging, and false deference."[10]

Elsewhere, peasants have presented their political demands more openly and aggressively. Contrary to Marx's expectations, the supposedly conservative peasantry was a critical actor in most twentieth-century revolutions, including communist upheavals in Russia, China, Vietnam, and Cuba, as well as in noncommunist insurgencies in Bolivia and Mexico.[11] More recently, they have been the backbone of guerrilla movements in Colombia, El Salvador, Peru, Cambodia, Nepal, the Philippines, and parts of India. In the mid-1990s, *Zapatista* rebels from the indigenous communities of Chiapas, Mexico, established a de facto zone of self-rule and forced the national government to the negotiating table. And in many other LDCs, ranging from India to Ecuador, many well-organized peasant groups also have become influential actors in democratic political systems.

We will examine the role of the peasantry in revolutionary movements in greater detail in Chapter 8. For now, however, suffice it to say that peasants are neither inherently conservative nor intrinsically radical. Rather, they vary considerably in their ideological propensities and their capacity for collective political action. To understand why so many peasants accept the political status quo, while others choose to resist or even rebel, we must first examine the relationship between the powerful and the weak in the countryside. Although traditional landlords frequently exploit their tenants or neighboring smallholders, mutually understood boundaries usually limit the extent of that exploitation. Links between landlords and peasants are usually grounded in long-standing patron–client relationships involving reciprocal obligations. Despite the landlords' superior power, these relationships are not always exploitative. For example, landowners frequently provide their tenants with land and financial credit in return for labor on their estate. And they may fund religious festivals or serve as godparents of their tenants' children.

As long as landlords fulfill their obligations, peasants generally accept the traditional order despite its many injustices. However, should rural modernization and the commercialization of agriculture induce rural patrons to cease discharging their traditional responsibilities, the peasantry may conclude that the previously existing "moral economy" has failed them.[12] In some cases, rural modernization may also give landlords (who can afford farm machinery and irrigation pumps) a competitive advantage over peasants (who cannot afford them) and eventually force the smallholders off the land. Eric Wolf has noted that the transition from feudal or semifeudal rural relations to capitalist economic arrangements often strips peasants of the certainty and protection afforded them by the old order (even an unjust old order). Frequently, the result is rural upheaval. Thus, he argued, communist revolutions in China, Vietnam, Cuba, and other Third World nations originated with the threats to the peasants' traditional way of life posed by the rise of rural capitalism.[13] This in no way suggests that rural modernization and the transition to capitalism *always* radicalize the peasantry or drive them to revolutionary activity. But when peasants feel that their way of life is threatened, they will resist change or at least try to channel it into forms more beneficial to their interests. How effectively they engage in collective political action and how radical or moderate their demands are depend on a number of factors: the extent to which they perceive themselves to be exploited; how desperate their economic condition is; the degree of internal cohesion and cooperation within their communities; their ability to form political linkages with peasants in neighboring villages or in other parts of the country; the extent to which they forge political ties with nonpeasant groups and leaders; the type of outside groups with whom they ally (be it the Catholic Church in the Philippines or Maoist revolutionaries in parts of rural India); the responsiveness of the political system to their demands; and the types of political options that the political order affords them.

The last two factors suggest that the probability of radical peasant insurrection depends as much on the quality of the political system as it does on the nature of the peasantry. Given a meaningful opportunity to implement change peacefully, peasants rarely opt for revolution. Rebellion—which brings obvious danger to their own lives and to the lives of their families—is an act of desperation normally entered into only when other options are unavailable. It is perhaps for that reason that no democratic political system has ever fallen to revolutionary insurgency.

In recent decades, the spread of the mass media throughout the countryside, increased rural educational levels, and the broadening of voting rights in many LDCs (such as extending the vote to illiterates) have greatly increased the political influence of peasant voters in electoral democracies. In countries such as India, South Korea, Turkey, Bolivia, and Ecuador, politicians must now consider the interests of the rural poor more seriously. Still, voting power is of little use in many nondemocratic nations in Africa, the Middle East, and Asia. And even in competitive party systems, the peasantry's political power is normally not proportional to their numbers.

On the whole, the range of peasant political activity runs the gamut from the far Left to the far Right, from peaceful to violent. As Samuel Huntington has noted, "The peasantry . . . may be the bulwark of the status quo or the shock troops of revolution. Which role the peasant plays is determined by the extent to which the existing system meets his immediate economic and material needs as he sees them."[14] In India, many peasants vote for the BJP—the conservative, Hindu fundamentalist party (see Chapter 3). In Latin America, on the other hand, peasants often vote for moderately left-of-center candidates. And in countries such as China, Vietnam, Nicaragua, and Colombia, still other peasants have supported revolutionary insurrections. Whatever their political inclinations, the peasants' economic and political concerns usually revolve around four broad issues: the prices they receive for their crops, consumer prices (of goods they buy), taxes, and the availability of land. The issue of land has been the most volatile and the most critical to the political stability of many Third World nations, and it is to this issue that we now turn our attention.

THE POLITICS OF AGRARIAN REFORM

In those areas of the Third World where landownership is highly concentrated, agrarian reform has long been an issue in the national political debate. To be sure, the pressure for reform has waxed and waned and other models of rural development have become more popular in recent years. Still, the issue lingers in many LDCs. Agrarian reform typically involves redistribution of farmland from landlords to landless peasants or to smallholders who need more land to support their families. In other instances, it entails distribution of public property, including previously uncultivated lands. Successful reforms require government credit, technical assistance, and improved access to markets. Unfortunately, many agrarian reform programs fail to redistribute enough land or to offer sufficient government support. Agrarian reforms that follow peasant-based revolutions sweep out the old systems of inequality, but often establish state-dominated landownership and management systems that deny the rural poor the control that they had fought for. Thus, with notable exceptions such as Japan, Taiwan, and South Korea, land reform programs frequently have fallen short of the peasants' goals.

Patterns of Land Concentration

In much of the Third World, especially Asia, landless peasants constitute a large portion of the rural population. In Bangladesh, for example, about half the rural population is landless. The proportion in India is about 40 percent. In Brazil, there are about 5 million landless rural families. In addition, millions of peasant smallholders own plots too small to support their families adequately. In countries such as Bangladesh, Rwanda, El Salvador, and Peru, the ratio of rural families to arable land (land suitable for cultivation) is so high that even an equitable distribution of farmland would fail to meet all the peasants' needs. But in many LDCs, where the ratio of rural families to arable land is more favorable, the concentration of agricultural land in a small number of hands is what causes landlessness and land shortages.

As we have noted, unequal distribution of land is most pronounced in Latin America, where large estates, sometimes measuring thousands of acres, control a substantial proportion of the region's farmland. In Brazil, for example, a mere 2 percent of the nation's farms, each exceeding 1,000 hectares (2,500 acres),* has owned more than 55 percent of all farmland.[15] In the Dominican Republic, where large estates are not nearly as vast as in Brazil, farms larger than 50 hectares have constituted less than 2 percent of the nation's agricultural units; nevertheless, they too have controlled more than 55 percent of the country's farmland. The largest of these estates—those exceeding 500 hectares—represented a mere 0.1 percent of all Dominican farms but held 27 percent of the nation's agricultural land. At the other end of the spectrum, peasant smallholders (owning units of 5 hectares or less) owned nearly 82 percent of the country's farms, but held merely 12.2 percent of all farmland.[16] Similar patterns have prevailed in much of Latin America. Prior to the 1979 Sandinista revolution, an astounding 43 percent of Nicaragua's rural families were landless. Yet a mere 2 percent of the rural population owned 36 percent of the farmland, including a full 20 percent that belonged to the ruling Somoza family alone.[17]

With different historical traditions and far higher population density, Asia does not have agricultural estates as large as Brazil's or Argentina's. In nations such as Indonesia, India, and Pakistan, farm holdings have rarely exceeded 50 hectares.[18] Still, in many cases a high proportion of farmland is concentrated in relatively few hands. For example, in Bangladesh, one of the

---

* A hectare, rather than an acre, is the standard measurement of farmland area in most of the world. One hectare is equivalent to 2.47 acres.

world's most densely populated countries, the largest farms are relatively small, rarely exceeding 5–10 hectares. Yet less than 3 percent of these units controlled more than 25 percent of the country's agricultural land. In the Philippines, virtually identical data showed 3.4 percent of the country's farms accounting for 26 percent of the land.

The Case for Agrarian Reform

Given the powerful interests opposing land redistribution, supporters of agrarian reform have needed to defend their objectives on several grounds, including social justice and equity, greater political stability, improved agricultural productivity, economic growth, and preservation of the environment. An examination of each of these arguments reveals the complexity of the debate.

Social Justice and Equity Because of the concentration of agricultural holdings in Latin America and parts of Africa and Asia, many analysts feel there is a *prima facie* case for some form of land redistribution based on social justice and human rights.[19] As previously noted, the millions of rural families with little or no land are among the poorest of the Third World's poor. They are trapped in a web of poverty, malnutrition, and illiteracy from which few escape. Usually they are politically powerless as well, controlled by landlords or local political bosses. For those peasants, agrarian reform is a fundamental step toward achieving greater political and socioeconomic justice.

Political Stability From the perspective of government policy makers, perhaps a more compelling justification for agrarian reform has been that it limits peasant unrest or averts the possibilities of future unrest. Samuel Huntington has starkly linked land reform to political stability:

> Where the conditions of land tenure are equitable and provide a viable living for the peasant, revolution is unlikely. Where they are inequitable and where the peasant lives in poverty and suffering, revolution is likely, if not inevitable, unless the government takes prompt measures to remedy those conditions.[20]

Indeed, statistical analyses indicate that the likelihood of revolutionary activity in developing countries increases wherever farmland is very unequally distributed and where there are many landless peasants.[21] Without the threat of peasant unrest, however, most policy makers have been relatively indifferent to the injustices of land tenure patterns. Ironically, then, the end of the Cold War and the threat of communist insurrection have reduced U.S. interest in promoting land reform, reforms it had advocated in El Salvador during the 1980s and in South Korea decades earlier.

Productivity One of the most hotly debated aspects of land reform is its effect on agricultural productivity. Opponents of agrarian reform maintain that land redistribution lowers agricultural output, thereby diminishing food supplies for the cities and curtailing export earnings. Citing "economies of scale," they argue that large agricultural units are generally more productive than smallholdings because they are more easily mechanized and use rural infrastructure (such as irrigation and roads) more effectively. Second, they insist that peasant cultivators have less technical knowledge than large landowners and are, therefore, less-productive farmers.

Advocates of agrarian reform counter that, in fact, smallholders are generally more efficient producers than larger landlords. Although a growing number of large landowners now study agricultural sciences and employ modern productive techniques, many of the landed elite still farm their land ineffectively. For example, in Latin America, where land is an important source of prestige and political power, landlords have often owned more land than they can efficiently cultivate. Peasant cultivators, on the other hand, tend to farm their plots very intensively because their families' living standards depend on raising productivity. This does not mean that small, peasant-run units are *always* more efficient. Peasant beneficiaries of land reform in some regions lack skills necessary for managing their own plots. Consequently, land transfers in such cases sometimes have caused short-term declines in efficiency.[22] In these cases, the beneficiaries of land reform may require supplemental government assistance as they become landowners.

The comparative efficiency of landlords and smallholders also varies according to which crop or animal they are raising. For example, production of meat, wheat, and sugar are more likely to benefit from economies of scale (i.e., output per acre will usually rise significantly as the result of capital investment). On the other hand, most of the grains, tubers, fruits, and vegetables that constitute the core of Third World food consumption, along with some exports such as coffee, do best on small farm units. These variations notwithstanding, data collected in Asia and Latin America reveal that labor-intensive smallholders (peasants who invest large amounts of physical labor on small units) generally have higher yields per acre than large-scale, capital-intensive (mechanized) producers.[23]

The economic efficiency of small farms may surprise many Americans accustomed to believing that larger units are inherently more productive. But in underdeveloped rural societies with a surplus of labor (i.e., many people who are underemployed and who will work for low wages), it is often more cost-effective to use family or hired labor intensively rather than invest in machinery. Out of economic necessity, peasant cultivators work hard, exploiting their own family labor. On the other hand, most large estates are farmed by tenants or hired laborers, neither of whom gain directly from raising productivity. That difference in motivation helps explain why the agricultural yields of peasant landowners in Japan, South Korea, and Taiwan and of near-owners in China are generally over twice as high as those of Filipino tenant farmers with comparable plots of land but less motivation to raise productivity.[24]

In recent decades, the disparity between large and small units in agricultural productivity has diminished. By using more advanced technology such as high-yield seeds and complementary irrigation, some large farmers have narrowed the efficiency gap.[25] But even if large farm units were more efficient (as measured by yield per hectare), smallholding operations would still be more productive to society than large landlords in other ways. For example, large landowners tend to import a sizable portion of their machinery, fuel, and chemicals, thereby expending much of the country's scarce foreign exchange. On the other hand, peasant farms draw upon family labor, a cheap input found in abundance. It is for this reason that the former president of the Overseas Development Council argued that "a land and capital scarce (but population plentiful) country should favor 40 two-and-a-half acre farms over a single-owner 100-acre farm in order to make optimum use of available land, labor, and capital."[26]

Economic Growth   In addition to its positive effect on agricultural productivity, land redistribution often brings broader benefits to the economies of developing countries. In nations such as Bolivia and Cuba, agrarian reform gave peasants a greater economic stake in the countryside, thereby reducing rural-to-urban migration and alleviating the tremendous strain on resources experienced by so many Third World cities (see Chapter 7).

When successfully implemented, land reform improves the living standards of the rural poor. And, as their purchasing power increases, they consume more of their country's manufactured goods, thereby stimulating industrial growth.[27] Indeed, Japan's, Taiwan's, and South Korea's postwar economic booms were initially partly stimulated by land reforms.[28] At the same time, reform also improved income equality in those East Asian nations. That equality brought political stability and supported rapid economic growth. In contrast, Latin America's pattern of concentrated landownership has contributed to the region's highly inequitable income distribution, extensive rural poverty, and lower economic growth.

Environmental Preservation   Another, more recent argument for agrarian reform relates to environmental protection. For example, Brazilian ranchers and farmers deliberately burn tracts of the Amazonian rainforest to clear land for agriculture, annually destroying a forest area equal to the size of New Jersey. The fires are so vast that they contribute to the *greenhouse effect* on world climate. Although large landowners create a substantial portion of this burn-off, peasant settlers also contribute. Driven out of the nation's poorest regions by desperation, land-hungry peasants colonize the jungle in search of a better life. Once there, however, they discover that cleared jungle soil quickly loses its nutrients. So, they must soon move on, clearing yet more forest land. Land reform in Brazil's nonforested regions would reduce landlessness and give tenant farmers a greater stake in the land they farm, thus reducing migration to the Amazonian basin.

Environmentalists advance similar arguments for land reform in other parts of the world. For example, Bangladesh's severe population pressure and concentrated landownership have forced many poor farmers to push the frontiers of agriculture beyond its ecologically desirable limits. In their search for farmland, landless peasants often move to coastal regions unsafe for habitation. There many of them fall victim to the typhoons that periodically sweep across the region, killing thousands of people.

TYPES OF AGRARIAN REFORM

In the past century, various forces brought about agrarian reform. At times, reform followed foreign occupation or pressure; occasionally, it resulted from peasant-based revolutions; and sometimes, it was introduced by national governments anxious to garner peasant support and maintain political tranquility. In each case, the underlying forces that stimulated reform have influenced the types of programs that emerged.

Externally Imposed Reform

The most successful externally imposed reforms occurred in East Asia after World War II. In Japan, the U.S. occupation command limited landownership to 10 acres while it transferred 41 percent of the country's farmland from landlords to their tenants and controlled rents for the remaining tenant population. The number of landless peasants fell from 28 to 10 percent of the rural population, making the countryside a bastion of stability.[29] In Taiwan and South Korea, U.S. pressure encouraged similar reforms designed to avert rural unrest. Farm ownership was limited to small parcels, and about one-third of each country's farmland was transferred to tenants, some 60 percent of whom benefited from the land transfers.[30] In all three nations, the transformation of rural society was enormously successful, raising agricultural productivity, improving rural living standards, and strengthening political stability. Consequently, East Asia's agrarian reforms have been viewed as benchmarks for evaluating programs elsewhere in the world.

In view of these impressive early achievements, it is striking how infrequently and ineffectively Washington has promoted Third World land reform since that time. In retrospect, it appears that there were three unique conditions in postwar East Asia that have rarely been replicated subsequently. First was the depth of American commitment to reform. At the start of the Cold War, fearing that peasant-based revolutions would spread from China to other Far Eastern nations, American policy makers endorsed land reform as the best way to contain Communism. A second unique condition was the enormous pressure that the United States could exert on those East Asian governments in the years following World War II. The Japanese were under U.S. military occupation, while the South Korean and Taiwanese governments were deeply beholden to the United States for liberating them from Japan and then protecting them from their communist neighbors (North Korea and China). In subsequent years, the United States lacked comparable influence. Although it favored land reform in South Vietnam (in the 1960s) and Central America (1980s), it was unwilling or unable to exert sufficient pressure on those conservative governments to attain effective programs.

This leads us to East Asia's last unique characteristic: Its landowning elites were so weakened at the end of World War II that they were ill-equipped to defend their own interests. In Japan, U.S. occupation authorities, supported by most of Japan's political elite, could impose their will on the country's previously powerful rural landlords. In South Korea, many of the country's landlords had collaborated with Japan during its 35 years of occupation. Hence, when Japanese occupation ended at the close of World War II, the Korean landed elite had little legitimacy or political influence. And in Taiwan—where the Kuomintang (KMT) government had fled after being driven out of China by the revolutionary army—government leaders recognized that their earlier failure to implement agrarian reform on the Chinese mainland had contributed to the communist victory there. Furthermore, many of Taiwan's largest landlords were Japanese (the island had been a Japanese colony for 50 years) who had fled back to Japan when that country surrendered to the Allies. So, with U.S. support, the KMT was ready to reform the Taiwanese countryside.

But, in the decades that followed, U.S. efforts on behalf of land reform were far less effective. Within the nations of Southeast Asia and Central America, large landlords used their extensive political power to obstruct rural reform. At the same time, when peasant unrest erupted in countries such as South Vietnam and El Salvador, the United States lacked the capacity, and perhaps the will, to promote real reform in the face of determined opposition by conservative elites.

Revolutionary Transformation

From the Mexican and Chinese revolutions through more recent insurgencies in the Philippines, El Salvador, Colombia, and Nepal, most twentieth-century insurrections were peasant based (Chapter 8). Therefore, agrarian reform was a fundamental rallying cry in both Marxist revolutions (China, Vietnam, Cuba, and Nicaragua) and non-Marxist insurgencies (Mexico, Bolivia, and Algeria). In the 1930s and 1940s, for example, the Chinese communists gained considerable peasant support by transferring land to the rural poor. Following their victories, revolutionary parties continued far-reaching land redistribution.

After coming to power in 1949, the Chinese communists distributed almost half of the country's arable land to about 60 million peasant households, totaling over half the nation's population at that time. Like the U.S.-sponsored reforms in East Asia (Japan, South Korea, and Taiwan), China's agrarian reform initially disbursed the land to peasant smallholders. But soon, arguing that privately owned peasant plots would reintroduce rural inequalities and class divisions, the government forced the peasantry to join state-directed cooperatives.[31]

Because they had vanquished the rural, landowning elite prior to taking power, revolutionary governments were free to redistribute their land. In countries such as Cuba, Nicaragua, and Vietnam, the government converted the larger agricultural estates to state farms and redistributed other land to peasant smallholders. Similarly, following their anticolonial revolutions, Algeria and Kenya redistributed farmland that had belonged to the ousted European settlers. In Mexico, some 40 percent of peasant families benefited from agrarian reform, receiving more than 40 percent of the country's agricultural and forest areas. Eighty percent of Bolivia's farmland was transferred to three-fourths of its rural families.[32]

While revolutionary reforms are generally more far-reaching than any of the other approaches discussed in this chapter, peasants have frequently been bitterly disappointed by the way the government organized the new agricultural units. Rather than break up the old landed estates and distribute the small plots directly to needy peasants (the East Asian model), most Marxist regimes created large collective or cooperative farms dominated by the state. The peasant recipients, then, essentially became employees of the new state farms without the power to manage its use or the ability to pass on smallholdings to their children. Worse yet from the perspective of those peasants who had already owned their own plots, revolutionary authorities often forced smallholders to merge their land into collective farms as well. In countries such as the Soviet Union, Vietnam, Ethiopia, and China, peasants who resisted collectivization were crushed, sometimes at the cost of many lives. Furthermore, in countries such as China, North Korea, and Ethiopia the disruptions in food production brought about by forced collectivization caused millions to die of starvation. Indeed both Joseph Stalin (the Soviet Union) and Ethiopia's leaders promoted policies to induce starvation in areas of peasant resistance. In North

Korea, more than 40 years after collectivization, inefficient state farms were still not producing enough to feed the country. In the mid-1990s, famine and related diseases took the lives of more than a million people. The country continues to be incapable of feeding its population.

China illustrates the dangers of forced collectivization, not only at the time the peasants were coerced into joining collective farms but years later as well. As we have noted, a brief period of family farming soon gave way to collective farming. The process reached its apex during the Great Leap Forward (1958–1961), when the government created huge agricultural communes. Over-centralization of agricultural decision making and poorly informed government policies caused enormous food shortages. In the massive famine that resulted, some 25 million people or more died of starvation or disease.[33] Although the government eventually abandoned its plans for huge communes, it expanded collective farming once again during the Chinese Cultural Revolution (1966–1976).

Several factors convinced various communist regimes to introduce collective farming, whether through state farms or state-directed peasant cooperatives. A fundamental objective was to establish state control over agriculture, so that government administrators could dictate which crops peasants grew and what they were paid for them. In China, for example, the government required agricultural communes to concentrate on the production of basic food grains such as rice and wheat, which were then sold to the general public at controlled prices. From a political standpoint, communist governments believed that collectivization was a means of controlling the peasants' individualistic impulses and reorienting them toward the public good. Arguing that private farming inevitably leads to inequalities between villagers and creates a "bourgeois mentality" among peasant smallholders, government leaders dismissed family farming as an undesired form of capitalism.* Finally, supporters of collectivization maintained that large, centrally controlled farms were more efficient than smallholdings.

To be sure, large state farms *are* often more efficient in one respect. They facilitate government delivery of social service. Thus, it is easier to deliver clean water, medical care, and schools to large collective farms than to provide those services to widely scattered private farms. However, as we have seen, the assumption that large state farms are more efficient *producers* than peasant smallholdings was usually quite mistaken. In fact, production data from Cuba, Ethiopia, Nicaragua, and China demonstrate that, for most food crops, private peasant plots have *higher* yields per acre than do collective farms.[34]

Private peasant plots are generally more productive than collective farms in large part because peasant smallholders gain directly when they and their families work harder and produce more. In contrast, workers on state farms get a set wage and see no gains for themselves in working harder or more effectively. Small wonder that a number of years ago, the Cuban government admitted that the average state farmworker, while being paid to work an eight-hour day,

---

* But some Marxist regimes allowed private farming. Poland and Yugoslavia, for example, did not collectivize agriculture during the communist era. Nicaragua and Cuba established large collectivized farms, but also allowed smallholders to keep their land.

actually worked about four. Government research revealed that they spent the remaining time taking breaks or, in some cases, illegally moonlighting as workers for nearby private farmers.

In recent decades, faced with growing evidence that smallholdings are more productive than collective farms, many of the Third World's remaining communist governments have set aside their ideological preferences and accepted more pragmatic policies. When Deng Xiaoping succeeded Mao Zedong as China's political leader, he introduced the "Household Responsibility System," which converted China's farm communes back to peasant-controlled, private farms.[35] In what amounted to a second agrarian reform (or, as one expert called it, "a second revolution"), the government broke up large communal farms and distributed the land to the peasants as family plots. The ensuing "unleashing [of] the entrepreneurial talents of China's peasants" led to striking gains in farm productivity. From 1980 to 1984 alone, the value of agricultural output rose an astonishing 40 percent.[36] That surge was a major factor contributing to a vast improvement in rural living standards from the early 1980s to the mid-1990s and raised many millions of Chinese out of absolute poverty. More recently, other revolutionary and reformed Marxist regimes in Asia, most notably Vietnam, have also decollectivized agriculture.

In Nicaragua, agrarian reform officials in the Sandinista revolutionary government initially preferred state farms over any other type of agricultural unit. They saw peasant-run cooperatives as next best, and ranked private smallholdings last. Not surprisingly, surveys showed that the peasants' preferred rankings were exactly the opposite. During the economic crisis of the 1980s, the government, which was more pragmatic and less ideologically rigid than most Marxist regimes, conceded that peasant farms were more efficient. Moreover, as it fought a bitter civil war against the Contras (U.S.-backed antirevolutionary guerrillas), the government realized that giving land to family farms would give peasant recipients incentive to support the Sandinista army. Consequently, the regime altered its priorities to accommodate peasant preferences.[37] Similarly, during its severe economic crisis in the 1990s, Cuba's government reversed gears and converted many of the country's centrally run agricultural cooperatives into family-run units. Cuba's new president, Raúl Castro, allegedly favors a more intensive shift to private farming similar to China's reforms.

Moderate Reformism

Most agrarian reform programs stem neither from foreign intervention nor revolution. Countries such as Egypt, Iran, India, Bangladesh, Zimbabwe, Chile, Venezuela, and Peru have redistributed agricultural land in various ways. In each case, however, the government introduced reform as a means of soliciting peasant support. Following the Cuban revolution, the United States and various Latin American governments concluded that the region needed rural reform in order to contain the spread of peasant unrest. Chile, Venezuela, and Peru all enacted moderate land reform programs in the 1960s. Twenty years later, the challenge of guerrilla insurgency prompted limited reform in El Salvador.

Elsewhere, rising rural literacy rates or, especially, the abolition of literacy requirements for voting has enfranchised a growing numbers of peasants, creating a large voting bloc supporting rural reform. Once minor players in the electoral process, peasants have become an important voting constituency in many countries, wooed by competing political parties. Running on platforms calling for agrarian reform, Chile's Christian Democratic Party, Peru's *Acción Popular*, and Venezuela's *Acción Democrática* all won national elections in the past with the help of broad peasant support. Once in office, all these governments introduced land reforms of varying magnitudes. Similarly, in Asia, some mix of incipient rural unrest and electoral politics contributed to modest reforms in the Philippines and parts of India.[38]

Moderate reformism has one obvious advantage. It is relatively free of the violence and excesses often associated with revolutionary programs. But with rare exception, its scope is far more limited than either externally induced redistribution or revolutionary change. For example, revolutions in Cuba, Bolivia, Mexico, and Nicaragua introduced Latin America's most extensive land redistribution programs, far exceeding moderate reformism. Similarly, reformism in Asia (Bangladesh, Thailand, the Philippines, and India) has also produced meager results when compared to revolutionary land redistributions in China and Vietnam.

Reformism generally produces a less-sweeping agrarian transformation because the government must deal with landed elites who are still strong enough to limit the scope of change. For example, reformist programs generally grant monetary compensation to landlords who have lost property. Because most Third World governments are strapped for funds and have other important spending needs, those payments limit the degree of land redistribution. In addition, bureaucratic obstacles and court challenges frequently slow the pace of redistribution to a crawl.

One notable exception to this pattern was the Peruvian agrarian reform. There, the government implemented a sweeping reform in the absence of either external pressure or internal revolution. A left-leaning, nationalist, military government led by General Juan Velasco expropriated most of the country's large agricultural and ranching estates, turning them over to the peasants and farm laborers who had been working on them. The military regime had the power to sweep aside objections from Peru's rural oligarchy, a group despised by Velasco and his colleagues. In all, the military government transferred approximately 40 percent of the country's farmland to 30 percent of the nation's peasant families.[39] Initially, the land was largely organized into cooperatives, but subsequently, as administrative and labor problems arose, most co-ops were subdivided and converted into peasant smallholdings.[40]

Ultimately, however, the military's agrarian reform failed to reduce Peru's pervasive rural poverty (discussed below). What it did accomplish was to destroy the once-considerable power of the landowning class and thereby transform the country's political and economic structure. The virtually unchallenged power of a military dictatorship, like the might of a revolutionary regime, allowed the government to ignore the demands of the rural aristocracy in a way that a democratic government never could. However, no other military government in Latin America has been equally dedicated to comprehensive rural change (though military rulers introduced more modest agrarian reforms in Panama and Ecuador).

In contrast, democratic governments, no matter how committed to helping the peasantry, cannot launch that type of frontal assault on the landed elite. For example, Venezuela's democratically elected *Acción Democrática* government, with strong backing from peasant voters, introduced a relatively ambitious agrarian reform. But because of political and financial restraints, much of the land transferred was previously uncultivated public property in the nation's jungle regions. Although this transfer permitted the government to sidestep landlord objections, such land was typically of marginal quality and not very accessible.

Currently, two far-reaching, moderate agrarian reforms are being implemented in Latin America—in Bolivia and Venezuela. In both cases, the president and his government have semi-Marxist ideologies that are more similar to revolutionary governments than to more centrist, elected regimes. These reforms promise to be more extensive than the programs of moderate agrarian reforms elsewhere in the region. While both presidents Evo Morales (Bolivia) and Hugo Chávez (Venezuela) were democratically elected, both have governed in a somewhat autocratic manner allowing them to often ignore the desires of the large landowners.

The Limits of Agrarian Reform

While the experiences of Taiwan, South Korea, Cuba, and China demonstrate that agrarian reform can substantially improve peasant living standards, few programs elsewhere have matched their success. Peru illustrates how even sweeping change initiated by a well-intentioned government may not achieve its objectives. That program transferred a high percentage of national farmland to the peasantry compared to other Latin American agrarian reforms and was, thus, more comparable to revolutionary transformations in Cuba, Mexico, and Nicaragua. The military regime stripped powerful Andean and coastal land-lords of their land and its associated political power, undercutting the elite that had once dominated the countryside. Yet these radical changes failed to improve peasant living standards as anticipated. The military's attempts at rural political change were often heavy-handed and counterproductive. But even if the government had better executed its reforms, expropriating the nation's largest haciendas and plantations would not have satisfied the peasants' requirements. There simply was not enough arable farmland to go around. Ultimately, less than one-third of the rural families in need received any land, and the poorest of the poor were frequently overlooked.[41] Even most of the program's beneficiaries found that their added land was insufficient to alleviate their deep poverty.

While the military regime narrowed the gap between rich and poor in the countryside, it did nothing to bridge the larger gulf between rural and urban living standards. As in most LDCs, the nation's economic structure has long favored the urban population over the peasantry. Despite substantial poverty in the cities, average urban income remains several times higher than rural earnings. Consequently, a substantial improvement in peasant living standards was impossible without a shift of wealth and government resources from urban areas to the countryside. Given the tremendous political power of the urban upper class, middle class, and organized working class, such a transfer of wealth and resources was more than even the armed forces were prepared to implement. Absent that change, agrarian reform merely "redistributed poverty" within the countryside.

Revolutionary agrarian reforms have limitations as well. Mexico still suffers from substantial rural poverty and landlessness, despite a reform that affected half the nation's peasants and a similar proportion of agricultural land. Beginning in the 1930s, the government organized reform beneficiaries into *ejidos*, cooperative units designed to channel state aid to the peasantry and increase their productivity. Following World War II, however, government agricultural policy changed in favor of larger commercial farms, failing to deliver adequate credits, infrastructure, and technology to the *ejidos*. As a consequence, poor farmers were unable to compete in the marketplace. Many lost their farms and poured into the nation's cities or across the border to the United States. Since 1970, the government has developed several programs designed to bolster peasant agriculture. While these programs had some positive impact, they were cut short after 1982 by the country's debt crisis and severe economic recession.[42] Current government policies encourage the privatization of the *ejidos'* communal property. This may benefit the most productive peasants, because they may now buy and sell land more readily. However, it also forces less-competitive peasants off their family plots into Mexico's already overcrowded cities or across the U.S. border.

The shortcomings of reform efforts in Mexico and Peru do not suggest that agrarian reform is without value. Rather, they indicate that redistribution of land must be supported by additional government measures if it is to be effective. Evidence from elsewhere in Latin America and from South Asia indicates that successful reform programs usually require some degree of peasant organization and mobilization.[43] That is to say, the state is more likely to provide land recipients with needed technical assistance, infrastructure, education, and financial credit if it is pressured to do so by effective peasant organizations. Government also needs to allow peasants a fair price for their crops.[44] The administrative apparatus governing reform must be simple, and peasant beneficiaries must be given a strong role in the decision-making process. In countries where rural elites maintain substantial political power, landlords losing property must receive reasonable payments if the program is to be politically viable. At the same time, peasant beneficiaries must only pay an amount they can afford if the program is to be economically feasible for them.[45] Wherever possible, Third World governments must reduce the tremendous gap that typically separates urban and rural living standards.

In recent years, a number of LDCs have introduced or continued land reform programs. Most programs, however, are very limited or exist in name only. As I have indicated, only a few governments are implementing significant reforms. In Venezuela, Hugo Chávez's leftist government has introduced a program to redistribute currently unused state and private lands to needy peasant families and to urban migrants who wish to return to the countryside. Venezuela's situation is uniquely favorable to rural reform in a number of ways: the rural population is very small (about 10 percent of the national total); the country has low population density with significant government landholdings (though much of that is unusable for agriculture); and, the boom in petroleum prices gave the state substantial economic resources for a while (until prices fell). Despite all these advantages and despite the existence of a powerful reform-oriented government, so far the number of beneficiaries has been modest and only state-owned land has been touched. Elsewhere in Latin America, Bolivia's government, led by Chávez's ally, Evo Morales, issued an executive order for land redistribution in 2006. In 2009, Bolivian voters approved a new constitution, which placed much tighter limits on the maximum size of agricultural holdings. Because Morales' primary political support comes from Bolivia's peasants, the effects of the reform are likely to be far-reaching, but it is still too early to judge its effectiveness.

Elsewhere in the developing world, modest land reform programs have been implemented in the Philippines and South Africa, but they have only touched the surface. The same can be said of a large number of reforms in Asia, Africa, and the Middle East. Zimbabwe's broader reform program has transferred land, which had been owned by Whites since the colonial era, to the Black rural population. However, this program has been plagued by a number of serious problems. The Mugabe government seems more interested in using agrarian reform for political gain than for improving rural conditions. It has distributed land almost exclusively to government supporters without regard to the recipients' qualifications or need. The government has often encouraged its militants to seize land violently, thereby leading many large landowners to cease investing in production. Finally, because the farms seized so far and those in danger of future expropriation produce much of Zimbabwe's food exports and because rural production has been badly disrupted, the national economy has suffered, and a substantial portion of the population are now malnourished. Domestic food production has fallen as well. In contrast, mindful of the violence and economic problems generated by agrarian reform programs in Zimbabwe and elsewhere, South Africa's government has moved very cautiously in redistributing land owned by wealthy White farmers to Black peasants. As a result, many rural Blacks complain that the government has not moved fast enough and that their living conditions have not improved significantly since the end of White rule. And, in Ethiopia, the brutal agrarian reform forced large numbers of villagers to migrate to new areas, resulting in substantial starvation.

Finally, in recent decades, a very different type of land reform has taken place in several communist nations that have been moving in the direction of free-market economies. Farmlands that had been seized from big landowners during their revolutions and turned into state farms or state-controlled peasant cooperatives have been decollectivized and broken into smaller, peasant-owned farms. As we have seen, the most extensive reform of this kind was in China during the 1970s and 1980s under the "Household Responsibility System." Since the end of the 1980s, Vietnam has carried out a comparable agrarian decollectivization program. And, a similar process has taken place through the privatization of state-controlled farmland in Russia and the former communist nations of Eastern Europe.

Even the most intelligently executed reform programs, however, will not be equally successful in every country. In nations such as Peru, El Salvador, and Bangladesh, there simply is not enough quality land to satisfy peasant needs. In such cases, the government and the private sector need to create alternative employment for the rural poor in other sectors of the economy. Ultimately, each nation's agrarian-reform package must be carefully designed to meet its own specific needs.

OTHER APPROACHES AND ISSUES

Since the 1970s, few governments have introduced significant agrarian reform programs. But there have been some notable exceptions including Bolivia, El Salvador, Mozambique, Nicaragua, South Africa, Venezuela, and, in a more controversial form, Ethiopia and Zimbabwe. Critics on the Right have long believed land redistribution programs undermine allegedly more efficient, large-scale agribusiness. Critics on the Left have found the fruits of moderate reformism disappointing, claiming that often it has benefited capitalists and state bureaucracies more than the peasantry.[46] And, powerful urban interests fear agrarian reform will curtail agricultural production and raise the cost of food. At the same time, rural pressures for reform have generally diminished. Vast numbers of peasants have migrated to the cities, many having despaired of change in the countryside. Most governments now attach less importance to peasant agriculture than to large-scale, export-oriented, commercial farming, which earns the country foreign exchange. While land redistribution programs continue in some LDCs, for now at least, efforts at rural reform have largely shifted to other issues and other types of programs.

Crop Pricing

In addition to their lack of sufficient farmland, peasants often have suffered from unfavorable government price policies. Anxious to ensure a supply of cheap food for the urban population, many governments, particularly in Africa and the Middle East, have imposed price controls on food staples such as rice, potatoes, and sugar. Price controls were also designed to promote industrialization by providing workers with cheap food, thereby helping employers keep wages down and facilitating greater capital investment.[47] But by holding crop prices below their free-market levels, these controls have further impoverished peasant producers.

In Africa, governments have also commonly controlled export crops, forcing farmers to sell their produce to the state at controlled price and then exporting it for a higher, free-market price, retaining the price difference as a de facto tax. One early study found that African farmers often received less than two-thirds, and in some cases less than half, of the value of their export crops.[48] Although designed to provide the country's urban poor and middle class with cheaper food and to generate government revenues from exports, price controls on crops ultimately have a perverse effects. They lower the incomes of poor farmers and are a disincentive to greater food production by larger farmers. In Egypt, for example, when the government controlled the prices of basic food grains, large landlords reduced the supply of badly needed grains by switching to other commercial crops whose prices were not controlled. Peasants were less capable of switching crops and thus suffered declining incomes.[49] Throughout Africa, price controls have decreased food output by driving many farmers out of business and reducing production incentives for the rest. For decades, per-capita food production declined, and the continent became increasingly dependent on food imports and foreign aid. While there is no single cause for that deterioration, some studies of African famine argue that government price controls and inefficient government bureaucracies have aggravated the problem.[50]

Unfortunately, once governments embark on the path of commodity price regulation, they are soon trapped by a conflict between short-term political pressures and long-term production needs. Lifting price controls leads quickly to sharply higher prices of basic foods. Consequently, when officials remove them (often in response to external pressures from the IMF or World Bank), they often face protests or even riots by irate, urban consumers. Not surprisingly, for many years few governments were willing to risk such unrest, particularly because the urban middle class, one group adversely affected by price hikes on food, is normally a vital pillar of government support. In the longer term, however, higher crop prices stimulate greater food production, ultimately causing food prices to come down. Since the 1980s, as many developing nations have introduced neoliberal economic policies (reducing government economic intervention), more and more are slashing or eliminating price controls on agriculture (see Chapter 10).*

Integrated Rural Development

As the LDCs' food consumption has grown and environmental constraints have limited the cultivation of new lands, Third World governments have tried to increase yields on peasant smallholdings. At the same time, in electoral democracies such as Brazil and India, the rural poor have increasingly organized to demand better public services. In recent decades, as the possibilities of further agrarian reform and land redistribution have diminished, a number of Third World governments and international development agencies have turned to "integrated rural development." This involves some combination of technical assistance for farmers, greater peasant access to credit, better access to markets (including building more and better roads), improved irrigation, creation of alternative sources of income (such as China's rural, industrial cooperatives), improved educational opportunities, and better health care. Normally, villages are lucky to receive help in any of those areas and virtually no community receives all of these benefits.

Many of the rural foreign aid projects supported by the United States and other industrialized nations have pursued a comprehensive and integrated approach to rural development. In 2000, the 192 members of the United Nations and a number of international organizations signed an agreement called the Millennium Project, in which they established eight major goals (and 21 specific targets) designed to dramatically improve Third World living standards. Targets for the year 2015 included:

1. Reducing the number of people living in absolute poverty and the number suffering from malnutrition to one-half the 1990 levels.
2. Reducing the level of child mortality to one-third of its 1990 level.
3. Eliminating the gender gap in all levels of education so as to attain equality for females.
4. Reducing the spread of AIDS, malaria, and other major diseases.

---

* Neoliberalism rejects most of the state intervention in the economy (including state regulation and ownership of key assets) that was prevalent in developing economies and instead favors free-market mechanisms.

In 2008, the United Nations reported significant progress in many areas: Six of the ten geographical regions designated by the UN (including the most populous) have reached 95 percent gender equality in education; eight of those regions have enrolled at least 95 percent of all children in primary school; deaths from measles have been cut from 750,00 annually to less than 250,000; 80 percent of all children have been vaccinated against measles; and 1.8 billion people have gained access to clean drinking water since 1990. There has been far less progress, however, reaching a number of other goals and targets.[51]

CONCLUSION: DEMOCRACY AND RURAL REFORM

For decades, Third World development policies have emphasized industrial growth and urban modernization, often to the detriment of the rural sector. In many cases, the consequences have been stagnant agricultural production, growing food imports, rural poverty, and heavy rural-to-urban migration. In some instances, rural poverty has led to peasant insurrection. Most notably in Africa and Latin America, government bias in favor of urban areas, along with the forces of capitalist modernization, have driven many peasants into the working class in a process known as *proletarianization*.[52] Pessimistic scholars have predicted the inevitable spread of large, mechanized farms to the detriment of peasant family farming.

More recently, research in countries such as Bolivia, Ecuador, and Colombia has revealed that, in at least some regions, innovative peasants have adapted skillfully to the forces of rural capitalism and modernization. Many have taken advantage of new commercial opportunities to compete successfully in the marketplace.[53] In Africa and Asia, peasant smallholders remain an even more important component of rural society. Rather than abandoning the peasantry as a relic of history, Third World governments and international agencies need to promote balanced economic and political development that gives proper weight to the rural sector and its peasant population.

The relationship between democracy and rural reform is somewhat paradoxical. On the one hand, democratic governments in countries such as Venezuela have broadened their base of political support by implementing agrarian reform and other types of assistance to the rural poor. As we noted earlier, experts such as Samuel Huntington argued that agrarian reform was the LDCs' best defense against revolution. However, the fact remains that the most far-reaching land reforms in the past century were implemented by revolutionary regimes in China, Vietnam, Mexico, Bolivia, Cuba, and Nicaragua, rather than by democratic governments. Military regimes redistributed significant amounts of land in Peru and Egypt. And authoritarian governments under pressure from the United States introduced sweeping agrarian reforms in South Korea and Taiwan. By contrast, in democratic countries such as Brazil, India, and the Philippines, landlords have formed powerful interest groups and have become influential in a number of major political parties, enabling them to block meaningful reform.

Institutions such as the U.N.'s Food and Agricultural Organization (FAO) continue to support rural reform in the developing world and to advocate its expansion. Arguing that current national agricultural policies stress increased production to the exclusion of other important needs, such as improving the living standard of the rural poor and sustaining the environment, FAO sees agrarian reform as central to those other objectives. As they noted at a 2006 conference on agrarian reform and rural development,

> While globalization, industrialization, and (often subsidized) commercial agriculture are creating wealth for some, they are also dramatically increasing the socio-economic disparities within and between countries, further exacerbating land concentration . . . Investment has tended to favor the development of the industrial, urban and service and often military sectors, at the expense of agriculture and rural development.[54]

Since 2002 (and particularly in 2007–2009), substantial increases in world food prices caused extensive malnutrition in many LDCs and gave rise to food riots and other forms of violent unrest. Food riots shook at least 20 developing countries in 2008 alone. Several factors contributed to this phenomenon, particularly the many farmers who have switched production from food grains to grains used in biofuels. Mounting hunger and political unrest convinced many of the First World's major food and foreign aid donors to rethink their attitudes toward peasant farming in the LDCs. Despite the financial advantages of large landholders and the pervasive government neglect of peasant farming, smallholders still produce about 60 percent of the food consumed in the developing world. Coming into the July 2009 G8 summit of the world's major economic powers, its participants pledged $15 billion in contributions over three years to aid food production, largely by peasants, in Africa and other very poor developing nations. At the summit itself, President Obama convinced the members to raise that pledge to $20 billion. The purpose of that aid would be to "transform traditional aid beyond simply donated [food to alleviate famines] to assistance building infrastructure and training farmers to grow their own food and to get it to market more efficiently."[55] Several months later (October 2009), Bill Gates announced that the Bill and Melinda Gates Foundation will be changing its philanthropic focus from fighting Third World diseases to aiding the LDCs' poor farmers, whom he described as the key to eradicating world hunger. Given how his foundation had become the fulcrum of the battle against malaria and other devastating Third World diseases—donating billions of dollars and inducing the United States and other governments to contribute billions more—it is likely that Gates's decision will have a major impact.

While many analysts hailed this new emphasis on Third World food production, a number of respected NGOs, such as Oxfam International, reacted skeptically. To begin with, they considered the $20 billion totally inadequate, particularly because the developing world had lost far more than that amount in the current global financial crisis. Second, G8 countries had a notoriously poor record of coming through with the aid pledged at previous G8 (and other) meetings. In the worst-case example, of all the aid that Italy has pledged in previous G8 summits over the years, it has delivered only three percent to this point. Third, unfortunately many of the countries targeted for this aid have notorious records of government corruption that siphons off large portions of any aid that is actually given. Finally, foreign assistance often falls into the hands of those who are best politically connected rather than those who need it the most or can best use it (i.e., larger farmers rather than peasants). Still, at the very least, G8 nations have come to realize that advancing the previously neglected peasant agricultural sector is a key to Third World development.

DISCUSSION QUESTIONS

1. Peasants were the major foot-soldiers in most twentieth-century revolutions (China, Cuba, Mexico, and Vietnam). Is that likely to be true of twenty-first century revolutions in the developing world? Why or why not?
2. What kind of rural reform or development projects do you think would most benefit the rural poor? Why?
3. Although Third World agrarian reform programs have fallen out of favor in contemporary government policies, there are those who still argue for their value. What are some arguments for restarting agrarian reform in the developing world?

NOTES

1. Where not otherwise indicated, the statistics in the first two paragraphs come from United Nations Population Division, *World Urbanization Prospects: The 2005 Revision Population Database*, http://esa.un.org/unup/.

2. Shaohua Chen and Martin Ravallion, *Absolute Poverty Measures for the Developing World, 1981–2004* (Washington, DC: World Bank Policy Research Working Paper 4211, April 2007) Tables 1–3. http://ideas.repec.org/p/wbk/wbrwps/4211.html.

3. George Foster, "Introduction: What Is a Peasant?" in *Peasant Society*, eds. Jack Potter, George Foster, and May Diaz (Boston: Little, Brown, 1967); Teodor Shanin, "The Nature and Logic of the Peasant Economy," *Journal of Peasant Studies*, vol. 1, no. 1–2 (1974).

4. Eric R. Wolf, *Peasants* (Upper Saddle River, NJ: Prentice Hall, 1966), 10.

5. Roy L. Prosterman and Jeffrey M. Riedinger, *Land Reform and Democratic Development* (Baltimore, MD: Johns Hopkins University Press, 1987), 41. Undoubtedly, those figures have changed in the last 20 years (in both directions), but they are still useful for cross-national comparisons.

6. Karl Marx, *Capital*. Quoted in Teodor Shanin, "Peasantry as a Political Factor," *Sociological Review*, vol. 14 (March 1966), 6. See also, Marx, *The Eighteenth Brumaire of Louis Bonaparte* (New York: International Publishers, 1964).

7. Robert Redfield, *Peasant Society and Culture: An Anthropological Approach* (Chicago: University of Chicago Press, 1965), 77.

8. Phyllis Arora, "Patterns of Political Response in Indian Peasant Society," *Western Political Quarterly*, vol. 20 (September 1967), 654.

9. Ronald J. Herring and Charles R. Kennedy Jr., "The Political Economy of Farm Mechanization Policy: Tractors in Pakistan," in *Food, Politics and Agricultural Development: Case Studies in the Public Policy of Rural Modernization*, eds. Raymond F. Hopkins, Donald J. Pachula, and Ross B. Talbot (Boulder, CO: Westview Press, 1979), 193–226.

10. James C. Scott, *Weapons of the Week: Everyday Forms of Peasant Resistance* (New Haven, CT: Yale University Press, 1986).

11. One of the most insightful books on the role of the peasantry in twentieth-century revolutions is Eric R. Wolf, *Peasant Wars of the Twentieth Century* (New York: Harper & Row, 1969).

12. James C. Scott, *The Moral Economy of the Peasant: Rebellion and Subsistence in Southeast Asia* (New Haven, CT: Yale University Press, 1976).

13. Wolf, *Peasant Wars*.

14. Samuel P. Huntington, *Political Order in Changing Societies* (New Haven, CT: Yale University Press, 1968), 375.

15. Anthony L. Hall, "Land Tenure and Land Reform in Brazil," in *Agrarian Reform and Grassroots Development*, eds. Roy L. Prosterman, Mary N. Temple, and Timothy M. Hanstad (Boulder, CO: Lynne Rienner Publishers, 1990), 206.

16. Carrie A. Meyer, *Land Reform in Latin America: The Dominican Case* (New York: Praeger, 1989), 38.

17. Rupert W. Scofield, "Land Reform in Central America," in *Agrarian Reform and Grassroots Development*, 154–155.

18. D. P. Chaudhri, "New Technologies and Income Distribution in Agriculture," in *Peasants, Landlords and Governments: Agrarian Reform in*

the Third World, ed. David Lehmann (New York: Holmes and Meier, 1974), 173; Howard Handelman, "Introduction," in *The Politics of Agrarian Change in Asia and Latin America*, ed. Howard Handelman (Bloomington: Indiana University Press, 1981), 4.

19. Joseph S. Nye Jr., "Ethical Dimensions of International Involvement in Land Reform," in *International Dimensions of Land Reform*, ed. John D. Montgomery (Boulder, CO: Westview Press, 1984), 7–29.

20. Huntington, *Political Order*, 375.

21. Bruce M. Russet, "Inequality and Instability: The Relation of Land Tenure to Politics," *World Politics*, vol. 16 (April 1964), 442–454; Prosterman and Riedinger, *Land Reform*, 24.

22. William Thiesenhusen, "Introduction," in *Searching for Agrarian Reform in Latin America*, ed. William Thiesenhusen (Boston: Unwin Hyman, 1989), 18.

23. Ibid., 16–20; Peter Dorner, *Latin American Land Reforms in Theory and Practice* (Madison: University of Wisconsin Press, 1992), 21–29.

24. Riedinger, "Philippine Land Reform," 19.

25. Dorner, *Latin American Land Reforms*, 23–25; Berry, "Land Reform," 72.

26. James Grant, "Development: The End of Trickle Down," *Foreign Policy*, vol. 12 (Fall 1973), 43–65.

27. Bruce F. Johnston and John W. Mellor, "The Role of Agriculture in Economic Development," *American Economic Review*, vol. 51 (September 1961), 566–593.

28. Dorner, *Latin American Land Reforms*, 29–31. That is not to suggest that agrarian reform was the most important development leading to economic growth, but it was a factor.

29. Ronald P. Dore, *Land Reform in Japan* (London: Oxford University Press, 1959); Mikiso Hande, *Modern Japan* (Boulder, CO: Westview Press, 1986), 347–348.

30. Shirley W. Y. Kuo, Gustav Ranis, and John C. H. Fei, *The Taiwan Success Story* (Boulder, CO: Westview Press, 1981); Gregory Henderson, *Korea: Politics of the Vortex* (Cambridge, MA: Harvard University Press, 1968).

31. John W. Bruce and Paula Harrell, "Land Reform in the People's Republic of China: 1978–1988," *Land Tenure Center Research Paper No. 100* (University of Wisconsin-Madison, 1989), 3–4; Vivienne Shue, *Peasant China in Transition—The Dynamics of Development Toward Socialism, 1949–56* (Berkeley: University of California Press, 1980).

32. Thiesenhusen, *Searching for Agrarian Reform*, 10–11.

33. Harry Harding, *China's Second Revolution* (Washington, DC: Brookings Institution, 1987),

12. Some experts put the death toll as high as 40 million.

34. For a crop-by-crop analysis of state and private sector farm productivity in Cuba, see Nancy Forster, "Cuban Agricultural Productivity," in *Cuban Communism*, 7th ed., ed. Irving Louis Horowitz (New Brunswick, NJ: Transaction, 1989), 235–255.

35. Nicholas Lardy, "Agricultural Reforms in China," *Journal of International Affairs* (Winter 1986), 91–104. Deng announced the program in 1978, but the government did not begin implementing it until 1980.

36. Harding, *China's Second Revolution*, 106.

37. Forrest D. Colburn, *Post-Revolutionary Nicaragua: State, Class and the Dilemmas of Agrarian Policy* (Berkeley: University of California Press, 1986) and Laura J. Enríquez, *Harvesting Change: Labor and Agrarian Reform in Nicaragua* (Chapel Hill: University of North Carolina Press, 1991), offer contrasting analyses.

38. Riedinger, "Philippine Land Reform," and Ronald Herring, "Explaining Anomalies in Land Reform: Lessons from South India," in *Agrarian Reform and Grassroots Development*, 15–75.

39. Howard Handelman, "Peasants, Landlords and Bureaucrats: The Politics of Agrarian Reform in Peru," in *The Politics of Agrarian Change*, 103–125; Cristóbal Kay, "The Agrarian Reform in Peru: An Assessment," in *Agrarian Reform in Contemporary Developing Countries*, 185–239.

40. Michael Carter and Elena Alvarez, "Changing Paths: The Decollectivization of Agrarian Reform Agriculture in Coastal Peru," in *Searching for Agrarian Reform*, 156–187.

41. Howard Handelman, "Peasants, Landlords and Bureaucrats," 103–125; Kay, "The Agrarian Reform in Peru," 185–239.

42. Merilee S. Grindle, *Searching for Rural Development: Labor Migration and Employment in Mexico* (Ithaca, NY: Cornell University Press, 1988).

43. Ronald J. Herring, "Explaining Anomalies in Agrarian Reform: Lessons from South Asia," in *Agrarian Reform and Grassroots Development*, 73.

44. Thiesenhusen, "Conclusions," in *Searching for Agrarian Reform*, 483–503.

45. Prosterman and Riedinger, *Land Reform and Democratic Development*, 177–202.

46. de Janvry, *The Agrarian Question*; Merilee S. Grindle, *State and Countryside: Development Policy and Agrarian Politics in Latin America* (Baltimore, MD: Johns Hopkins University Press, 1986).

47. Charles Harvey, ed. *Agricultural Pricing Policy in Africa* (London: Macmillan, 1988), 2.

48. Robert H. Bates, *Markets and States in Tropical Africa: The Political Basis of Agricultural Policy*

(Berkeley: University of California Press, 1981), 29; see also Michael J. Lofchie, *The Policy Factor: Agricultural Performance in Kenya and Tanzania* (Boulder, CO: Lynne Rienner Publishers, 1989), 57–59.

49. Marvin G. Weinbaum, *Food, Development, and Politics in the Middle East* (Boulder, CO: Westview Press, 1982), 61.

50. Michael F. Lofchie, "Africa's Agricultural Crisis: An Overview," and Robert H. Bates, "The Regulation of Rural Markets in Africa," in *Africa's Agrarian Crisis: The Roots of Famine*, eds. Stephen K. Commins, Michael F. Lofchie, and Rhys Payne (Boulder, CO: Lynne Rienner Publishers, 1986), 3–19, 37–54.

51. United Nations, *The Millennium Development Report 2008,* http://www.un.org/millennium-goals/pdf/The%20Millennium%20Development%20Goals%20Report%202008.pdf

52. David Goodman and Michael Redclift, *From Peasant to Proletarian: Capitalist Development and Agricultural Transitions* (Oxford, England: Basil Blackwell, 1981).

53. Nola Reinhardt, *Our Daily Bread: The Peasant Question and Family Farming in the Colombian Andes* (Berkeley: University of California Press, 1988).

54. F72 and Rural Development (March 7–10, 2006), "FAO's Contribution to Good Policies and Practices in Agrarian Reform and Rural Development: A Brief Overview," p. 3, http://www.fao.org/participation/bibdb/retrieval/det_scr.asp?unid=5800&langsel=en.

55. Peter Baker and Rachel Donadio, "Obama Wins More Food Aid but Presses African Nations on Corruption," *New York Times* (July 11, 2009).

CHAPTER 7

RAPID URBANIZATION AND THE POLITICS OF THE URBAN POOR

E ach day, in the villages of Bangladesh, China, Kenya, Egypt, and Brazil, thousands of young men and women pack up their meager belongings and board buses, trucks, or trains for the long trip to Dhaka, Shanghai, Nairobi, Cairo, or Rio. Often they travel alone, sometimes with family or friends. They are a part of the largest and most dramatic tidal wave of human migration in world history. Despairing of any hope for a better life in the countryside and seeking new opportunities for themselves and their children, millions of villagers leave the world they have known for the uncertainties of the city. In Africa, refugees fleeing civil wars and famine have augmented the legions of migrants. In the aftermath of Rwanda's 1994 ethnic genocide, that country's urban population grew by an astounding 11.6 percent *annually* between 2000 and 2005. By 2030, the proportion of its population living in urban areas will have climbed from only 18.3 percent (in 2003) to 58.5 percent.[1] At the same time, as migration adds to the size of Third World cities, urban populations are also growing as a result of "natural increase"—the annual total of births minus deaths—among those already living in cities.

THE THIRD WORLD'S URBAN EXPLOSION

Not long ago, the United Nations Population Fund (UNFPA) looked back to a prediction that it had made a decade earlier: "the growth of cities," it had said in 1997, "will be the single largest influence on development in the 21st century." Now, the Fund observes, "this statement is proving more accurate by the day." In 2008, the number of people living in cities through out the world exceeded the rural population for the first time in human history. The proportion of city dwellers in the LDCs is still only about 40 percent, but will pass 50 percent by 2017. Although, the rate of rural-to-urban migration has been slowing and birth rates have generally declined, the world's urban population will still nearly double from 2007 to 2050, an increase of more than 3 billion people. Nearly all of that growth (95 percent) will come from the LDCs (see Table 7.1).[2]

Most migrants maintain close links with their rural roots long after they have left the countryside. Some of them intend to accumulate savings and eventually return to their villages. "Others alternate between city and country in a permanent pendular pattern."[3] Indeed, in various parts of West Africa and Southeast Asia, more than half the urban migrants are temporary, including those who repeatedly circulate between village and city.[4] In China prior to the

TABLE 7.1   Urbanization in the Developed and Less Developed Worlds

	2000	*2025*	*2050*
Urban Population			
Developed Countries	872,925,000	994,720,000	1,071,393,000
Less Developed Countries	1,980,984,000	3,589,513,000	5,326,899,000
Annual Urban Growth Rate			
Developed Countries (%)	0.56[a]	0.46[b]	0.19[c]
Less Developed Countries (%)	2.96[a]	2.07[b]	1.26[c]
Percentage Urban			
Developed Countries	73.1	79.0	86.0
Less Developed Countries	40.2	53.2	67.0

[a]Average annual growth rate for 1995–2000
[b]Average annual growth rate for 2020–2025
[c]Average annual growth rate for 2045–2050

Source: United Nations Population Division, *World Urbanization Prospects: The 2007 Revision Population Database*, http://esa.un.org/unup/.

1980s, government restrictions made it difficult to migrate to the cities. Even now, most urban migrants still live in a bureaucratic limbo without assurance of permanence. Known as China's "floating population," they currently number more than 150 million people and that figure is expected to double by 2025. Some stay permanently, but most do not. Although not officially counted as part of the urban population (because their official documents supposedly restrict their residence to their home villages), they actually account for about one-fifth of China's urban residents. In Shanghai, China's largest city and its economic hub, 6 million migrants constitute one-third of the population. In contrast, Latin America's cityward migrants tend to settle permanently. Whatever their initial aspirations, the Third World's rural-to-urban migrants continue to crowd the urban slums and shantytowns they have come to call home.

Swelled by the influx of migrants in recent decades as well as natural increase, Third World urban populations have ballooned and will continue to grow rapidly in the coming years. Table 7.1 shows that between 2000 and 2050, the urban population of the world's *developed* nations will grow by nearly 200 million (from nearly 873 million people to 1.07 billion), an increase of approximately 22 percent. On the other hand, Third World cities will expand by approximately 260 percent (from nearly 2 billion people to over 5.3 billion). Further, Table 7.1 indicates that during the last 5 years of the twentieth century, the urban population of the developed countries grew by only 0.56 percent annually, whereas cities in the LDCs expanded more than five times as fast (2.96 percent). During the first half of this century, urban growth will slow down in both regions, but Third World cities will continue to grow at about 5–6 times the rate of industrialized nations. At the start of this century, less than one-half of the LDCs' population (40.2 percent) lived in cities, but by mid-century that figure will increase to 67 percent.

The magnitude of that expansion has placed tremendous strains on public services, housing, public health, and personal safety in these large cities. In Latin America, the rate of growth was most rapid in the middle of the twentieth century. In just a single decade (1950–1960), the populations of Bogotá (Colombia) and Caracas (Venezuela) doubled, while Lima (Peru) nearly tripled. Since the 1970s, the *rate* of growth in the region's largest metropolises has slowed, but in absolute terms, there is still considerable migration to both primary and secondary cities. African cities, though starting from a smaller base, expanded at an even faster pace. Between 1960 and 1983, Kinshasa (Congo) grew by nearly 600 percent and Abidjan (Côte d'Ivoire) by more than 800 percent.[5] Today, a number of major, Third World cities are still doubling their populations in two decades or less. As Table 7.2 indicates (column 3), Latin America and the Caribbean are by far the most urbanized regions in the developing world, reaching 78 percent in 2007. Currently, Mexico City's population of more than 18 million people makes it the world's second largest metropolitan area (behind Tokyo). Elsewhere in Latin America, São Paulo, Brazil (4th largest), and Buenos Aires, Argentina (8th), are close behind.[6]

As of 2007, the urban areas of South Asia (31 percent), sub-Saharan Africa (36 percent), and East Asia (42 percent) represented a far lower percentage of the population than in Latin America (Table 7.2, column 3). On the other hand cities in sub-Saharan Africa and South Asia are now growing far more rapidly than in Latin America and by 2050, they will have closed the gap considerably (see columns 3 and 4). In 1960, Casablanca (Morocco) and Cairo (Egypt) were the only African cities with more than 1 million people. By 1983, nine cities in the region reached or surpassed that size.[7] As Table 7.3 indicates, in a number of sub-Saharan African metropolises—such as Addis Ababa (Ethiopia) and Lagos (Nigeria)—populations will continue to skyrocket. Indeed, greater Lagos and Dhaka (Bangladesh) are expected to have populations exceeding 24 million and 19 million respectively by 2015, making them two of the world's largest megacities.[8]

TABLE 7.2   Percentage of the Third World's Population in Urban Areas (by Region)

Region	Percentage Urban 1975	Percentage Urban 2007	Projected Percentage Urban 2050
Third World	27	44	67
Arab States	42	51	72
East Asia and the Pacific	21	42	73
Latin America and the Caribbean	61	78	89
South Asia	21	31	57
Sub-Saharan Africa	21	36	61

Source: United Nations, Department of Economic and Social Affairs, Population Division, "*Urban and Rural Areas, 2007*," http://www.un.org/esa/population/unpop.html, United Nations Development Programme, *Human Development Report 2007/2008*, Human Development Indicators, Table 5, http://hdr.undp.org/en/media/HDR_20072008_EN_Complete.pdf.

TABLE 7.3   Populations of Third World Metropolitan Areas, 1995–2015

City	Population	
	1995	*2015 (predicted)*
Mexico City	16,562,000	19,180,000
Tegucigalpa	995,000	2,016,000
Santiago	4,891,000	6,066,000
Cairo	9,690,000	16,530,000
Casablanca	3,101,000	4,835,000
Addis Ababa	2,431,000	6,578,000
Lagos	10,287,000	24,640,000
Bangkok	6,547,000	9,844,000
Dhaka	8,545,000	19,486,000

Source: United Nations Development Programme, *Human Development Report, 1998* (New York: Oxford University Press, 1998), 174–175.

Of course, within each Third World region, the proportion of people residing in cities varies considerably from country to country. As Table 7.4 (column 3) indicates, the percentage of the population living in cities in individual countries in 2007 ranged from around 17 percent in Ethiopia to approximately 88 percent in Chile. Note, however, the enormous urban expansion in several African and Asian nations: Ethiopia's urban population is projected to grow from about 17 percent (in 2007) to 42 percent by mid-century. Indonesia and China were less than 20 percent urban in 1975, but have climbed to about 50 percent in 2007 and will reach 73–79 percent by 2050.

TABLE 7.4   Percentage of the Population Living in Urban Areas (by Country)

Country	*Percentage Urban 1975*	*Percentage Urban 2007*	*Percentage Urban 2050 (estimate)*
Egypt	39	43	62
Ethiopia	10	17	42
Nigeria	23	48	75
Sudan	19	43	74
Indonesia	19	50	79
China	17	42	73
Chile	78	88	94
Dominican Republic	46	68	86

Source: United Nations, Department of Economic and Social Affairs, Population Division, "*Urban and Rural Areas, 2007,*" http://www.un.org/esa/population/unpop.html, *United Nations Development Programme,* Human Development Report, 2007, Table 5, http://hdr.undp.org/en/media/HDR_2007 2008_EN_Complete.pdf.

THE POLITICAL CONSEQUENCES OF URBAN GROWTH

Surprisingly, the Third World's urban population explosion since the mid-twentieth century is not without precedent. From 1875 to the early 1900s, Western nations experienced enormous, urban growth *rates*. What makes the LDCs' experience unique, however, is the sheer volume of people involved. The current population of the developing world is much larger than that of nineteenth-century Europe and North America. It is one thing for a nineteenth-century European city to grow from 80,000 to 400,000 people in a 25-year period. It is quite another for Seoul (South Korea) to swell from 1 million to nearly 7 million, for Kinshasa (Congo) to spiral from 400,000 to more than 2.5 million, and for Lagos to expand from 10 million to more than 25 million in the same number of years. Massive population shifts such as these obviously place enormous pressures on urban housing, education, and transportation, among others.

This chapter examines two important aspects of urban politics in the developing world. First, it looks at the problems that exploding urban populations present to political leaders and government planners. Specifically, it asks how poor countries can provide city dwellers with needed jobs, housing, sanitation, and other services, while also protecting them from crime. What is the government's role in those areas, and how do state policies interact with private-sector activities and self-help efforts? Second, we examine the political attitudes and behavior of city dwellers in the LDCs, focusing particularly on the politics of the urban poor. To what extent do the inhabitants of urban shantytowns and slums have political orientations that are distinct from both those of the rural poor and those of the urban middle and upper classes? Is rapid urbanization likely to contribute to political development, or does it carry the seeds of political instability?

THE SEARCH FOR EMPLOYMENT

Contemporary Third World urbanization differs from the West's earlier urban explosion in two important respects. First, as we have noted, the number of urban migrants and the size of Third World cities during the twentieth to twenty-first centuries dwarf the extent of the West's urban explosion in the eighteenth and nineteenth centuries. Second, the urban explosion in Europe and North America occurred during an era of unprecedented industrialization and economic growth. Modern capitalism was coming of age and could accommodate—indeed required—the wave of migrant and immigrant laborers. By contrast, the economies of most contemporary LDCs have failed to provide sufficient employment for their growing urban workforce.

To be sure, many people do find jobs, and some low-income workers achieve impressive upward mobility. For example, one study of Howrah, an industrial city in West Bengal (India), found that "several hundred men who started with almost nothing now own factories large enough to employ twenty-five [or more] workers," placing them "among the richest people in the community."[9] There are similar examples in the other regions of the developing world. Still, these cases are very exceptional. A host of other workers have achieved much more modest success. However, most of the urban poor must engage in an ongoing struggle for economic survival. For example, even during Mexico's impressive economic boom in the 1960s and 1970s, the country's expanding modern sector was able to provide regular employment for only about half the people seeking to enter the urban workforce. The severe recessions that gripped Africa and Latin America in the 1980s, parts of Asia in the late 1990s, and much of the world today all exacerbated urban poverty, as industrial employment plummeted in scores of countries. Furthermore, at times, various countries in Latin America and Africa have suffered from high rates of inflation, making it impossible for people, even those who were regularly employed, to support their families adequately.

Many of the urban poor who are unable to find work in the so-called *formal sector* of the urban economy (the government and more modern, private-sector enterprises) turn to the *informal economy* for jobs. As noted in Chapter 5, this sector is defined as the part of the economy that is "unregulated by the institutions of society [most notably the state], in a legal and social environment in which similar activities are regulated" and taxed.[10] Most of the workers in the informal economy are self-employed (an estimated 70 percent) in occupations ranging from garbage recyclers to shoeshine boys, street vendors, mechanics, electricians, plumbers, and drivers of unlicensed taxis. Others work in "underground" factories or other business that operate outside the law.

Of course, informal-sector activity is not limited to the developing world. In recent years, cities such as New York, Los Angeles, and Milan have seen substantial expansion in the number of unlicensed street vendors, underground sweatshops, and other endeavors that are "off the books." In the Third World, however, the informal economy represents a far greater proportion of total urban employment. According to a 2005 World Bank estimate, the informal sector may have generated as much as 70 percent of urban employment and 30 percent of the LDCs' gross domestic product.[11] Those figures have undoubtedly increased during the current global economic crisis.

In the vast garbage dumps of Cairo and Mexico City, hordes of entrepreneurs sift through the refuse looking to recycle marketable waste. On the commercial boulevards of Manila (Philippines) and Nairobi (Kenya), an army of street vendors sells food, household appliances, and bootleg DVDs. In Lagos and Lahore (Pakistan), shoemakers and carpenters, working out of their homes, sell their wares to appreciative clients. All belong to the informal economy. While outside observers once assumed that people working in this sector were particularly impoverished, we now know that their earning power varies greatly and that some of them have higher incomes than the average factory worker does.

Over the years, government planners and social scientists have debated the informal economy's merits and faults. Critics point out that its workers are not protected by minimum wage laws and do not have access to government health and welfare programs such as social security. Proponents respond that the informal economy not only employs vast numbers of people who would otherwise have no work, but it also contributes a substantial proportion of the Third World's consumer goods and services. Consequently, these analysts argue, Third

World governments should cease trying to regulate and license the informal sector and instead should allow it to flourish and expand.

Another source of employment is the public sector. Third World governments employ significant numbers of white-collar workers and bureaucrats. These jobs are a boon to the urban middle class since there is insufficient employment in the private sector. In addition, many governments own various economic enterprises (parastatals)—including the oil industry, railroads, electric power plants, and steel mills—which provide relatively well-paid, blue-collar jobs in economies generally plagued by high unemployment.

Unfortunately, there have been two major problems with public-sector employment. First, in their efforts to gain popular support, the government or the ruling party have often padded bureaucratic and parastatal payrolls with unneeded employees. While this creates some badly needed jobs, it adds to government deficits and makes these institutions highly inefficient. Second, public-sector employment is frequently treated as a political plum, with jobs going to ruling party activists and government supporters, rather than to the most qualified applicants. In many countries, government bureaucracies hire unneeded white-collar workers as a form of political patronage. In fact, many employees never show up except to collect their paychecks. At the start of the 1990s, some 40 percent of all government bureaucrats and state workers in Sierra Leone were "ghosts," employees on the payroll who never worked.

As we will see, in the past two decades, faced with spiraling government spending and large external debts, most LDCs have been forced to reduce the size of their state sectors substantially, often under pressure from the International Monetary Fund (IMF). While these cuts were necessary in order to cut huge government budget deficits and reduce inflation, they have imposed a heavy burden on white- and blue-collar workers who have been laid off and on young workers who faced limited opportunities for future employment.

Only in communist countries such as China and Cuba has the state been a major employer. Those governments have considered employment to be a fundamental workers' right and a source of legitimacy for the system. Until recently, some communist governments created as many jobs as necessary to achieve full, or nearly full, employment, no matter how economically inefficient many of these jobs might be. Under China's "iron rice bowl" policy, factory workers were essentially guaranteed a job for life. But as the country has moved toward a capitalist economy, it has closed many inefficient plants and no longer guarantees workers their employment.

In other Third World countries, the state has always been a limited employer. Therefore, governments primarily influence the urban job market indirectly, through their **macroeconomic policies**. Two areas of economic policy have particularly influenced the job market: the government's industrialization strategy and its handling of inflation. Differences in government industrialization policies led to very different employment outcomes in Latin America and East Asia.*

Starting as early as the 1930s and 1940s, governments in the larger, more developed Latin American nations—including Mexico, Argentina, and Brazil—introduced economic policies designed to stimulate domestic manufacturing of

---

* I will discuss macroeconomic policy in greater detail in Chapter 10. The reader wishing to better understand the economic analysis offered briefly in this section is referred to that chapter.

consumer goods that until then had been largely imported. Toward that objective, those governments introduced tariff walls and other protectionist measures limiting competing imports. Furthermore, the state offered national industries financial stimuli, such as cheap credit, designed to nourish them. These policies had various purposes—including diversifying the economy and reducing the country's dependency on foreign imports—but one of the most important goals was creating industrial employment for the urban working class. Not surprisingly, the so-called **populist parties** that promoted these policies were able to win the support of both the business community and the labor unions.

However, while state-supported industrialization expanded impressively into the 1960s and created a substantial number of skilled, well-paying jobs, the government's trade and financial policies also enabled local manufacturers to import machinery for their factories at relatively low prices. Given that opportunity and faced with the prospect of dealing with Latin America's many militant labor unions, new industries were often capital-intensive (i.e., heavily mechanized and using imported, modern technology), thereby providing comparatively fewer additional jobs (we will soon contrast that with Asia's very different industrialization strategy). At the same time, government trade protectionism that largely shielded local industries from import competition gave domestic firms little incentive to improve the quality of their products or lower their prices. Consequently, few of the goods manufactured in Latin America could compete in the international market. In time, a combination of inefficient industries, excessive government spending, and growing trade deficits brought the region to a major economic crisis in the 1980s. In contrast, East Asia's developing economies—Hong Kong, Singapore, South Korea, Taiwan, Thailand, Malaysia, and Indonesia—also began with protectionist industrialization policies like Latin America's but soon reduced or removed those measures, forcing domestic manufacturers to compete with foreign imports. That competition forced Asian firms to produce goods whose quality and price were competitive both at home and in the export market. Furthermore, the East Asian model was labor-intensive, relying less on imported machinery and more on cheap, nonunionized labor. During the last decades of the twentieth century, the unparalleled growth of the region's export-oriented industries created many new jobs in the cities. Indeed, in time, labor shortages developed, driving up wages. The current world economic crisis has slowed or reversed that trend for now in many Asian countries, but urban employment will surely expand once again, when this crisis ends. Since the 1980s, Latin America has largely abandoned its earlier protectionist measures and tried to emulate the East Asian success story by stressing manufactured exports.

Beginning in the 1970s and 1980s, many Third World countries—particularly in Africa and Latin America—experienced severe inflation rates, largely caused by excessive government deficit spending. In some of the worst cases, annual inflation rates reached as high as 3,000 percent annually in Argentina and Brazil and 8,000 percent in Peru.* More recently (2008), annual inflation in the African

---

* To appreciate what 8,000 percent inflation would feel like in the United States, imagine a car that cost $10,000 on January 1. After a year of 8,000 percent inflation that car would cost over $800,000.

country of Zimbabwe surpassed an incredible *230 million percent* before the government stopped printing new Zimbabwean dollars in early 2009 (one of the worst cases of hyperinflation in world history). Encouraged or pressured by the IMF, the World Bank, and private foreign banks, many heavily indebted African and Latin American countries adopted macroeconomic policies, designed to slash inflation rates. These measures sought to lower large budgetary and trade deficits by slashing government spending, cutting public-sector employment, devaluing the national currency, and privatizing state enterprises (selling them to private investors). These policies—officially called structural adjustment and monetary stabilization programs, but widely known as austerity programs—were usually quite successful in curtailing high inflation rates. In doing so, they were extremely helpful to urban consumers, especially the poor. At the same time, however, stabilization entailed major cutbacks in government and private-sector employment. For example, when the Mexican government privatized the previously state-owned steel industry, the new owners laid off half of the industry's workforce. Austerity programs also reduced employment in the public sector and cut government spending on education, public health, and welfare programs that had benefited the poor.

THE URBAN POOR'S STRUGGLE FOR HOUSING

Of all the problems facing the urban poor, particularly the wave of new migrants, none is more serious than finding adequate housing. With many metropolitan areas doubling in size every 10–25 years, private-sector housing cannot possibly expand fast enough to meet the need. Besides, most of the new homes and apartment houses built for private sale or rental are built for the middle and upper classes, because there is little profit to be made in building low-income housing. At the same time, while many Third World governments have invested in public housing, their rents are commonly too high for most low-income families to afford. Therefore, lacking adequate options in the private or state sectors, many of the urban poor live in squatter settlements and other forms of "self-help" (occupant-built) housing, collectively called "spontaneous shelter."* Others crowd into existing urban slums (decaying tenements). The poorest city dwellers, lacking the resources to rent or build, are often homeless, residing in doorways, unused construction material, or the like. In Cairo, several hundred thousand people, with nowhere else to go, live amidst cemetery tombs.

In all, the total population of slum dwellers (living either in squatter settlements or dilapidated older housing) and homeless persons account for close to half the population of Third World cities. UN data from earlier in the decade indicate that about 30 percent of the urban population in North Africa, Latin America, and the Caribbean live in slum (substandard) housing. That number rises to 57 percent in South Asia and 72 percent in sub-Saharan Africa. Looking

---

*While squatter settlements (also called shantytowns) are poor neighborhoods, not everyone living in them is poor. A minority of shantytown residents are white-collar workers or well-paid blue-collar workers. Some of them achieved upward mobility since first settling there, but have remained there because of attachments to friends and community.

at individual nations, about 40 percent of the urban populations live in slums or squatter settlements in Brazil, Egypt, and Turkey. In urban India, that figure rises to about 55 percent. The slum and squatter population accounts for about 70–80 percent of all urban residents in Kenya, Pakistan, and Nigeria, and jumps to 86 percent in Haiti and 98 percent in Afghanistan.[12] Millions of the Third World's urban poor, including many of them who have built their own homes, have no direct access to clean water or sanitation facilities.

Today, the availability of basic urban services in low-income neighborhoods varies considerably from region to region. For example, a recent survey of eight low-income neighborhoods in Latin America—located in Rio de Janeiro and Aracajo (Brazil) as well as Santiago and Temuco (Chile)—found that nearly all of the inhabitants had running water and electricity. On the other hand, a parallel study of eight poor, African neighborhoods—in the cities of Abidjan and Man (both in Côte d'Ivoire) and Nairobi and Kisumu (Kenya)—revealed that almost all the residents had to buy their drinking water in cans (a minority had nearby wells, while virtually no families had tap water in their homes). Similarly, very few homes in any of the eight African neighborhoods studied had electricity, which was either unavailable or too expensive.[13] In light of these glaring needs, developing nations frequently have searched for appropriate state responses.

Public Housing and the Role of the State

Throughout the developing world, many governments have constructed public housing to alleviate housing shortages. In China, workers in state enterprises are commonly assigned apartments linked to their employment. Cuba's revolutionary government has built large apartment blocks, some of them housing 25,000–40,000 persons on the outskirts of its largest cities. During Venezuela's petroleum boom in the late 1970s and early 1980s, the government constructed as many as 34,000 urban housing units annually.[14] Hugo Chávez's populist government built many additional units during the most recent oil boom. In the 1960s and 1970s, various African governments established housing agencies with far more limited resources. One of the continent's most ambitious programs was in the Côte d'Ivoire, where some 40,000 units were constructed during the 1970s, almost all in the capital city of Abidjan. By the close of that decade, the Kenyan government was building more than 3,000 units annually.[15]

In time, however, it has become clear that public housing cannot provide sufficient shelter for the poor, and, in some cases, such housing projects actually worsen their plight. In the capital cities of India, Senegal, and Nigeria, for example, government housing projects have often been designed to eradicate "urban blight," that is, "unsightly," low-income slums built near the city center. To make the central city more aesthetically pleasing to the political elite, urban planners, middle-class residents, and foreign tourists, the government has sometimes eradicated those slums and replaced them with government buildings or government-built middle-class housing. Rarely did the poor families who had been evicted from their homes subsequently secure a home in low-income public housing projects. Even those who received alternate housing were usually relocated on the edges of town, far removed from their workplace. Diana Patel describes how Zimbabwe's government periodically ousted the same squatters from their settlements in different parts of the nation's capital, in effect "chasing them around town." Instead, many of the urban poor turn to self-built housing, often in sprawling shantytowns located in remote parts of town. Many government planners, viewing these shacks from a middle-class perspective, believed that unless the squatters can afford "decent" urban housing with plumbing and multiple rooms for their families, they would be better off returning to the countryside.[16]

In fact, we have noted that most public housing projects do not serve the poor at all. In order for the government to recoup its construction costs, it must sell or rent the new housing units at higher rates than the urban poor can afford. Consequently, the state faces two options: it can subsidize rents and mortgages to bring their cost down to a level that the poor can afford, or it can rent or sell the dwellings to those who have enough money to live there without state subsidies, namely the middle class.

Despite its obvious value as a welfare benefit for the poor, subsidized housing has several drawbacks. First, even if the government wants to subsidize low-income housing, it is too costly for most developing nations to sustain. For example, following the Cuban revolution, the government committed itself to providing homes for the urban lower class. To demonstrate its generosity and gain public support, the government poured far more into these projects than it charged the new tenants. As one political scientist observed, "early housing policies reflected Fidel Castro's belief that nothing was too good for the working class."[17] Projects such as Santiago's José Martí provided schools, day-care centers, theaters, clinics, and stores for its 40,000 inhabitants. However, by lavishing excessively "luxurious" housing on early recipients, the government soon ran out of funds for the many others needing shelter. Thus, the East Havana project, planned for 100,000 dwelling units, ultimately contained only 1,500. Furthermore, Castro's government, like many other communist regimes, placed a greater priority on building hospitals, schools, stadiums, and other public places, than on housing. And even though the state lacked the resources to meet the country's housing needs, it discouraged or prohibited private and self-help housing (i.e., units built by the owner) for many years. Not surprisingly, Cuba, like most communist regimes, has suffered chronic housing shortages.

Second, in many LDCs, subsidized housing has become a political plum, in which allocation of units is based, not on need, but rather on the applicants' activism on behalf of ruling party or their support for the government. Because political patronage plays such an important role, police officers, government bureaucrats, and teachers, are often among the first served.[18] Consequently, residents in state housing are often middle or lower middle class. They can afford to pay higher rents than low-income families can and have the political connections to secure access to public housing.

Singapore and Hong Kong are among the very few cities that provide low-income, public housing to a large portion of the population, including low-income residents. However, they have unique circumstances that make it highly unlikely that other LDCs will or can replicate their records. First, they are very densely populated city-states (Singapore) or virtual city-states (Hong Kong) with very little unused land. So they have no room for sprawling shantytowns and no alternative but to house the poor in high-rise housing projects. Second, both are among the Third World's most affluent cities and, hence, can afford the cost of extensive, state-subsidized, low-income housing. With the exception of several small, oil-rich Gulf States, the governments of other LDCs lack the resources to provide housing for a large segment of the urban poor. Consequently, many analysts believe that the government should not try to provide relatively costly, completed housing units to poor families, but instead should support cheaper alternatives that can serve far more people. With developing nations cutting back on government spending since the 1980s, the case for cheaper, but more widely disbursed, housing solutions has become yet more powerful.

Spontaneous Housing

For years, many social scientists and urban planners have maintained that the most effective remedy for housing shortfalls in Third World cities is spontaneous (or self-built) shelter—that is, the very shantytowns and squatter settlements that are so widely viewed as urban blights. In cities throughout the developing world, the poor have built their own homes, sometimes with hired or volunteer assistance. While living in these dwellings, many proprietors, particularly in Africa, also rent space to needy individuals or families. In some cases, the property owners are squatters, living on land that has been occupied illegally, often with the compliance of government authorities.[19] Others, residing in so-called "pirate settlements," have purchased their lots from land speculators but lack ownership titles because their community does not conform to government zoning requirements.[20]

Spontaneous housing settlements range in size from a few isolated homes to communities of many thousands. For example, on the dried-up marshlands outside Mexico City, the municipality of Netzahualcóyotl began as a pirate settlement in the 1940s. By 1970, it housed 600,000 people.[21] Organized protests eventually persuaded the national government to provide badly needed urban services and to grant the squatters legal title to their homes. Elsewhere, up to 40 percent of Nairobi's population and one-fourth to one-third of the inhabitants of Jakarta, Karachi, and Lima live in squatter settlements.[22] These homes, argued John F. C. Turner, often have been erroneously viewed by politicians and planners as a problem, when, in fact, they are a major part of the solution to urban housing needs.[23] Rather than building public housing, he insisted, Third World governments can serve many more people by removing legal and political obstacles to spontaneous housing settlements, giving squatters title to their land, and helping residents upgrade the dwellings that they have built.

Self-built homes have several important advantages over public housing.[24] First, they actually serve the poor, whereas most public housing does not. Second, they afford occupants the opportunity to upgrade their homes continuously. For example, in Lima's vast network of shantytowns, one can observe many wood and straw shacks whose owners are building brick walls around them, slowly constructing a better home as funds become available. Third, precisely because they are self-built, these homes better address the needs and desires of their owners than do units built by government planners. Finally, squatter settlements have the "churches, bars, and neighborhood stores that help create a sense of community" that is too often lacking in large, impersonal public housing projects.[25] Given these advantages, proponents of spontaneous housing argue that the state's most constructive role would be to stop evicting illegal squatters and grant them land titles and other assistance needed to improve their homes. Over the years, the governments of Peru, Brazil, and other nations have given millions of illegal squatters title to their plots of land and provided public services such as sewage or drinking water.

Sites-and-Services Programs

Other analysts who favored a more active role for the state viewed the Turner's thesis as a convenient excuse for governments that did not wish to spend much on the poor. Championing self-help housing charged these critics, merely perpetuated the status quo, and allowed the state to direct its limited housing resources toward the middle class.[26]

Ultimately, many Third World governments, the World Bank, and other foreign-aid donors have pursued a middle ground between providing expensive, fully built public housing units and a **laissez-faire** policy that leaves the government with little role to play. In countries as diverse as Colombia, India, Malawi, and Turkey, the state has sold or rented parcels of land to the poor with basic services such as running water, sewage, and electricity. Buyers then build their own homes on the sites as they do with spontaneous housing. In some cases, governments provide credit, technical assistance, or low-cost construction materials.[27]

These "**sites-and-services**" programs have several obvious advantages. First, they allow the government to steer self-built housing to locations that are safer and more environmentally sound. By contrast, unregulated spontaneous shelters in Caracas illustrate the dangers of unzoned squatter settlements. There, more than half a million people live on precarious hillsides in shacks that are sometimes washed away during the rainy season by mudslides. Second, in contrast to many sprawling squatter communities, inhabitants of sites-and-services settlements have electricity, sanitation, and other basic services from the outset. Furthermore, although occupants must purchase their sites, the lots are far more affordable than are fully built, state housing units.

Critics of sites-and-services programs concede that the communities developed on those sites are generally healthier, safer, and more aesthetically pleasing than spontaneous shelter, but they point out that they still fail to help the very poor, who cannot afford even these lots. In addition, they charge that these programs draw away the most talented and successful residents of existing slums and shantytowns, thereby leaving the older communities bereft of leadership. Moreover, they note that governments tend to locate sites-and-services projects in remote areas of town in order to remove the poor from downtown business areas. Consequently, their inhabitants live far from their jobs and from important urban facilities.[28]

Such criticisms notwithstanding, we have seen that sites-and-services programs have some clear advantages over unaided spontaneous shelters and clearly benefit the poor more than fully built public housing does. Unfortunately, these programs often have not been self-financing (i.e., government income from the rent or sale of lots has not covered their cost). Consequently, during the periodic economic crises that LDCs have faced over the years, many governments have abandoned them, once again leaving the poor to fend for themselves. Finally, in time, both sites-and-services programs and unregulated squatter settlements have faced a growing obstacle—because of increasing urban sprawl, cities have ever-diminishing space for any type of self-built housing.[29]

THE PROBLEM OF URBAN CRIME

Escalating crime is a problem in many Latin American and African cities, but East Asia's major urban areas are generally safer than large American cities.[30] In places such as Rio de Janeiro and Nairobi, large, well-armed youth gangs escalate the level of violence. For example, in Nairobi's massive Mathare slum (housing some 500,000 people), a recent war between two tribally based gangs resulted in 10 deaths and 600 homes burned to the ground in a period of five days. Thousands of families fled the area, seeking shelter in makeshift refugee camps in other parts of Nairobi. In late 2007 and early 2008, the massive slum was the scene of violent, ethnically based protests against apparently fraudulent vote tallies in the 2007 presidential election. In many developing countries, crime is more than a personal concern. It has become an important political issue, eliciting mass demonstrations and angry demands for better protection from robbery and violent crime. Just as in the United States and other industrialized nations, the origins of criminal activity often lie in poverty, discrimination, income inequality, inadequate schools, and broken families. Its victims come from all social classes—poor, middle class, and, less frequently, the rich. However, throughout the world, the urban poor represent a disproportionate percentage of the perpetrators *and* the victims of crime. The confluence of poverty and social decay helps explain why violent crime rates in Africa and Latin America are generally much higher than in economically advanced nations.

Nevertheless, some countries and regions do not fit that pattern. For example, the rates of homicides and rapes are a good deal higher in the United States, a very wealthy country, than in other advanced industrial countries and even exceed the levels in Third World countries such as South Korea, Indonesia, Hong Kong, Malaysia, Singapore, Tunisia, and Kuwait. Conversely, despite its substantial poverty, Asia's violent crime rates tend to be substantially lower than in the United States or even Western Europe.[31] Indeed, the United States has a homicide rate about five times as high as Indonesia's, four times as high as Tunisia's, and two to three times as high as South Korea's and Chile's.[32] One possible explanation for these anomalies is that income *inequality* may be a more important factor than is the *absolute* rate of poverty in determining the crime rate. Countries such as the United States, South Africa, and Brazil—all of whom have particularly high income inequality—tend to have higher violent crime rates than other countries with comparable or lower per-capita incomes but greater equality. Thus, Asian countries such as Bangladesh, Indonesia, India, and Pakistan, though housing large, impoverished populations, have less income inequality than the United States does.

African and Latin American cities (largely poor *and* unequal) tend to suffer from high rates of crime. For example, Colombia and South Africa, with some of the world's most extreme income inequality, often suffer the world's highest annual rates of urban homicide and rape. Rio de Janeiro is among the world's leaders in robbery and sexual assaults, while Kingston (Jamaica), Kampala

(Uganda), and Gaborone (Botswana) also suffer from exceptionally high levels of violent crime. All of them also have very high concentrations of income and wealth. Like almost any correlation, the association between inequality and crime is not absolute. For example, while income is very unequally distributed in Chile's cities, the country (mostly urban) has a low violent crime rate. Similarly, both Hong Kong and Singapore, though they have moderately high concentration of income and wealth, are among the safest cities in the world. In these cases, other factors likely influence crime rate. These include cultural values, the strength of nuclear families, and the likelihood of being caught and punished by the criminal justice system. For the most part, however, the level of income equality is an excellent predictor of the level of criminal activity.

Comparative homicide statistics are informative, but may not always tell the whole story. For example, highly industrialized nations have superior medical facilities (including trauma centers) compared to poorer countries. Therefore, many violent crime victims who die in countries such as El Salvador or Angola survive in American or French hospitals and do not add to the murder rate. In general, the homicide statistics released by groups such as the United Nations and the CIA are fairly consistent with each other (e.g., all data sources agree that Colombia and Mexico have high murder rates, while Saudi Arabia and Indonesia have low rates). Nevertheless, people in some countries may be less prone to report violent crimes (such as rapes and honor killings) than others. And some criminal justice systems are far more competent than others in recording crime statistics accurately.

Table 7.5 offers a different means of measuring and comparing crime rates. About a decade ago, researchers conducted surveys in cities located in the major regions of the world. Rather than accepting official crime statistics, the study asked respondents directly whether they had been a victim of crime in the *previous 5 years*. The table reflects the percentage of the urban population that claimed to have been victimized during that period. Column 2 indicates the percentage of the population that had been a victim of violent crimes. Column 3 indicates the percentage of the respondents who had suffered either violent or nonviolent crimes. Because the data were obtained through interviews of crime victims, they do not include homicides since existing survey techniques do not enable us to interview murder victims.

TABLE 7.5 Percentage of the Urban Population Victimized by Crime within the Previous 5 Years

Region	Victims of Violent Crimes[a] (Other than Homicide) (%)	Victims of All Crimes (Other than Homicide) (%)
Western Europe	15	60
North America	20	65
South America	31	68
Asia	11	44
Africa	33	76

[a]Rape, assault, muggings, grievous bodily harm.

Source: Franz Vanderschueren, "From Violence to Security and Justice in Cities," *Environment and Urbanization*, vol. 8, no. 1 (April, 1996), 94.

This table indicates that crime rates are much lower in Asia than in any other region, underdeveloped or developed. "Only" 44 percent of all respondents had been crime victims in the previous 5 years, considerably lower than 60 percent in Western Europe, the 65 percent in North America or 76 percent in Africa. Violent crimes were also far less common in Asia, with only 11 percent of the population victimized, about half the rate in North America and one-third the level of South America and Africa. Europe was the next safest region, with South America and Africa suffering the highest rates of violent crime.

In addition to normal criminal activity, residents of many cities must deal with "government crime" in the form of corruption. In many Mexican cities, for example, the police will not respond to a homeowner's report of a burglary unless he or she has previously paid the local police officer a small monthly bribe for protection. In polls conducted in a range of locations, only 0.1 percent of British residents (one in a thousand) and 0.2 percent of Americans responded that they had been asked to pay a bribe to a government official (including police) during that year or expected to be asked to pay one before the end of the year. That proportion increased to 19.5 percent in Kampala (Uganda), 29.9 percent in Jakarta (Indonesia), and 59.1 percent in Tirana (Albania).[33] The situation is yet more disturbing when police are themselves involved in criminal activities. In recent years, hundreds of thousands of angry citizens marched in Buenos Aires and Mexico City to protest pervasive police involvement in each city's alarmingly mounting rates of kidnapping. As one Argentine sociologist has observed,

> Each division [of the Buenos Aires police department] dedicates itself to the area of crime that it is supposed to be fighting. The robbery division steals and robs, the narcotics division traffics drugs, auto theft controls the stealing of cars and the chop shops, and those in fraud and bunko, defraud and swindle.[34]

All too sadly, the same can be said of police forces in many other Third World cities. In Mexico City and elsewhere, there has been occasional evidence of police involvement in kidnapping rings. Rampant crime and, especially, extensive police corruption not only threaten the security of all city dwellers (regardless of economic status) but undermine the government's legitimacy.

THE POLITICS OF THE URBAN POOR: CONFLICTING IMAGES

How do the urban poor react politically to their daily struggles for jobs, shelter, and personal safety? As with discussions of peasant politics, social scientists have presented sharply contrasting images of the politics of the urban poor.[35] When political scientists and sociologists first noted the flood of Third World migration and urban growth, many viewed the sprawling slums and squatter settlements as potential hotbeds of unrest or revolution. In a highly influential early work on the LDCs, James Coleman warned that "there exist in most urban centers elements predisposed to anomic activity [behavior caused by alienation, often lacking societal or moral constraints]."[36] Samuel Huntington maintained that the first generation of urban migrants was unlikely to challenge the existing order, but their children often would: "At some point, the slums [and shantytowns] of

Rio and Lima are likely to be swept by social violence, as the children of the city demand the rewards of the city."[37] And economist Barbara Ward, taking note of shantytown poverty and the rise of radical urban movements, insisted that "unchecked, left to grow and fester, there is here enough explosive material to produce . . . bitter class conflict . . . erupting in guerrilla warfare, and threatening, ultimately, the security even of the comfortable West."[38]

As we will see, the urban poor have, indeed, contributed to several recent Third World revolutions. In addition, urban mass violence periodically threatens political stability. For example, the surge in food prices in 2007–2008 provoked urban riots in a large number of countries, including Bangladesh, Cameroon, the Dominican Republic, Egypt, Haiti, Somalia, and Yemen. Nonetheless, the urban conflagrations that many analysts had once expected have been rare. For the most part, the poor have shunned radical political activity and violence. Even at the ballot box, they have been as likely to vote for right-wing or centrist political candidates as for radicals. It now seems clear that initial expectations of a violent or radicalized urban lower class were based on erroneous premises. Many social scientists had assumed that urban migrants, coming to the cities with raised expectations and heightened political sensitivities, would surely turn militant when those expectations were not satisfied. Instead, however horrendous the slums of Cairo, Calcutta, or Caracas may appear to an outside observer, most migrants find them preferable to their previous life in the countryside. For example, the urban poor are far more likely than their rural counterparts to have access to electricity, sewage, tap water, and nearby schools. In many countries, urban migration provides an escape from semifeudal social controls or ethnic civil war. Small wonder that surveys of migrants to Ankara, Baghdad, Bogotá, Mexico City, Rio de Janeiro, and other cities have indicated that most respondents feel better off in their urban hovels than they had in their rural villages.[39] A study of 13 low-income neighborhoods in Bogotá (Colombia), Valencia (Venezuela), and Mexico City revealed that between 64 and 76 percent of those surveyed believed that their settlement was "a good place to live," while only 11–31 percent felt they lived in a "bad place."[40] Periodic economic downturns, including the present crisis, have lowered urban living standards for a while and have undoubtedly embittered some of the poor and middle class. Yet surveys over the years have shown that urbanites generally remain optimistic about the future, particularly their children's future.

When early expectations of urban radicalism and political violence generally failed to materialize, some scholars jumped to the opposite conclusion. For example, based on his studies of low-income neighborhoods in Mexico and Puerto Rico, anthropologist Oscar Lewis concluded that most of the urban poor are prisoners of a "culture of poverty." By that he referred to an underclass that lacks class consciousness, economic and political organization, or long-term aspirations. While distrustful of government, they feel powerless and fatalistic about effecting change. The culture of poverty, Lewis argued, is inherently apolitical and, hence, quite unlikely to generate radical or revolutionary activity or, for that matter, any pressure for change.[41]

A related body of literature describes the urban poor as "**marginal**"—outside the mainstream of the nation's political and economic life. This suggests a vicious cycle in which the exclusion of the poor magnifies their political apathy, which, in turn, isolates them further. They demonstrate a "lack of active participation due to the fact that . . . marginal groups make no decisions; they do not contribute to the molding of society."[42] Like the victims of Lewis's culture of poverty, marginals allegedly show little class consciousness or capacity for long-term collective action.

While it may be true that many poor city dwellers feel incapable of advancing their own lives or influencing the political system—often with good reason—they do not necessarily suffer from the apathy or helplessness that scholars such as Lewis ascribed to them. Levels of fatalism or optimism vary from place to place and from time to time, depending on both the community's cultural values and its socioeconomic experience. When poor slum dwellers in Côte d'Ivoire and Kenya—low-income African countries—were asked whether they believed that "when a person is born, the success he/she is going to have is already decided" (an obvious measure of fatalism), nearly 60 percent of them strongly agreed and an additional 11 percent agreed somewhat. In Brazil, a much more economically developed country with one of the world's most unequal income distributions, only about 15 percent strongly agreed, but some 30 percent agreed somewhat. Finally, in Chile, which has experienced the most rapid economic growth in Latin America since the start of the 1990s and has enjoyed a sharp decline in urban poverty, a mere 4 percent of the respondents strongly agreed, while only 15 percent agreed somewhat.[43] In short, the level of fatalism or optimism among the urban poor varies considerably across nations and seems to correspond to objective economic conditions more than to any culturally embedded values.

Just as initial predictions of radicalism and political violence among the urban lower class have turned out to be greatly exaggerated, so too have the reverse assertions that the poor are invariably apathetic and fatalistic. To be sure, low-income communities generally are not highly politicized. In his study of the poor in Guatemala City, Bryan R. Roberts found that "they claim to avoid politics in their local work, and to them the term *politician* is synonymous with deceit and corruption."[44] Yet those assessments do not originate in the slum dwellers' innate apathy or fatalism. Rather, they come from the realistically "perceived impracticality of [the urban poor] changing the existing order" and, in countries such as Guatemala, from living in a repressive political system.[45] On the other hand, when given the opportunity to organize (i.e., when their political activity is not repressed) and when there is a realistic chance of attaining some benefits from the political system, many low-income communities have seized the opportunity. The slums and shantytowns of Caracas, Lima, and Rio, for example, have spawned numerous, well-organized and politically effective community groups. Furthermore, their leaders often have a keen understanding of how to operate within and manipulate the political system.

In time, social scientists came to question the concepts of marginality and the culture of poverty. In the previously mentioned survey of poor neighborhoods in four African cities (in Côte d'Ivoire and Kenya) and four Latin American cities (in Brazil and Chile), political attitudes, levels of political interest, and political knowledge varied considerably. In all four countries, a majority of the people surveyed responded that they were *not* interested in politics. The portion of those expressing "no interest" ranged from 51 percent in Brazil to 62 and 63 percent in Côte d'Ivoire and Chile.[46] The Chilean figures are noteworthy since 25–30 years earlier the shantytowns of Chile's largest cities were among the most politicized and radicalized in the world. However,

17 years of a repressive military dictatorship, during which many left-wing political activists were jailed or killed, had led many Chileans to disengage from politics.

Yet, despite their professed disinterest, many of these slum dwellers were well informed and communicative about politics. In Chile, Côte d'Ivoire, and Kenya roughly half of them reported talking occasionally with other people "about the problems which [their] country has to face today." That proportion rose to almost two-thirds in Brazil. Moreover, although 51–63 percent of them professed to have no interest in politics, about half of those surveyed in Chile and Côte d'Ivoire claimed that they regularly followed political news. In Brazil and Kenya, that portion fell to about one-third. When asked to name important government leaders, most were quite knowledgeable. In all four nations, at least two-thirds were able to name the president of their country (ranging from 69 percent in Brazil to 94 and 96 percent in Kenya and Chile). Moreover, about half the respondents in Chile and Kenya, and two-thirds in Brazil and Côte d'Ivoire could name the mayor of their town. Most impressively, more than 70 percent of the poor Kenyans and Ivorians could name the president of at least one *other* African country, while almost half the Chileans could name the president of another Latin American country (Brazilians were less knowledgeable). One suspects that these figures exceed the percentage of Americans who can name the president of Mexico or the prime minister of Canada. In short, these low-income city dwellers seemed to have a greater interest in politics than they were willing to admit. Perhaps the question on their level of political interest may have meant something different to them than it did to the people conducting the survey.

On the negative side of the ledger, in all four countries the urban poor tended to take a rather dim view of their political system and their elected representatives. More than 80 percent of those surveyed in each of the four countries believed that "those we elect to parliament lose touch with people pretty quickly," with that number reaching 94 percent in Chile. When asked whether they believed that "public officials care what people like me think," a significant majority in all of the eight cities said "no." The number who believed that public officials *do* care ranged from a low of 15 percent in Chile to a high of 40 percent in Côte d'Ivoire. Perhaps most surprisingly, Ivorians, living in a country that was not democratic, were most positive about their public officials (the poll took place prior to the outbreak of civil war in 2002). On the other hand, Chileans, who live in the most democratic and politically responsive of the four nations, were least likely by far to believe that their government officials care about them and were also least likely to believe that their parliamentary representative keeps in touch with low-income constituents. Perhaps Chileans had harbored unrealistically high expectations of their new political leaders with the restoration of democracy in 1990, ending General Augusto Pinochet's 17-year dictatorship. Another important factor may be that Chilean parties, renowned for their strong linkages to the lower classes prior to the dictatorship, had become elitist and distant during their years in exile.

Thus, that limited sample of Third World cities reveals a wide variety of political attitudes among the urban poor. Similarly, while the poor neighborhoods of, say, Santiago in 1973 or Tehran (Iran) in 1979 may have boiled with unrest, the same neighborhoods may be tranquil or passive years later. Clearly, a more nuanced view of Third World urban politics requires us to ask: Under what circumstances do the poor organize politically? What goals do they seek, and how do they pursue them? What factors determine whether their political organization is peaceful or violent, conservative or radical, reformist or revolutionary?

FORMS OF POLITICAL EXPRESSION AMONG THE URBAN POOR

Political scientists have long understood that the urban poor tend to be better informed and more politically active than their rural counterparts. Indeed, early scholarship on the Third World used a nation's level of urbanization as an indirect indicator of its level of political participation. Lower-income city residents have higher levels of literacy than peasants do, greater exposure to the mass media, and more contact with political campaigns and rallies. This does not mean, however, that most of them are highly politicized. To the contrary, as we have noted, many of them are indifferent, apathetic, or fatalistic about political events (just as many Americans are). Nor does it mean that political activists in the community are necessarily radical or indignant about local living conditions or prone to violent protest. What it does mean is that the urban poor generally vote in higher numbers and follow politics more closely than the peasantry. Furthermore, it appears that many low-income neighborhoods carefully calculate what benefits they can secure from the political system and then organize to secure them. Contrary to initial expectations that the disoriented and frustrated urban poor would riot and rebel, they have tended, instead, to be rather pragmatic and careful in their political behavior.

Individual Political Behavior

For most slum and shantytown dwellers, opportunities for individual political activity are rather restricted. Until recently, voting had a limited political impact in most developing nations. Despite the impressive spread of Third World democracy during the past decades, most countries in Africa and the Middle East, and many in Asia, are still dominated by a single party or leader who controls the election results (e.g., the 2009 presidential elections in Iran and Afghanistan). And even in electoral democracies, where many candidates court the support of the urban poor, they tend to forget those voters between elections.

An alternative, often more fruitful, type of individual political activity takes the form of **clientelism**. Members of the urban lower class often advance their interests by attaching themselves to an influential patron within the government, an influential political party, or an organized political movement. Clientelism (patron–client relationships) involves "the dispensing of public resources as favors by political power holders/seekers . . . in exchange for votes or other forms of popular support."[47] While it does offer concrete advantages to the less-powerful partner (i.e., the client), clientelism is at its heart "a strategy of elite-controlled political participation fostering the status quo."[48] Potentially frustrated or radicalized individuals and groups are thereby co-opted into the political system with the lure of immediate, though limited, gains.

Of course, patron–client relations were also common tools of America's urban political bosses in the late nineteenth and early twentieth centuries. Big-city political machines often aided recently arrived immigrants by giving them help—such as jobs, access to local government authorities, or Christmas turkeys—in exchange for their support at the polls. Today, in cities throughout the Third World, the poor use clientelistic relations to secure credit, government employment, and other economic goods. Dictators such as Zaire's Mobutu Sese Seko and Nicaragua's Anastasio Somoza maintained their regimes for years by dispensing patronage. And in electoral democracies, such as India, Uruguay, and the Philippines, political bosses garner votes and volunteers primarily through patronage.

For most of the urban poor, however, collective rather than individual activity appears to be the most productive form of political participation. Many low-income neighborhoods have organized rather effectively to extract benefits from the political system. Often, one of their first goals is to secure land titles for their homes along with basic services such as sanitation, sewage, tap water, schools, and paved streets.

Collective Goals: Housing and Urban Services

On the outskirts of Lima, Peru, several million people live in squatter communities. For the most part, these settlements were started through organized invasions of unoccupied land—either government property or land whose ownership had been in dispute:

> Some invasions involve relatively small groups of families who cooperate on an informal basis shortly before the occupation of the land. Others involve hundreds of families and are planned with great care. The leaders of these invasions often organize well before the invasion occurs and meet many times to recruit members, choose a site, and plan the occupation itself.[49]

Although these land seizures were obviously illegal, one study found that nearly half of the earliest ones were carried out with either explicit or tacit local government approval. While the authorities did not want invasions to get out of hand, they understood that permitting a controlled number of them onto low-value land (much of it public) enabled the poor to build their own homes with little cost to the state. There were political benefits to be gained as well. By protecting the invaders from police eviction, a political leader or a party could secure future electoral support from that community. In many cases, squatters paid off local authorities prior to their invasions.

When a leftist, military regime seized power in Peru, it was anxious to mobilize the urban poor but, at the same time, it also wanted to preempt independent, grassroots, political activity. The generals issued an urban reform law legalizing most of the existing squatter communities. It tried to mobilize, yet control, the poor through SINAMOS, a state-run political organization for the rural and urban masses. Henry Dietz's study of six poor neighborhoods in Lima reveals that community leaders in several locations were quite adept at switching their tactics from Peru's earlier competitive electoral politics to the new rules of enlightened authoritarianism.[50] Mobilized neighborhoods used an impressive array of tactics to secure assistance from the military regime. These included working through SINAMOS, enlisting the aid of a sympathetic Catholic bishop whom the church had assigned to the shantytowns, gaining the support of foreign nongovernmental organizations (NGOs), publishing letters in major newspapers, pressuring local government bureaucrats, and directly petitioning the president.

Although Lima's squatter settlements have been unusually well organized, the urban poor in many other developing countries have also established useful ties between their neighborhoods and the state. For example, in her study of low-income neighborhoods in Mexico City, Susan Eckstein described how neighborhood leaders became active in the long-ruling political party at the time (the PRI) thereby establishing themselves as the links between the government and their communities. Because these community organizations were controlled from the top down and tended to be short-lived, Eckstein was skeptical about how much the poor really gained through Mexico's clientelistic system. Still, she conceded that, over the years, poor neighborhoods had successfully petitioned the government for such benefits as running water, electricity, local food markets, schools, and better public transportation.[51] Following the PRI's defeat in the 2000 presidential election (after 71 years in power) and Mexico's transition to democracy, many low-income neighborhoods have been forced to establish new clientelistic relationships.

The politics of low-income neighborhoods throughout the Third World generally resemble the Peruvian and Mexican models in two important respects: the scope of their claims and their relationship to the national political system. Studies of politics in India, Pakistan, the Philippines, and other LDCs demonstrate that the poor usually have limited and pragmatic demands. For example, when their demands focus on housing, as they often do, they may simply request protection against eviction from their illegal settlements. Beyond that, they may ask for basic services (water, electricity) and titles to their plots so that they can build their own homes.[52] Established neighborhoods often request a medical clinic, a market, or a preschool lunch program. None of these objectives presents a challenge to the established political system or a call for major redistribution of economic resources.

In fact, the very nature of their political organizations limits the demands of low-income neighborhoods. Their patron–client links to the state, powerful political parties, and political bosses filter political inputs from the poor. Political organizations are often based in particular neighborhoods; or they may be tied to ethnic, religious, or racial identities; or they may simply be formed around powerful political figures. In the slums of Madras, India, where politics is closely linked to the film industry, clientelistic organizations grow out of local fan clubs for politically active movie stars.[53] Whatever its base, patron–client politics inherently reinforces the status quo. In return for votes or other forms of political support, the state or political party delivers some of the goods or services that residents need. In many cases, a neighborhood's rewards are very paltry. Elsewhere, political systems are far more generous. In either case, however, the state or local political bosses engage in "divide and rule" politics, as poor urban districts compete with each other for limited government resources.[54]

Critics of clientelistic politics point to the limits of the benefits gained by poor neighborhoods. Although better-organized communities get water, electricity, or medical clinics, many other neighborhoods are left out. Moreover, even successful neighborhoods find it difficult to maintain pressure on the system for an extended period because their political organizations generally atrophy after a number of years. Consequently, as Alan Gilbert and Peter Ward charge, "The [the government's] main aim [in supporting] community-action programs is less to improve conditions for the poor . . . than to legitimate the state . . . to help maintain existing power relations in society."[55] As an alternative to clientelism, its critics favor a more independent, and perhaps more radical, form of mobilization that would raise the urban poor's political consciousness and lead to more sweeping redistributive policies benefiting far more people.

Other analysts, however, hold a more positive view of clientelism. While recognizing its shortcomings, they insist that the benefits that it brings are clearly better than nothing. Viewed in the broader context of society's tremendous inequalities, paved streets, clean drinking water, a clinic, or a food market may not seem like sufficient improvements to some outside observers. Nevertheless, the low-income neighborhoods that receive them appreciate their value. A radical regime might redistribute more to the poor, but, that often is not a viable option. Furthermore, the performance of Third World radical regimes in helping the poor has been mixed. Marxist governments often redistribute significant resources to the urban poor soon after taking power. However, with the notable exception of China (after it transformed to a capitalist economy), they have usually had a poor record of generating further economic growth.

The benefits of clientelism vary from country to country, depending on the nature of the political system and the health of the economy. In relatively open and democratic systems, the poor have broader opportunities to organize, demonstrate, petition, and vote. Consequently, their capacity to *demand* rewards from the state is normally greater than under authoritarian regimes. At the same time, the level of benefits clientelistic systems can allocate to low-income neighborhoods is also constrained by the state's economic resources. During their petroleum booms, the Mexican and Venezuelan governments could be more generous to the urban poor. Even in more difficult economic times, the Mexican government used revenues from the sale of state enterprises to finance public works projects in the urban slums. Until the recent slump in oil prices, Venezuela's petroleum wealth enabled Hugo Chávez to finance extensive antipoverty programs, which have earned him strong support among the urban poor. On the other hand, the remaining dictatorships in sub-Saharan Africa, such as Zimbabwe, have neither the economic resources nor the political will to aid impoverished urban neighborhoods.

During the 1980s, a number of independent, grassroots organizations emerged in many of Latin America's poor urban neighborhoods. Known as "new social movements," they avoided clientelistic linkages with the government or political parties, including sympathetic, leftist parties. For example, in Monterrey (Mexico), radicalized squatters in the community of *Tierra y Libertad* (Land and Liberty) hijacked several buses, forcing the public transport company to extend its routes further into their neighborhood. Ultimately, however, Mexico's independent movements had limited life spans.

By the 1990s, they were overshadowed by President Carlos Salinas's public works network for low-income neighborhoods known as the National Solidarity Program. Using traditional clientelistic techniques, his administration won the support of many poor neighborhoods by delivering new schools, clinics, and the like through government-affiliated groups. However, when the Mexican economy plummeted after Salinas left office, those programs were cut back.

Whatever the merits or limits of clientelism, its scope and range refute certain earlier assumptions about the politics of the urban poor. On the one hand, their often delicate and complex patron–client negotiations demonstrate that many low-income neighborhood leaders are more politically skilled than some outside analysts had given them credit for. While many of the urban poor suffer from fatalism and excessive individualism, others are capable of sophisticated political organization and tough bargaining with the state or political parties. On the other hand, the universality of clientelism indicates that poor rarely engage in the radical politics, violent upheavals, or revolutionary activities that other political scientists had expected. During the current global economic crisis and in regional economic meltdowns in the 1980s and 1990s, various urban neighborhoods have erupted in violence. Nevertheless, the extent of rioting and social unrest has remained surprisingly limited.

Radical Political Behavior

While most of the Third World's urban poor favor moderate and pragmatic forms of political expression, there have been important exceptions. In some countries, such as Chile in the early 1970s, Peru in the 1980s, and El Salvador since the mid-1990s, low-income neighborhoods have voted in substantial numbers for Marxist political candidates. And, in a few cases, residents of urban slums and shantytowns have been important players in revolutionary upheavals. In 1970, Salvador Allende, candidate of Chile's leftist Popular Unity (UP) coalition, became the developing world's first democratically elected Marxist president. Allende received considerable electoral support in the *campamentos* (squatter settlements) that ring the capital city of Santiago. In fact, a number of *campamentos* were politically organized either by the UP or by the MIR (Revolutionary Left Movement), a group to the left of the UP that periodically engaged in armed action.[56] In 1983, the poor of Lima played a major role in electing a Marxist mayor, Alfonso Barrantes. These examples, as well as the Communist Party's electoral successes in several large Indian cities, indicate that the poor do support radical political parties under certain circumstances. However, they will favor those parties only if they have a realistic chance of winning at the local or national level so that they can be in a position to deliver tangible benefits to their supporters. Thus, even a slum dweller's decision to vote for a radical candidate is often based on very pragmatic calculations. Not long after supporting Barrantes for mayor, Lima's poor gave him few votes when he ran for the nation's presidency, believing that his Marxist policies might succeed in Lima but were not viable at the national level.

More often, the urban poor are attracted to charismatic populists (such as Venezuelan president Hugo Chávez) or to moderate leftists (such as Brazilian president Luiz Inácio Lula da Silva). Squatters or slum dwellers are much less likely to embrace urban guerrillas or other revolutionary movements. Teodoro Petkoff, a former leader of the Venezuelan communists' urban guerrilla wing, noted that residents of Caracas's poor barrios, even those who belonged to leftist unions, rejected the guerrillas. Blue-collar workers often elected communist union representatives in those days, Petkoff observed, because they felt that those union militants would deliver more at the bargaining table. On the other hand, in national elections, the urban poor were more likely to vote for the two mainstream parties (Social Democrats and Christian Democrats) or the country's former right-wing dictator, all of whom were more capable of delivering rewards to their supporters than the guerrillas were.[57]

In the 1980s and 1990s, Peru's *Sendero Luminoso* (Shining Path) guerrillas had some success in the shantytowns of Lima. However, as often as not they only earned that "support" through intimidation. For example, when a popular, women's political organizer in the large shantytown, Villa El Salvador, failed to cooperate with it, the guerrilla group assassinated her in front of her family and neighbors.

This is not to suggest that the urban poor never support revolutions. Josef Gugler notes that during the second half of the twentieth century, the cities played a central role in four of the Third World's revolutions—Bolivia, Cuba, Iran, and Nicaragua.[58] However, in most cases, other social classes took the lead: miners, unionized blue-collar workers, artisans, the lower-middle class, and the national police in Bolivia; students and university graduates in Cuba; theology students and petroleum workers in Iran. In contrast, Douglas Butterworth's study of the former inhabitants of a Havana slum, *Las Yaguas*, conducted almost 20 years after the revolutionary victory, found that most respondents were barely aware of Fidel Castro's existence during his rise to power.[59]

CONCLUSION: FUTURE URBAN GROWTH AND DEMOCRATIC POLITICS

While the *rate* of urbanization has slowed in parts of the Third World, *absolute increases* in urban populations (i.e., the increases in raw numbers) will be greater than ever in the coming decades (Tables 7.3 and 7.4). Thus, governments will have to heed urban needs, including those of the poor. Still, even with the best-intentioned public policies, developing economies will be hard-pressed to provide sufficient jobs, housing, sanitation, and social services. Various economic crises over the past 2–3 decades have made the task all the more difficult, at least temporarily. Urban crime, pollution, and AIDS will add tremendously to the burdens on the political and economic systems. In countries such as South Africa, Guatemala, and Iraq, the fall of authoritarian regimes has led to a surge in crime.

Given the current weakness of the revolutionary Left, however, and the tendency of the poor to engage in adaptive behavior, urban unrest is more likely to express itself in occasional rioting than in mass insurrection. Perhaps the one exception may be in the Middle East, where segments of the urban lower and middle classes may turn to militant Islamic fundamentalism, as many have already done in Algeria, Egypt, Iran, and Iraq. Elsewhere, crime and drug usage are more likely than radical politics to threaten stability in the proximate future. In the long run, Third World governments may be able to cope with those problems if they can generate sustained economic growth. In the short term, however, the possibility of increased state repression persists in many countries as the military and middle class become fearful of urban crime and disorder.

We have noted previously that poor, urban neighborhoods generally receive more government assistance from democratic governments than from authoritarian ones. In countries where democracy has been consolidated, the urban poor will have to refine their strategies for securing state resources. Similarly, if newly democratic governments are to endure, they will need to become more responsive to the poor and more cognizant of the vast inequalities that plague Third World cities. Studies of urban slums and shantytowns generally suggest that while the poor are not as radical as once thought, they are not necessarily committed to democratic values either. Faced with rising crime rates and economic deprivation, they may become disillusioned with democracy (Chapter 2). At the same time, rising crime and urban unrest may cause the middle and upper classes to support authoritarian government as well. Democratic governments will have to prove to all of them that they are more helpful than alternative authoritarian regimes. In addition, political parties and other institutions need to spread democratic cultural values among the affluent and the poor alike.

DISCUSSION QUESTIONS

1. Discuss the political orientations of the urban poor. What does survey research tell us about the way that the urban poor look at their present circumstances and their views on prospects of improving them?
2. Discuss the growth of urban crime in the Third World, the major obstacles to reducing crime, and the possible political consequences of rising crime rates.
3. How might rapid urban growth contribute to the growth of democratic government in the LDCs? Under what circumstances might it *undermine* democracy?

NOTES

1. United Nations, Department of Economic and Social Affairs, Population Division, "Urban and Rural Areas, 2003," http://www.un.org/esa/population/publications/wup2003/2003 Urban_Rural.pdf.

2. United Nations Department of Economic and Social Affairs—Population Division, "World Urbanization Prospects: The 2007 Revision," http://www.un.org/esa/population/publications/wup2007/2007wup.htm.

3. Stella Lowder, *The Geography of Third World Cities* (New York: Barnes and Noble, 1986), 19.

4. Sally Findley, "The Third World City," in *Third World Cities*, eds. John Kasarda and Allan Parnell (Newbury Park, CA: Sage Publications, 1993), 14–16.

5. R. A. Obudho, "Urbanization and Urban Development Strategies in East Africa," in *Urban Management*, ed. G. Shabbir Cheema (New York: Praeger, 1993), figures extrapolated from Table 4.2, p. 84.

6. "Largest Cities in the United States & the World," http://www.mongabay.com/igapo/cities.html. The data are drawn from the United Nations, with estimated future populations calculated by Mongabay. Data from different sources vary somewhat, particularly about projected populations, but agree on general trends. See Table 7.3 for population statistics for major metropolitan areas in other periods.

7. Obudho, "Urbanization and Urban Development Strategies," 84.

8. United Nations Population Information Network, *World Populations Prospects* (2003 and 2005), http://esa.un.org/unpp/.

9. Raymond Owens, "Peasant Entrepreneurs in an Industrial City," in *A Reader in Urban Sociology*, eds. M. S. A. Rao, Chandrashekar Bhat, and Laxmi Narayan Kadekar (New Delhi, India: Oriental Longman, 1991), 235.

10. Manuel Castells and Alejandro Portes, "World Underneath: The Origins, Dynamics and Effects of the Informal Economy," in *The Informal Economy: Studies in Advanced and Developing Economies*, eds. Alejandro Portes, Manuel Castells, and Lauren A. Benton (Baltimore, MD: Johns Hopkins University Press, 1989), 12.

11. Vincent Palmade and Andrea Anayiotos, "Rising Informality—Reversing the Tide," *Knowledge Resources for Financial and Private Sector Development* (The World Bank), note number 298, August 1, 2005, http://www.cipe-arabia.org/files/pdf/artid945_en.pdf.

12. UN-Habitat (United Nations Human Settlements Programme), Statistics, http://ww2.unhabitat.org/programmes/guostatistics.asp.

13. Silvia Schmitt, "Housing Conditions and Policies," in *Poverty and Democracy*, eds. Dirk Berg-Schlosser and Norbert Kersting (London and New York: Zed Books, 2003), 61.

14. Howard Handelman, "The Role of the State in Sheltering the Urban Poor," in *Spontaneous Shelter*, ed. Carl V. Patton (Philadelphia: Temple University Press, 1988), 332–333.

15. Richard Stern, "Urban Housing in Africa: The Changing Role of Government Policy," in *Housing Africa's Urban Poor*, eds. Philip Amis and Peter Lloyd (Manchester, England: Manchester University Press, 1990), 36–39.

16. Diana Patel, "Government Policy and Squatter Settlements in Harare, Zimbabwe," in *Slum and Squatter Settlements in Sub-Saharan Africa*, eds. R. A. Obudho and Constance Mhlanga (New York: Praeger, 1988), 205–217.

17. Handelman, "The Role of the State," 339.

18. Susan Eckstein, *The Poverty of Revolution: The State and the Urban Poor in Mexico*, 2d ed. (Princeton, NJ: Princeton University Press, 1988), 41; Howard Handelman, *High-Rises and Shantytowns* (Hanover, NH: American University Field Staff, 1979), 17; B. Sanyal, "A Critical Look at the Housing Subsidies in Zambia," *Development and Change*, vol. 12 (1981), 409–440.

19. David Collier, *Squatters and Oligarchs* (Baltimore, MD: Johns Hopkins University Press, 1976).

20. Gilbert and Gugler, *Cities, Poverty and Development: Urbanization in the Third World*, 2nd ed. (New York: Oxford University Press, 1992), 123.

21. Alan Gilbert and Peter Ward, *Housing, the State, and the Poor* (New York: Cambridge University Press, 1985), 86–87.

22. Diana Lee-Smith, "Squatter Landlords in Nairobi," in *Housing Africa's Urban Poor*, 177; Douglas Butterworth and John Chance, *Latin American Urbanization* (New York: Cambridge University Press, 1981), 147; Collier, *Squatters and Oligarchs*, 27–28.

23. John F. C. Turner and Robert Fichter, eds., *Freedom to Build* (New York: Macmillan, 1972); see also William Mangin, "Latin American Squatter Settlements: A Problem and a Solution," *Latin American Research Review*, vol. 2, no. 3 (1967), 65–98.

24. Gilbert and Gugler, *Cities, Poverty and Development*, 117–130.

25. Handelman, "The Role of the State," 328.

26. R. Burgess, "Petty Commodity Housing or Dweller Control? A Critique of John Turner's Views on Housing Policy," *World Development*, vol. 6 (1978), 1105–1133.

27. Handelman, *High-Rises and Shantytowns*; A. A. Laquian, "Whither Site and Services," *Habitat*, vol. 2 (1977), 291–301.

28. Ernest Alexander, "Informal Settlement in Latin America and Its Policy Implication," in *Spontaneous Shelter*, 131–133; Lisa Peattie, "Some Second Thoughts on Sites-and-Services," *Habitat International*, vol. 6 (Winter 1982), 131–139.

29. Gilbert and Ward, *Housing, the State, and the Poor*.

30. Portions of this section are drawn from Howard Handelman, *The Security and Insecurities of Democracy in the Third World*, vol. 12, no. 1 (Milwaukee: University of Wisconsin-Milwaukee, Global Studies Perspectives: Occasional Paper Series of the Center for International Education, 2004).

31. Andrew Morrison, Mayra Buvinic, and Michael Shifter, "The Violent Americas: Risk Factors, Consequences, and Policy Implications of Social and Domestic Violence," in *Crime and Violence in Latin America*, eds. Hugo Frühling and Joseph Tulchin (Washington, DC: Woodrow Wilson Center Press, 2003), 96.

32. *Seventh United Nations Survey of Crime Trends and Operations of Criminal Justice Systems, Covering the Period 1998–2000* (United Nations Office on Drugs and Crime, Centre for International Crime Prevention) as reported by Nationmaster.com. http://www.nationmaster.com/graph/cri_mur_percap-crime-murders-per-capita.

33. All the crime and corruption data in this paragraph come from the UNDP, *Human Development Report 2000*, 220–221.

34. *New York Times* (August 4, 2004).

35. Joan Nelson, *Access to Power* (Princeton, NJ: Princeton University Press, 1979), chap. 4; Howard Handelman, "The Political Mobilization of Urban Squatter Settlements," *Latin American Research Review*, vol. 10, no. 2 (1975), 35–72.

36. James Coleman, "Conclusion: The Political Systems of Developing Nations," in *The Politics of Developing Areas*, eds. Gabriel Almond and James Coleman (Princeton, NJ: Princeton University Press, 1960), 537.

37. Samuel Huntington, *Political Order in Changing Societies* (New Haven, CT: Yale University Press, 1968), 283.

38. Barbara Ward, "Creating Man's Future Goals for a World of Plenty," *Saturday Review*, vol. 9 (August 1964), 192.

39. Joan Nelson, *Migrants, Urban Poverty, and Instability in Developing Nations* (Cambridge, MA: AMS Press and the Harvard University Center for International Affairs, 1969), 18–20; Eckstein, *The Poverty of Revolution*, 41.

40. Gilbert and Ward, *Housing, the State, and the Poor*, 215.

41. Oscar Lewis, *The Children of Sanchez* (New York: Random House, 1961).

42. Jorge Giusti, "Organizational Characteristics of the Latin American Urban Marginal Settler," *International Journal of Politics*, vol. 1, no. 1 (1971), 57.

43. Barbara Happe and Sylvia Schmit, "Political Culture," in *Poverty and Democracy*, eds. Berg-Schlosser and Kersting, 130.

44. Bryan R. Roberts, *Organizing Strangers: Poor Families in Guatemala City* (Austin: University of Texas Press, 1973), 299.

45. Alejandro Portes and John Walton, *Urban Latin America* (Austin: University of Texas Press, 1976), 108.

46. Happe and Schmit, "Political Culture," in *Poverty and Democracy*, 125. All of the survey results that follow come from that chapter (pp. 121–152) or from Norbert Kersting and Jaime Sperberg, "Political Participation," in *Poverty and Democracy*, 153–180.

47. A. Bank, "Poverty, Politics and the Shaping of Urban Space: A Brazilian Example," *International Journal of Urban and Regional Research*, vol. 10, no. 4 (1986), 523.

48. Ibid.

49. Collier, *Squatters and Oligarchs*, 41 and 44.

50. Henry Dietz, *Poverty and Problem Solving Under Military Rule* (Austin: University of Texas Press, 1980).

51. Eckstein, *The Poverty of Revolution*, chap. 3.

52. Turner, "Barriers and Channels."

53. Joop de Wit, "Clientelism, Competition and Poverty: The Ineffectiveness of Local Organizations in a Madras Slum," in *Urban Social Movements in the Third World*, 63–90.

54. Jan van der Linden, "The Limits of Territorial Social Movements: The Case of Housing in Karachi," in *Urban Social Movements in the Third World*, 101.

55. Gilbert and Ward, *Housing, the State and the Poor*, 175.

56. Handelman, "The Political Mobilization of Urban Squatter Settlements: Santiago's Recent Experience," *Latin American Research Review*, vol. 10, no. 2 (1975), 35–72.

57. My conversations with Petkoff in 1976 and 1978.

58. Josef Gugler, "The Urban Character of Contemporary Revolutions," in *The Urbanization of the Third World*, 399–412.

59. Douglas Butterworth, *The People of Buena Ventura* (Urbana: University of Illinois Press, 1980), 19–20.

CHAPTER 8

REVOLUTIONARY CHANGE

The opening decades of the twentieth century ushered in the Mexican and Russian revolutions. The closing decades witnessed the collapse of Soviet Communism, the transformation of the Chinese and Mexican revolutions, and the weakening of Cuba's revolutionary government.* No era in world history encompassed more revolutionary upheaval. Yet as the twenty-first century begins, the force that had once promised (or threatened) to transform the face of the Third World appears to be spent, at least for the time being.

Karl Marx, the foremost prophet of revolution, expected insurrections to take place in industrialized European nations where the organized working class would rise up against the oppressive capitalist system. Instead, modern revolutionary movements have been largely a Third World phenomenon, fought primarily by the peasantry. And, even Europe's internally generated communist revolutions—Russia and Yugoslavia—occurred in countries where capitalism and industrialization were relatively underdeveloped. The remaining communist governments in Central Europe were installed by Soviet military intervention, not through popular uprisings.

In the LDCs, the appeal of revolutionary change has been its pledge of rapid and sweeping solutions to the problems of underdevelopment. It promised to end colonial rule, terminate dependency, protect national sovereignty, reduce social and economic inequalities, accelerate economic development, mobilize the population, and transform the political culture. Not surprisingly, many of the LDCs' poor and oppressed, along with numerous intellectuals and alienated members of the middle class, have found revolutionary platforms and ideologies quite appealing.

Some revolutionary governments—in China, Cuba, and Mexico, for example—were able to deliver on a number of their promises. Under Mao Zedong's leadership, the Chinese Communist Party redistributed land to the peasantry, industrialized the economy, and transformed the country into a world power. Fidel Castro's government implemented extensive land reform, an impressive adult literacy campaign, and significant public health programs. Mexico's revolutionary party reestablished national sovereignty over the country's most-valued natural resources (most notably petroleum), initiated agrarian reform, and transformed the nation into a Third World industrial power.

Often, however, these gains have come at great cost, including political repression, considerable human suffering, and rampant corruption. As a result of their revolution, the Chinese people now enjoy far better medical care, education, and general living conditions than ever before. At the same time, however, some

---

* China's Leninist regime remains in place, but the government has abandoned communist economics and class-based politics.

30 million people starved to death in the 1950s due to the mistaken experiments of Mao's Great Leap Forward. Millions more suffered humiliation or imprisonment and perhaps 400,000 people died during the ultra-radical period called the Cultural Revolution (1966–1976). Many other communist governments had their own *gulags* (networks of prisons or forced labor camps) for real and imagined political opponents. In Vietnam, the revolutionary government sent many suspected dissidents to "reeducation" camps, and in Cuba a smaller, but still significant, number were imprisoned.

In the most unfortunate cases—Angola, Mozambique, and Cambodia (Kampuchea)—huge portions of the population died as the result of the revolutionary conflicts and their aftermaths, with little or nothing positive to show for it.* In Cambodia, the fanatical Khmer Rouge government murdered or starved more than a million people, including much of the country's educated class, while failing to accomplish anything for its people. Over the years, even some of the more idealistic revolutionary regimes changed into corrupt bureaucracies, run by a new generation of opportunistic *apparatchiks* (party or government bureaucrats) who had never risked anything for the revolution's ideals.

After examining the meaning of the term *revolution* and classifying different types of twentieth-century revolutions, this chapter will discuss the causes of revolutionary upheavals, their principal sources of leadership and support, and the policy objectives of their leaders once in power. Finally, it will discuss the decline of the revolutionary model at the end of the twentieth century.

DEFINING REVOLUTION

Scholars have argued endlessly about what constitutes a revolution and whether particular upheavals such as the American Revolution or Iran's Islamic revolution were, in fact, true social revolutions. Thus, Chalmers Johnson notes, "half the battle will lie in answering the question, 'What is revolution?'"[1] In its broadest and least precise usage, the term is applied to any violent government overthrow. Peter Calvert offers perhaps the most open-ended definition when he maintains that revolution is "simply a form of governmental change through violence."[2] That kind of definition, however, seems too broad because it encompasses military coups and other upheavals that do little more than change the heads of government. Most scholars insist on a more rigorous definition, arguing that revolutions must bring fundamental political, economic, and social change. Samuel Huntington has suggested,

> A revolution is a rapid, fundamental, and violent domestic change in the dominant values and myths of society, in its political institutions, social structure, leadership and government activity and policies. Revolutions are thus to be distinguished from insurrections, revolts, coups and wars of independence.[3]

---

* In Angola and Mozambique, most of the killing was carried out by counterrevolutionary forces. For the hundreds of thousands of innocent civilians butchered, however, it mattered little which side killed them.

To be sure, it is frequently difficult to make the distinctions that Huntington proposes at the end of his definition. For example, some "wars of independence" (sometimes called "wars of national liberation"), such as Algeria's and Mozambique's, are generally considered authentic social revolutions because they ushered in fundamental societal change.[4] On the other hand, Theda Skocpol accepts Huntington's starting definition but narrows it by claiming that "social revolutions are accompanied and in part effectuated through [massive] class upheavals."[5] She adds,

> Social revolutions are set apart from other sorts of conflicts by the combination of two coincidences: the coincidence of societal structural change with class upheaval; and the coincidence of the political with social transformation.[6]

Skocpol concedes that according to her more restrictive, class-based definition, only "a handful of successful social revolutions have ever occurred." The most clear-cut cases are the three she has studied in great detail: France (1789–1799), Russia (1917), and China (1911–1949). Other less-restrictive definitions of revolution apply to Mexico, Bolivia, Cuba, Nicaragua, Algeria, Ethiopia, Mozambique, Angola, Eritrea, Vietnam, Cambodia, Turkey, and Iran, among others. What is common to all of them is that insurgency brought sweeping changes to the country's political, economic, and social systems.

Because revolutions involve a fundamental transfer of political and economic powers, rather than a mere change in political leaders (as is the case in most military coups), they are invariably violent. Not surprisingly, the government officials and social classes that have long held (and often abused) power and now face bleak futures invariably fight to stay on top. If the revolutionaries triumph, they remove old elites from power and install new ones. And, at least in some respects, they broaden political, economic, and social participation to include those further down the social and economic ladder. This does not imply that revolutionary governments are democratic. They virtually never are. But they are frequently more broadly participatory and egalitarian than the regimes that they have toppled.

I classify as a revolution any insurgency that brings about these kinds of comprehensive political and socioeconomic changes. The insurrection may be rooted in class struggles (China and Nicaragua), as Skocpol insists, or, contrary to Huntington, it may be a war of national liberation (Algeria and Angola), as long as it overturns critical political and economic institutions and changes the country's underlying power structure and social values. In fact, the borderline between nationalist and class-based revolutions is often difficult to discern. The Vietnamese revolution most clearly combined anticolonial and class struggles. Moreover, even primarily class-based revolutions, such as China's, Mexico's, Cuba's, and Nicaragua's, had important nationalist, anti-imperialist components to them.

Revolutions may be Marxist (China, Russia, Vietnam, Cambodia, and Cuba), partly Marxist (Nicaragua), or non-Marxist (Mexico, Bolivia, and Iran). Marxism was particularly appealing to many revolutionaries because it promised the ideological rigor, social and economic "justice," and new political myths that they sought. But the revolutionary's vision of social justice need not be communist. It may also come from nationalism, Islam, or other ideologies and religions.

Revolutionaries generally come to power either through mass uprisings—featuring strikes, protest marches, and street riots (Russia, Bolivia, and Iran), guerrilla warfare (China, Vietnam, and Cuba), or a combination of both (Nicaragua). There have also been a few "elite revolutions" in which military officers or upper-level bureaucrats have overthrown the government and instituted far-reaching socioeconomic changes that far transcended the objectives of mere coups.[7] Primary examples include Mustafa Kemal Ataturk's military revolt in Turkey (1919), Gamal Abdel Nasser's officers' revolt in Egypt (1952), and Peru's "revolution from above" (1968)—all led by reformist military officers (see Chapter 9).

UNDERLYING CAUSES OF REVOLUTION

Just as experts have disagreed about the definition of revolution, they have also differed over the causes of revolutionary insurrection. Some theories focus on broad historical trends, including changes in the world order that make revolution possible or likely. Other explanations center on weaknesses in the *ancien régime* (the old political and socioeconomic systems), examining factors that caused the pre-revolutionary state to fall. And yet others concentrate on the revolutions' major players, particularly the peasantry, seeking the factors that cause them to revolt.

Inexorable Historical Forces

Karl Marx viewed revolution as an unstoppable historical force growing out of class inequalities that are rooted in the ownership of the means of production. Those who command the economic system, he argued, control the state as well. Over time, however, subordinate classes will become alienated from the political-economic order and will attain sufficient political skills and vision (class consciousness) to overthrow the existing order. Thus, Marx maintained, that an ascendant *bourgeoisie* (property owners, particularly capitalists)—who had toppled the old order dominated by the aristocracy and landed oligarchy—had led the British Civil War (Revolution) of 1640 and the French Revolution (1789). Both of those were part of a broader European transition from agrarian feudalism to industrial capitalism. Although Marx believed that this new capitalist order presented a more advanced and more productive historical stage, he also argued that it depended on the exploitation of the working class (proletariat). In time, he predicted, as the exploitation of the proletariat became more apparent and as workers developed sufficient class consciousness, they would overthrow capitalism and install revolutionary socialism.[8]

More than any other revolutionary theorist, Marx influenced the course of history, as most of the leaders of the twentieth-century's major revolutions—including V. I. Lenin, Mao Zedong, Ho Chi Minh, Che Guevara, and Fidel Castro—fervently believed in his ideology. His writings evoked the centrality of class struggle in most revolutionary movements. But as even sympathetic analysts have noted, "He was, first and foremost a nineteenth-century man" whose ideology was closely linked to the era in which he lived.[9] "Marx's theoretical approach," writes Irving Zeitlin, "enabled him to explain the past but failed him in his predictions."[10] Indeed, *no* country has ever had the succession of revolutions that he predicted, first capitalist, then socialist.* Instead, the primary locus of modern revolution has been the Third World—not advanced capitalist nations—and the major protagonists have been peasants rather than industrial workers.

Mao Zedong, the leader of the Chinese Revolution, accepted Marx's view of revolution as part of a historical dialectic.† Like other Third World Marxists, he viewed capitalist exploitation and its resulting class conflict as the root causes of communist upheavals. However, the Chinese Communist Party's military defeats in the 1920s convinced him that its orthodox commitment to proletariat revolution was not viable in a country in which the working class constituted only a small percentage of the population. Consequently, he reinterpreted Marxist theory to make it more applicable to China and other parts of the developing world. Mao developed a model of peasant-based struggle and a military strategy designed to encircle and conquer China's cities following a period of protracted rural guerrilla conflict.[11] The success of his strategy in the world's most populous country and its frequent use elsewhere in the Third World made Mao the most influential practitioner of revolutionary warfare in the twentieth century.

In Vietnam and Cuba, Ho Chi Minh and Che Guevara refined Mao's vision of "peoples' war" to make it more compatible with conditions in Southeast Asia and Latin America. While all of them demonstrated that communist revolutions could take place in countries that are not highly industrialized, those leaders still adhered to Marx's theory of history and his vision of class struggle.

Regime Decay

Even before the collapse of the Soviet bloc, it had become obvious that there was no *inevitable* march toward revolution and that, in fact, successful revolutions have been rather rare. Theda Skocpol argues that neither the repression of the masses nor the skills of revolutionary leadership alone can bring about successful social revolutions. These factors may be necessary, but they are not sufficient. Rather, true revolutions succeed only when international pressures such as war, economic competition, or an arms race undermine the state. The modernization of Britain and other European powers, she contends, created severe military and economic pressures on LDCs within and outside Europe. Some of those states, such as royalist France, Czarist Russia, and imperial China, were unable to adjust to these challenges and, hence, fell victim to revolutionary challenges.[12]

---

* In other words, no Marxist revolution has taken place in a country where capitalism was entrenched. And, by the end of the twentieth century, in a complete reversal of Marxist theory, communist regimes in the Soviet Union and Central Europe were changing to capitalism.

† The term *dialectic* indicated that major ideas or historical forces (the thesis) are eventually opposed by rival ideas or forces (the antithesis), and out of their conflict emerges a "synthesis" that draws upon both sides.

In Russia, excessive military entanglements, foreign indebtedness, and a disastrous involvement in World War I undermined the Czarist state. Successive military defeats in two wars—first by the Japanese (1905) and then by the Germans (1917)—helped undermine the Czarist regime. Similarly, China's Manchu dynasty, having been fatally weakened by European and Japanese imperialism, was toppled by Nationalist forces in 1911, who, in turn, were overthrown by the communists nearly 40 years later. Elsewhere, stronger regimes were able to withstand comparable challenges, but the Russian and Chinese states were too weak. Ultimately, disgruntled soldiers, workers, and peasants, led by "marginal elites" (university students and middle-class professionals alienated from the system), toppled the old orders.[13] Ironically, just as military competition undermined the Czarist government and set the stage for the Russian Revolution, some 70 years later, the Soviet-American arms race undercut the Soviet Union's financial health and contributed to the system's collapse.

Thus, Skocpol and others have argued that the most significant factor contributing to a successful revolutionary struggle is not the revolutionary leadership's strategy, tactics, or zeal, but rather the internal rot of the decaying old order. For example, Japan's invasion of China prior to World War II undercut the legitimacy of the Kuomintang government. The Japanese occupation demonstrated that the Nationalist regime was too corrupt and incompetent to resist a foreign threat, while the communist People's Liberation Army (PLA) was far more effective. When the Chinese revolutionary war resumed after World War II, many of the areas in which the communists won major military victories were the same ones in which they had organized mass resistance against the Japanese.[14]

In fact, military defeats have frequently delegitimized the existing political order, setting the stage for subsequent revolutions. Thus, the destruction of the Ottoman Empire in World War I and the Japanese capture of British, French, and Dutch colonies in Asia (including Burma, Vietnam, and Indonesia) during World War II all undermined the imperial or colonial governments' legitimacy and led, respectively, to the "Young Turks" military revolt in Turkey, the communist revolution in Vietnam, and various independence movements in South and Southeast Asia.[15] Similarly, Egypt's defeat by Israel (1948–1949) helped precipitate Colonel Nasser's revolution from above in that country.

War has the additional effect of disrupting peasant life, forcing many of them to seek the new social structure and physical protection offered by the revolutionary forces. For example, in accounts of life in rural China during its civil war and the Japanese invasion, "one is struck by the number of peasants . . . who had their routines upset through the [war-related] death of their kin before they joined revolutionary organizations."[16]

Of course, there are other factors besides military defeats that may undermine governments. In Cuba and Nicaragua, prolonged dictatorships became obscenely corrupt. Fulgencio Batista rose from the rank of army sergeant in 1933 to become Cuba's dominant political actor over the next two decades. During that period, corruption infested all ranks of government. Batista's links to the American mafia helped turn Havana into a playground for affluent foreign tourists seeking gambling and prostitution. Elsewhere, members of the ruling Somoza dynasty commandeered a huge share of Nicaragua's economy for decades. The National Guard—virtually the Somozas' personal army—enriched themselves as well. For example, when an earthquake leveled the nation's capital (Managua), the Guard intercepted and sold U.S. relief supplies to the needy.

A further element undermining the legitimacy of both the Cuban and the Nicaraguan dictatorships was their subservience to the United States, which offended their peoples' national pride. Because the U.S. military had occupied both countries for years early in the twentieth century, this was a particularly sensitive issue. The occupying American Marines had installed Anastasio Somoza Sr., the dynasty's founder, as the first commander of Nicaragua's hated National Guard (the country has no army), a position that he subsequently used to seize the presidency. Decades later, in the years preceding their Sandinista revolution, Nicaraguans derisively referred to his son President Anastasio Somoza Jr. a graduate of West Point, as "the last Marine." In both Cuba and Nicaragua, the combination of rampant corruption and injuries to nationalist sensibilities united people across class lines against the government—from peasants to students to business owners. Lacking any real commitment to Batista's corrupt dictatorship, the undisciplined army offered surprisingly little resistance to Fidel Castro's small guerrilla force. In Nicaragua, the National Guardsmen, knowing that they faced popular retribution if they lost power, put up a stronger fight against the Sandinista revolutionaries, but also fell relatively quickly.[17]

Revolutionary opportunities may also arise when the economy deteriorates, standards of living decline, and the government is unable to meet long-standing economic responsibilities to its population. For example, runaway inflation undermined support for China's Kuomintang government. Declining living standards also helped spark the Kenyan rebellion against British colonialism. Thus, maintains Charles Tilly, one cause of revolution is "the sudden failure of government to meet specific obligations which members of the subject population regarded as well established and crucial to their welfare."[18]

While Skocpol, Tilly, and others emphasize the decay of state authority at the *national* level, revolutions can also arise from the breakdown of authority at the local level. We observed earlier (Chapter 6) that a web of patron–client relationships linking peasants to their landlords and other local power brokers helps maintain stability in the countryside. Peasants will tolerate considerable injustice if their landlords and the village political bosses compensate by providing villagers with needed benefits, such as secure access to land, credit, and protection from harassment by the police. However, if the expansion of market forces makes rural patrons unwilling or unable to continue providing benefits that peasants had come to expect, their authority will likely break down. At this point, the state may try to replace the traditional patrons by providing social services such as credit, technical assistance, schools, and clinics. If, however, government authorities fail to satisfy the peasants' needs as well, the rural poor may turn to revolutionary groups as their new patrons and protectors.

Challenges from Below

While revolutionary movements generally succeed only against discredited or weakened governments, they must also mount a well-organized and politically coherent challenge from below. Without that, the old regime, weak though it may be, will either cling to power (the Third World has numerous incompetent and discredited governments that linger on) or the society may collapse into disorder or anarchy (as in Somalia).

Charles Tilly contends that three things must happen before a revolutionary movement can succeed: first, the revolutionaries must establish themselves as an "alternative sovereignty"; that is, the rebel leadership must convince its would-be supporters that it can function as a viable alternative government. Second, a sizable portion of the population must support that revolutionary alternative. Finally, the established government must be incapable of suppressing the revolutionary opposition.[19] There are a number of well-known cases in which revolutionaries successfully established alternative sovereignties. Following the collapse of Czarist rule in Russia, the Bolsheviks (Communist Party) established a network of workers' soviets (local political committees) to challenge the sovereignty of Alexander Kerensky's moderate provisional government. Asia's protracted guerrilla wars also illustrate the phenomenon. During the Chinese Revolution, the PLA (the Communist Party's military arm) controlled "liberated zones" in which the communists distributed land to the peasants, organized military and political support, and demonstrated their ability to govern. The same was true of South Vietnam's National Liberation Front (Viet Cong).

But, even after understanding these broad preconditions for successful revolutionary activity, we still must ask what causes a revolution to break out in a particular country, at a particular time and not in others. Samuel Huntington maintains that the probability of a successful insurrection is determined by the balance of power between the capabilities of government political institutions, on the one hand, and the level of antigovernment political and social mobilization, on the other. Most revolutions, he notes, occur neither in highly traditional societies nor in modern nations. Rather, they are most likely to erupt in modernizing countries—those in transition from traditional culture to modernity. As greater urbanization, increased education and literacy, and expanded mass-media communication stimulate widespread political mobilization, civil society (the network of organized groups independent of government control) makes increased demands on the political system. Unless the governing order can create appropriate institutions capable of accommodating this increased political participation in a timely manner, the system will become overloaded and, hence, more unstable.

Huntington then distinguishes two distinct revolutionary patterns: a *Western* model in which "the political institutions of the old regime collapse followed by the mobilization of new groups into politics and then by the creation of new [revolutionary] political institutions" (i.e., regime decay *precedes* a full challenge from below); and an *Eastern* (Asian) revolutionary model that "begins with the mobilization of new groups into politics and the creation of new [revolutionary] political institutions and ends with the violent overthrow of the political institutions of the old order."[20] The French, Russian, and Mexican revolutions fit the Western model, while communist revolutions in China and Vietnam followed the Eastern model.*

---

* Not all Asian revolutions followed the Eastern model, nor did all Latin American insurgencies conform to the Western model.

James C. Davies shifts our attention from the broad historical-social forces that make revolution possible to the question of why particular individuals choose to join a revolt or a revolution. He asserts that, contrary to what we might expect, people rarely rebel when they are experiencing prolonged or permanent suffering. "Far from making people revolutionaries, enduring poverty makes for concern with one's solitary self or solitary family, at best resignation, or mute despair at worst."[21] To uncover the source of political upheavals, Davies combines economic and psychological explanations. Unlike Marx, Skocpol, or Tilly, his analysis lumps together mass revolutions with local uprisings and military "revolutions from above." Drawing upon historical data ranging from Dorr's Rebellion (an 1842 uprising in Rhode Island) to the Egyptian military revolution of 1952, he concludes that each upheaval took place after a period of sustained economic growth was followed by a sharp downturn. A diagram of that growth and subsequent downturn (Figure 8.1) produces what Davies called the "J-curve."* As a country's economy grows for a period of time, he suggests, people's expectations rise correspondingly (parallel to the long side of the "J"). However, those expectations continue to rise even after the economy experiences a downturn. What emerges is "an intolerable gap between what people want and what they get."[22] Davies argues that this economic J-curve also explains the American and French revolutions, the American Civil War, the rise of German Nazism, student unrest in the United States during the 1960s, and the African American civil rights movement.

Using twentieth-century data from 17 LDCs, Raymond Tanter and Manus Midlarsky confirmed Davies's thesis in Asia and the Middle East but not in Latin America. Interestingly, their Asian and Middle Eastern cases also indicated that the higher the rate of economic growth prior to a downturn and the sharper the slide immediately preceding the outbreak of unrest, the longer and more violent the upheaval will be.[23]

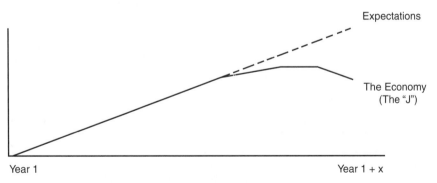

Expectations

The Economy
(The "J")

Year 1   Year 1 + x

FIGURE 8.1   Davies's Psychological Model Showing the Gap Between People's Expectations and Economic Reality

---

* More precisely, the economic pattern he described can be drawn as the letter "J" tipped over, with the long side representing the period of economic growth and the rounded part depicting the downturn.

Davies's theory is one of the most influential psychologically based explanations of revolutionary behavior. There is, however, an important limitation to his findings. He based his conclusions exclusively on data from countries which have experienced revolts or revolutions. That raises the question of whether there are countries that experienced a J-curve in their economies (growth followed by a downturn) yet did not have social upheavals. In fact, Davies admits that there are. For example, he notes the absence of mass unrest in the United States during the Great Depression, a devastating economic downturn. The same holds true for many Latin American countries that enjoyed strong economic growth in the 1960s and 1970s followed by a precipitous decline in the 1980s. Argentina had a comparable cycle from 1990 to 1998. Thus, as Davies concedes, his theory identifies common but not sufficient conditions for unrest. Although a J-curve often leads to revolution, it does not necessarily do so.

Ted Gurr has also developed a psychological model examining the gap between expectations and reality. Like Davies, he examines various types of civil violence, not just revolution. Gurr argues that "the necessary precondition for violent civil conflict is relative deprivation defined as [the] actors' perception of the discrepancy between their value expectations [i.e., what people believe they deserve from life] and value capabilities . . . conditions that determine people's perceived chances of getting . . . what they . . . expect to attain."[24] In other words, *relative deprivation* is the gap between what people want or expect from life and what they actually get.

Unlike Davies's theory, however, Gurr's notion of relative deprivation is not solely economic. Thus, he posits that there is also a high probability of civil unrest if many people are deprived of an important, noneconomic benefit that they have come to expect, or if they have suffered a blow to their status and their preferred social order. For example, although Westerners admired the Shah of Iran's attempts to modernize women's dress (prohibiting the veil) and improve their status, many of these changes violated the "preferred social order" of the nation's Shi'ite population. This, as we have seen, helped set the stage for the Islamist revolution. Furthermore, adds Gurr, the closer people are to attaining their goals, the greater will be their frustration if they fail to achieve them. Note, for example, the growing radicalization of Palestinians (expressed by the victory of the Islamist Hamas party in the most recent parliamentary elections) as the once-promising peace process between Israelis and the PLO had stalled and the dreams of a Palestinian state had faded.

Finally, Gurr maintains that the type of civil violence that a country experiences will depend on which segments of society are experiencing relative deprivation. If the poor alone feel frustrated, there may be political "turmoil" (spontaneous, disorganized violence) but not a revolution. Only if important elements of the middle class and the elite—more educated and politically experienced individuals who can provide political leadership—also suffer relative deprivation can there be revolutionary upheaval.

Causes of Revolution: A Summary

None of these theories of revolution offers a single "correct" explanation. For one thing, they often focus on different aspects of the question. For example, while Gurr and Davies ask why individuals join revolts or revolutionary movements, Skocpol focuses on the international economic and military factors that have weakened the state prior to successful revolutionary insurrections.

Clearly, revolutions are never inevitable and, in fact, successful revolutions are rare. While the causes of unrest may lie in relative deprivation and the regime's loss of legitimacy, the ultimate success or failure of revolutionary movements also depends on the relative military and political capabilities of the contending forces. Only by comparing the political-military strength of those who rebel with the state's capacity to defend itself can we understand why some revolutionary movements succeed, while others fail.

As we have seen, revolutions often occur after a country has been defeated or badly weakened in war (Russia, China, Turkey, and Egypt) or after its government has been ousted temporarily (in Vietnam and other parts of Asia, European colonial rule was disrupted by the Japanese during World War II). They may also take place when a government is particularly corrupt (Cuba and Nicaragua) or subservient to foreign powers (Cuba, Mexico, and Nicaragua). In all of these cases, the incumbent regime lost its legitimacy. Thus, Russia's Czarist regime and China's Kuomintang government both fell when they proved incapable of defending their people's sovereignty against foreign armies. Similarly, Cuba's president Fulgencio Batista lost his legitimacy when he turned Havana into "the brothel of the Caribbean" in league with the American mafia. And, the Shah of Iran lost his legitimacy after his modernization program offended Iran's Islamic clerics. British, French, and Dutch colonial rule in Asia was secure as long as the indigenous population believed that Europeans were too powerful to topple and perhaps better equipped to govern. When the Japanese ousted the colonial governments of Burma, Malaysia, Vietnam, and Indonesia, they demonstrated that Asian armed forces could defeat European powers. Once the Europeans lost their aura of invincibility, they were unable to reestablish sustained colonial rule after World War II.

Finally, the very authoritarianism of many Third World governments often ultimately undermines them. Cuba's Batista, the Shah of Iran, and Nicaragua's Anastasio Somoza Jr. illustrate that point. Because their governments had never been legitimized through free and honest elections, they could not convincingly claim to represent the people. Ignoring that issue during the Cold War, the United States supported authoritarian governments in countries such as El Salvador, Nicaragua, Chile, Zaire (Congo), South Korea, Iran, and Pakistan. Responding to criticisms by human rights groups, Washington argued that, whatever their faults, these repressive governments were the last remaining fire walls against communist subversion and the rise of totalitarianism. In truth, however, a democratic government offers the best inoculation against revolution. Indeed, no consolidated democracy has ever been toppled by a revolution.*

---

* The only case of a communist regime replacing a democratic government is in postwar Czechoslovakia. But the new government took power through a Russian-supported coup, not through revolutionary insurgency.

LEVELS OF POPULAR SUPPORT

Che Guevara, the leading military strategist of the Cuban Revolution, once observed that those who undertake revolutions either win or die. Though perhaps overstating his point, Guevara's remark highlights the tremendous risk revolutionary fighters take, be they poor peasants or radicalized university students. Rebels almost always face superior firepower and a range of formidable state institutions (the police, the military, special intelligence units, etc.). Not surprisingly, most of the time the insurgents lose. One study counted 28 guerrilla movements in Latin America from 1956 to 1990. Of that total, only two succeeded (Cuba's July 26 movement and Nicaragua's Sandinistas).[25] Asia and Africa are also littered with the corpses of dead revolutionaries and failed insurgents. Even victorious revolutions, such as Vietnam's and China's, leave behind vast numbers of fallen rebel fighters and supporters. Those who survive often return home to devastated villages and suffering families. Not surprisingly, then, peasants, workers, students, and professionals do not take lightly the decision to join a revolutionary force.

What portion of the population must support a revolution if it is to succeed? What types of people are most likely to join the movement? The answer to the first question is ambiguous. There is no fixed or knowable percentage of the population that must support an insurrection in order for it to triumph. Following World War II, a majority of Ukrainians are believed to have supported a separatist movement fighting to end Russian control, yet that uprising was crushed by the powerful Soviet army. On the other hand, insurgencies elsewhere have succeeded with the active support of less than 20 percent of the civilian population.

Any evaluation of popular sentiment during a revolutionary upheaval needs to identify at least five different groups. First, there are those who strongly support the incumbent government and believe that their own fates are linked to the regime's survival. Government officials, military officers, landowners, and businesspeople with close links to the pre-revolutionary state normally fall in this category. It may also include ethnic groups tied to the regime (such as the Hmong people of Laos), people ideologically committed to the political system, and an assortment of others with a stake in preserving the status quo.

A second group in society also supports the government but more conditionally. For example, during the 1960s, most Venezuelans supported the government's battle against Marxist guerrillas. Even though many of them shared the guerrillas' objections to the country's severe inequality and poverty, they were repulsed by the rebels' use of violence and their refusal to work within the country's new democratic framework. Because the government's public support was broad but thin (i.e., many Venezuelans were conditional supporters), it could easily have lost its advantage had it used the repressive antiguerrilla tactics so widely employed elsewhere in Latin America. By showing moderation, the government held its ground.

A third, often critical, segment of the population supports neither the revolutionaries nor the government. Its members are generally alienated and probably dislike both sides. In the 1980s and 1990s, many Peruvian Indian villages were victimized by the *Sendero Luminoso* (Shining Path) guerrillas, an extremely fanatical and brutal revolutionary Marxist movement. At the same time, these peasants also were often brutalized by the Peruvian army, which flagrantly violated their human rights. Not surprisingly, most peasants feared and hated both sides. Caught in the middle, for their own preservation they avoided taking sides, though some did join government-supported defense militias.

A fourth group—drawn primarily from the peasantry, workers, the urban poor, and alienated members of the middle class who sympathize with the revolutionary cause—occasionally lends support to the insurgents but does not actually join them. For example, sympathetic peasants in China, Cuba, and Vietnam offered intelligence information, food, and shelter to rebel guerrillas. In countries such as China and El Salvador, where the guerrillas controlled "liberated zones" for long periods of time, these support networks were very extensive. In other countries where the revolution was fought primarily through urban street protests rather than guerrilla war (Iran) and in revolutions with important urban and rural components (Mexico, Nicaragua), revolution-aries also depended on the sympathy and occasional support of the urban poor, workers, and parts of the middle class.

Finally, there is a relatively small portion of the population that fully involves itself in the revolutionary struggle. In Cuba, Mexico, and Nicaragua, for example, committed students, teachers, and professionals assumed leadership positions. In those countries, as well as in China, Vietnam, and El Salvador, many peasants (including women and teenagers) became the revolution's foot soldiers. Given the enormous risks involved for the participants and their families, it is not surprising that only a small portion of the people took up arms. Some peasants joined out of desperation, because the armed forces had destroyed their farms or villages or because they feared being drafted into an army that they despised. Others were attracted to the revolutionaries' promises of a more just social order.

One can only guess the proportion of a country's population in each of these five groups at a particular point in time. Public opinion surveys in countries experiencing revolutionary upheavals are unlikely to elicit honest responses. But we do know that if they are to succeed, revolutionary movements must attract a core of firmly committed activists willing to risk their lives for the cause, as well as a larger circle of sympathizers. How large their numbers must be depends on the extent of government decay and loss of legitimacy. It also depends on how well-armed and committed government troops are, how effectively those troops fight, and how much foreign support they have. Thus, for example, Fidel Castro's small rural force of only a few hundred troops (supported by a comparable number of urban guerrillas) defeated Batista's much larger but dispirited army. On the other hand, El Salvador's FMLN—a far larger and better-equipped guerrilla army than Castro's—could not unseat a government that was bolstered by extensive American economic and military aid. Yet even the United States' commitment of massive military assistance and many thousands of American troops could not save the South Vietnamese government from the Viet Cong guerrillas and their North Vietnamese allies.

The people in the second category (mild government supporters) and the third (neutrals) are equally important targets for any revolutionary movement. In developing countries that have substantial urban populations, governments can maintain power in the face of considerable peasant unrest and rural guerrilla activity as long as they control the cities and retain the support of the urban middle class, particularly civil servants, businesspeople, and professionals.

These middle-class groups are not normally radical, but they can become disenchanted with particularly corrupt, repressive, or ineffectual regimes. In Iran, the tide turned in favor of the revolutionary mullahs when Tehran's bazaar shopkeepers lost confidence in the Shah's government.

Nicaragua's revolution also illustrates this point. Because the Somoza family had expropriated such a large share of the national economy, its greed not only damaged the poor but hurt the business community as well. As the Sandinista uprising spread and the National Guard became increasingly repressive, Nicaragua's private sector grew increasingly alienated from the government. Prominent business leaders—including the head of the country's Coca-Cola bottling plant, the nation's most prominent newspaper owner, and the directors of several important banks—demanded Anastasio Somoza Jr.'s resignation and organized business shutdowns to express their opposition. While most of these people were wary of the Sandinista movement (which made no secret of its leftist ideology), they shared its desire to oust the Somoza regime.

While flying from Panama to Miami during the height of the insurrection, I found myself seated next to the chief executive of an important Nicaraguan agrochemical plant. In the course of our conversation about events in his country, he declared, "Somoza has to go. He's too damned corrupt and he's wrecking the country." "But what if reformist business leaders such as you have to share power with the [Marxist-oriented] Sandinistas after he falls?" I asked. "I don't like those guys," he replied, "but if sharing power with them is what it takes to get rid of Somoza, then we'll have to do it." In the face of such broad ideological and cross-class opposition to the government, it was just a matter of time before the Somoza regime fell.*

In short, if a revolutionary movement is to gain power, there must be wide-scale alienation from the government, a disaffection that reaches beyond the ranks of the poor and the oppressed to the heart of the middle class and the business community. It is neither likely nor necessary for a large portion of those groups to actively support the insurrection. For the revolution to succeed, it is only essential that some of them, including a highly committed core, do so, while many others, like the Nicaraguan business executive on the plane, simply cease supporting the government.

PEASANTS AS REVOLUTIONARIES

Let us now turn our attention to the ranks of committed revolutionary supporters, particularly the last group, revolutionary activists. With rare exception, Third World revolutions have been fought primarily by peasants. The Chinese Red Army and the Viet Cong, for example, consisted overwhelmingly of the rural poor. Indeed, almost all African and Asian revolutionary movements have been overwhelmingly rural in character. And even in Latin America's revolutions, where the urban populations often played key roles, peasants were also very important actors. Consequently, it is important to ask, "What factors induce some peasants to risk joining a revolution, and what types of peasants join?"

---

* After the rebels ousted the Somoza regime, the Sandinista-led government did initially include progressive business leaders, but the two sides soon parted ways.

Why Peasants Rebel

In our analysis of Third World rural society (Chapter 6), we noted that traditional peasant culture tends to be rather conservative. Because early economic modernization frequently affects them negatively, they have good reason to cling to tradition. But the intrusion of market forces into their communities sometimes so unsettles their world that it radicalizes them as they struggle to protect what they have. For one thing, increasing numbers of subsistence farmers (peasants producing primarily for their family's consumption) in a modernizing economy are induced or pressured to enter the commercial market for the first time. Once involved in commercial agriculture, however, they must deal with fluctuations in the price of their crops, including volatile shifts that they are ill-equipped to handle.

At the same time, rural landlords, whose precapitalist exploitation of local peasants had been constrained by their neofeudal obligations, now viewed their tenants merely as factors of production in the new market economy. In Latin America, many landlords who had previously funded their peons' *fiestas* or lent them money when they were in special need, concluded that such expenditures were no longer financially prudent in the more competitive market environment. Other landlords entering the commercial market decided to mechanize production and evict tenant farmers from their land.

For all of these reasons, rural society's transition from neofeudal to capitalist production precipitated many of the Third World's twentieth-century revolutions.[26] James Scott notes that the pain peasants suffered during that transformation was not merely economic or physical but also *moral*. To be sure, the precapitalist rural order had its share of grave injustices, but those inequities were somewhat mitigated by a web of reciprocal obligations between landlords and peasants and among peasants. It is the collapse of that "moral economy," Scott argues, that drives many peasants to revolution.[27] Similarly, as noted in Chapter 6, Eric Wolf insists that in countries as disparate as Cuba, Mexico, Algeria, Vietnam, and China, most peasant participants in revolutionary movements were not trying to create a new socialist order. Rather, they were seeking to restore the security of their old way of life.

Which Peasants Rebel

Even in a single country or region, peasants are not a homogeneous mass. Some of them, called *kulaks*, own larger plots of land and employ other peasants to work on their farms with them. Others are landless or own extremely small plots. And still others work as wage laborers on large estates or rent parcels of land from the landlord, paying their rent in cash, labor, or sharecropping.* Each group has distinct political and economic needs.

The peasants most threatened by the economic modernization of the countryside are the ones most likely to join local revolts or broader revolutionary movements. Analyzing data collected from 70 developing nations over a 22-year period, Jeffrey M. Paige found that the peasant groups most

---

* Sharecroppers are tenant farmers who pay their rent by giving the landlord a percentage of their crop.

liable to join insurgencies were wage laborers and sharecroppers who worked for landlords who, in turn, earned all their income from their land.[28] Not only are these peasants particularly vulnerable to changing economic conditions, but their landlords are also less likely to grant them financial concessions because they depend exclusively on their farmland for their incomes. Research on Latin American guerrilla movements reveals that squatters (poor farmers who illegally occupy land) and other peasants who face eviction from the land that they cultivate are also more prone to rebel.[29]

But even peasants with more secure access to the land feel threatened by declining crop prices. For example, in Peru's Ayacucho province, the birthplace of the Shining Path guerrilla movement, peasants experienced declining terms of trade for two decades; that is, the cost of the goods they consumed had been rising faster than the price of the crops that they sold. Caught in an ongoing financial squeeze, they felt increasingly insecure and, hence, became more receptive to the Shining Path's appeals.[30]

All of the peasants who are more prone to support revolutions, then, have one element in common—they were threatened by the prospect of losing their land and/or their livelihood. Conversely, the most conservative peasants are those with secure title to their landholdings and relatively stable prices for their crops. It is for this reason that many analysts maintain that the best protection against rural revolution is an agrarian reform program that distributes land and offers the recipients secure titles and support services (see Chapter 6).

Peasant insurrections are also more likely to occur in areas that have historical traditions of rebellion. For example, the revolutionary forces in China, Vietnam, Cuba, Mexico, and Nicaragua all received their greatest support in regions that had traditions of peasant resistance, what one author calls a "rebellious culture."[31] Fidel Castro's home province of Oriente, known as "the cradle of the Cuban Revolution," had a long history of unrest dating back to nineteenth-century slave revolts against their owners and against Spanish colonial rule. China's Hunan province (Mao Zedong's home) and the area around the Sandinista stronghold of León also had rebellious traditions. Some revolutionary movements take root in areas without a record of prior rebellions but with a tradition of lawlessness and hostility toward the legal authorities. For example, Mexican revolutionary leader Pancho Villa operated in a region known for cattle rustling and other forms of social banditry. And Villa himself was a bandit-turned-revolutionary. Similarly, Castro's July 26 guerrillas based themselves in the Sierra Maestra Mountains, a region with a history of smuggling, marijuana production, and banditry.

REVOLUTIONARY LEADERSHIP

Although peasants furnish the foot soldiers for revolutions, they rarely hold the highest leadership posts. They may stage spontaneous uprisings or even more extensive revolts on their own, but they usually lack the organizational and political skills needed to lead a broader social revolution. Consequently, the top revolutionary leaders and many at the middle level are typically people with more education and greater political experience. To be sure, there are exceptions. Mexico's Emiliano Zapata was a horse trainer from a peasant family who only became literate as an adult.[32] Pancho Villa was also of humble origins. Today, peasants hold important leadership posts in the Colombian Revolutionary Armed Forces of Colombia (FARC) guerrillas. Ultimately, however, their political inexperience and lack of external contacts proved costly. Thus, Villa and Zapata jointly conquered Mexico City, the nation's capital, but then left it because neither man felt equipped to run the country.

More typically, then, the top revolutionary leadership comes from middle-class or even upper-class origins. In Latin America, for example, "they are drawn disproportionately from the intelligentsia, not only highly educated, but also largely involved in the production of theories."[33] Trained as a librarian, China's Mao Zedong was the son of a rural grain merchant. In Vietnam, Ho Chi Minh, the son of a rural school teacher, practiced a number of professions, including photography, while living in Paris, where he became a French Communist Party activist. Fidel Castro received a law degree at the University of Havana, where he was a leader in student politics. His father, a Spanish immigrant, had started life in Cuba as a worker, but eventually became a well-to-do landowner. Castro's comrade, Che Guevara, was a doctor whose parents, though not rich, were of aristocratic origin. Similarly, most of the nine *comandantes* who directed Nicaragua's Sandinista revolution came from solid middle- or upper-class families and were well educated. For example, President Daniel Ortega and his brother, Defense Minister Humberto Ortega, were the sons of an accountant-businessman. Luis Carrión, the son of a millionaire, had attended an American prep school. Only one *comandante*, Henry Ruiz, came from a poor urban family, and none were of peasant origin.[34] Finally, a Vietnamese Communist Party study of nearly 2,000 party activists (conducted after World War II, at the start of their long revolutionary struggle) revealed that 74 percent of them were either intellectuals or were from bourgeois families, while only 7 percent were the children of workers, and 19 percent came from peasant families.[35] These are remarkable statistics for a party trying to speak for the country's peasantry and working class.

Not surprisingly, a larger number of lower-ranking revolutionary leaders are of peasant or working-class backgrounds. Compared to Latin America, more of the rural poor have held leadership positions in Asia's revolutionary governments (including China, Vietnam, and Cambodia), in countries where peasants accounted for most of the national population. During their two-decade revolutionary struggle and after taking power, the Chinese Communist Party (CCP) and its Red Army offered peasant activists unprecedented opportunities for upward mobility. From its early days, the party gave peasants and children of peasants—heretofore at the bottom of the social ladder—preference for admission to its ranks. And as recently as 1985, decades after it took power, one-third of all CCP members were peasants (some 25 percent of whom were illiterate).* Similarly, many of the lower- and middle-level guerrilla leaders in El Salvador and Peru were of

---

* Although the percentages of peasants and illiterates in the party were still well below the corresponding shares of the general population, they were higher than in most LDCs. Since the late 1980s, however, the educational level and professional training of mid-level party leaders has risen, meaning that they are more skilled but somewhat less representative of the population.

peasant origin, although lots of them were upwardly mobile children of peasants who had become teachers, health workers, and the like.

The educational and social gaps separating aspiring revolutionary leaders from the peasant rank and file can be considerable problems unless those leaders have a firm understanding of the local culture. Although Mao Zedong was an urban intellectual, his rural upbringing had given him an understanding of village life. Fidel Castro was no peasant, but his childhood on his father's farm had familiarized him with the region's rural poor. And in Venezuela, several of the FALN commanders were sons of local landlords who built on their father's patron–client ties to the local peasants.[36]

On the other hand, the rural poor often turn away aspiring guerrilla organizers who come to them with little understanding of their problems. Hence, they generally reject the overtures of radical university students from other regions of the country, other countries, or other ethnic backgrounds. Given their history of exploitation, peasants tend to be understandably wary of outsiders. The wider the linguistic, cultural, or racial gaps between would-be revolutionary leaders and the local villagers, and the greater the peasants' prior suspicion of outsiders, the harder it is for aspiring organizers to break through that wall of distrust. In Cuba, where racial and ethnic divisions were relatively less important, the peasants of the Sierra Maestra Mountains accepted Che Guevara, an, urban, middle-class Argentinean. So when he later ventured to Bolivia to spread the revolution, Guevara was ill-prepared for the Indian peasants' deep mistrust of White outsiders such as himself. There, an antiguerrilla unit of the Bolivian armed forces captured and killed him, aided by local villagers who saw no reason to risk their safety for an outside agitator. Similarly, Hector Béjar, a failed Peruvian guerrilla leader, later wrote candidly in his memoirs about how he—a coastal, White journalist and poet—was unable to gain the trust of the highland Indians whom he had hoped to lead.[37]

Revolutionaries in Power

While many comparative studies have examined the causes of revolution, there is less cross-national research on the *policies* revolutionary regimes implement once in office. Perhaps guerrilla fighters in the hills have inspired more interest and romanticism (or fear) than have revolutionary bureaucrats in the corridors of power. The record suggests that Third World revolutions in the developing world have accomplished more than their detractors admit but less than their supporters claim.

A major goal of many revolutionary governments (especially Marxist ones) has been to achieve greater socioeconomic equality. That quest usually begins with the struggle for power itself, when revolutionary leaders use egalitarian appeals to garner support from downtrodden peasants and workers. Recognizing the critical importance of that support, Mao Zedong wrote that the peasantry is to the guerrilla army what water is to a fish. To win their loyalty, the Red Army treated peasants whom they encountered with greater respect than other Chinese military forces or governments had.[38] Similarly, in Cuba, "the army's brutal treatment of the peasants" contrasted with "Castro's policy of paying for the food purchased from the peasants . . . and putting his [mostly urban] men to work in the . . . fields."[39]

Once in power, revolutionary governments have generally continued to emphasize economic and social equality. In addition to redistributing land and other economic resources, they also introduce egalitarian cultural reforms. We have noted, for example, that at meetings of Cuba's Committees for the Defense of the Revolution (CDRs), neighbors may pressure husbands to share household tasks with their spouses. Efforts at economic and social egalitarianism have been more limited in non-Marxist revolutions. Still, insurgencies such as Bolivia's and Mexico's have improved the social status of the rural poor, including indigenous (Native American) peoples.

As we have seen, revolutions open up new channels of upward social mobility for peasants and workers who previously had few such opportunities. To be sure, people of middle-class origins hold most of the government and party leadership positions. And ethnic minorities are also underrepresented at that level. For example, Cuba's Black and Mulatto populations and China's (non-Han) ethnic minorities have been severely underrepresented in their Communist Party politburos and government cabinets. But many revolutionary activists from humble backgrounds *do* hold political positions that they could never have attained under the old order. Consequently, revolutionary parties and mass organizations such as Cuba's CDRs often give peasants and workers a greater sense of participation in the political system.

Finally, revolutions usually decrease economic inequality, though the degree of change varies from country to country. Agrarian reform programs in China, Vietnam, Bolivia, Cuba, Mexico, and Nicaragua redistributed land from the rural oligarchy to the peasantry. Many Marxist regimes have offered guaranteed employment, subsidized food and housing, state-sponsored medical care, and other measures that particularly benefit the poor. In countries such as Cuba, government wage policies have reduced income inequalities. In contrast, in more moderate revolutions, such as Mexico's, the pre-revolutionary concentration of income has remained or even worsened.

To be sure, inequalities persist even in radical revolutionary societies. For example, while many of them have reduced disparities between rural and urban living standards, significant gaps remain. As China implements free-market reforms, income inequality—which declined substantially in the 1980s—has increased sharply since that time. In fact, currently economic inequality (as measured by the Gini index) is greater in China than in the United States, India, Thailand, Mexico, or any country in Europe. On the other hand, other communist countries in Asia—Vietnam, Laos—as well as many former communist nations—Mongolia, Eastern Europe, and the former republics of the Soviet Union—have relatively low income inequality.[40]

At the same time, a new form of inequality usually emerges in revolutionary societies as newly entrenched party and government officials begin to appropriate special perquisites for themselves and their families. Many years ago, Milovan Djilas, a disillusioned former leader of Yugoslavia's communist government, complained about the rise of a "new class" in revolutionary regimes, an elite of party officials who enjoy special privileges and a better standard of living.[41] Today in China, the foremost Communist Party leaders are well known for their lavish lifestyles, while the children of the party cadre are despised for their arrogance and corruption. While the effect of this "new class" is not sufficient to substantially affect their nations' Gini indexes, it usually demoralizes the public. Widespread government corruption (even technically legal corruption) is disheartening in any setting, but even more so in a population that fought a revolution in the name of equality.*

Another major revolutionary objective has been mass political mobilization. As Samuel Huntington notes, "a full-scale revolution involves the rapid and violent destruction of existing political institutions, the mobilization of new groups into politics, and the creation of new political institutions."[42] Thus, in China, Vietnam, Cuba, and Nicaragua, government incentives and pressures induced a large portion of the population to join revolutionary support groups. At one time, close to 90 percent of Cuban adults belonged to their neighborhood CDRs. In the 1980s, substantial portions of the Nicaraguan population joined Sandinista Defense Committees (CDSs).

At its best, mass political mobilization has increased the government's capacity to build the economy by mobilizing volunteer labor and spreading labor discipline. At times, revolutionary support groups have also helped combat sexism, racism, and crime. At their worst, these groups have been used as vigilantes against alleged counterrevolutionaries and as agents of thought control. At Cuban CDR meetings, government spokespersons familiarize the members with current government political position, while citizens are encouraged to volunteer for projects such as planting neighborhood gardens and are imbued with greater revolutionary consciousness.[43] But in Mao Zedong's China, mass mobilization often involved brutal political campaigns that called upon citizens to root out and punish alleged enemies of the revolution. Hundreds of thousands, perhaps more, were persecuted, jailed, or killed during the government's Anti-Rightist Campaign (1957) and its Cultural Revolution (1966–1976).[44]

Mass mobilization can be used either to activate citizens who support the revolution's goals or to isolate and persecute those who do not. Most revolutionary regimes are led by a dominant party, such as the Chinese Communist Party or the Mexican PRI, which stands at the center of the mobilization process. Opposition parties are either prohibited or are only tolerated in a weakened condition. Among Marxist governments, only Nicaragua's Sandinistas ever allowed themselves to be voted out of office. Elsewhere, a number of non-Marxist revolutionary parties have lost favor over time. They may resort to fraud when faced with the prospect of losing control (as in Mexico until 2000), cancel elections that the opposition is expected to win (Algeria), or hand over the reins of power and become just another competing party (Bolivia and, most recently, Mexico).

In short, while revolutionary regimes often have broad popular support, as we have already noted, they are *not* democratic. Because they view themselves as the *only* legitimate voice of the people and the sole custodians of the general good, most radical regimes tend to regard opposition groups as enemies of the people who should be denied political space. Nicaragua's Sandinista government, a rare exception, allowed opposition parties and interest groups to function, even if they were occasionally harassed. Although

---

* The British essayist George Orwell (himself an active radical) foresaw this danger in his famed novel, *Animal Farm* (1945). It notes that "all animals are equal, but some animals are more equal."

the major opposition newspaper, *La Prensa*, was periodically censored or shut down briefly, it continued to vigorously, and sometimes outrageously, attack the government right up to the time its publisher, Violeta Chamorro, was elected the nation's president. For the most part, however, even communist governments that have opened up their economies to free-market reforms (China and Vietnam) have maintained a repressive political structure that tightly limits opposition voices.

While members of the first generation of revolutionary leaders tend to be true believers in their movement's ideology, the next generation is frequently more corrupted by power. In China and Vietnam—where rapid economic growth and the expansion of the private sector have opened up new opportunities for corruption—bribing the right state official is often a necessity for doing business.[45] Cubans, who generally had believed that their revolutionary leaders were more honest than their extremely corrupt predecessors, were shocked by the "Ochoa affair (1989)," which revealed that high-ranking military and security officers were involved in drug trafficking. Since that time, government corruption of a more mundane nature has become far more pervasive as a result of the severe economic scarcities of the 1990s.[46] And, after the Sandinistas left office in 1990, disillusioned Nicaraguans learned that top party officials had kept for themselves some of the luxurious mansions that had been confiscated from the Somoza regime.* It is not that these revolutionary regimes are more corrupt than other Third World governments; often they are less so. Thus, Transparency International's most recent rating of international corruption ranks Cuba and China better than average (i.e., less corrupt than over half the countries on the list), when compared to other Third World countries.[47] It is just that their supporters, some of whom made considerable sacrifices for the revolutionary cause, had expected more.

CONCLUSION: REVOLUTIONARY CHANGE AND DEMOCRACY

Revolutionary change was an important force in much of the Third World throughout the twentieth century. Its impact was probably greatest in Asia, where the Chinese Revolution transformed the lives of one-fifth of humanity and where revolutionary struggles in Vietnam, Laos, and Cambodia involved France and then the United States in major wars. Elsewhere in Asia, there were failed communist insurgencies in the Philippines and Malaysia and, most recently, a partially successful one in Nepal. Most of Africa's revolutions were wars of national liberation from European colonialism (Algeria, Angola, and Kenya, among others) or secessionist wars (including Biafra, Eritrea, and southern Sudan). In some African nations, military rulers imposed revolutions from above—most notably in Ethiopia—usually with unfortunate results. Latin America experienced two Marxist revolutions (Cuba and Nicaragua), two non-Marxist insurrections (Bolivia and Mexico), and a number of unsuccessful revolutionary movements (Argentina, Colombia, El Salvador, Guatemala, Peru, Uruguay, and Venezuela). Both the revolutions and the failed insurgencies had spillover effects on neighboring countries. For

---

* In 2006, Sandinista leader, Daniel Ortega, was once again elected president.

example, the Cuban Revolution prompted a number of Latin American governments to initiate agrarian reform programs designed to avert "another Cuba." The Nicaraguan Revolution inspired both agrarian reform and intensified government repression in neighboring El Salvador.

However, in the past two decades, revolution's appeal, particularly Marxist revolution, has waned considerably. Indeed, today's world is a veritable graveyard of failed insurrections. The Soviet Union, once the fountainhead of Communism, collapsed, and its most important successor state, Russia, still is struggling to overcome the errors of its Marxist-Leninist past. Communism is equally discredited throughout Eastern and Central Europe, where it held sway until recently. In Nicaragua, an American-backed counter-revolutionary war and the Sandinista regime's own errors undid most of the revolution's early social and economics gains and led to the Sandinistas' defeat in the 1990 presidential election. Cuba's impressive achievements in education and health care were partially eroded in the 1990s after the collapse of the Soviet Union, previously a major source of economic assistance. Elsewhere in the Third World, other revolutionary governments performed far more poorly. Countries such as Angola, Cambodia, Ethiopia, and Mozambique suffered enormous losses of life and economic devastation, having achieved little or nothing in return.

Judging the accomplishment and failures of revolutionary change in countries such as China, Cuba, and Vietnam is not easy because evaluations are invariably influenced by the analysts' ideological orientations. Furthermore, even the most objective social scientist finds it difficult to isolate the effects of revolutionary policy from a host of other overlapping factors. For example, critics of the Chinese Revolution argue that the socioeconomic gains attained under Mao were achieved in spite of his radical policies, not because of them. They further insist that the country's rapid economic growth since the 1980s demonstrates the advantages of free-market reforms. On the other hand, other analysts maintain that China could never have achieved its market-based economic boom without the revolution's earlier advances in education.

In the same way, the Cuban Revolution's detractors contend that the country's progress in health care and education could have been achieved under a democratic system, noting that Costa Rica (one of the strongest democracies in the region) has made comparable gains in social welfare. Furthermore, they maintain that Cuba's strong record in those areas was only possible because of massive Soviet aid over a period of 30 years. Nevertheless, more sympathetic observers note that Cuba achieved its impressive educational and health gains in spite of an American economic embargo.*

Neither side can definitively prove its position because there are so many independent variables that make it difficult or impossible to establish causal relationships. In any event, while there may yet be future revolutions in the developing world, it is likely that *the age of revolution* is drawing to an end. The demise of Soviet and Central European Communism exposed more clearly the deficiencies of Marxism-Leninism. So too have China's and Vietnam's introduction of free-market (capitalist) components into their

---

* Prior to the revolution, the United States was Cuba's dominant trading partner.

economic systems. With Communism discredited, even among some of its once-fervent followers, it is unlikely to find many adherents willing to risk their lives fighting for its ideals. Marxist ideology, once chic among Third World intellectuals and political activists, has become far less fashionable.[48] At the end of the 1980s, facing defeat by its mujahideen opponents, Afghanistan's then-ruling People's Democratic Party (a communist party beholden to Moscow at the time), renounced its Marxist ideology in a failed effort to maintain power. One of its leaders dismissed the party's long-standing communist position by claiming that it had adopted that ideology at "a time when Marxism-Leninism was quite in fashion in underdeveloped countries." In Angola, where the governing party made a similar ideological conversion, the president explained that continuing to support the Marxist-Leninist model "would be rowing against the tide [of capitalist democracy]."[49] Similar transformations have occurred within Nicaragua's Sandinista party and El Salvador's FMLN, both former revolutionary movements that subsequently transformed themselves into democratic socialist political parties. In his successful 2006 campaign to regain the presidency, Sandinista leader Daniel Ortega insisted that Jesus Christ, not Marx, was his first inspiration when he led the country's revolution nearly 30 years earlier. Modifying his earlier leftist views, he declared that "in this new context, to which we had to adjust, the market economy plays its role."

How many revolutionary upheavals will take place in the coming years is hard to predict, and the answer may be partly an issue of semantics (i.e., how we choose to define a revolution). However, now that colonialism has come to an end in Africa and Asia, there are few possibilities for wars of national liberation. There still may be other mass-based revolutions in societies that suffer from severe socioeconomic inequalities, sharp rural–urban divisions, or repressive governments. However, as we have noted, the collapse of the Soviet bloc, the abandonment of Marxist economics in China and Vietnam, the weaknesses of the Nicaraguan revolutionary government, and Cuba's economic problems after it lost Soviet aid have all substantially diminished the appeal of revolutionary Marxism. Thus, for example, in 1992, El Salvador's FMLN guerrillas ended their 12-year revolutionary war, signed a peace treaty that promised some of the reforms that they had long fought for, and converted themselves into a legal political party. In a series of national elections in 2009, the FMLN first won a congressional plurality and then won the presidency ending the 20-year rule of the conservative, ARENA party.

Any future insurgencies are likely to occur in Africa, the Middle East, and parts of Asia. Perhaps, there also will be scattered uprisings by indigenous peoples (Indians) in Latin America, as there already have been in Bolivia, Ecuador, and Peru. Fundamentalist Islamic upheavals are a distinct possibility in the Middle East or North Africa. Whether these struggles can properly be called revolutions, however, is debatable. They fail to satisfy most social science definitions of the word. Hence, it is probably more accurate to call them civil wars, secessionist rebellions, religious uprisings, or ethnic conflicts, rather than revolutions. Successful revolutions, in the sense that Skocpol or even Huntington defines them, appear unlikely in the foreseeable future.

DISCUSSION QUESTIONS

1. What conditions or developments have convinced Third World inhabitants to join revolutionary movements?
2. What is the likelihood of further revolutions in the twenty-first century? What kinds of revolutions are most likely to occur?
3. Discuss some of the major accomplishments and failures of revolutionary governments.

NOTES

1. Chalmers Johnson, *Revolution and the Social System* (Stanford, CA: Hoover Institution, 1964), 2.

2. Peter Calvert, "Revolution: The Politics of Violence," *Political Studies*, vol. 15, no. 1 (1967), 2; and *Revolution and Counter Revolution* (Minneapolis: University of Minnesota Press, 1990).

3. Samuel P. Huntington, *Political Order in Changing Societies* (New Haven, CT: Yale University Press, 1968), 264.

4. Norman R. Miller and Roderick R. Aya, *National Liberation: Revolution in the Third World* (New York: Free Press, 1971).

5. Theda Skocpol, "France, Russia, China: A Structural Analysis of Social Revolutions," *Comparative Studies in Society and History*, vol. 18, no. 2 (1976), 176.

6. Theda Skocpol, *States and Social Revolutions: A Comparative Analysis of France, Russia and China* (Cambridge, England: Cambridge University Press, 1979), 4.

7. Ellen Kay Trimberger, "A Theory of Elite Revolutions," *Studies in Comparative International Development*, vol. 7, no. 3 (1972), 191–207.

8. Karl Marx and Frederick Engels, *Manifesto of the Communist Party* (New York: International Publishers, 1948).

9. A. S. Cohan, *Theories of Revolution* (London: Thomas Nelson and Sons, 1975), 72.

10. Irving M. Zeitlin, *Marxism: A Re-examination* (Princeton, NJ: Princeton University Press, 1967), 142.

11. Stuart R. Schram, *The Political Thought of Mao Tse-tung* (New York: Praeger, 1969).

12. Skocpol, *States and Social Revolutions*.

13. Skocpol, "France, Russia, China."

14. Chalmers Johnson, *Peasant Nationalism and Communist Power* (Stanford, CA: Stanford University Press, 1962).

15. Johnson, *Revolution and the Social System*.

16. Joel Migdal, *Peasants, Politics and Revolution* (Princeton, NJ: Princeton University Press, 1974), 252.

17. Ramón L. Bonachea and Marta San Martín, *The Cuban Insurrection, 1952–1959* (New Brunswick, NJ: Transaction Books, 1974); John A. Booth, *The End and the Beginning: The Nicaraguan Revolution* (Boulder, CO: Westview Press, 1982).

18. Charles Tilly, *From Mobilization to Revolution* (New York: Addison-Wesley, 1978), 204–205.

19. Charles Tilly, "Does Modernization Breed Revolution?" *Comparative Politics*, vol. 5, no. 3 (April 1974), 425–447.

20. Huntington, *Political Order in Changing Societies*, 265–266.

21. James C. Davies, "Toward a Theory of Revolution," *American Sociological Review*, vol. 27, no. 1 (February 1962), 7.

22. James C. Davies, "Toward a Theory of Revolution," reprinted along with other articles on the causes of revolution in *When Men Revolt and Why*, ed. James C. Davies (New York: Free Press, 1971).

23. Raymond Tanter and Manus Midlarsky, "A Theory of Revolution," *Journal of Conflict Resolution*, vol. 11, no. 3 (1967), 264–280.

24. Ted Robert Gurr, "Psychological Factors in Civil Violence," *World Politics*, vol. 20, no. 2 (1967–1968), 252–253; see also Ted Robert Gurr, *Why Men Rebel* (Princeton, NJ: Princeton University Press, 1970).

25. Timothy P. Wickham-Crowley, *Guerrillas and Revolution in Latin America* (Princeton, NJ: Princeton University Press, 1992), 312.

26. Eric R. Wolf, *Peasant Wars of the Twentieth Century* (New York: Harper & Row, 1969). For a discussion of similar factors in the capitalist transformation of Europe, see Karl Polanyi, *The Great Transformation* (New York: Rinehart, 1957).

27. James C. Scott, *The Moral Economy of the Peasant: Rebellion and Subsistence in Southeast*

Asia (New Haven, CT: Yale University Press, 1976).

28. Jeffrey M. Paige, *Agrarian Revolution: Social Movements and Export Agriculture in the Underdeveloped World* (New York: Free Press, 1975), chaps. 1–2.

29. Wickham-Crowley, *Guerrillas and Revolution,* chap. 6.

30. Cynthia McClintock, *"Sendero Luminoso:* Peru's Maoist Guerrillas," *Problems of Communism,* vol. 32, no. 5 (September–October 1983), 19–34.

31. Wickham-Crowley, *Guerrillas and Revolution,* 246–250; Wolf, *Peasant Wars.*

32. John Womack Jr., *Zapata and the Mexican Revolution* (New York: Vintage, 1968).

33. Wickham-Crowley, *Guerrillas and Revolution,* 213.

34. Dennis Gilbert, *Sandinistas: The Party and the Revolution* (New York: B. Blackwell, 1988).

35. Thomas H. Green, *Comparative Revolutionary Movements* (Upper Saddle River, NJ: Prentice Hall, 1974), 18.

36. Wickham-Crowley, *Guerrillas and Revolution,* 143.

37. Hector Béjar, *Peru 1965: Notes on a Guerrilla Experience* (New York: Monthly Review Press, 1970).

38. Among the many writings on Maoist ideology and strategy, see Stuart R. Schram, *The Political Thought of Mao Tse-tung* (New York: Praeger, 1963); Arthur Cohen, *The Communism of Mao Tse-Tung* (Chicago: University of Chicago Press, 1964); Cohan, *Theories of Revolution,* 93–110.

39. Sebastian Balfour, *Fidel Castro* (New York: Longman, 1990), 49.

40. All of these Gini indices are found in the United Nations Development Program, *2007/20008*

Human Development Report, "Inequality in income or expenditure," http://hdrstats.undp.org/indicators/147.html. Data are not available for Cuba or North Korea.

41. Milovan Djilas, *The New Class* (New York: Praeger, 1957).

42. Huntington, *Political Order in Changing Societies,* 266.

43. Richard R. Fagen, *The Transformation of Political Culture in Cuba* (Stanford, CA: Stanford University Press, 1969); Domínguez, *Cuba: Order and Revolution.*

44. There is a voluminous literature on the Chinese Cultural Revolution. Liang Heng and Judith Shapiro, *Son of the Revolution* (New York: Vintage, 1983), offer a moving personal account of both the Anti-Rightist Campaign and the Cultural Revolution. See also K. S. Karol, *The Second Chinese Revolution* (New York: Hill and Wang, 1974).

45. *The Guardian: Unlimited,* "Corruption: China's Mushrooming Problem" (August 3, 2007), http://www.guardian.co.uk/china/story/0,, 2141185,00.html; *The Economist,* "Vietnam's Corruption" (September 12, 2002), 9.

46. Sergio Díaz-Briquets and Jorge Pérez López, *Corruption in Cuba: Castro and Beyond* (Austin: University of Texas Press, 2006). There has been widespread corruption since the economic crisis of the 1990s.

47. "The 2006 Transparency International Corruption Perception Index," *Infoplease,* http://www.infoplease.com/ipa/A0781359. html.

48. On this theme, see Forrest Colburn, *The Vogue of Revolution in Poor Countries* (Princeton, NJ: Princeton University Press, 1994).

49. Both quotations come from *The Vogue of Revolution,* 89.

CHAPTER 9

SOLDIERS AND POLITICS

For many years, military governments were common in much of the developing world—most notably in Latin America, Africa, and the Middle East. More recently, as democracy has advanced in much of the Third World, military government has become comparatively rare. However, military officers (or former officers) still govern a number of countries, including Guinea, Libya, and Myanmar. In countries such as Algeria and Egypt, a façade of apparent civilian government covers the reality of military rule.

Of course, men emerging from the military ranks occasionally head even the most advanced industrial democracies. American president Dwight Eisenhower, French president Charles de Gaulle, and Israeli Prime Minister Ehud Barak all used distinguished military careers as stepping stones to the leadership of their nation. But each of them entered politics as a private citizen, having first retired from the armed forces. Moreover, they achieved high office through democratic elections, not military coups.*

Over the years, Third World politics has been distinguished by its high degree of military interference, either through direct rule or as a dominant interest group. Unlike their counterparts in industrialized democracies, soldiers in the LDCs often reject any dividing line between military and political activity. A pronouncement by the Indonesian armed forces prior to their assumption of power in the 1960s illustrates that perspective well:

> The army, which was born in the cauldron of the Revolution, has never been a dead instrument of the government, concerned exclusively with security matters. The army, as a fighter for freedom, cannot remain neutral toward the course of state policy, the quality of government, and the safety of the state.[1]

To be sure, there are countries such as India, Malaysia, Kenya, Tunisia, Mexico, and Costa Rica where the armed forces have not ventured deeply into politics for decades. But, until the 1980s, such restraint was the exception rather than the rule. Indeed, until recently, the military's political involvement in most of the Third World was so pervasive that it was almost a defining characteristic of political underdevelopment.

One early study of military intervention revealed that the 59 developing nations scrutinized had had a total of 274 attempted coups between 1946 and

---

* A military coup is a sudden and illegal removal of the incumbent government and the seizure of political power by the armed forces or a faction of the military, using violence or the threat of violence. Usually, the coup makers install themselves in power, but sometimes they install another civilian government or call new elections. Coups occasionally bring about far-reaching changes in government policies, but usually they do not.

1970.[2] At the start of the 1980s, most countries in South America—most notably Argentina, Brazil, Chile, and Peru—was governed by the armed forces. During that decade the armed forces also dominated politics in much of Africa, including Algeria, Ghana, Nigeria, and Sudan. From 1958 to 1984, there were more than 62 successful and 60 failed coup attempts in sub-Saharan Africa alone, affecting more than 80 percent of the nations in that region.[3] During the 1980s, on an average year, military rulers governed 65 percent of Africa's population. Noting the absence of elections in the region for most of that period, one analyst argued that "coups had become the functional equivalent of elections, virtually the sole manner of ousting incumbent political leaders."[4] As democracy began to spread in the 1980s, the number of coups in the region shrank somewhat from its high point during the previous decade (from 24 to 18), but rose again slightly in the 1990s. In all, sub-Saharan Africa had 80 coups and 108 failed coup attempts from 1956 to 2001, affecting 41 of the region's 48 countries. Three African countries (including Nigeria, the continent's most populous nation) had six successful coups each.[5]

Military intervention was less prevalent in Asia, where India, Sri Lanka, and Malaysia, among others, were able to maintain elected civilian government. Elsewhere in Asia, authoritarian civilian governments in Singapore, Taiwan, and China also kept the armed forces in check. Still, military takeovers in some countries continued into the twenty-first century.

Although several Arab nations in North Africa (including Algeria, Libya, and Sudan) have often been controlled by the armed forces or by military strongmen, indirect military dominance is more common in the Middle East. President Husni Mubarak of Egypt and Syria's long-time strongman Hafez al-Assad (1970–2000) entered politics as military men. Elsewhere in the region, monarchs in Morocco, Jordan, Saudi Arabia, Kuwait, and the smaller Gulf States have so far successfully controlled the armed forces.

The last 25 years or so have seen a sharp decline in the number of Third World coups and military regimes. With rare exception, such as Thailand, coups since the early 1990s have only taken place in the world's poorest nations. That change has been most dramatic in Latin America, where democratically elected government has become the norm. In a remarkable turnabout, military coups have virtually ended in the region since the end of the Cold War.* In Asia, military regimes fell in countries such as Indonesia, Bangladesh, and South Korea. But, after having stepped down in favor of civilian governments, military rulers returned to power for a period in Pakistan (1999–2008) and Thailand (2006–2008), while in Bangladesh the armed forces postponed national elections in 2006 and installed a military-controlled caretaker government that served until the December 2008 elections restored civilian government. Finally, the military government in Myanmar (in power since 1962) still endures as one of the oldest and most repressive dictatorships in the world.

Even in Africa, where military government persisted into the 1990s, important transitions to civilian government have occurred in such nations as Nigeria and Ghana, leaving few military regimes in power (though there continue to be some coups and attempted coups). In that region, the rate of new military coups

---

* In 2009, however, the Honduran military, working with elected politicians, ousted the elected president and installed another civilian elected official in his place.

dropped from 2001 through 2007, with only three *successful military* takeovers, all in very small nations. While far fewer African countries remain under formal military rule today, in several cases armed-forces leaders have resigned their positions and subsequently become presidents through rigged elections. Moreover, of late there has been a renewed surge (though still a small one) in armed-forces intervention. In only a 7-month period from August 2008 to March 2009, there were successful military coups in Guinea (Conakry), Guinea-Bissau, Mauritania, and Madagascar (where the armed forces installed the civilian opposition leader as president). Moreover, during this century, there have been a number of unsuccessful coup attempts (multiple times in some nations), which destabilized their political systems.

While the number of Third World military governments has declined substantially, the armed forces continue to wield considerable political influence over many civilian regimes. For example, they may be able to veto the decisions of elected civilian officials in certain policy areas and to influence appointments to important government posts. In some countries, military leaders protect their own budgets, determine who serves as defense minister, or control military promotions. Thus, for example, although elected civilian presidents have governed Guatemala since 1985, they still hesitate to pursue policies that threaten the army's interests. In some countries, such as Algeria, Bangladesh, Nigeria, Pakistan, Syria, and Turkey, the armed forces remain a commanding force in politics.[6] On the other hand, in a number of nations once dominated by the military (such as Argentina and Brazil), the generals now fully accept civilian control.

In order to examine military involvement in Third World politics and the changing nature of civil–military relations, this chapter explores a series of interrelated questions: What accounts for extensive armed forces involvement in politics? How do the structures of military regimes differ from one another? What do the armed forces hope to accomplish when they seize power? How successfully have military regimes achieved their political and economic goals? Is military rule generally beneficial or detrimental to Third World economic and political development? What factors have induced military regimes to step down in recent decades? What political roles do the armed forces continue to play after the establishment or reestablishment of civilian rule? How can civilian governments best control the military?

THE CAUSES OF MILITARY INTERVENTION

Political scientists have offered two alternative perspectives for explaining the frequency and nature of military intervention in developing countries. The first focuses on the *internal characteristics* of the armed forces themselves. The second stresses the broader *political environment* in which the military operates, most notably the weakness of civilian regimes.

The Nature of the Armed Forces

In early research on Third World politics, many analysts maintained that the armed forces enjoyed greater organizational cohesion and clarity of purpose than did civilian political institutions, hence their penchant for intervention. As one leading analyst concluded, "The ability of officers to intervene in domestic politics and produce stable leadership is [directly] related to internal [military] social cohesion."[7] In their efforts to better understand the military's inner workings, scholars examined the class origins, educational levels, ideological orientations, and internal organization of the officer corps. These factors all seemed to affect the probability of military involvement in politics and to influence the officers' goals.

Obviously, the officers' education and training greatly influence their political values. In his highly influential book, *The Soldier and the State*, Samuel Huntington argued that a country wishing to keep the military out of politics must impart "professional" values to its officers. Ideally, as military training and tactics become more sophisticated, officers develop specialized and complex military skills, while distancing themselves from politics. Under those circumstances, Huntington claimed, "a clear distinction in role and function exists between military and civilian leaders."[8] However, he warned, such a division of function only will develop if military training focuses on external threats such as wars with other nations. Should the focus of military education shift toward internal warfare—controlling guerrilla unrest or other civil insurrection—professionalization will not suffice to keep the military out of politics.[9]

Building on this theme, Alfred Stepan distinguished between "old" and "new" military professionalism. The former, typical of developed countries such as the United States, emphasizes skills relevant to "external security." As military officers train to repel foreign enemies, Stepan agreed, we can expect them to remove themselves from domestic politics. In many developing nations, however, military training (the new professionalization) has primarily prepared officers for internal warfare against class-based or ethnically based insurgencies.[10]

In his study of civilian relations with the military over time, Michael Desch found that the level of civilian control over the armed forces correlates with the level of external threat that the country faces from a foreign adversary and the extent of any domestic threat from internal upheaval. He argues that civilian control over the military is likely to be strongest when the country faces a high external threat and a low internal threat. Conversely, civilian control is generally weakest when the country faces a low external threat and a high internal threat, precisely the situation that has prevailed in many Latin American and African nations in the recent past.[11]

The Nature of Civil Society

Although research into the internal structure and dynamics of the armed forces is very useful, it fails to tell the entire story. In other words, we cannot ascertain the probability of military intervention in politics and the objectives of that intervention merely by evaluating internal military factors such as the armed forces' cohesion, size, or ideological orientation. For example, there is surprisingly little correlation between the military's size or its firepower, on the one hand, and its propensity to topple civilian governments, on the other. Indeed, Africa, home to some of the world's smallest militaries, has had one of the highest incidences of military rule. In Togo, an army of only 250 men and a small number of retirees from the former French colonial force carried out West Africa's first military coup. "In Dahomey [now called Benin], General Sogol [*sic*] who had come to power by a coup d'état, was [later] overthrown by sixty paratroopers."[12] Indeed, small and poorly armed military units executed a number of other takeovers in the region. In the closing years of the twentieth century, of nearly 45 African countries, 35 had armed forces of fewer than 30,000, and 23 of those had fewer than 10,000 men.[13] In contrast, China, India, Israel, Sweden, and the United States—with far larger, more skilled, and more internally cohesive militaries—have never suffered a coup.

Ultimately, then, the military's propensity to intervene in politics is less a function of its own capabilities than a consequence of the weaknesses of civilian political institutions. As Huntington insisted, "the most important causes of military intervention in politics are not military, but political and reflect, not the social and organizational characteristics of the military establishment, but the political and institutional structure of society."[14] Hence, the second group of explanatory theories focuses its attention on the nature of civil society.

If a civilian government enjoys substantial support from relevant elites, influential political parties, and the general public, and if it provides political stability and a healthy economy, it is relatively immune to military coups. Conversely, "in times of uncertainty and the breakdown of [civilian political] institutions, soldiers come into their own; when there is no other effective organization of society, even a small, weak army may take command over a large, unorganized mass."[15] In his classic study of civil–military relations, *The Man on Horseback*, Samuel E. Finer maintained that the quality of a nation's political culture helps determine whether or not its civilian government can resist military intervention. Countries are relatively safe from coups if their citizens (including political and military elites) believe that that only *civilian* political leaders and institutions are legitimate and that elections are the only legitimate means of changing governments. Civilian government is also more secure if a country has a strong civil society, a network of independent groups such as labor unions and business organizations.[16] But, in many developing nations, civilian governments have low legitimacy. Consequently, disgruntled military leaders have more opportunity to overthrow them, while other troops and civilians are less likely to risk their lives defending them.

From an institutional perspective, civilian regimes are strongest when broadly based political parties support them. Where party systems are deeply entrenched in the fabric of society and elicit widespread support, the likelihood of military intervention is greatly diminished. In fact, a country's susceptibility to coups is more strongly influenced by the degree to which its party system penetrates and organizes society than by how democratic it is. Thus, once-authoritarian governments in Mexico and Taiwan (dominated by a single party) controlled the military effectively for years, just as the autocratic Chinese government does now. But when placed under great stress, not even a strong party system can fully immunize a political system from military interference. For example, strong party systems, which had kept Uruguay and Chile free of military coups for decades, collapsed under the strains of intense class conflict in the 1970s.

Civilian governments are most vulnerable during periods of economic decline or high inflation. They are also at risk when they are perceived as corrupt and when they are unable to maintain political stability. All these circumstances undermine their legitimacy and often increase popular expectations (or hopes) that military rule could improve the situation. In nations such as Nigeria, Thailand, and Pakistan, soon after taking power military leaders declared their intention to root out widespread corruption. In such cases, military intervention often has initially drawn broad support from civil society. Following severe economic and political crises in Argentina, Brazil, Chile, and Uruguay, the new military dictatorships committed themselves to crush leftist movements, restore social order, and reinvigorate the economy.

As modernization theory would lead us to believe, countries that are more socioeconomically developed are less likely to suffer military takeovers.

> Countries with per-capita GNPs of $1,000 or more [in 1995 dollars] do not [normally] have *successful* coups; countries with per-capita GNPs of $3,000 or more do not have coup *attempts*. The area between $1,000 and $3,000 per-capita GNP is where unsuccessful coups occur, while successful coups ... were [most common] in countries with per-capita GNPs under $500.[17]

While there have been a few exceptions to that claim, it has remained largely true (assuming that per-capita GNP is expressed in constant dollars).

In summary, a nation's propensity for military intervention reflects, in large part, the strength of its political institutions, the values of its political culture, and its level of economic development. Yet, these factors alone do not account for all the variations in civil–military relations. Elite values and behavior also play an important role. For example, India and Costa Rica, with political and socioeconomic circumstances comparable to those of their neighbors, have experienced far less military intervention in politics. The explanation may lie in the values of their political and economic elites: elected officials, government bureaucrats, political party leaders, business leaders, and labor leaders, as well as military officers themselves.*

India illustrates this point well. Located near several countries with long histories of military intervention (Pakistan, Bangladesh, Myanmar, and Thailand), it has been governed exclusively by civilians since independence. There is little to suggest that the Indian public, still heavily rural and one-third illiterate, has a political culture more modern or informed than that of its neighbors. Nor, until the 1990s, was its economy much more advanced than theirs (indeed it trailed Thailand). It appears, however, that political and economic elites in India have endorsed civilian control more strongly than have their counterparts in neighboring countries.

Elite values, however, may change more quickly than entire political cultures do. In a process of "political learning," a nation's civilian leaders may understand from previous experience how better to avert military coups. The armed forces governed Venezuela for much of the first half of the twentieth century. From 1959 into the mid-1990s, nearly four decades of elected government transformed the country into one of Latin America's most stable democracies until government corruption and a declining economy undermined the political

---

* Costa Rica is the first country in the world to abolish its armed forces and remains one of the very few that have done so.

establishment's legitimacy. While a number of factors contributed to the prolonged period of civilian governance, one critical element was a change in the attitudes of political elites following the collapse of Venezuela's first experiment with democracy (1945–1948). Recognizing that political polarization had precipitated a 1948 military coup, leaders of the major political parties agreed to moderate their political conflict. In 1958, the foremost democratically oriented political parties signed the Pact of Punto Fijo, which increased interparty cooperation and set the basis for decades of civilian political dominance. Viewed until recently as a model for democratic reform in the region, Venezuela was one of the only Latin American countries to avoid military rule in the 1970s and 1980s. Indeed, elite political pacts, often modeled after Punto Fijo, helped terminate civil wars and establish democratic government in several Central American countries.

By the end of the 1980s, however, Venezuela's deep economic crisis and its pervasive government corruption had severely eroded civilian support for the political parties that had dominated government since the interparty pact. An unsuccessful coup attempt in 1992 received considerable popular approval and turned the coup's leader, Lieutenant Colonel Hugo Chávez, into a national hero, at least among the poor. Elected government has survived, but Chávez, who spent 2 years in jail for his coup activity, easily won the 1998 presidential elections. The two political parties that had dominated Venezuelan politics for the past 40 years were practically wiped off the electoral map. Since then, Chávez has subverted some of the country's democratic institutions and given the armed forces a much greater foothold in politics. Still, while not panaceas, political pacts such as Punto Fijo have often been valuable tools for establishing more stable civilian government.

PROGRESSIVE SOLDIERS AND MILITARY CONSERVATIVES

Having examined the factors that either promote or inhibit military intervention, we will now consider the political behavior and policies of military regimes once they have established control. Given the disorder and conflict that characterize so many Third World nations, we must ask whether military rule produces greater political stability and socioeconomic development, at least in the short run. Also, once in office, are the generals and colonels likely to be a force for progressive change or defenders of the status quo? Many of the foremost early modernization theorists felt strongly that the armed forces could contribute to development. Marion Levy was impressed by the military's alleged rationality, disciplined organization, and commitment to modern values. Taking their critics to task, he maintained that the armed forces might be "the most efficient type of organization for combining maximum rates of modernization with maximum levels of stability and control."[18] Lucian Pye also saw the military as one of the best-organized national institutions in otherwise "disorganized transitional societies." It was, said Pye, at the forefront of technical training and a leader in imparting the values of citizenship to the public.[19] For Manfred Halpern, the Middle Eastern military was "the vanguard of nationalism and social change."[20]

Positive evaluations such as these predominated in the early modernization literature.[21] They frequently were based on an idealized vision of the professional soldier: trained in modern organizational skills, nationalistic, and, above narrow tribal, class, and regional interests. At times, these writings reflected the authors' strong preference for order and stability, coupled with the assumption that the military could bring order out of political and economic chaos. Occasionally, they drew on a few military success stories and projected them onto a larger screen. One early model was the Turkish military revolt led by Mustafa Kemal (Ataturk) in 1922. During the next two decades, Ataturk and his followers (the "Young Turks") modernized the country before eventually turning it over to civilian rule. Another frequently cited military reformer was Egypt's Colonel Abdul Gamal Nasser, who rose to power in the 1950s seeking to reform his country's social and economic institutions while strengthening its military. Subsequently, reformist officers elsewhere in the developing world often have been labeled "Young Turks" or "Nasserites."

Over the years, very different kinds of officers (and sometimes enlisted men) have seized power in the Third World, promising to modernize their country through industrialization, greater labor discipline, expanded education, agrarian reform, or other fundamental reforms. In countries such as Upper Volta, Libya, and Peru, left-wing militaries have promoted one or more of the following causes: economic redistribution, greater state intervention in the economy, mass mobilization, agrarian reform, and a struggle against imperialism. On the other hand, conservative generals in Brazil, Chile, Indonesia, and South Korea repressed mass political participation while encouraging investment by domestic firms and multinational corporations (MNCs).

Why have some military regimes championed the poor, while others have supported wealthy corporate and landowning interests? To find the answer, we must examine the class origins of the officers' corps, their nation's level of socioeconomic development, and the class alliances that had developed in their political system. Research in a range of LDCs has shown that officers tend to come from middle-class backgrounds, particularly in Asia and Latin America. Typically, their fathers were military officers, shopkeepers, merchants, midsized landowners, teachers, or civil servants. Not surprisingly, then, military regimes have commonly identified with the goals and aspirations of their nation's middle class.

But what are those goals, and what political ideologies and development policies have emerged from these men? In the least developed Third World countries, officers have often viewed economic elites, including large landowners and MNCs, as the source of their country's backwardness. Members of the middle class frequently resent those same elites for obstructing their own rise to political and economic prominence. In such a setting, both the armed forces and the civilian middle class may perceive the relatively unmobilized lower class as a potential ally in the battle against the oligarchy. For example, soon after taking power, Peruvian general Juan Velasco blamed the traditional landowning class and Peru's economic dependency for the nation's underdevelopment. In the following years, the military's ambitious land redistribution, shantytown reform, expropriations of property belonging to MNCs, expansion of the state economic sector, and mass mobilization greatly altered the country's political and economic landscape. Elsewhere, "General Omar Torrijos of Panama railed against oligarchic control and encouraged the lower class to participate in politics."[22]

Muammar Qaddafi's government in Libya and a number of Marxist military regimes in Africa were cut from a similar cloth.

In more modern and industrialized Third World nations, however, with greater lower-class mobilization, the military confronts a different political panorama. Urbanization, the spread of secondary and university education, and economic development all enlarge and strengthen the middle class, enabling it to wrest a share of political power from the economic elites. At the same time, industrialization increases the size of the working class and enhances the trade union movement. Urbanization also creates a growing and sometimes organized shantytown population. And the commercialization of agriculture often triggers unrest in the countryside. Not surprisingly, the middle class (having achieved a share of political influence) and its military partners sees the more galvanized and politicized lower classes as a threat rather than a useful ally.

If left-wing political parties and trade unions have gained considerable mass support and if there has been growing political unrest, the military is also more likely to ally itself with the economic elite and to repress mass mobilization. In Chile, the election of Salvador Allende's Marxist government and the accompanying mobilization of workers, peasants, and urban poor polarized the country along class lines. In nearby Uruguay, the Left's electoral appeal was not as strong, but labor–industrial conflict was intense, and the Tupamaros, a potent urban guerrilla group, were engaged in a campaign of political kidnappings and insurgency. In both countries, the perceived threat of guerrilla groups, mass mobilization, and an ascendant Left (including strong leftist political parties) caused the military to topple long-standing democracies.

In short, then, the more underdeveloped a country is and the weaker its middle class, the greater the likelihood that the country will have a left-of-center military.* However, notes Eric Nordlinger, "the soldiers who have power in countries with an established middle class . . . act as more or less ardent defenders of the status quo."[23] Similarly, Samuel Huntington observes,

> In the world of the oligarchy, the soldier is a radical; in the middle class world, he is a participant and arbitrator; as mass society looms on the horizon he becomes the guardian of the existing order. . . . The more advanced a society becomes, the more conservative and reactionary becomes the role of the military.[24]

The conservative military officers' concerns are not limited to leftist mass movements. They generally oppose any mobilization of lower-class groups that threaten the nation's stability. For example, in recent times, the Algerian and Egyptian armed forces have stood in the way of mass mobilization by Islamic fundamentalists.

---

* But the armed forces in the least developed nations are not *always* reform oriented. In Africa and other impoverished areas, the military often seize power out of self-interest or for narrow ethnic or tribal goals. Similarly, while the military has often been progressive in the less developed nations of South America, Africa, and the Middle East, it has generally been reactionary in Central America and the Caribbean, where it was co-opted by the upper class.

THE TYPES AND GOALS OF MILITARY REGIMES

Having observed the range of ideological orientations amongst military governments, we now examine the structures and goals of those regimes.

Personalistic Regimes

In the least developed countries—those with low levels of military professionalization, limited mass political participation, extensive political corruption, and little semblance of representative government—military officers frequently seize power for their own personal enrichment and aggrandizement, usually with little or no interest in economic or political reform. Their governments tend to be personalistic; that is, a single charismatic officer with a strong personal following leads them. In order to bolster his support, however, the leader allows some government plunder to pass on to the military and civilian cliques surrounding him. "Legitimacy is secured through patronage, clientelistic alliances, [and] systemic intimidation."[25]

In Latin America, personalistic dictatorships were most common in the less developed political and economic systems of Central America and the Caribbean. One of the most prominent examples was the Somoza dynasty in Nicaragua. As leader of the country's National Guard (its only military force), General Anastasio Somoza Sr. overthrew the government in 1937, primarily seeking his own enrichment. Governing a small and impoverished nation, he amassed a fortune of several hundred million dollars using state resources to purchase construction firms, urban real estate, electrical power plants, air and shipping lines, cement factories, and much of the nation's best farmland. Following Somoza's assassination in 1956, his political and financial empire passed to his two sons, who ruled the country in succession until the 1979 Sandinista revolution.[26] Other personalistic regimes in the Americas included the Batista government in Cuba (eventually toppled by Fidel Castro's revolutionary army) and Alfredo Stroessner's long-lived dictatorship in Paraguay. Batista had links to the American mafia's gambling and prostitution operations in Havana. Stroessner and his associates enriched themselves by collaborating with international smugglers and drug dealers.*

Personalistic military regimes have been especially common in sub-Saharan Africa, sometimes led by upwardly mobile junior officers or even enlisted men such as Ghana's flight sergeant Jerry Rawlings and Liberia's sergeant-major Samuel Doe. While some, like Rawlings, were well intentioned, most have done little to develop their countries. The most infamous personalistic dictators in the continent have been Uganda's Idi Amin Dada, the Central African Republic's Jean-Bédel Bokassa, and Zaire's Mobutu Sese Seko. Ironically, in light of his regime's enormous brutality, Amin initially justified his coup by citing the human rights violations of ousted President Obote. Enamored of power as much as wealth, Amin played upon and exacerbated Uganda's ethnic divisions during his

---

* To be sure, a few personalistic dictators, such as Argentina's Juan Perón and Venezuela's Hugo Chávez, introduced broad social and economic reform programs. But even benevolent personalistic military regimes are usually corrupt and concentrate excessive power in the hands of one person.

brutal 8-year reign (1971–1979). He not only expelled the country's sizable Asian population (mostly Indian) but also murdered an estimated 300,000–500,000 civilians, most notably members of the previously influential Langi and Acholi tribes. Seeing enemies at every turn, he even executed one of his wives. In an attempt to maintain absolute control over the armed forces, he purged or executed a large portion of the officers' corps, eventually creating an army composed largely of foreign troops (principally Sudanese and Zairian).

Equally megalomaniacal, the Central African Republic's Marshal Bokassa unleashed a reign of death and terror on his country following his takeover in 1965. Plundering the treasury of one of the world's more impoverished nations, he concluded that the presidency was not a sufficiently exalted position, so he lavished millions of dollars on his own coronation as the country's new emperor. In time, Amin and Bokassa so outraged the world community that they were ousted through external intervention. Amin fell to a Tanzanian invasion, while a French-sponsored coup toppled Bokassa.

Because most personalistic dictators lack a meaningful ideology or program to legitimize their regime, they typically must share some of the spoils with their military and civilian supporters in order to maintain themselves in office. For example, Zaire's president Mobutu, Africa's most enduring military dictator (1965–1997), made himself one of the richest men on earth while opening up the floodgates of corruption to benefit his military and civil service. In this manner, he kept himself in office for decades while bankrupting the national government and destroying a once-dynamic economy. By the late 1990s, however, as the Zairian economy collapsed, his regime unraveled, falling rapidly to a rebel force whose new government, unfortunately, turned out to be almost as corrupt and even more repressive.* More recently, warlords (regionally based, military/political bosses who plunder the region they control) in Sierra Leone and Liberia overthrew the government with few goals other than looting the country. In Nicaragua, the Somoza dynasty maintained the National Guard's critical support by allowing its officers to enrich themselves. In the most egregious example, following an earthquake that devastated the nation's capital, Guard officers appropriated relief supplies sent from the United States and sold them for a profit.

Institutional Military Regimes

As Third World political and economic systems modernize, corresponding changes take place in military institutions and attitudes. Frequently, officers attend advanced military academies at home or abroad. Sometimes, they enroll in specialized seminars with civilian leaders, establishing links with politicians, businesspeople, and academics. These programs more deeply expose military officers to their country's political and economic problems.

If these "new soldiers" seize power, they are likely to govern collectively rather than vest authority in the hands of a single leader. To be sure, many institutional military regimes have been dominated by a single figure, such as

---

* Following events in the Congo can be confusing because Mobutu changed the country's name from the Congo to Zaire. After he was overthrown, the name changed to the Democratic Republic of the Congo, not to be confused with its smaller neighbor, the Republic of the Congo.

Libya's Muammar Qaddafi, Indonesia's Suharto, and Chile's Augusto Pinochet. Like purely personalistic dictators, some of these men are motivated by "covert ambition, fear, greed, and vanity."[27] Still, even in such cases, a substantial number of officers hold influential government positions (not just the paramount leader), and there is a degree of institutional decision making. In Indonesia, for example, active and retired military officers at one time held nearly half the positions in the national bureaucracy and some two-thirds of the provincial governorships.[28] Furthermore, the goals of these institutional regimes are broader than any single leader's ambitions.

Institutional military governments have generally been headed by councils or juntas such as Niger's Supreme Military Council, Myanmar's Revolutionary Council, or Argentina's governing junta. Comparable groups have governed Algeria, Brazil, Ethiopia, Thailand, Uruguay, and a number of other countries. These are relatively small governing committees made up of officers from the various branches of the armed forces.* Typically, one active or retired officer serves as president and wields the most influence. Often, however, his term of office is limited. For example, in Argentina and Brazil, the military juntas limited the president to a single term. In contrast, Chile's General Augusto Pinochet was all-powerful and was not constrained by term limits. In some countries, including South Korea, Brazil, and Indonesia, the armed forces tried to legitimize its rule by forming a government political party that ran candidates in tightly controlled elections. Frequently, presidents and other leading government officials retire from active military duty before taking office. And in Egypt and Syria, military and civilian elites have joined together to form a ruling political party.

Institutional military regimes can be as repressive and brutal as personalistic dictatorships—sometimes even more so. Their day-to-day governing style, however, is generally more bureaucratic and sophisticated—commonly drawing on the talents of highly trained civilian technocrats. Moreover, unlike self-aggrandizing personalistic leaders, they are more likely to support the aspirations of the middle class, more prone to espouse a coherent political ideology, and more likely to champion nationalistic goals.

Most institutional military governments pursue four broad objectives, or at least claim to do so. *First*, they usually justify their seizure of power by denouncing the alleged corruption of the government that they have ousted. Thus, when Bangladesh's lieutenant general Hussain Muhammad Ershad led a 1982 army coup, he charged that the outgoing administration had "failed totally because of [its] petty selfishness . . . and unbounded corruption."[29] Incoming military leaders in Uruguay, Pakistan, Thailand, and much of Africa have made similar proclamations. All of them promised to clean up the mess.

A *second* goal—one not normally publicly articulated or acknowledged—is the advancement of the military's own corporate interests. As Ruth First observed, while African coup leaders may claim to have acted for the good of the nation or other noble political purposes, "when the army acts, it generally

---

* In some cases such councils have been mere façades, with one officer really in power. Thus, it is not always easy to distinguish between personalistic and institutional military regimes. Ultimately, the determining factor is where real power resides rather than what the formal structures is.

acts for army reasons."[30] When officers are unhappy with their salaries, the defense budget, or the quantity and quality of their weapons, they often take action. They also react negatively to civilian "interference" in military affairs, such as the president deviating from normal officer promotion practices or lessening the armed forces' autonomy.

Ever since the 1960s—a decade featuring coups in Togo, Ghana, Mali, Congo-Brazzaville, and Algeria—a number of African armies have taken power to protect themselves from competing military units (such as presidential guards), to increase their troop strength, to raise their salaries, or to augment their budgets. In South Asia, repeated coups in Bangladesh have been motivated by resentment over civilian interference in military promotions and by desires for greater military spending.[31] In Southeast Asia, "neglect of [military] corporate interests" by civilian governments has only been "a *background factor* contributing to a general sense of alienation [among the armed forces] rather than an immediate cause of intervention." Still, the military's concerns about the defense budget contributed to several coups in the region.[32]

A *third* common goal is maintaining or restoring order and stability. Institutional coups have often occurred during periods of civil unrest, guerrilla insurgencies, or civil war. For example, the army first involved itself deeply in South Korean politics when student demonstrations and labor protests challenged the civilian administrations of Syngman Rhee and Chang Myon. Thailand's many coups have frequently followed strikes and street demonstrations in Bangkok.

Military officers are particularly troubled by radical challenges to the political and economic order and by threats to the safety and integrity of the armed forces. During the early 1960s, Indonesia's civilian president, Sukarno, moved his regime leftward and became increasingly dependent on the country's large communist party, much to the discomfort of his conservative military commanders. Their fears intensified in 1965, when a small group of leftist officers assassinated Lieutenant General Ahmad Yani and five other officers, claiming that these men had been plotting a coup against Sukarno. The country's top military command responded with a massive attack against the communist party, eventually killing some half million alleged party supporters. At the same time, many Indonesian civilians used the chaos as an opportunity to loot and kill members of the country's more prosperous Chinese minority. In time, army chief General Suharto ousted Sukarno and established a military dictatorship that lasted more than 30 years.*

Similarly, in Argentina, Brazil, Chile, and Uruguay, the generals' fear of leftist unions, guerrillas, and radical political parties prompted extended military dictatorships. In 1992, the Algerian armed forces terminated parliamentary elections that seemed certain to result in victory for the FIS (Islamic Salvation Front), a party of militant, Islamic fundamentalists.

A *final* goal of many institutional military regimes has been to revive and stimulate the economy. As we have noted, coups frequently follow periods of rampant inflation, labor conflict, or economic stagnation. For example, one analysis of military intervention in 38 sub-Saharan African governments over

---

* Like many Indonesians, both Suharto and Sukarno have only one name and do not use a family name.

a two-decade period revealed that coups were most likely to occur after an economic downturn.[33] Asian and Latin American coups have frequently followed that pattern as well.

Third World militaries are frequently committed to industrialization. For one thing, industrial growth can provide them with arms and supplies that previously needed to be imported. In the least developed countries, such production may be limited to uniforms or rifles. On the other hand, in countries such as Brazil, Indonesia, and South Korea, highly advanced arms industries now produce planes, tanks, and other sophisticated weaponry for both domestic consumption and export. Even when it has no direct military payoff, industrialization contributes to national pride and international prestige. Small wonder, then, that many Latin American and Asian countries have seen a political alliance between industrialists and the armed forces.

Having reviewed the goals of institutional military governments in general, we now focus on two distinct regime types that have received considerable attention in recent years: the bureaucratic authoritarian regime and the revolutionary military regime. While each type has only represented a minority of Third World military governments, they have had a significant impact both within and outside their borders, particularly in Latin America and Africa.

Bureaucratic Authoritarian Regimes   Beginning with the Brazilian coup d'état of 1964, through the 1973 coups in Uruguay and Chile, to the Argentine military takeovers of 1966 and 1976, four of the most socioeconomically developed countries in South America succumbed to authoritarian rule. Furthermore, Chile and Uruguay had also been the strongest democracies in the region, free of military domination for decades. Thus, their coups contradicted the widely held assumption that both socioeconomic development and the creation of a strong party system limit military intervention.

Once in power, these regimes lasted longer than typical military governments in the region, from 12 years (in Uruguay) to 21 (Brazil). These dictatorships suspended political party activity, crushed labor unions and other grassroots organizations, prohibited strikes, and jailed and tortured many suspected political dissidents. In Argentina and Chile, thousands of people were murdered or "disappeared" (covertly taken away, never to be seen again).

Argentine political scientist Guillermo O'Donnell referred to these military governments as "bureaucratic authoritarian (BA) regimes." Compared to previous military dictatorships, they had a more extensive bureaucratic structure that included like-minded civilian technocrats. They penetrated more deeply into civil society, established close links to MNCs, and were particularly repressive.[34] O'Donnell focused on the closely related economic and political factors that explained the rise of these BA regimes in Latin America's most developed nations. First, he noted, economic growth in these countries had begun to stagnate by the 1960s. Many analysts argued that further growth would require investment in capital goods industries and new technologies, which only MNCs had the resources to provide. But the MNCs (as well as domestic companies) had been reluctant to invest because of the rising labor strife, civil unrest, and leftist electoral strength, all caused by the countries' economic stagnation, high inflation, and declining living standards.

Not surprisingly, growing radicalism among the poor and portions of the middle class, and the resulting political polarization of society deeply alarmed the armed forces. In Argentina, Chile, and Uruguay, urban guerrillas added to the perceived threat. The goals of the new BA regimes, then, were to crush leftist political parties, unions, and guerrilla movements; limit workers' wages; create a "stable environment for investment"; and work closely with MNCs and domestic corporations to control inflation and reinvigorate the economy. Beyond repressing the Left, the generals wanted to depoliticize society and terminate most forms of political participation for an extended period. In addition, BA regimes wanted to extend the role of the private sector and roll back state economic activity, including welfare programs, minimum wage guarantees, and public ownership of economic resources.

Revolutionary Military Regimes   In a number of developing nations, the military has pursued goals diametrically different from those of the conservative BA regimes. Rather than excluding most of the population from the political system, they instead *extended* political and economic participation to formerly excluded groups. At the same time, however, their authoritarian political structure tightly controlled mass participation. In Africa, a number of Marxist military regimes proclaimed policies of cultural nationalism, anti-imperialism, peasant and working-class political mobilization, expansion of the state's economic role, and redistribution of economic resources to the poor.

Revolutionary coups have usually been led by radicalized officers from the middle ranks (captains, majors, colonels), rather than generals. In a speech outlining the goals of Upper Volta's military government, Captain Thomas Sankara articulated the Marxist rhetoric typical of such regimes:

> The triumph of the Revolution [i.e., the military takeover] . . . is the crowning moment of the struggle of the Volta People against its internal enemies. It is a victory against international imperialism and its internal allies. . . . These enemies of the people have been identified by the people in the forge of revolutionary action. They are: the bourgeoisie of Volta [and] . . . reactionary forces whose strength derives from the traditional feudal structures of our society. . . . The People in our revolution comprises: The working class . . . the petty bourgeoisie . . . the peasantry . . . [and] the lumpen proletariat.[35]

Military governments in Ethiopia, Sudan, Somalia, Congo-Brazzaville, Benin, and Madagascar made similarly radical declarations. Like most African military regimes, however, these governments have been led by men without significant political skills or advanced education. Consequently, their Marxist ideals were "self-taught, ideologically immature and crude, and riddled with inconsistencies."[36] For some of them, Marxism simply expressed their strong nationalism and distaste for the European nations that had colonized the continent. For others, revolutionary rhetoric came almost as an afterthought, a means of justifying their earlier seizure of power and authoritarian control. Thus, the government of Colonel Mengistu in Ethiopia, perhaps Africa's most prominent radical military regime, did not embrace Marxism-Leninism until it had been in office for 3 years. In

Dahomey, General Mathieu Kerekou declared his government to be Marxist and created "revolution committees" simply as a pretext for spying on the civil service.

In other world regions, leftist (though not Marxist) military regimes have governed countries as disparate as Libya, Myanmar, Panama, and Peru. Peru's military came to power seeking to curtail the influence of the rural oligarchy and incorporate the peasantry, working class, and urban poor into the political system. Finally, military regimes in Panama and Ecuador introduced comparable, though far more modest, reform programs.

THE ACCOMPLISHMENTS AND FAILURES OF MILITARY REGIMES

How successfully have military governments achieved their goals and how well have they served their country? Little needs to be said about personalistic military dictatorships. With a few notable exceptions, they are rarely seriously interested in benefiting their country. Even those with broader goals have had blatantly self-serving objectives. Thus, it would be impossible to argue seriously that dictators such as Batista (Cuba), Somoza (Nicaragua), Stroessner (Paraguay), Amin (Uganda), or Bokassa (Central African Republic) contributed to the long-term political or economic growth of their nation. Consequently, the analysis in our next section focuses exclusively on the record of institutional military governments, which often have serious intentions, be it for left-wing or right-wing reform.

Combating Corruption

Let us first look at one of the most commonly professed objectives of institutional regimes—eliminating government corruption. Because government malfeasance is so pervasive in the Third World, denouncing corruption is a convenient means of legitimizing the armed forces' unconstitutional seizure of power. Yet, most soldiers in office prove every bit as corrupt as their predecessors, or more so. To be sure, a few military regimes have been quite honest, but they are the exceptions. As one leading scholar has observed,

> Every Nigerian and Ghanaian coup . . . has had as its prime goal the elimination of deeply ingrained corruption from society. Yet, not one military administration has made truly consistent efforts in that direction . . . or for that matter remained immune to it itself. . . . [Elsewhere in Africa] in two . . . military regimes—Guinea and Burkina Faso—nepotism and accumulation of wealth commenced the very day the officers' hierarchy took office.[37]

Ironically, the continent's constant military intervention has tended to increase corruption in the civilian governments that they oust. "The fear that [civilian] power may not last encourages the incoming politicians to grab what is grabbable."[38] In Asian nations such as Thailand and Indonesia, the military's record has been equally disappointing. Indeed, Harold Crouch has noted that "often military officers have already become entangled in this web [of corruption] even before the coup takes place."[39] In those few military governments that avoid *gross* corruption, the more modest lure of contraband automobiles and tax-supported vacation homes often proves irresistible. In short, even those military governments that seized power with noble intentions are generally soon corrupted.

Defending Military Interests

When it comes to pursuing their second major objective—advancing their own corporate interests—not surprisingly, military governments have been more successful, at least in the short term. More often than not, military rulers enhance the nation's defense budget. Unfortunately, however, those expenditures draw government resources away from badly needed programs such as health care and education.

Typically, military governments increase spending on armaments, military salaries, military housing, and officers' clubs. In much of Asia, officers have benefited from "lucrative public-sector employment, foreign postings, and preferential treatment in the disbursal of governmental contracts."[40] After leading a coup in Libya, Colonel Qaddafi insured his officers' loyalty by doubling their salaries, thereby making them the highest paid army in the Third World. In their first 5 years in office, Uruguay's generals raised the military and security share of the national budget from 26.2 percent to more than 40 percent.[41] A parallel "bias in favor of army, police and civil-service salaries and benefits can be observed in practically every military regime in Africa."[42]

Throughout the LDCs, even when soldiers do not actually govern, the mere specter of intervention has often led civilian governments to bestow salary hikes and expensive weapon systems on the armed forces. For example, it would be very imprudent for elected leaders in the Philippines or Thailand to slash their country's defense budget. Even Malaysia and Singapore, with no history of coups d'état, pay their officers generously to keep them out of politics. Similarly, Colombia and Venezuela, with two of Latin America's most long-lived civilian governments (though military involvement in politics has risen sharply in both since the 1990s), have supported healthy defense budgets aimed at keeping the generals at bay.

But, although military rule may enlarge military budgets, it also damages the armed forces in the long run by reducing their institutional cohesion. Eventually, generals, colonels, and admirals begin to squabble over resource allocation and other policy issues. As new economic and political challenges arise, they drive a wedge between the officers in command. Furthermore, even military regimes that took power with considerable popular support usually lose their legitimacy as they confront difficult economic and social problems. As a consequence, in some regions, most notably sub-Saharan Africa, internal coups (one military faction ousting another) have produced a series of unstable military governments. Nearly half of Africa's twentieth-century coups and failed coup attempts sought to topple incumbent military regimes.[43] But, for the most part in the recent decades, Third World militaries have returned to the barracks to avoid further internal divisions, restoring the government to civilian hands.

Patterns in Military Spending

Unfortunately, the major "accomplishment" of most military governments in the LDCs—budgetary gains for the armed forces itself—is frequently the nation's loss. Military expenditures are frequently higher than their country can afford, thereby reducing badly needed social and economic investment. Countries in South America that have not fought an international war in decades have spent fortunes on naval vessels and state-of-the-art combat jets. And in Africa, home to many of the world's poorest countries, military budgets are particularly disproportionate to economic capacities. For example, in the 1980s, despite having per-capita national incomes well below half of Latin America's, African governments spent one-third more per soldier.[44] Africa's defense outlays generally declined from 1988 to 1998, but have increased sharply since (see Table 9.2).[45] Currently, defense consumes a disproportionate share of that continent's gross domestic product (GDP) and thereby limits government spending on education, health care, rural development, and other social needs. In the 1990s, military budgets were particularly large in countries that were engaged in either internal or international warfare, such as Eritrea, Ethiopia, Uganda, Rwanda, Sudan, and Angola. For example, in 1999, when Eritrea, one of the world's poorest countries, was at war with Ethiopia, it devoted an astounding 37.5 percent of its GDP to military expenditures.

Table 9.1 demonstrates that, while some developing nations have tightly limited their military spending, others, particularly those facing external military threats or civil war, have enormous military budgets relative to their social expenditures. The table compares government spending on health and education with outlays for the military in four groups of countries: highly industrialized democracies (the United States and Japan), relatively wealthy Third World nations (Singapore), "middle-income" developing nations (Mexico, Ghana, and Jordan), and very poor LDCs (Burundi, Ethiopia, and Eritrea). The second column indicates the percentage of each nation's GDP that was devoted to public welfare programs as measured by total government spending on health

TABLE 9.1   Public Welfare (Health and Education) versus Military Expenditures as a Percentage of GDP (2002)

Country	Health and Education Expenditures (% of GDP)	Military Expenditures (% of GDP)	Health and Education Spending as Percentage of Military Spending
United States	10.1	3.4	297
Japan	9.5	1.0	950
Singapore	4.8	5.2	92
Mexico	6.9	0.5	1380
Ghana	6.3	0.6	1050
Jordan	9.2	8.4	109
Burundi	6.6	5.2	126
Ethiopia	5.0	7.6	66
Eritrea	7.6	23.5	32

Source: Stockholm International Peace Research Institute (SIPRI) 2004, http://www.sipri.org/.

and education. The next column shows the percentage of each country's GDP spent on the armed forces. Obviously, poorer countries, such as Ghana and Ethiopia, cannot possibly spend nearly as much money on either public welfare or the military as Singapore and Japan do. But, Table 9.1 enables us to compare each country's expenditures relative to the size of its economy (GDP). The last column in the table compares those two budget items, expressing welfare spending as a *percentage of military outlays*. If a country spends more on *welfare* than on the military (as the United States, Japan, Mexico, Ghana, and Burundi do), the figure in the last column will exceed 100 percent. On the other hand, if it spends more on the *military* than on welfare, the figure in the last column will be less than 100 percent. Thus, this column tells us that in 2002 the United States spent almost three times as much on health and education combined as on the military (297 percent). In contrast, Eritrea spent about three times as much on *the military* as it did on public welfare (32 percent).

Third World and industrialized countries alike devote widely varying proportions of their GDP to military spending (see Table 9.1). For example, in 2002, Eritrea, whose bloody war with Ethiopia (1998–2000) had recently ended, still devoted an enormous portion of its GDP—more than 23 percent—to the military. That was probably the highest percentage in the world and about 6–7 times the international average. Military expenditures also consumed a very high percentage of the GDP in Jordan (8.4 percent) and Ethiopia (7.6 percent), as well as a smaller, but considerable, share in Burundi and Singapore (both at 5.2 percent). All of these countries faced hostile or potentially hostile neighbors, while Ethiopia and Burundi also confronted internal ethnic unrest. All of them had authoritarian governments of varying stripes. On the other hand, the armed forces consumed less than 1 percent of the GDP in Mexico and Ghana, countries that have recently democratized and that face no foreign or internal military threats. For the sake of comparison, while the absolute level of military spending by the United States has long dwarfed that of any other country in the world, its military budget as a percentage of national GDP was only a modest 3.4 percent. Japan's allocation was even lower (1 percent of GDP).

The last column—comparing public welfare with military spending—is particularly revealing. Undoubtedly, the poorest nations in the table (Burundi, Ethiopia, and Eritrea) had the greatest need for health and educational expenditures and could, therefore, least afford high military outlays. Yet, Eritrea and Ethiopia spent far more on the armed forces than on public welfare. Although the United States has the largest military budget in the world, the *ratio* of welfare expenditures to military spending is far higher in the United States than in Burundi. That ratio was also significantly higher than Burundi's in Japan, Mexico, and Ghana. While Singapore had a high military budget relative to welfare spending, it is so much wealthier and healthier than the other Third World nations in the table that, in spite of its high military spending, it could still serve its citizens' health and education needs.

Throughout the developing world, civilian governments with strong control over the armed forces and low security threats have been best equipped to reduce military budgets substantially. As the Third Wave of democracy strengthened the legitimacy and authority of newly elected, civilian governments, a number of LDCs made such cuts in the 1980s and 1990s. For example, from 1983 to 1987, following the restoration of democracy in Argentina, military spending fell by almost 50 percent.[46] From 1985 to 1993, defense expenditures as a share of GDP fell from 2.9 to 1.7 percent in Argentina, from 6.8 to 2.1 percent in Chile, and from 4.4 to 1.6 percent in El Salvador.[47] Some nondemocratic governments also cut military outlays. Thus, military expenditures in Cambodia fell from 4.6 percent of GDP (in 1997) to 2.7 percent (2003).

For the most part, however, the demise of so many military governments during the 1980s and 1990s has *not* caused widespread cuts in defense spending, at least not since the mid-1990s. Table 9.2 indicates the *absolute* volume of military spending, as expressed in U.S. dollars, over an 18-year period in the principal regions of the Third World. Dollar allocations for all years have been converted to their equivalent value in constant dollars, thereby eliminating the effects of inflation. The last column in the table indicates the percentage changes in military spending for each region between 1998 and 2007. Between 1988 (toward the end of the Cold War) and 1998 (columns 2 and 3), military outlays fell sharply in sub-Saharan Africa and modestly in South America, while rising in the Middle East, East and South Asia, and Central America. From 1998 to 2007 (last column), the percentage of military spending rose relatively modestly in Central and South America and sharply in sub-Saharan Africa, East Asia, South Asia, and, especially, the Middle East. In some cases, regional conflicts contributed to increased expenditure. For example, the seven countries that devote the highest percentage of their GDP to the military are all in the Middle East (including, Saudi Arabia, Iraq, Jordan, and Israel).[48] Tense relations between India and Pakistan contribute to higher military spending in South Asia. In other cases, increase military outlays were made possible by rapid economic growth (much of East Asia) or greater oil revenues (the Arab world).

Because these statistics do not distinguish between defense expenditures in democratic countries (including newly democratized nations) and those in military regimes, they fail to tell us whether the spread of democracy influenced military spending. However, they clearly suggest that military expenditures were influenced, not only by regime type (democratic or authoritarian), but by other factors as well, particularly by the extent of international and domestic conflict in

TABLE 9.2   Trends in Regional Military Expenditures, 1988–2007: Billions of (constant) Dollars

Region	1988	1998	2006	Percentage Increase 1998–2007
Sub-Saharan Africa	9.0	5.6	9.0	51
Central America	2.4	3.6	3.5	14
South America	23.9	23.2	29.1	25
East Asia[a]	76.4	100.0	138.0	51
South Asia	15.0	20.2	30.7	57
Middle East	40.2	49.3	72.5	62

[a]East Asian data exclude Myanmar, North Korea, and Vietnam.

Source: Stockholm International Peace Research Institute (SIPRI), "*World and Regional Military Expenditure Estimates,*" *SIPRI Yearbook, 2006;* SIPRI, "Recent Trends in Military Expenditure," 2008. http://www.sipri.org.

the region. Countries such as Cambodia, El Salvador, and Ethiopia, which ended their civil wars, sharply cut their military expenditures (as a percentage of national GDP). Ethiopia slashed the size of its armed forces—Africa's largest at that time—from 438,000 in 1991 to 120,000 in 1996, while Mozambique and Nigeria made sizable cuts as well. However, in countries such as Chad and Sudan, where internal warfare has continued, troop strength has grown considerably.

Finally, Table 9.3 presents statistics on trends in military spending (expressed as a percentage of national GDP) in two developed nations (France and the United States) and six Third World nations that have large military budgets. Recall that Table 9.2 demonstrated that, between 1988 and 2006 (columns 2 and 4), the *absolute* level of military spending (expressed in constant dollars) *increased* in all but one region of the developing world (sub-Saharan Africa). Yet, in every nation in Table 9.3, military outlays *as a percentage of GDP* have steadily *decreased* during that same period. What this means is that, although the actual amount of military spending rose for most nations after 1988, their GDPs typically grew faster. As Table 9.3 indicates, for some developing nations, such as Ethiopia, that decrease (from 8.1 percent of its GDP to 1.7) has been dramatic. While not *all* LDCs enjoyed as large a reduction, in the vast majority of them military outlays as a percentage of GDP have declined. Even in countries such as Saudi Arabia and Eritrea, which allocate an unusually large percentage of their GDPs to military expenditures, this trend has persisted. Critics insist that many LDCs (especially the poorest) still spend too much on the military relative to national welfare needs (as demonstrated in Table 9.1), but the tendency, at least for now, is for lower military budgets as a percentage of GDP.

Establishing Stability

Military officers almost always react negatively to popular unrest and political instability. For one thing, disorder violates their hierarchical view of society. Furthermore, it frequently threatens the interests of their middle-class and industrialist allies. In other instances, it poses an imminent danger to the armed

TABLE 9.3 Trends in Military Expenditures as a Percentage of GDP, 1988–2007

Country	1988 (%)	1998 (%)	2007 (%)
France	3.6	2.7	2.3
United States	5.7	3.1	4.0
India	3.6	2.8	2.5
Indonesia	2.0[a]	1.1	1.2[a]
Saudi Arabia	15.2	14.3	9.3
Chile	5.0[a]	3.4	3.4
Nigeria	0.8	0.9	0.6
Ethiopia	8.1	6.7	1.7

[a]Estimates

Source: Stockholm International Peace Research Institute (SIPRI), *"The SIPRI Military Expenditure Data Base,"* http://first.sipri.org/non_first/milex.php.

forces themselves. The generals and colonels of Latin America, for example, have been keenly aware that Marxist revolutions in Cuba and Nicaragua destroyed the old military establishment. In Cuba, a number of Batista's officers faced the firing squad, while in Nicaragua, many National Guardsmen were imprisoned or had to flee the country. In Chile and Brazil, leftist political leaders threatened the officers' hierarchical control of the armed forces. Similarly, the generals in Algeria felt endangered by the growing strength of Islamic fundamentalism. Even "revolutionary soldiers" in Ethiopia, Libya, and Peru preferred to dictate change from the top, with tight government controls over mass mobilization.

In many respects, military governments are particularly well suited for controlling civil unrest. They can use force with impunity to combat guerrilla insurrections, disperse street demonstrations, and ban strikes. In some cases, their extensive intelligence agencies, such as South Korea's KCIA and Chile's DINA, enabled them to penetrate deeply into society to control dissent. The Argentine, Chilean, and Uruguayan armies used mass arrests, torture, and death squads to crush potent urban guerrilla movements. In Indonesia, the military destroyed one of the world's largest communist parties and later decimated various separatist movements.

But the generals restored order in these countries at a tremendous cost in human suffering. Some 20,000–30,000 people died in the Argentine army's "dirty war" against the Left, while many more were imprisoned and tortured. Students and other young people were the primary victims, many of them incorrectly identified as part of the leftist opposition. In Chile, thousands of intellectuals and professionals fled the country, devastating one of the Third World's most advanced university systems and artistic communities. Some 3,000 Chileans died; many others were the victims of torture. During Indonesia's "year of living dangerously," perhaps 500,000 communists and ethnic Chinese were massacred, while some 150,000 other people died subsequently (largely from starvation) in the army's struggle against East Timorian separatists. Another 12,000 died in the separatist struggle in Aceh (or Ache). Of course, many military regimes are not very repressive. However, it is precisely those that seize power to restore order in highly polarized societies that normally are the most brutal.

Moreover, *in the longer term*, the military has not been particularly successful in providing political stability. To be sure, in several Asian and Latin American countries, state repression, coupled with technocratic development policies, has either co-opted or decimated opposition groups. In South Korea, sharply improved living standards and a gradual political transition paved the way to stable elected government. And in Argentina, Chile, and Uruguay, the BA regimes' brutality against radical movements convinced political leaders on both sides of the ideological spectrum (but especially the Left) to moderate their positions so as not to provoke further military intervention. Ironically, all three countries now have democratically elected leftist governments, not what the BA regimes hope to achieve.

But these "successes" are the exception. Despite their brute strength, the armed forces' hold on power has generally been relatively brief. Eric Nordlinger's pioneering study of military governments found that, on average, they dissolved in 5–7 years.[49] Karen Remmer's later work on 12 South American military regimes between 1960 and 1990 showed four to be quite durable (12–35 years); the remaining eight, however, averaged less than 7 years in office.[50] Moreover, military rule, no matter what its accomplishments, ultimately impedes the maturation of political parties and other civilian institutions necessary for long-term stability.

In Africa, more often than not, coups have only led to further coups, hampering political development as they turn politics into a Hobbesian game. The brutal regime of Sergeant Samuel Doe exposed Liberia to a devastating civil war and a far more sinister ruler who fomented unspeakably brutal internal warfare at home and in nearby Sierra Leone. Military rule in Ethiopia and the Sudan only worsened ethnically based civil wars. Elsewhere, extended suppression of dissident groups in countries such as Myanmar will likely lead to greater upheavals after those regimes eventually fall.

Improving the Economy

Earlier we noted that coups often are provoked by economic recessions or severe inflation. Consequently, many newly installed military governments promise to impose fiscal discipline and revitalize the economy. In South Korea, Indonesia, Brazil, and Chile, for example, conservative military regimes curtailed union activity in order to suppress wage demands. By reducing strike activity and weakening unions, the generals expected to lower inflation and attract multinational investment.

Proponents of military dictatorships assert that they can more easily make economic decisions consistent with the national interest because they need not pander to special interest groups. Critics counter that soldiers lack the expertise to manage an economy. Even when well intentioned, they tend to allocate excessive funds to defense and to wasteful chauvinistic projects. Examining the economic performance of specific military governments provides evidence to support both sides of the debate. South Korea demonstrated that a military government can oversee a very successful economic development program. Following General Park Chung Hee's seizure of power in 1961, the armed forces governed the country for more than 25 years. During that period, the Republic of Korea changed from an underdeveloped economy into one of the world's most dynamic industrial economies. Moreover, the country enjoyed sustained economic growth while still maintaining very equitable income distribution. Indeed, economists frequently cite South Korea as a model of well-executed economic modernization.

Elsewhere in Asia, Indonesia's military also presided over rapid economic growth from the mid-1960s to late 1990s. During the 1970s and early 1980s, the Suharto dictatorship plowed back a portion of the country's extensive petroleum revenues into labor-intensive export industries. At the same time, rural development programs and mass education improved income distribution and, coupled with economic growth, substantially reduced the number of Indonesians living in poverty. Nearby Thailand, governed by the military for much of the last 70 years, has also enjoyed an economic boom, though it was somewhat flawed by corruption and "crony capitalism" (plentiful government loans and contracts awarded to politically connected businesspeople).

Two of Latin America's major bureaucratic-authoritarian regimes—Brazil and, especially, Chile—also had relatively successful economic records. After several false starts, Chile's pro-business, export-oriented policies ushered in a period of strong economic expansion with low inflation. Those achievements, however, followed a period of severe economic hardship, which forced the poor to bear a disproportionate share of the sacrifice. As with other BA regimes, income distribution deteriorated. After the restoration of democracy in 1990, the civilian governments of Patricio Aylwin and Eduardo Frei maintained high growth rates while using targeted programs to reduce poverty. During that decade, that combination of high growth and remedial programs for those left behind halved the number of Chileans living in poverty.

Brazil's BA regime achieved dramatic economic growth during the late 1960s and 1970s, turning the country into an important industrial power. The benefits of that growth, however, were very poorly distributed, leaving many of the poor worse off than before. Moreover, Brazil's "economic miracle" was built on excessive foreign borrowing that turned the country into the Third World's largest external debtor. Currently, President Luiz Inácio Lula da Silva has somewhat altered the country's economic model in an attempt to better serve the needs of the poor.

Many other Latin American military governments, including the BA regimes in Argentina and Uruguay, performed poorly in the economic sphere. They spent far too much on defense, borrowed excessively, were corrupt, and frequently failed to understand development economics. In Africa, the armed forces' economic record has ranged from poor to disastrous.

Moving beyond examinations of individual cases such as these, some analysts have engaged in more systematic statistical comparison regime types. Examining data on economic indicators such as growth rates and inflation, they have compared the economic performance of military and civilian governments in specific regions or throughout the Third World. Unfortunately, these comparisons face a number of methodological problems. For example, the fact that some military governments in the 1990s had higher GDP growth than many civilian governments have today largely reflects the effects of the '90s global economic boom compared to the global crisis today, rather than the military governments' economic skills. Moreover, a military regime's economic policies may either negatively or positively influence the performance of civilian government that replaces it. Thus, for example, some military governments have stimulated short-term economic growth by borrowing excessively from foreign banks or institutions. But in doing so, they bequeathed high inflation and a debt crisis on their civilian successors. Few analytical comparisons have been able to control for all such factors. For the most part, though, cross-national statistical research has uncovered *little difference* between the economic growth rates of democratic and military regimes, though in some regions (such as sub-Saharan Africa), civilian governments seem to outperform military regimes.

MILITARY WITHDRAWAL FROM POLITICS

Once the armed forces have become entrenched in the political system, dislodging them is usually no easy task. Domestic upheavals (Indonesia) or external intervention (Uganda) sometimes induce the military to withdraw from power. More often, however, the armed forces voluntarily relinquish power for one or more of the following reasons: having accomplished their major objectives, they see no value in retaining power; deteriorating economic conditions make continued rule unappealing; extended rule has undermined internal military cohesion; or, the regime becomes so unpopular that staying in office would reduce the military's legitimacy as an institution.

Many military governments come into office as "caretakers" whose goal is to restore stability or solve a particular problem and then quickly return control to civilians. In Ecuador, for example, the armed forces frequently ousted elected leaders whom they considered too demagogic, too populist, or too incompetent. After ruling relatively briefly, they then voluntarily stepped down.

Because the perpetrators of institutional coups usually take power with expectations of augmenting military budgets and accelerating economic growth, their interest in governing, not surprisingly, wanes if the economy turns sour (as it does for at least a period of years in most LDCs). In countries such as Peru, Uruguay, and Thailand, economic downturns have convinced military governments to step down. These declines may also aggravate internal divisions within the armed forces.

In sub-Saharan Africa, military rule may also aggravate ethnic tensions within the armed forces, particularly when officers from one tribe or religion dominate top government positions. For example, in Nigeria, the military's entry into the political arena unleashed four internal coups in a 10-year span, with ethnic divisions playing an important role. Two heads of government and a number of other senior officers were killed in the military's internal struggles. Elsewhere, other military governments, fearing similar deteriorations in the armed forces' cohesiveness, have preferred to step down, leaving the nation's problems to civilians. In some countries, soldiers from one tribe or ethnic group may dominate the armed forces. For example, in Togo as of 2005, the Kabyé tribe made up only 15 percent of the country's population but constituted 70 percent of all soldiers and 90 percent of the officer corps. Ultimate power has been in the hands of a Kabyé military dictator who ruled the country for 38 years (1967–2005) and his son who has ruled since 2005.[51]

Just as military coups are most likely when civilian governments lack legitimacy, the army is most likely to return to the barracks when its own legitimacy declines. This happens most dramatically when the country has been defeated in war. For example, following its humiliating defeat by Britain in the Falklands (or Malvinas) war, the Argentine military regime was forced to step down. And Pakistan's military had to transfer power to its leading civilian critic, Zulfiqar Ali Bhutto, after it lost East Pakistan (now Bangladesh) in a war with India.

In recent years, influential nations and international organizations in both developed countries and LDCs have taken a stronger stance against military takeovers. Thus countries such as Madagascar and Ecuador, which have had coups or attempted coups in recent times, found themselves isolated in the African Union (AU) or the Organization of American States (OAS) until they restored civilian government. Indeed, in 2009, the OAS unanimously ousted Honduras from that organization shortly after that country's armed forces removed an elected president, who was replaced with a more conservative civilian official. The coup was universally condemned by governments of all political stripes, whereas such a coup would have gone virtually unnoticed in decades past. Later in that year, both the European Union and the Economic Community of West African States (ECOWAS) imposed an arms embargo on Guinea when its military government's soldiers fired on an opposition protesters, killing some 150 of them.

During the Cold War (1945–1991), the United States had worked closely with a number of military governments, occasionally even encouraging military coups against elected leftist governments (in Brazil and Chile, for example). Since the 1990s, however it has opposed almost all military takeovers, though it has made exceptions, such as cooperating with Pakistan's recent military strongman, General Pervez Musharraf. President Obama has taken a particularly firm stance against military takeovers, though some have criticized his administration for not taking stronger action against Honduras's recent coup. In general, however, members of the world community have toughened their position toward military governments.

But these international pressures are usually ineffective unless the military has also lost its legitimacy at home. In Uruguay, economic decay and public revulsion against the regime's political repression so weakened the military government that it unexpectedly lost a national referendum that it had been confident it could tightly control.[52] Eventually, popular discontent induced the generals to negotiate a return to civilian government. Similarly, in 1992, in Thailand, massive student-led, pro-democracy demonstrations convinced the armed forces to withdraw. And most recently, mass demonstrations led by Pakistan's lawyer's association brought down the Musharraf dictatorship.

While some combination of these factors has accounted for the departure of most military regimes, it has not guaranteed that the armed forces would stay out of power. Indeed, until the 1980s, the soldiers were likely to return to power. Talukder Maniruzzaman examined 71 instances of military withdrawal from office in the Third World from 1946 to 1984. He only considered cases in which military rulers were replaced by civilian government. In 65 percent of these cases examined, the armed forces were back in power within 5 years.[53] In 2006 the Thai military returned to power and the Pakistani military has been in and out of power a number of times.

These cases notwithstanding, however, since the 1990s those military regimes that have stepped down have been more likely to stay out of office. In most of the Third World, there has been a dramatic decline in military rule. That trend has been weaker in Africa, where military regimes or quasi-military governments remain in such nations as Equatorial Guinea, Egypt, Guinea-Bissau, Guinea (Conakry), Libya, Sudan, Togo, Chad, Uganda, and Rwanda.* For example, as of 2009, the Latin American nations of Argentina, Ecuador, Brazil, Guatemala, and El Salvador, all with long histories of armed-forces intervention, had enjoyed anywhere from 20 to 31 years without military government. In South Korea, decades of military dominance ended in 1993. Even in Africa, military regimes in several countries, including Nigeria, Ghana,

---

* Quasi-military governments are nominally headed by civilians but are really run either by a former military strongman or a civilian who is under military control.

Benin, and Congo-Brazzaville, have given way to elected civilian governments since the early 1990s.[54]

In some cases, years of misrule undermined the military's institutional legitimacy. The brutality and incompetence of Argentine military dictatorship (1976-1983) so discredited it that succeeding civilian governments were able to reduce the armed forces to one-third their previous size. Elsewhere, as in Mozambique, El Salvador, and Nicaragua, peace treaties ending long civil wars mandated sharp reductions in the size of the military.

Ultimately, if the armed forces are to relinquish political power and not return, they will need to find new responsibilities to justify their role in society and their share of the national budget. This is particularly true in countries that face no serious foreign threats. In Latin America and much of Africa, for example, wars between nation-states, as opposed to civil conflicts, have been quite rare. In assigning the military new roles, however, civilian governments must be careful not to involve it in tasks that may draw it back into politics— a danger some analysts see in the Latin American military's growing involvement in the "war on drugs." Furthermore, to *maintain* their restored political power and their control over the armed forces, civilian governments will to have to establish more effective civil–military relationships.

New Roles for the Armed Forces

Many of the proposed "new roles" for the military are not really entirely new. They include combating drug trafficking (in parts of Latin America, the Caribbean, and Asia), antiterrorist activity, and emergency relief efforts following natural disasters. Unfortunately, in the past some of these activities have brought as many new problems as solutions. In Mexico, Colombia, the Caribbean, and Central America, antidrug efforts have frequently corrupted the armed forces, as some officers have changed from enforcers to well-paid protectors of the drug cartels. In Mexico, for example, there have even been gun fights between military antidrug units and soldiers who were paid by the drug cartels to protect them. Furthermore, in countries such as Colombia and Sri Lanka, the armed forces have often used their mandates to combat terrorism and internal subversion as carte blanche for violating human rights and crushing peaceful and legitimate political opposition groups.

Another popular activity is military **"civic action"**—using troops in projects that are beneficial to the civil population, especially the poor, such as building roads, medical clinics, sanitation projects, and schools. During the Cold War, U.S. military missions in the LDCs, particularly in Central America, encouraged and financed civic action designed to win local support for the government. Many governments have continued similar projects in countries such as Senegal, Thailand, and the Philippines. Unfortunately, these activities have been far too limited to make a significant dent in national poverty.

Finally, another role for Third World militaries has emerged in recent times. Countries such as Argentina, India, Pakistan, and Uruguay have participated in United Nations peacekeeping forces in trouble-spots such as Bosnia, Cambodia, and the Congo. In addition to the U.N. missions, West African regional peacekeeping forces helped settle a bloody civil war in Liberia.

Most recently, the African Union has dispatched peacekeepers to Darfur and Somalia. UN and other peacekeeping troops have sometimes been very effective. But, in cases such as Darfur, they have failed to effectively protect the civilian population. Sometimes—most notably in Burundi, the Congo, Haiti, Liberia, and Sudan—"peacekeeping" troops have been guilty of raping and pillaging some of the people they were sent to protect.

Improved Civil–Military Relationships

Although there are far fewer Third World, military regimes today, the danger of political interference by the armed force still remains, particularly in countries with prior histories of military dominance. Consequently, civilian governments need to shore up their positions by modernizing and improving civil–military relationships. They must create or strengthen political institutions, attitudes and behavior that reinforce civilian control.

One important area is the education of military officers. They are normally trained at military academies, often after graduating from military high schools. In the larger and more developed Third World countries, many senior officers continue their educations through much of their careers, with the most promising ones attending advanced academies for specialized training. All of these schools are critical in socializing military officers into the values of both the armed forces and the political system. If those officers are to refrain from interfering in national politics, their training must stress the importance of civilian control over the armed forces.

Second, the nation's constitution and legal system must bestow upon the chief executive (president or prime minister) final control over the armed forces. Unfortunately, in some countries, the constitution requires the civilian president to secure the approval of the military high command before appointing the defense minister or promoting the most senior generals and admirals. Other nations require the defense minister to be a military officer. To establish civilian control, governments need to eliminate such restrictions. Indeed, it is best if only civilians can be appointed as defense ministers.

Third, the country's political institutions must give the civilian president and defense minister clear and direct control over the armed forces. In the United States, for example, the president is legally the commander-in-chief and officers who criticizes his policies publically are often relieved of duty. In addition, it is important that the country's parliament or congress determines the defense budget and have some level of oversight (through committee hearings and the like) over the armed forces.

Fourth, an important, but rarely discussed, requirement for civilian dominance is that civilian officials control military intelligence activities. Primarily these intelligence activities involve clandestine gathering of information at home and possibly abroad regarding national security. But often they also include covert operations. In countries such as Chile under General Pinochet and Pakistan today, military intelligence units have operated as an independent force in defense, foreign, and even domestic policy.[55] For example, in the past, Pakistan's powerful Directorate for Inter-Service Intelligence (ISI) has assisted the Afghan Taliban and perhaps Al Qaeda in the hopes of having an Afghan ally against India. It is quite possible that it continues such aid, on a reduced scale, today. It also has maintained links to the Pakistani Taliban (a faction of which almost surely assassinated former Prime Minister Benazir Bhutto, the wife of the current national president, Asif Ali Zardari) and to Muslim terrorist groups operating in the Indian-controlled portion of Kashmir.

Finally, government leaders need to walk a fine line in their relationships with the armed forces. While insisting on civilian control, they also need to fund the military sufficiently to protect national security, and they must take seriously the opinions of military commanders in matters related to national defense. To do otherwise would be to invite a coup attempt.

CONCLUSION: DEMOCRACY AND THE MILITARY

By definition, the spread of democracy has reduced the number of Third World military governments. This does not mean that the specter of military takeovers has disappeared. But, since the 1990s, attempted military coups have been largely limited to sub-Saharan Africa and, to a lesser extent, Asia.

Even in democratically elected governments, the armed forces often exercise considerable political influence in certain policy areas. Furthermore, in a number of countries, the military remains outside civilian control. For example, in Chile, where General Pinochet's outgoing dictatorship was able to dictate the terms of the 1989 transition to democracy, the new constitution afforded the armed forces considerable influence. The military was granted amnesty for most of its human rights violations, including the murder of some 2,000–3,000 civilians. The elected president lacked authority to remove the military's chief of staff, and the armed forces appointed several members of the senate. General Pinochet himself, as a former president, served initially as senator for life. It took more than 10 years until the Chilean Congress was able to end those special powers.

In order to consolidate democracy, LDCs must do more than merely restore elected government. Stable and secure democracy requires a professionalized military that is committed to staying out of politics. In other words, there must be both "a high level of . . . professionalism and recognition by military officers of the limits of their professional competence" and "subordination of the military to the civilian political leaders who make the basic decisions on foreign and military policy" as well as domestic policy.[56] Officers must largely limit their professional role to defending their country from potential external threats and must recognize that their involvement in national politics will only divide the armed forces and diminish their professional capacity. But just as the generals and colonels must keep out of national politics, civilian political leaders must respect the military's domain and not attempt to politicize the armed forces. All too often, aspiring political leaders who are unable to gain office through legitimate channels have approached the military for support. As David Mares has noted,

> If civilians are willing to accept democracy as a value, it is hard to see how a professional military would be drawn into politics. And if civilians, especially powerful corporate groups, do not accept the rules of the democratic game, it is difficult to see how democracy could be consolidated whether or not the military intervenes.[57]

Even the most successful military governments inhibit political development. They do so because their very rationale for taking office is "the politics of antipolitics." With their hierarchical perspective and their distaste for disorder, soldiers believe in a managed society. Most reject the give and take of political competition and the compromises inherent in politics. Consequently, they

> fail to see the functional aspects of the great game of politics: They severely restrict the free flow of the political process and force would-be politicians into a long period of hibernation. . . . The opportunity for gaining political skills by a people once under a military regime is continually postponed by every new military regime.[58]

DISCUSSION QUESTIONS

1. Why do most political sciences have a negative view of military rule in the LDCs? Under what circumstances, if any, might military government be a good thing for the country?
2. Discuss why you think the armed forces of developed countries such as the United States or Canada do not attempt military coups.
3. Where have military regimes successfully developed Third World economies and where have they failed to do so? What seems to account for the difference?

NOTES

1. Harold Crouch, *The Army and Politics in Indonesia* (Ithaca, NY: Cornell University Press, 1978), 345.

2. William Thompson, "Explanations of the Military Coup," Ph.D. dissertation, University of Washington, Seattle, 1972, 11. Quoted in Amos Perlmutter, *The Military and Politics in Modern Times* (New Haven, CT: Yale University Press, 1977), 115.

3. Claude E. Welch, "Military Disengagements from Politics: Incentives and Obstacles in Political Change," in *Military Power and Politics in Black Africa*, ed. Simon Baynham (New York: St. Martin's Press, 1986), 89–90.

4. Samuel Decalo, *Coups and Army Rule in Africa* (New Haven, CT: Yale University Press, 1990), 2.

5. Patrick J. McGowan, "African Military Coups D'état, 1956–2001: Frequency, Trends and Distribution," *Journal of Modern African Studies*, vol. 41, no. 3 (September 2003), 339.

6. Steven Cook, *Ruling But Not Governing: The Military and Political Development in Egypt, Algeria, and Turkey* (Baltimore: Johns Hopkins University Press, 2007).

7. Morris Janowitz, *Military Institutions and Coercion in the Developing Nations: Expanded edition of the Military in the Political Development of New Nations* (Chicago: University of Chicago Press, 1977), 105.

8. Samuel P. Huntington, "Civilian Control of the Military: A Theoretical Statement," in *Political Behavior: A Reader in Theory and Research*, eds. Heinz Eulau, Samuel Eldersveld, and Morris Janowitz (New York: Free Press, 1956), 380–381.

9. Samuel P. Huntington, "Patterns of Violence in World Politics," in *Changing Patterns of Military Politics*, ed. Samuel P. Huntington (New York: Free Press, 1962), 19–22.

10. Alfred Stepan, "The New Professionalism of Internal Warfare and Military Role Expansion," in *Armies and Politics in Latin America*, rev. ed., eds. Abraham Lowenthal and J. Samuel Fitch (New York: Holmes and Meier, 1986), 134–150.

11. Michael C. Desch, *Civilian Control of the Military: The Changing Security Environment* (Baltimore, MD: The Johns Hopkins Press, 1999).

12. Ruth First, *The Barrel of a Gun: Political Power in Africa and the Coup D'état* (London: Allen Lane/Penguin Press, 1970), 208, 4.

13. Michel Louis Martin, "Operational Weaknesses and Political Activism: The Military in Sub-Saharan Africa," in *To Sheathe the Sword: Civil-Military Relations in the Quest for Democracy*, eds. John P. Lovell and David E. Albright (Westport, CT: Greenwood Press, 1997), 89.

14. Samuel P. Huntington, *Political Order in Changing Societies* (New Haven, CT: Yale University Press, 1968), 194.

15. Robert Wesson, "Preface," in *New Military Politics in Latin America*, ed. Robert Wesson (New York: Praeger, 1982), v.

16. Samuel E. Finer, *The Man on Horseback: The Role of the Military in Politics*, 2d ed. (London: Penguin Books, 1976), 78–82.

17. Samuel P. Huntington, "Reforming Civil-Military Relations," in *Civil–Military Relations and Democracy*, eds. Larry Diamond and Marc F. Plattner (Baltimore, MD: Johns Hopkins University Press, 1996), 9. Italics added.

18. Marion J. Levy Jr., *Modernization and the Structure of Societies* (Princeton, NJ: Princeton University Press, 1966), Vol. 2, 603.

19. Lucian W. Pye, "Armies in the Process of Political Modernization," in *The Role of the Military in Underdeveloped Countries*, ed. John J. Johnson (Princeton, NJ: Princeton University Press, 1962), 69–89.

20. Manfred Halpern, *The Politics of Social Change in the Middle East and North Africa* (Princeton, NJ: Princeton University Press, 1963), 75, 253.

21. For a summary of those writings, see Henry Bienen, "The Background to Contemporary Study of Militaries and Modernization," in *The Military and Modernization*, ed. Henry Bienen (Chicago: Atherton, 1971), 1–33; First, *The Barrel of a Gun*, 13–20.

22. Karen L. Remmer, *Military Rule in Latin America* (Boston: Unwin Hyman, 1989), 3.

23. Eric A. Nordlinger, *Soldiers in Politics: Military Coups and Governments* (Englewood Cliffs, NJ: Prentice Hall, 1977), 173; also Huntington, *Political Order*, chap. 4.

24. Huntington, *Political Order*, 221.

25. Decalo, *Coups and Army Rule in Africa*, 133.

26. John Booth, *The End and the Beginning: The Nicaraguan Revolution*, 2d ed. (Boulder, CO: Westview Press, 1985).

27. Decalo, *Coups and Army Rule in Africa*, 11. Decalo argues that in Africa personalities, more than broad socioeconomic or political variables, have explained military intervention.

28. Edward A. Olsen and Stephen Jurika Jr., "Introduction," and Harold W. Maynard, "The Role of the Indonesian Armed Forces," in *The Armed Forces in Contemporary Asian Society*, eds. Edward A. Olsen and Stephen Jurika Jr. (Boulder, CO: Westview Press, 1986), 18, 207–208.

29. Jeffrey Lunstead, "The Armed Forces in Bangladesh Society," in *The Armed Forces in Contemporary Asian Society*, 316.

30. Ruth First, *Power in Africa* (New York: Pantheon Books, 1970), 20.

31. Craig Baxter and Syedur Rahman, "Bangladesh's Military: Political Institutionalization and Economic Development," in *Civil-Military Interaction in Asia and Africa*, eds. Charles H. Kennedy and David J. Louscher (Leiden, The Netherlands: E. J. Brill, 1991), 43–60.

32. Harold Crouch, "The Military and Politics in South-East Asia," in *Military-Civilian Relations in South-East Asia*, eds. Zakaria Haji Ahmad and Harold Crouch (New York: Oxford University Press, 1985), 291. Italics added.

33. Seitz, "The Military in Black African Politics," in *Civil-Military Interaction*, 61–75.

34. The most useful analysis of O'Donnell's rather complex theory is contained in David Collier, ed. *The New Authoritarianism in Latin America* (Princeton, NJ: Princeton University Press, 1979).

35. "The Political Orientation Speech Delivered by Captain Thomas Sankara in Ouagadougou, Upper Volta, on October 2, 1983," in *Military Marxist Regimes in Africa*, eds. John Markakis and Michael Waller (London: Frank Cass, 1986), 145–153 (selected portions).

36. Samuel Decalo, "The Morphology of Radical Military Rule in Africa," in *Military Marxist Regimes in Africa*, 123.

37. Samuel Decalo, "Military Rule in Africa: Etiology and Morphology," in *Military Power and Politics in Black Africa*, 56, 58.

38. J. Bayo Adekanye, "The Post-Military State in Africa," in *The Political Dilemma of Military Regimes*, eds. Christopher Clapham and George Philip (London: Croom Helm, 1985), 87.

39. Crouch, "The Military and Politics in South-East Asia," in *Military-Civilian Relations*, 292–293.

40. Charles H. Kennedy and David J. Louscher, "Civil-Military Interaction: Data in Search of a Theory," in *Civil-Military Interaction in Asia and Africa*, eds. Charles H. Kennedy and David J. Louscher (Leiden, The Netherlands: E. J. Brill, 1991), 5.

41. Howard Handelman, "Uruguay," in *Military Government and the Movement towards Democracy in South America*, eds. Howard Handelman and Thomas Sanders (Bloomington: Indiana University Press, 1981), 218.

42. Decalo, *Coups and Army Rule in Africa*, 20.

43. McGowan, "African Military Coups D'état, 1956–2001," 347.

44. Claude E. Welch Jr., "From 'Armies of Africans' to 'African Armies': The Evolution of Military Forces in Africa," in *African Armies: Evolution and Capabilities*, eds. Bruce E. Arlinghaus and Pauline H. Baker (Boulder, Co: Westview Press, 1986), 25.

45. Elisabeth Sköns et al., "Military Expenditures." summarized on the SIPRI Web site (http://www.sipri.se/).

46. J. Samuel Fitch, *The Armed Forces and Democracy in Latin America* (Baltimore, MD: The Johns Hopkins University Press, 1998), 77–78.

47. Juan Rial, "Armies and Civil Society in Latin America," in Diamond and Plattner (ed.), *Civil–Military Relations and Democracy*, 57.

48. CIA, "Country Comparison—Military Expenditures," *The 2008 World Factbook,* http://www.cia.gov/library/publications/the-world-factbook/index.html.

49. Nordlinger, *Soldiers in Politics*, 139.

50. Remmer, *Military Rule*, 40.

51. Issaka K. Souaré, *Civil Wars and Coups d'Etat in West Africa* (Lanham, MD: University Press of America, 2006), 101

52. Howard Handelman, "Prelude to the 1984 Uruguayan Election: The Military Regime's Legitimacy Crisis and the 1980 Constitutional Plebiscite," in *Critical Elections in the Americas,* eds. Paul Drake and Eduardo Silva (San Diego: University of California Press, 1986), 201–214.

53. Talukder Maniruzzaman, *Military Withdrawal from Politics: A Comparative Study* (Cambridge, MA: Ballinger Publishing, 1987), 21, 24–25.

54. Michael Bratton and Nicolas van de Walle, *Democratic Experiments in Africa* (New York: Cambridge University Press, 1997), 197–203.

55. Thomas Bruneau and Kenneth Dombrowski, "Reforming Intelligence: The Challenge of Control in New Democracies," in *Who Guards the Guardians and How: Democratic Civil-Military Relations,* eds. T. Bruneau and Scott Tollefson (Austin: University of Texas Press, 2006), 147. Many of the ideas in this section drew on this book.

56. Samuel P. Huntington, "Reforming Civil-Military Relations," 3–4.

57. David R. Mares, "Civil-Military Relations, Democracy, and the Regional Neighbors," in *Civil-Military Relations,* ed. David R. Mares, (Boulder, CO: Westview Press, 1998), 59–75, 18.

58. Brian Loveman and Thomas M. Davies Jr., eds. *The Politics of Antipolitics: The Military in Latin America,* 2d ed. (Lincoln: University of Nebraska Press, 1989), 6.

CHAPTER 10

THE POLITICAL ECONOMY OF THIRD WORLD DEVELOPMENT

A lmost every Third World government, except the most corrupt and incompetent, wishes to promote economic development. Economic growth coupled with reasonably equitable income distribution offers the promise of improved living standards and, presumably, increased popular support for the ruling regime, at least in the long run.* It also provides added tax revenues, which enhance government capacity. And economic development can augment a nation's military strength, diplomatic influence, and international prestige. But the obvious benefits of growth should not obscure the many difficult questions that economic development policy entails. How can nations promote economic growth, and how can the conflicting goals of economic development be reconciled? How should countries share the inevitable sacrifices required for generating early economic development? How can a country achieve economic development without doing irreparable harm to the environment?

During the 1980s, the optimism of early modernization theorists looked ill-founded in light of sharp economic declines in Africa and Latin America.[1] Today, the war on poverty often seems unwinnable in South Asia, sub-Saharan Africa, and other developing regions. On the other hand, East Asia's spectacular growth since the 1960s and India's takeoff since the mid-1990s appear to belie dependency theory's pervasive pessimism about the limits of economic development in the periphery.

In recent decades, a substantial amount of the scholarship on the Third World has focused on its *political economy*. Martin Staniland defines this field as the study of "how politics determines aspects of the economy, and how economic institutions determine the political process," as well as "the dynamic interaction between the two forces."[2] This chapter focuses on several important issues: What are the major strategies for development? What should be the role of the state in stimulating and regulating economic growth and industrialization? How should countries deal with the deep economic inequalities that normally persist, or even increase, during the modernization process?

---

* Of course, we have seen that in the short term, economic growth may be politically destabilizing. However, if growth is coupled with equitable income distribution, the chances of unrest diminish.

THE ROLE OF THE STATE

The question of the state's proper economic role has been at the center of political and economic debates for hundreds of years, first in Western industrial economies, and more recently in the LDCs. During the sixteenth and seventeenth centuries, major European powers were guided by the philosophy of *mercantilism*, which looked at a nation's economic activity as a means of enhancing the political power of the state and its monarch. Consequently, mercantilists saw government as "both source and beneficiary of economic growth."[3] That perspective, however, drew the fire of the eighteenth-century, Scottish economist Adam Smith, who favored a very limited state that gave market forces a free hand. The following century, Karl Marx, reacting to the exploitative nature of early capitalism, proposed giving the state a dominant economic role, at least initially, through ownership of the means of production and centralized, state, economic planning. Finally, the twentieth-century economist, Sir John Maynard Keynes, responding to the Great Depression, advocated a substantial degree of government economic intervention, but rejected Marxist prescriptions for state ownership and centralized planning.

Today, the collapse of the Soviet bloc's centrally controlled "command economies" and the poor economic performance of the world's remaining communist nations have discredited the advocates of state-controlled economies. At the same time, however, no government embraces full **laissez faire** (i.e., allowing market forces complete free reign, with no government intervention). All countries, for example, no matter how capitalistic, have laws regulating banking, domestic commerce, and international trade. Most have introduced some environmental regulations and work-safety rules. In the real world, then, governments must decide where to position themselves between the extreme poles of an unregulated economy and a command economy.

For a number of reasons, that choice is particularly contentious in the developing world. The fragile nature of many economies, their high level of poverty, their poor distribution of wealth and income, their dependence on international market forces, and their endangered environments all have encouraged many governments to assume an active role in the economy. Moreover, many developing nations also lack a strong entrepreneurial class and sufficient private capital for investment. As a consequence, their governments have often built the steel mills, railroads, and sugar refineries that the private sector could not or would not provide. More recently, governments have been asked to protect the environment against the ravages of economic development. Not surprisingly, then, state economic intervention traditionally has been more pronounced in the developing world than in the West. Since the 1980s, however, the spread of *neoliberal* economic policies—characterized by free trade, free markets, and relatively unrestrained capitalism—has sharply reduced government economic intervention in both the developing and the developed worlds.*

---

* Originally, liberalism—first formulated as an ideology in the eighteenth century—advocated greater individual liberty (hence the name *liberal*) and less government intervention into people's lives, including their economic activities. Today, outside of the United States, the terms *liberal*, *neoliberal policies*, and **economic liberalization** normally refer to policies that *reduce* the role of government in the economy, contrary to the way the term *liberal* is used in the United States.

This chapter discusses a number of alternative models prescribing the role of the state in Third World economies, ranging from command economies, such as North Korea's, to very limited state intervention, as in Hong Kong. In considering these alternatives, the reader should keep in mind that these are ideal types. Few countries fit any of these models perfectly. Cuba's Marxist government, for example, permits private farming and some other small businesses. Also, many nations have introduced some mix of these approaches. While the options discussed below are not exhaustive, they cover the models most widely used in the LDCs today.

The Command Economy

Marxism began as a critique of capitalism in the Western world during the early stages of industrial development. Inherently, argued Karl Marx, capitalism produced an inequitable distribution of wealth and income, with those who control the means of production (industrialists, landlords) exploiting those who worked in or on them (the working class, peasants). One of Marxism's appeals to its supporters was its promise of great equality and social justice. In modern times, economic inequality has usually intensified as countries have moved from the lower to the middle levels of development. Consequently, it is not surprising that Marxist ideology initially appealed to many Third World government leaders or radical opposition figures who were troubled by the deep injustices in their own economic systems. It was particularly attractive in Latin America and parts of Africa, which have had the greatest disparities between rich and poor.

A second assertion by Marxist leaders was that only a revolutionary political-economic system could free Third World countries from the yoke of dependency. Because most dependency theorists believed that capitalist trade and investment in the developing world created an exploitative relationship between core industrial nations and the periphery, they argued that only "socialist" developing countries could achieve economic independence and development.*

Finally, another of communism's appeals was its centralized, state control of the economy. A *command economy*, first established in the Soviet Union, has two central features. First, the state largely owns and manages the means of production. That includes factories, banks, major trade and commercial institutions, retail establishments, and, frequently, farms. While all communist nations have allowed some private economic activity, the private sector has been quite limited, aside from nations such as China and Vietnam, which have

---

* The term *socialist* can describe two very different political and economic models, thereby confusing many readers. In Western Europe, socialist parties and governments in nations such as Sweden, France, Germany, and Spain have supported liberal democracy and a high level of civil liberties (sometimes even more than their conservative opponents have). While they advocate a significant degree of government involvement in the economy—including extensive welfare programs and, at least until recently, some state ownership—they also favor a major role for private enterprise. On the other hand, the term *socialist* is also applied, as it is here, to countries that are allegedly in the early stages of Communism, such as the USSR (Union of Soviet *Socialist* Republics). Thus, self-proclaimed "socialist" countries such as Cuba, the USSR, and China, have concentrated political power in a single political party (normally the only party permitted) and placed dominant economic power in the hands of the state.

largely abandoned Marxist economics in recent years. Second, in a command economy, state planners, rather than market forces, shape basic decisions governing production (including the quantity and price of goods produced).

Interestingly, Marxism viewed market (capitalist) economies as anarchistic because they leave the most fundamental decisions about the allocation of resources and the determination of prices to the "whims" of supply and demand. Thus, Adam Przeworski has satirized the orthodox Marxists' attitude toward capitalism's "**invisible** [guiding] **hand**": People in capitalist countries such as Britain and the United States get up each morning and find their newspapers or milk bottles already sitting outside their doors without even knowing who delivered them. Yet, Przeworski noted wryly, orthodox Marxist theory insisted that the paper or milk bottle could not possibly have arrived without a central planner guaranteeing its delivery.[4] But, in fact, he observes, under a centrally planned economy not only is home delivery unreliable, but there are recurrent shortages of paper, milk bottles, and milk. Indeed, the collapse of Soviet and Eastern European Communism revealed the organizational failures of centralized command economies.

In fact, the command economy's flaws are now so obvious that most people are unaware of its earlier accomplishments. By dictating the movement of people and resources from one sector of the economy to another, communist countries such as the Soviet Union and China were able to jump-start their industrial takeoffs. During the 1920s and 1930s, "entire industries were created [in the USSR], along with millions of jobs that drew peasants away from the countryside and into higher-paying jobs and higher living standards."[5] Western estimates of Soviet economic performance during its early industrialization phase indicate that between 1928 and 1955, GNP grew at a robust average annual rate of some 5 percent.[6] During the first decades of its revolution, China also moved quickly from a backward, agrarian economy to a far more industrialized society. According to one leading authority, between 1952 and 1975, that country's economy grew at an average annual rate of 8.2 percent, while industrial output surged ahead at 11.5 percent annually.[7] These rates far exceeded the norms in either capitalist developing nations or industrialized democracies.[8] Other analysts believe that its growth rate could not have been that high because of the setbacks of the Great Leap Forward and the Cultural Revolution. Still, all agree that compared to India, Pakistan, and most LDCs, China's growth during that period, like the Soviet Union's decades earlier, was absolutely impressive. Small wonder that, at one time, many Third World leaders were attracted to the Soviet and Chinese development models.

Finally, command economies have frequently made great strides toward reducing income inequalities. Indeed, it is in this area that some communist LDCs clearly outperformed their capitalist counterparts. In Cuba, for example, the revolution brought a substantial transfer of income from the richest 20 percent of the population to the poorest 40 percent.[9] The poor also benefited from land reform, subsidized rents, and free health care, though some of those gains were undermined in the 1990s, following the loss of Soviet economic assistance. An extensive adult literacy program and greater educational opportunities further advanced social equality. Nor was Cuba unique in this respect. Cross-national statistical comparisons indicate that communist countries as a whole have more equal income distribution than do capitalist nations at similar levels of development.[10]

Eventually, however, the weaknesses of command economies overshadow their accomplishments.* Lacking measures of consumer demand, state planners have little basis for deciding what to produce and how much. Moreover, centrally controlled economies typically reward producers for meeting their output quotas, with little concern for product quality. Furthermore, even in the best of circumstances, to be at all efficient, a centralized command economy would need a highly skilled and honest bureaucracy equipped with sophisticated and accurate consumer surveys. Unfortunately, Third World bureaucracies rarely have these qualities. Moreover, command economies handed inordinate power to state planners. And as Lord Acton once warned, "Power tends to corrupt, and absolute power tends to corrupt absolutely."

Thus, for example, Chinese business entrepreneurs know that the price of doing business is bribing government officials (cadres) or their adult children. Elsewhere as well, command economies have featured a large privileged class of state and party bureaucrats (*apparatchiks*), who enjoy perquisites unavailable to the rest of the population. Furthermore, while the Soviet Union and China enjoyed rapid growth in the early decades of their revolutions, both economies eventually lost momentum as they became more complex and therefore harder to centrally control. Finally, command economies are more adept at building heavy industries such as steel mills or public works projects—activities more common in the early stages of industrialization—than they are at developing sophisticated high-tech production techniques or at producing quality consumer goods. The Soviet Union, for example, turned out impressive military hardware and powerful space rockets, but was unable to produce a decent automobile or home washing machine.

By the late 1970s in China and the 1980s in the USSR, as both economies deteriorated, their leaders (Deng Xiaoping and Mikhail Gorbachev) recognized the need for economic decentralization and reduced state economic control. China's subsequent transition to *market socialism* (a mixture of free market and socialist economics) has produced perhaps the world's fastest growing economy. However, in the Soviet Union and its major successor state, Russia, reforms resulted in an economic collapse that lasted for nearly a decade. The fall of Soviet bloc Communism and China's remarkable economic transformation have inspired market-oriented reforms in other command economies. Vietnam, for example, has transferred state farmland to the peasantry, attracted billions of dollars in foreign investment, and transferred a substantial portion of its industrial production from the state to the private sector. Elsewhere in Asia and Africa, governments such as Myanmar and the Congolese Republic have privatized much of the state sector (i.e., sold government-owned enterprises back to private owners) and reduced government economic controls. The end of Soviet aid has undercut some of Cuba's gains in health care, nutrition, and education. Stripped of its primary benefactor, it too has been forced to accept limited free-market innovations.

In many former communist nations in Eastern and Central Europe, the demise of their command economies initially failed to improve living standards and often lowered them sharply. Only in China and Vietnam did the transition

---

* Command economies all are controlled by politically repressive governments. This chapter only analyzes the economic record of command economies and not their politics, which are discussed in Chapter 2.

toward free-market economics rapidly raise standards of living. In Eastern and Central Europe, especially Russia, it took a decade or more for living standards to equal or surpass their levels in the communist era.

Latin American Statism

Even in capitalist Third World countries, the state has often played a major economic role, hoping to be an engine of economic growth. In the period between the two World Wars, many Latin American nations first pursued state-led industrialization. That process accelerated during the Great Depression of the 1920s and 1930s, when countries in the region had difficulty finding markets for their food and raw material exports and, consequently, lacked foreign exchange for industrial imports. Argentina, Brazil, Chile, Uruguay, and Mexico were among the early leaders in the push toward industrialization.

Unlike communist countries, Latin American nations left most economic activity in the hands of the private sector and did not centralize control over the economy. But their governments often owned strategically important enterprises and invested in industries that failed to attract sufficient private capital. Consequently, prior to the recent privatization of state enterprises, many of the region's railroads, airlines, petroleum companies, mines, steel mills, electric power plants, telephone companies, and armaments factories were state owned.

However, in a number of ways state ownership contradict popular stereotypes. First, many government takeovers were supported by the business community. To begin with, the most important nationalizations (transfers of private firms to state ownership)—including the seizures of the petroleum industries in Mexico and Venezuela, mining operations in Chile and Peru, and railroads in Argentina—affected companies that were owned by foreign corporations rather than local capitalists. Second, after taking control of the petroleum industry, railroads, and utilities, the state often provided domestic, private-sector industries with subsidized and inexpensive transportation, power, and other needed resources. In fact, until the 1980s, conservative governments in the region were as likely to expand government ownership as were left-leaning or populist regimes. For example, during the 1960s and 1970s, Brazil's right-wing military regime substantially increased the size of the state sector. Moreover, such nationalizations typically were broadly popular and bolstered the government's legitimacy as a defender of national interests.

Along with its ownership of a number of essential enterprises, the state also played a pivotal role in fomenting private-sector industrial growth. In Latin America's largest economies, the government initiated import-substituting industrialization (ISI) programs in the early to mid-twentieth century. ISI (discussed more extensively later in this chapter) sought to replace imported consumer goods with domestically manufactured products. Import-substituting firms were normally privately owned, but depended heavily on government support. This included protective tariffs and quotas on competing imports, favorable exchange rates, subsidized energy and transport costs, and low-interest loans.

In countries such as Argentina, Brazil, Chile, Colombia, and Mexico, these government-supported development policies were initially quite successful. From 1945 to 1970, rates of investment in Latin America were higher than in the

Western industrial nations, and from 1960 to 1980, the region's manufacturing output grew faster as well.[11] Virtually every Latin American country began manufacturing basic consumer goods such as textiles, clothing, packaged food, and furniture. Larger nations such as Argentina, Brazil, and Mexico established automotive industries, steel mills, and other heavy industries. In time, industrialization altered the region's demographic and class structures. Massive rural migration to the cities transformed Latin America into the Third World's most urbanized region (see Chapter 7). Furthermore, for decades ISI created blue-collar jobs and expanded the size of the middle class.

But hidden beneath these accomplishments, this strategy also promoted economic inefficiencies and income inequalities. While government nurturing of industrialization was probably necessary in the early stages of economic development, Latin America maintained protectionist measures and subsidies too broadly and too long. Rather than serving as a finely calibrated tool for getting industrialization off the ground, ISI became a politically motivated juggernaut. With industrialists, the middle class, and organized labor all united behind these policies, elected officials were unwilling to wean established industries from government support and protection long after they should have become self-sufficient. Inefficient domestic industries received excessive protection; trade and fiscal policies designed to promote industrialization often harmed agricultural exports; and the income gap widened both between the urban and rural populations and between skilled and unskilled urban workers.

Mexico illustrates both the initial accomplishments and the subsequent weaknesses of statism in the region. From the mid-1930s to 1970, the national government supplied 35–40 percent of the country's total capital investment.[12] At the same time, the state-owned petroleum and railroad enterprises offered private industry subsidized energy and transportation by selling them below their free-market values. Government trade and labor policies protected Mexican companies from foreign competition and held down domestic wages as a means of stimulating domestic investment. As a consequence, between 1935 and 1970, industrial output grew at an average annual rate of nearly 10 percent, and GNP rose 6 percent annually, making Mexico one of the world's fastest growing economies at that time.[13] During the 1970s and early 1980s, however, the state's role in the economy spiraled out of control. By 1985, the government operated nearly 1,200 state enterprises (**parastatals**) involved in everything from petroleum drilling to food sales. At the same time, however, even during this era of enormous economic growth, Mexico's "economic miracle" left the rural population and the urban poor behind, creating a highly unequal distribution of income and leaving substantial pockets of poverty.

Finally, when the state petroleum monopoly (PEMEX) discovered vast new oil reserves in the 1970s at a time that the world price of petroleum was tripling, the government saw an opportunity to use this bonanza to help the poor. At the same time, however, more powerful groups also lobbied for their share in the form of greater consumer subsidies, increased state support for private industry, and new jobs in the parastatals. Soon, spiraling government expenditures exceeded new oil revenues, thereby contributing to huge budget deficits and enormous foreign indebtedness.

Overall, Latin America's development model introduced two important areas of inefficiency, both of which typify state-led industrial growth elsewhere in the developing world. First, a large number of state-owned enterprises were overstaffed and poorly run. Contrary to the common stereotype, state enterprises are not inherently inefficient. In advanced industrialized nations such as France and Norway, governments have operated some enterprises quite effectively. But few Third World governments have the skilled and disciplined personnel needed to perform at that level. Furthermore, given the high rate of unemployment in almost all the LDCs, their governments are under great political pressure to hire more employees, whether the state enterprises need them or not. Consequently, parastatals are typically substantially overstaffed, with many employees who do little or nothing.[14] At the same time, labor unions and middle-class groups also lobby state enterprises to sell the public consumer goods and services at highly discounted prices. For example, in the past Argentineans rode the state railroads for a nominal fee and received highly subsidized electricity in their homes. Elsewhere in the region, governments have subsidized or controlled prices for items such as gasoline, urban bus fares, and food. Ultimately, the combination of money-losing parastatals, consumer subsidies, and subsidies to private-sector producers helped bankrupt most Latin American governments. By 1982, virtually every government in the region was deeply in debt and experiencing severe fiscal problems.

A second important weakness of Latin America's development model was the inefficiency ISI policies encouraged in the private sector. To be sure, governments throughout the world have effectively used protectionist measures to help infant industries get started during the early stages of development. Typically, in the ISI model, the state creates a wall of high import tariffs and quotas to protect emerging local manufacturers from foreign competition. But over time, the government needs to scale back the level of protection or else domestic firms will have little incentive to become more efficient and internationally competitive. Instead, Latin American protectionism, rather than serving as a temporary stimulus, became embedded in the economy.

From the early 1980s to the mid-1990s, the region's severe debt crisis and economic depression compelled almost all Latin American nations to reverse their statist economic policies. In Mexico, the de la Madrid and Salinas administrations (1982–1994) closed or privatized more than 80 percent of the country's 1,155 state enterprises, including the national airline, telephone companies, and banks.[15] In Chile, the transition to a slimmed-down state began during the dictatorship of General Augusto Pinochet (1973–1990). But when democracy was finally restored, the new governing coalition (led first by two Christian Democratic presidents and subsequently by two Socialist party administrations) continued many of Pinochet's economic policies, which they had once denounced.

While these reductions in public-sector activity were usually necessary, they also carried a great human cost. Throughout Latin America in the 1980s and early 1990s, millions of public- and private-sector workers lost their jobs, and as the new owners of privatized parastatals fired "excess workers," as the region suffered its most serious economic recession since the 1930s. Many other state-owned, money-losing plants simply shut down. In Mexico, for example, the government's economic restructuring program eliminated an estimated 400,000 jobs. More than half the workers formerly employed in state steel mills were laid off when their companies were privatized.[16] Argentina, Chile, Peru, and Venezuela experienced similar layoffs. At the same time, reduced protectionism in much of the region opened the door to a surge of imported consumer goods, further slashing sales and jobs in domestic firms that were unable to compete. Finally, the reduction or elimination of government consumer subsidies sharply increased the cost of basic necessities including bread, milk, and other foods.

In Mexico and Argentina, just as in Chile, populist and leftist parties that had once been the leading advocates of government economic intervention reluctantly conceded that the state sector had grown too unwieldy and needed to be cut back. Excessive government spending coupled with the middle and upper classes' failure to pay their fair share of taxes had resulted in massive fiscal deficits and runaway inflation. Only by substantially cutting budgetary deficits since the 1980s have Latin America's governments been able to control inflation that had reached annual rates of 1,000–10,000 percent in Argentina, Brazil, Nicaragua, and Peru. The debt crisis and the related economic recession contributed to a sharp decline in Latin American living standards from the early 1980s to the early 1990s (the "lost decade"). In Peru and Venezuela, for example, **real incomes** fell by nearly 40 percent.[17] Beginning in the mid-1990s, the region experienced a gradual economic recovery. Most importantly, inflation rates, which had frequently reached 100 percent annually or higher, were brought under control. Economic growth picked up, but was somewhat sluggish and irregular in certain countries. During the 1990s, the region's GDP increased at an annual rate of 3.3 percent, nearly twice what it had been in the 1980s but far below its rate in the 1970s and substantially below the average for the Third World in the 1990s.[18] Living standards only recovered slowly and, as elsewhere, economic growth once again has been brought to a halt since the current economic crisis began in 2008. Thus, while most analysts agree that Latin America's level of state economic interventionism and protectionism had been excessive, neoliberal reforms designed to scale down government have generally failed to improve living standards, other than in Chile.

East Asia's Developmental State

While many Latin American economies have been struggling since the early 1980s, a number of Asian economies have grown at a phenomenal rate for most of the past 30 years. South Korea, Taiwan, Hong Kong, Singapore, and China have received the most attention. More recently, India has made tremendous strides. Their impact on world trade has been enormous. China is now the world's leading exporter of manufactured goods. In 2008, it was the leading source of U.S. imports and the third largest destination for American exports. But several Southeast Asian economies—Thailand, Malaysia, and Indonesia—have also grown dramatically. From the mid-1960s until the region's financial crisis in 1997–1998, Taiwan, South Korea, Singapore, Hong Kong, Thailand, Malaysia, Indonesia, and China all grew at annual rates ranging from 4 to 10 percent, and China and South Korea sometimes exceeded 10 percent.[19] In fact, from 1960 to the late 1990s, these economies grew almost three times as fast as Latin America's and five times as fast as sub-Saharan Africa's.[20] While a number of East and Southeast Asian economies suffered serious setbacks during the late 1990s crisis, they quickly resumed rapid development. Moreover, the benefits of East and Southeast Asia's rapid growth have been distributed relatively equitably, with a far narrower gap between the rich and poor than in Latin America or Africa.

With the partial exception of Communist China and Vietnam (which have mixed socialist and free-market economies and, therefore, lie outside the "East Asian model"), most East and Southeast Asian countries have tied their growth to the free market. More than in other Third World regions, the private sector has controlled most of the economy, with a relatively small state sector. Not surprisingly, this has led conservative economists to hail the East Asian economic miracle as a triumph of unfettered capitalism, a testimony to keeping government out of the economy.[21]

But many East Asian specialists insist that, on the contrary, governments in that region were key players in stimulating economic growth.[22] Examining the causes of Japan's spectacular postwar economic resurgence, Chalmers Johnson first formulated the notion of the *developmental state*.[23] We can best understand the meaning of that term by comparing the role of government in East Asia's high-growth capitalist nations (including Japan, South Korea, Singapore, and Taiwan) to its function in Western nations during their initial industrial expansions some 150 years earlier. At that time, Western nations created *regulatory states* in which "government refrained from interfering in the marketplace, except to insure certain limited goals" (e.g., banking regulation). In contrast, the East Asian developmental states "intervene actively in the economy in order to guide or promote particular substantive goals" (e.g., full employment, export competitiveness, energy self-sufficiency).[24]

Japan's powerful Ministry of International Trade and Industry (MITI), Johnson notes, directed that country's postwar industrial resurgence. Subsequently, South Korea, Taiwan, Singapore, Indonesia, and other industrializing nations in East and Southeast Asia adopted many features of Japan's state-guided capitalist development model.[25] Typically, each country had a powerful government ministry or agency "charged with the task of planning, guiding, and coordinating industrial policies."[26] They included South Korea's Economic Planning Board, Taiwan's Council for Economic Planning and Development, and Singapore's Economic Development Board, all modeled after MITI. Under the developmental state, their government economic intervention was far more extensive and direct than in the West, targeting entire economic sectors (such as agriculture or industry), whole industries (such as computers, software, and automobiles), and particular companies (such as South Korea's Hyundai).

All of the developmental states did not pursue identical policies. For example, the bonds between government and big business have been tighter in South Korea than in Taiwan, while state enterprises were more important in Taiwan than in Korea. In Singapore, government control over labor has been more comprehensive than in the other two countries.[27] But in all of them, the state played an important role, guiding the private sector toward targeted economic activities and stimulating growth in areas that the government wished to expand. Sometimes, government planners have even pressured particular industries or companies to specialize in certain products and abandon others.

For example, when the South Korean and Taiwanese governments wished to develop the electronics and computer industries, they intervened aggressively, rather than leaving it to the marketplace. They established relevant research institutes; granted firms in targeted industries preferential access to credit; temporarily required companies that had been importing those targeted products to switch to domestic manufacturers; and offered trade protection to new industries for limited periods of time. South Korea temporarily banned all imports of computers when it promoted that industry, and Taiwan did the same for textiles.[28]

While the East Asian development model's tremendous success has earned it widespread admiration, some observers have remained skeptical about its applicability elsewhere. One concern is the model's apparent political requirements. Chalmers Johnson notes that most developmental states have been authoritarian—or what he calls "soft authoritarian"—during their major industrialization push. Authoritarian rule allowed government to repress or control labor unions and to direct management. Taiwan, South Korea, and Indonesia all industrialized under authoritarian governments, though all have subsequently democratized. The governments of Malaysia and Singapore continue to repress democratic expression in varying degrees. Hence, there is some doubt about how the developmental state would perform under the democratic pressures now spreading across the Third World.

Another important question is the transferability of East Asian political and economic institutions and policies to other parts of the Third World. The developmental state seems to require qualities that are in short supply in other developing areas: a highly skilled government bureaucracy and close cooperation between business, labor, and agriculture. In Indonesia, for example, a team of government economists known as "the Berkeley Boys" (most of them holding doctoral degrees from the University of California at Berkeley) oversaw that country's economic development. South Korea's highly trained state technocrats worked closely with the country's all-powerful business conglomerates (*chaebols*), such as Hyundai and Samsung. Similar cooperation between sophisticated government planners and big business, along with a relatively docile working class, contributed to economic surges elsewhere in East and Southeast Asia. Outside of Asia, however, only Chile's "Chicago Boys" (economists trained at the University of Chicago) brought a comparable set of skills and enjoyed similar support from government and the business community.

While it is possible that the model will eventually spread, few African, Latin American, or Middle Eastern nations currently offer promising conditions for its use. Furthermore, current free-trade regulations and neoliberal prescriptions from the World Trade Organization (WTO) mean that future Third World industrial development will probably involve less state intervention than in the initial Japanese model.

The Neoclassical Ideal

Quite unlike the preceding models, the neoclassical (or neoliberal) ideal assigns government a very limited economic role.* The state, it argues, should provide certain fundamental "public goods" such as national defense, police protection, a judicial system, and an educational system. It may also supply a physical infrastructure, including sewers and harbors, when it is not feasible for private

---

* Neoclassical economics is a revised formulation of Adam Smith's "classical" economic approach.

capital to do so. And perhaps it should allocate some resources to meet the most basic needs of the very poor. But neoclassical economists believe that most Third World governments have injured their economies by moving far beyond that limited role. These critics attribute past Africa's and Latin America's economic development problems to excessive state intervention, while they credit East and Southeast Asia's success to their governments' allegedly limited role.

They insist that free-market forces should determine production decisions and set prices free of government interference. Consequently, they condemn state policies designed to stimulate industrial growth: protective tariffs and import quotas that restrict free trade and thereby drive up prices to the consumer; artificial currency exchange rates that distort the prices of exports and imports; state subsidies to producers and consumers; and government controls on prices and interest rates. All of these policies, they argue, distort the choices made by producers, consumers, and governments. Only when these artificial constraints are removed will the economy "get prices right" (by letting free-market forces determine them).

During the past two decades, the neoclassicists (also known as "neoliberals") have largely won the debate against advocates of extensive state intervention. As we have observed, governments throughout Africa and Latin America have **liberalized** their **economies** in recent years, deregulating the private sector, privatizing state enterprises, removing trade barriers, and freeing prices. They have reduced subsidies for industry and for consumers, often out of budgetary necessity. In part, these changes resulted from pressures on the LDCs exerted by international lending agencies—such as the World Bank and the International Monetary Fund (IMF)—and by the United States. But they have also sprung from the conviction of many Third World governments that earlier statist models have largely failed. Still, the growing consensus that government intervention had gotten out of hand does not mean that the neoclassical model has unequivocally triumphed. While conservative economists and politicians often depicted the East Asian economic miracle as proof positive of what free enterprise can do if government does not intervene in the economy, leading specialists on the region, such as Stephan Haggard and Alice H. Amsden, strongly disagree. They maintain that government intervention has been a fundamental ingredient of industrial growth in that region.[29] Far from "following the market," Robert Wade maintains, the East Asian developmental state has actively "governed the market."[30] So, while the neoclassicist's criticisms of statist policies often ring true, they seem to take their case too far when they claim that East Asian governments played a passive economic role.

In fact, the only East Asian economy that has almost fully conformed to the neoclassical model has been Hong Kong's. As the least regulated economy in the region, many free-market advocates cite it as a success story for unrestricted capitalism. But Hong Kong is such a unique case that it may not be a model that can be emulated in other countries. For one thing, it is largely a city-state with virtually no rural population. Like Singapore, and unlike most LDCs, it has not needed to deal with significant rural poverty and its daunting associated problems. Initially, Hong Kong's wealth derived from its location as a major port for Asian trade and an outpost of the British Empire (until 1997). Other developing nations obviously do not enjoy those benefits.

While analysts continue to disagree on the broader economic effects of neoliberalism, the evidence seems to indicate that reducing government intervention has usually stimulated economic growth, particularly in economies that had earlier imposed extensive state intervention. For example, when India and Chile substantially reduced government's economic role, both embarked on a period of rapid growth. At the same time, however, unfettered capitalist growth often has benefited only a portion of the population, leaving the poor behind. India illustrates this point well. The changeover to a predominantly free-market economy turned that nation into the world's second fastest growing major economy (after China), averaging about 8 percent annually in recent years. Yet, so far, less than one-third of the population has benefited from that growth—essentially city dwellers employed in the modern economy, especially the expanding middle class. To be sure, those beneficiaries constitute some 350 million people, certainly no small accomplishment. But, nearly two-thirds of the country's population—primarily the barely educated rural poor—have gained little or nothing from the boom. Many of the country's most rapidly expanding industries are in the high-tech or tech-support sectors, which primarily hire people with more advanced educations. Furthermore, many of the other new industries (such as auto manufacturing) are capital-intensive and generate comparatively few jobs. Thus, despite India's rapid economic growth, a 2006 government health survey revealed that 46 percent of the country's children were malnourished, essentially unchanged from the proportion in 1999 (47 percent). That level of childhood malnutrition is about the same as impoverished Bangladesh and Burkina Faso and over five times as high as in China. Indeed, some 2.5 million Indian children die of disease or malnutrition each year.[31]

Argentina has had a more irregular pattern of economic growth since it introduced neoliberal reforms in the late 1980s. At first, these changes ushered in a period of strong economic growth. However, the economy veered downward in the late 1990s and the country suffered a severe economic and political crisis in the last days of 2001. Yet, after just a few years of decline, the economy rebounded strongly in 2003–2006, with the highest growth rate in Latin America (about 8 percent annually). Still, as in India, the benefits of that growth have not reached a large portion of the population, and neoliberal reforms dismantled many of the country's extensive welfare programs. Argentina had long enjoyed one of the most equitable income distributions in Latin America. In the mid-1970s, the most prosperous 10 percent of the population had incomes that were, on average, 12 times higher than the poorest 10 percent. By the mid-1990s, following neoliberal restructuring, that ratio had risen to 18 to 1, and by 2002, the richest portion of the population earned 43 times as much as the poorest 10 percent.[32]

In addition to its tendency to widen income inequality, neoclassical economics has been strongly criticized by environmentalists. From their perspective, even a modified policy of laissez faire that acknowledges some state responsibility for the environment, is inadequate. As Richard Albin notes,

> The idea that private interest, operating within unfettered markets, will tend to produce a close approximation of the socially optimal allocation of resources, was close to the truth when output (population, too) was so much smaller.[33]

But, he argues, as the world's population and associated pollution have reached dangerous levels, society can no longer afford to let free-market mechanisms allocate penalties for pollution. Such remedies would come far too late. Further discussion of economic growth and its impact on the environment follows later in this chapter.

Finding a Proper Role for the State

Political scientists and economists will continue to debate the state's proper role in Third World economies. As time goes on, new models will undoubtedly emerge. Still, some areas of agreement have emerged in recent decades. On the one hand, the level of government intervention in both command economies and Latin American statism was excessive. At the same time, the extremely limited government role advocated by the neoclassicists is unrealistic and inadequate in most countries. East Asia's developmental state model has been the most successful. But, it is unclear whether it can be replicated elsewhere. Indeed, a model that succeeds in one country or region will not necessarily work in another. Countries vary greatly in size, human capital, natural resources, and the like. Thus, cookbook formulas will probably be inadequate. As we have noted, the strong hand of the stereotypical developmentalist state—in Japan, South Korea, Singapore, and Taiwan—would have to be modified to meet current trade regulations under the WTO. Finally, new crises—such as the oil shocks of the 1970s and 2000s, the Latin American and African debt crises in the 1980s, the 1997–1998 Asian financial crisis, and international terrorism in the first decade of the twenty-first century— force planners to alter and adapt development models.

INDUSTRIALIZATION STRATEGIES

Since the time of Britain's industrial revolution, governments have equated industrialization with economic development, national sovereignty, and military strength. Latin America's largest countries launched their major industrialization drives in the 1930s. Following World War II, a number of newly independent Asian and African countries also developed their industrial capacities. Steel mills and auto plants became symbols of national prestige.

Neoclassical economists frequently criticized industrialization programs in many LDCs, arguing that every country should specialize in economic activities for which it has a "comparative advantage." That is, it should produce and export those goods it can provide most efficiently and cheaply relative to other nations. Based on that argument, neoclassicists maintained that most Third World nations should abandon plans for industrialization and concentrate, instead, on the production and export of raw materials or agricultural products.[34] Rather than manufacture goods such as cars, washing machines, or fertilizers, they insisted, countries such as Sri Lanka or Kenya would be better off increasing tea or coffee exports, products for which they have a comparative advantage, so that they could use the additional earnings to import manufactured products. Similarly, they contended that it made little sense for Nigeria to build steel mills or for Uruguay to produce refrigerators. Still, many LDCs have been reluctant to depend fully on revenues from the export of "primary goods," in part because agricultural and raw-material prices are so volatile. One possible solution (easier said than done) is to pursue balanced growth, including some industrial development (presumably manufacturing products such as Indonesian wicker furniture, which draw on local natural resources and can be exported), while still stressing primary goods production for export.

Until now, industrializing nations have generally pursued one of two alternative strategies: import-substituting industrialization (ISI) and **export-oriented industrialization (EOI)**. In the first case, as we have seen, LDCs try to reduce their dependency on manufactured imports by producing more goods, especially consumer goods, at home. Similar to Latin America, Asian nations began industrialization by producing for their own consumption. But, unlike Latin American ISI, which focused on consumer goods for the home market, East Asian nations soon turned to EOI, linking their industrial development to manufactured exports. Although EOI has been most closely associated with East and Southeast Asia, it is a strategy now widely embraced in Latin America and other parts of the Third World as well. Having started that strategy later, Latin America and other developing areas have yet to catch up with Asia's export capabilities. Consequently, shirts, blouses, electronics, and running shoes sold in Western department stores are more likely to be manufactured in Singapore, Sri Lanka, Indonesia, or Thailand than in Honduras, Brazil, or Colombia.

Import-Substituting Industrialization

National economic policies are partly the product of deliberate choice and partly the result of political and socioeconomic opportunities and constraints. As we have seen, ISI emerged as a development strategy in Latin America during the 1930s as the worldwide depression sharply reduced international trade. Because the industrialized nations of North America and Europe reduced their purchases of Third World primary goods (Uruguayan wool, Argentine beef, and Brazilian coffee, for example), Latin American nations no longer were able to earn enough foreign exchange to import the manufactured products that they needed. So, the region's early industrialization was designed, in part, to produce consumer goods that Latin American countries could no longer afford to import. But although ISI began as a response to an international economic crisis, economic planners subsequently transformed it into a long-term strategy for industrial development. With substantial unemployment at home and an urban population pressing for economic growth, government leaders faced a political imperative to industrialize. Nationalist presidents such as Argentina's Juan Perón and Brazil's Getúlio Vargas forged populist political coalitions of industrialists, blue-collar workers, and the urban middle class, all committed to industrialization.

As we have seen, Latin American governments imposed quotas and tariffs on foreign *consumer* goods in order to protect emerging domestic industries from international competition. But, planners also wanted to facilitate certain other types of imports, namely capital equipment (primarily machinery) and raw materials that domestic manufacturers needed. To reduce the cost of those imports, governments often overvalued their own currencies. Eventually, most Latin American countries established multiple currency exchange rates, with differing rates for transactions tied to imports, exports, and other financial activities.

To further encourage industrial development, governments also offered domestic industrialists tax incentives, low-interest loans, and direct subsidies.[35]

Because of ISI's impressive record in Latin America from the 1940s into the 1970s, the strategy was emulated in many parts of Africa and Asia, sometimes with comparable success. Turkey, for example, enjoyed strong ISI growth before shifting to EOI during the 1980s.[36] Even East Asia began its industrial development using ISI. By the 1970s, however, the ISI strategy was undermining Latin America's economies. As John Sheahan notes, "It fostered production methods adverse for employment, hurt the poor, blocked the possible growth of industrial exports, [and] encouraged high-cost consumer goods industries."[37]

To understand how poorly Latin America's **newly industrialized countries** (**NICs**) fared in international trade compared to East Asian NICs, it is useful to compare Mexico (one of Latin America's major industrial powers) with East Asia's "four little tigers" (South Korea, Taiwan, Hong Kong, and Singapore). Mexico has a substantially larger population than the four Asian countries combined. It also has a considerable geographic advantage over them in the export market, being located thousands of miles closer to the United States, the world's largest importer, and closer to Western Europe. Yet, as of the mid-1980s (prior to the North American Free Trade Agreement, NAFTA), the combined value of *manufactured* exports of the four little tigers was 20 times higher than Mexico's at that time (since then the gap has narrowed somewhat).[38]

In many Latin American countries, export taxes and overvalued currencies put traditional primary goods exporters (agricultural products and minerals) at a competitive disadvantage, thereby depriving the country of needed foreign exchange income. At the same time, because local consumer-goods industries could import their needed capital goods (machinery and other manufactured products used to manufacture other goods) cheaply, the region never developed its own capital-goods industry and, instead, imported manufacturing technologies that were inappropriate to local needs. Subsidized imports of machinery and heavy equipment encouraged capital-intensive production (i.e., using relatively advanced technologies and machinery while employing fewer workers) rather than the labor-intensive production that predominated in Asia. The ISI model of industrialization benefited a small, relatively well-paid "labor elite" (i.e., skilled, unionized workers employed in highly mechanized factories). But it failed to provide enough jobs for the region's workforce, leaving too many Latin Americans unemployed and underemployed.

Ironically, although ISI was originally designed to make Latin America more economically independent, in the end it merely replaced dependence on consumer-goods imports with dependence on imported capital goods, foreign technologies, and credit. Traditional primary exports languished, while the government did little to develop new manufactured exports. Increased balance of trade deficits contributed to Latin America's spiraling foreign debt, leading eventually to a major debt crisis and a severe economic recession in the 1980s.[39] That crisis, in stark contrast to East Asia's rapid growth at that time, induced Latin American governments to abandon their inwardly oriented economic policies as they tried to emulate East Asia's export-driven model. The NAFTA treaty between Mexico, Canada, and the United States is the most dramatic manifestation of that region's move toward (EOI). Since that time, Latin American nations have established several regional trade associations, including Mercosur (involving two economic powers—Brazil and Argentina—and two smaller South American countries) and the Latin American Integration Association (LAIA). Chile, once among the most inward-looking economies in the hemisphere, has been at the forefront of export production and free trade, giving it the highest economic growth rate in the region in recent decades.

Export-Oriented Industrialization

East Asia's NICs began their industrialization drive through import substitution, just as their Latin American counterparts had done years earlier. Soon, however, they diversified into manufacturing for export. As governments phased out their early protectionist measures, they forced local companies to become more competitive in the world market. State planners shaped the market, pressuring industries and offering them incentives to export. By 1980, manufactured goods constituted more than 90 percent of all South Korean and Taiwanese exports but represented only 15 percent of Mexico's and 39 percent of Brazil's.[40] Fueled by their dynamic industrial export sectors, East Asia's booming economies became the envy of the developing world. More recently, India has enjoyed impressive growth based on the export of services as well as manufactured goods.

There are a number of reasons why East Asia decided to stress manufactured exports early in its industrialization drive, while Latin America failed to do so for decades. For one thing, East Asian industrialization began in a period of unprecedented expansion in world trade, inspired by the West's enormous postwar economic boom (from the mid-1940s through early1970s) and the broad assault on global trade barriers in the years following the General Agreement on Trade and Tariffs in 1947 (GATT)*. The opportunities offered by outward-oriented growth were obvious to Asian policy makers in the 1960s. Conversely, the expansion of Latin American industrialization started during the Great Depression of the 1930s, a period of greatly restricted world trade. Indeed, it was their very inability to export traditional products at that time that inspired Latin American nations to turn initially to ISI. In retrospect, Latin America should have moved to EOI after World War II, but ISI seemed to be working so well until the 1980s that there was little incentive to change. Ironically, another reason why East and Southeast Asian countries chose EOI was that their economic opportunities seemed more limited than Latin America's. Because of their smaller populations, Hong Kong, Singapore, and Taiwan (though not South Korea) did not believe that ISI, which relied upon the domestic market, was a feasible strategy for them as it had been for larger countries such as Mexico, Argentina, Brazil, and Colombia. Furthermore, with fewer agricultural goods or raw materials to export, East Asians turned their weakness into a strength by emphasizing manufactured exports.

---

* In 1995, the World Trade Organization (WTO) replaced the GATT.

GROWTH WITH EQUITY

Until this point, our discussion has focused on the size of the national economy. Indeed, production is the primary measure of economic development used in popular and scholarly analysis. Typically, a country is thought to be performing well when its GDP (or its GNP) is growing rapidly. Economists focus less frequently on how equitably that growth is distributed. It is to that important dimension that we now turn.

Early debate on Third World development often pitted mainstream social scientists against left-of-center scholars, with the first group primarily interested in the prerequisites of growth and the second focusing on the fairness of economic distribution. For example, while many mainstream economists were impressed with Brazil's rapid economic expansion in the late 1960s and early 1970s, critics pointed out that the country's extremely unequal income distribution meant that few benefits of rapid growth reached the poorest half of the population. On the other hand, although Cuba's income redistribution policies and social welfare programs favorably impressed left-leaning economists, conservative critics pointed to its weak economic growth since the late 1960s.

Many market-oriented economists insist that increased inequality is unavoidable, indeed desirable, in the early stages of economic development in order to concentrate capital in the hands of entrepreneurs, who can then invest more in the economy, expand their enterprises, and create jobs. Their critics countered that development of that sort did little to help the majority of the people. In many developing nations, they maintained, the bottom half of the population would benefit more from meaningful redistribution of wealth and income, even with little growth, than from strong economic growth without redistribution.[41]

In time, however, analysts of varying ideological persuasions have concluded that there is no intrinsic contradiction between these two goals. In fact, a proper development strategy entails "growth with equity." One study indicates that since the 1960s, countries with higher income equality have developed faster than those with highly concentrated patterns. East Asia's economic takeoff since the 1970s and 1980s demonstrates that point. For example, Taiwan and South Korea have coupled spectacular economic growth rates with relatively equitable income distributions.[42] Indeed, widely based purchasing power in both those countries has helped stimulate their economic growth. In South Korea, almost all peasant families own television sets, a feat hardly conceivable in Africa or Latin America. During the Korean television industry's takeoff, these domestic purchases supplemented exports in stimulating that industry's growth.

What accounts for the higher level of economic equality in East Asia compared to Africa or Latin America? One important factor is the pattern of land distribution in the countryside. For a number of reasons, farmland has historically been more equitably distributed in Asia (especially East Asia) than in Latin America. While the size of Latin America's largest landholdings has declined in recent decades, estates of several thousand acres still exist and were common in the recent past. Today, large landowners still dominate the countryside in nations such as Brazil and Colombia (see Chapter 6). While the largest farms in Africa are not nearly as big, landownership is still very concentrated in countries such as South Africa, Kenya, and Ethiopia. On the other hand, the largest holdings in Asia, where there is much heavier population pressure, are rarely more than one or two hundred acres and they are far smaller in countries such as South Korea.

Landholding patterns reflect both historical legacies and contemporary government policies. Spanish colonialism established an agrarian structure in Latin America and the Philippines dominated by *latifundia* (large estates). In Africa, landholding is most concentrated in countries that had substantial numbers of White settlers (who carved out large agricultural estates) during their colonial period. These include Kenya, Mozambique, Namibia, and Zimbabwe. On the other hand, Japanese colonial authorities in Korea and Taiwan encouraged smallholder farming. Although European colonial regimes established large export-oriented plantations in Southeast Asia, landownership there was still never as concentrated as in Latin America. It is surely not coincidental that the Philippines, the only country in East Asia to share Latin America's Spanish colonial heritage, also has the region's most concentrated land and income distribution. In the postcolonial period, South Korean and Taiwanese agrarian reform programs led to even more egalitarian land distribution in those countries, just as the American-imposed reform had done in Japan after the war. By reducing rural poverty, land reform contributed to greater income equality (see Chapter 6).

Another major component of national income distribution is the relationship between rural and urban living standards. Although city dwellers enjoy higher incomes and greater social services throughout the Third World, the urban–rural gap is particularly marked in Africa and Latin America. Residents of Mexico City, for example, have incomes averaging four to five times higher than those in the countryside. There are many reasons for such discrepancies, but government policy often plays an important role. In Chapter 6, we noted that, until recently, governments in both regions generally kept the prices of basic food crops below their market value in order to provide their urban political constituencies with cheap food.[43] By contrast, East Asian farmers generally have received the free-market price for their crops or even obtained subsidized prices above market value.

Industrial policy also affects income distribution. Latin America's ISI strategy encouraged the importation of capital equipment for domestic industries. Such capital-intensive development created many relatively skilled and well-paid industrial jobs, but left behind a far larger number of poorly paid, "unskilled" urban workers and rural peasants. Conversely, East and Southeast Asia's EOI strategy benefited from the region's large labor force, thereby producing a great number of low-wage jobs in emerging industries.

By initially using labor-intensive methods that utilized their pools of cheap labor, Hong Kong, Taiwan, and South Korea successfully exported cheap low-tech goods such as textiles, toys, and footwear. Over time, as these industries needed increasing numbers of workers, two changes took place. First, greater demand for labor in these low-end export industries caused factory wages to rise; second, rural-to-urban migrants seeking factory jobs reduced the supply of rural labor, thereby driving up wages for farmworkers in the countryside. What had begun as a policy exploiting cheap labor eventually promoted economic growth, higher wages, and greater income equality.[44] As factory wages rose substantially in the four little tigers, those countries shifted from low-tech manufactured products to more sophisticated exports such as electronics, commercial services (most notably in Singapore), computer software, computers, and automobiles (South Korea). Production of apparel and other low-wage items passed to lower-income Asian nations such as Malaysia, Thailand, Indonesia, Bangladesh, and Sri Lanka. China, which first became an industrial giant by manufacturing low-priced consumer goods and parts for foreign brands, is now also producing higher-end products, including some under Chinese brand names.

ECONOMIC DEVELOPMENT AND THE ENVIRONMENT

Throughout the world, economic development has inevitably caused environmental degradation. For example, prior to European settlement, the East Coast of the United States was covered with thick forest. Since then, increased human population, urban sprawl, and farming have destroyed almost all of that growth. Today, industrial and auto pollution in the United States and Europe contaminate the surrounding air and water, sometimes affecting areas thousands of miles away. In the LDCs, rapid population growth, natural-resource extraction, and industrialization have also brought substantial environmental decay. In Indonesia, for example, foreign-owned mines and logging firms have dumped health-threatening waste into nearby water systems and harvested vast tracks of jungle timber, bringing birth defects (in mining areas) and flooding (in timber regions) in their wake. Massive dams in China flood archeological treasures, farmland, and vacated villages. Since the 1970s, environmental groups in advanced industrialized nations have questioned the trade-offs between economic growth and the conservation of natural resources. Most ominously, the consequences of global warming may soon threaten living standards and lives throughout the world. Some of the more radical environmentalists in the United States and Europe have proposed zero-growth strategies for highly industrialized nations. That could require limiting population growth (already on the decline in those countries) and creating a less consumer-oriented society.

But the option of zero growth, or even of reduced economic growth, which has never attracted significant support in the developed world, is totally unacceptable in the Third World. In countries such as Bangladesh, Brazil, Egypt, Indonesia, and Nigeria, where a substantial portion of the population lives in abject poverty, it would be politically suicidal and ethically questionable for government leaders to propose limiting economic growth. Unless and until the environmental consequences of economic growth can be mitigated, the trade-off between growth and environmental decay presents a horrible ethical dilemma. It would be unconscionable to tell poor Pakistanis or Ethiopians that they should not hope for a higher standard of living. But barring major technological and political breakthroughs, achieving an acceptable standard of living for all Third World people could easily overtax the planet's resources.

Moreover, environmental regulations and controls are generally far weaker in the LDCs, because of their urgent desire for economic growth and because their "green" (ecology) movements developed much later than in the West and lack the political influence of their American and European counterparts. Moreover, LDCs often lack the government infrastructure to enforce environmental controls. Finally, polluting industries (both foreign and domestic) are often able to bribe public officials responsible for enforcing environmental laws.

The Costs of Growth

The world's industrialized nations continue to be the major consumers of natural resources, the leading polluters of air and water, and the greatest contributors to global warming, ozone-layer depletion, and other looming environmental disasters. Yet, ironically, it is those same developed countries that now insist that the LDCs become better environmental citizens. In response, Third World leaders often point out that the United States, with only 4 percent of the world's population, annually consumes 20–25 percent of the planet's energy.[45] Hence, many of them bristle at the suggestion that developing nations make special efforts to protect the environment. Even so, because of their more fragile economic and ecological conditions, a number of Third World nations face daunting environmental challenges. In African countries such as Sudan, Nigeria, and Burkina Faso, wood fires produce 75 percent or more of all energy, forcing peasants hungry for firewood to deplete the forests. Each year, rich cattle ranchers and poor peasants in Brazil both burn vast areas of the Amazonian jungle (about equal to the size of the state of New Jersey) to clear the land for agricultural production. In Malaysia and Indonesia, Japanese-owned logging firms cut down large tracts of rainforest. Since 1947, as much as 50 percent of the earth's tropical rainforests may have been destroyed, largely by slash-and-burn, peasant farming, expansion of plantations (especially palm-oil), logging, and cattle ranching. As a consequence, in places such as Central America, Indonesia, and sub-Saharan Africa, rains and waterways wash off topsoil, rainfall patterns shift, and both droughts and floods occur more frequently. In many parts of the developing world, the arable land area is declining and deserts are growing.

Third World cities such as Shanghai, Cairo, New Delhi, Nairobi, and São Paulo have grown tremendously in recent decades (Chapter 7), producing enormous quantities of raw sewage, auto emissions, and industrial waste. As cars and buses (most without proper emission controls) choke the streets, air quality rapidly deteriorates. Elsewhere, mines, oil fields, chemical plants, and factories, operating with few environmental safeguards, pollute their surroundings. The consequences for local populations are often tragic—including infections, respiratory illnesses, birth defects, and loss of farmland. Other environmental costs—such as destruction of rainforests, which further contributes to global warming—have consequences that extend far beyond the Third World.

Environmental Decay as a Third World Problem

The difficult trade-off between economic growth and environmental conservation is probably most starkly illustrated in China, the world's fastest growing economy and home to more than one-fifth of the earth's population. From the time that its government introduced free-market economic reforms in the 1980s through the current world economic crisis, that country enjoyed the world's highest rate of economic growth, averaging about 8 percent annually. Living standards have tripled, and millions of Chinese citizens have moved out of poverty. The number of people spared from hunger, disease, and early death is staggering. Balanced against those gains, however, are enormous increases in air and water pollution and extensive destruction of the country's farmland, raising the danger of future famine just when China has finally managed to feed its population adequately. Moreover, as the country has built an average of two new, coal-burning, electric-power plants annually, added over 6.5 million motor vehicles each year, and vastly expanded its industrial production, it has surpassed the United States as the world's largest producer of greenhouse gases (carbon dioxide (CO_2) emissions that trap the earth's heat and contribute to global warming).[46]

Attracted by higher urban living standards, over 100 million Chinese peasants have migrated to the cities, often abandoning farms in productive agricultural regions. In addition, substantial quantities of farmland have been paved over for highways, factories, and urban sprawl. Since the late 1950s, the country's total arable land has decreased by somewhere between 15 and 55 percent (depending on what estimate one accepts), while the nation's population has grown by some 80 percent. Though China's rate of population growth is currently relatively low (1 percent annually), loss of farmland caused by economic development continues to accelerate at an alarming rate. So far, the country has averted hunger by farming the remaining land more intensively, and some recent grain harvests have reached record or near-record levels. But this intensive use of fertilizers and pesticides eventually depletes the soil, and a food crunch probably looms in the coming decades. As this enormous country needs to import increasing amounts of food, it will likely drive up prices of grains and other foods in the world market, with serious consequences for the poor throughout the Third World.

Third World Environmental Decay and Global Warming: A Global Problem

Not only does environmental degradation pose dangers to LDCs within their own borders, but they threaten developed countries as well. And, of course, the developed world's environmental sins similarly endanger the Third World. Of all the environmental threats currently facing the world, the most menacing is surely global warming. Although there are still some scientists who feel that the future risks of global warming have been exaggerated, there is now a general consensus within the scientific community and among most world leaders that the earth has been warming over the long term, that the causes are in large part man-made, and that the consequences will be horrendous if nothing is done to stop it. As Michael Klare has warned,

> In general, adverse effects from global warming will produce suffering on an unprecedented scale. Many will starve; many more will perish from disease, flooding, or fire. Others, however, will attempt to survive in the same manner as their predecessors: by fighting among themselves for whatever food and water remains; by invading more favorable locales; or by migrating to distant lands, even in the face of violent resistance.[47]

Specific environmental consequences of warming may include increased drought in some regions, more frequent floods in others, declining food production (though some areas may produce more), widespread hunger and starvation, intensified hurricane and typhoon activity, and flooding of coastal cities and low-lying rural areas. Many countries in Africa will be among the hardest hit because they already suffer from frequent drought and severe food shortages and have the fewest economic resources to address the problem. But many other regions of the Third World will also suffer because of their limited resources and the likelihood that global warming will hit countries closest to the equator most severely. Moreover, developed nations, suffering from their own diminished agricultural production, will not be in a position to send famine relief to Africa and Asia as they have done so often before.

While these outcomes are already widely discussed, Klare points to a number of less well-known consequences that threaten to create conflict and violence. Some severely affected nations will probably invade neighboring states that have more water or arable land, especially if they are stronger militarily than their more climatically fortunate neighbors. Somalia, Ethiopia, and Sudan have already fought wars linked to water and land rights. Similarly, within nations, regions or ethnic groups that are more adversely affected may attack their neighbors. In many of the most poverty-stricken countries, economic disasters and internal violence may cause states to fail, opening up the way for roving bands and militia, as has already happened in Somalia. Finally, the combination of hunger, warfare, and internal violence is almost certain to intensify population movement from stricken areas to more affluent ones, including intensified emigration from Africa to Western Europe and from Latin America to the United States and Canada.

For the most part, then, First World (developed) countries are the primary sources of global warming, while developing nations—particularly in Africa and Asia—potentially will be its greatest victim. At the same time, rapid industrialization in Asia and Latin America has sharply increased the Third World's share of greenhouse gas emissions in recent years. As noted previously, China has surged past the United States as the world's largest source of these gases, while India now ranks third. Those two nations correctly respond that, since each of them is home to more than 1 billion people, they each pollute far less than the United States on a per-capita basis. Still, the additional gases produced by these two industrial nations are cause for great concern. In the 15-year span between 1992 and 2007, emissions rose by nearly 40 percent worldwide. While emissions actually declined during that period by almost 2 percent among the Western European members of the European Union (its 15 earliest members) and grew by only 11 percent in Japan, emissions grew by 20 percent in the United States and jumped 103 percent in India and 150 percent in China.

THE SEARCH FOR SUSTAINABLE DEVELOPMENT

Discussion of the environmental consequences of economic growth often focuses on the objective of *sustainable development*, defined as economic development that "consumes resources to meet [this generation's] needs and aspirations in a way that does not compromise the ability of future generations to meet their needs."[48] Whenever feasible, it involves the use of *renewable resources* (such as wind and water power for generating electricity) in place of resources that cannot be replaced (e.g., coal and petroleum) or that are being consumed at a faster rate than they can be replaced (such as tropical rainforests and ocean fishing grounds). It also embraces consumption of resources in ways that least pollutes the environment: limiting auto and industrial emissions, finding sustainable substitutes for pesticides and other agricultural chemicals that pollute the soil and the water system, and reducing the use of products that destroy the world's ozone layer.

In theory, these are goals to which all nations—rich and poor alike—can aspire. Even so, developed and developing nations have debated which of them should take the lead and which should bear the greatest economic costs. At the groundbreaking 1992 United Nations Conference on Environment and Development (UNCED) in Rio de Janeiro—often called the first Earth Summit—signatories made a nonbinding commitment to reduce greenhouse gas emissions (caused by the burning of carbon-based fuels, including oil, natural gas, coal, and wood) by the year 2000 and developed an action plan for sustainable development into the twenty-first century. The Rio Declaration listed 27 guiding principles on the environment and development, including the LDCs' right to economic development and the alleviation of poverty. Still, tensions between the First and Third Worlds were obvious. As one analyst observed,

> At the Rio Summit, the conflicts between the rich and poor became evident. The Northern [industrialized] countries, which felt vulnerable to global environment problems such as climate change and biodiversity loss, attempted to extract commitments on environmental conservation from the South [LDCs]. However, the South, which felt more vulnerable to perceived underdevelopment, was concerned with extracting [economic] transfers from the North.[49]

The difficult trade-off between growth and environmental protection was vividly brought home to this author at a meeting in Jamaica with local social scientists. After one U.S. scholar stressed the importance of preserving the island's ecology, a Jamaican economist sarcastically replied, "You Americans raped your environment in order to develop your country and raise your standard of living. Now we Jamaicans reserve the right to do the same." While such feelings are counterproductive, they are understandable. Third World leaders note that the industrialized countries ask NICs such as China and Mexico to reduce smokestack emissions and beseech Thailand and Brazil to sustain their rainforests. But it is the First World nations that have wreaked the greatest havoc on the environment and have offered the developing nations little help to defray the costs of environmental controls.

U.S. policies have created further problems. During the 8 years of the George Bush administration (2001–2009), the U.S. government questioned whether there was actually a danger of global warming and rejected mandatory caps on greenhouse gas emissions. In 1997, worldwide negotiations had produced the Kyoto Protocol, which envisioned a global contract binding industrialized nations to reduce their emissions of six greenhouse gases by 2012 to 5.2 percent below their 1990 level. That would be 29 percent below what they had been expected to have reached without an accord. President Bill Clinton never submitted the Kyoto agreement to the U.S. Senate, which had made it clear that it would not ratify unless it imposed mandatory targets on developing nations as well. In 2001, 178 nations agreed in Bonn, Germany, to meet objections from Japan and other nations by modifying the Kyoto agreement so as to lower the targeted 5 percent reduction to only 2 percent. In spite of these modifications, the United States upset its allies in the European Union and much of the world community by announcing that it would not ratify the Kyoto treaty or the Bonn modifications. The Bush White House—supported by a large segment of the business community and Congressional Republicans—had two major objections to the treaty: first, the Protocol called for no reduction in greenhouse gas emissions in the developing nations (including high-growth countries in Asia); second, it believed that Kyoto's mandatory environmental targets would undermine American economic growth.

By insisting that it would only accept voluntary targets, the United States reinforced the Third World's belief that it was being held to a double standard when it came to making economic sacrifices for the environment. Most of the international community has been determined to pursue Kyoto's goals. However, because the United States accounts for 25 percent of all greenhouse emissions (the world's largest share at that time), its decision to pull out made it harder to reduce overall levels. In early 2005, following Russian ratification, the Kyoto accord went into effect without U.S. participation. The Protocol is due to expire in 2012 and the next United Nations Climate Change Conference is scheduled for the end of 2009 in Copenhagen, where delegates will try to negotiate a new treaty.

Some Signs of Progress

Despite these obstacles, there are some hopeful signs of progress. Today, there are few powerful voices in the United States or elsewhere denying the existence and threat of global warming. At the very least, the governments of developing countries and international development agencies have become more conscious of the growth-environmental trade-off. Together many of them have begun searching for ways to achieve development that reduces damage to the environment. Many LDCs that previously saw the green movement as a Western conspiracy to keep them underdeveloped have come to realize that sustainable development is in their own interest. Conversely, the world's most developed nations have generally acknowledged that, to date, they have contributed the most to global warming and other environmental dangers and that they will have to help less affluent nations pay the costs of future environmental protection.

Recently, the European Union and Japan have both taken new, more vigorous initiatives to reduce greenhouse gas emissions. In the United States, Barrack Obama took office having made a strong commitment during his campaign to reduce greenhouse gas emissions as well by offering government support for several initiatives, including the development of more fuel-efficient, cleaner-burning automobiles; and greater use of alternative sources of energy, such as wind and solar power. An administration energy bill currently before Congress would establish caps (limits) on a firm's CO_2 emissions and would allow companies which come in under their caps to trade (sell) their unused quotas to other companies that had exceeded their caps. The Obama administration has ruled out joining the Kyoto Protocol, arguing that the treaty will expire in only 3 years and it is far too late for the United States to reach its targets. The White House's goal is to cut American greenhouse gas emissions 17 percent by 2020, bringing it back to the 1990 level and to reduce emissions 80 percent by 2050. But the fate of Obama's energy bill (like many of his conservation proposals) remains very uncertain. There is considerable Congressional opposition to the proposed "Cap and Trade" provision of the bill, much of it coming from Congressmen (including some Democrats) who represent districts fearful of being hurt by it. At the same time, many European countries (particularly Germany) believe that even the White House's goals are too modest.

Ultimately, even if the LDCs applied strict environmental measures, they still would not fully reconcile the tension between economic growth and environmental protection. Furthermore, environmental controls are generally expensive and often reduce productivity. If the world's industrial powers want the LDCs to make such sacrifices, they will probably have to underwrite much of the cost. This might involve debt forgiveness, subsidized technology transfers, and direct grants.

Which of the economic models discussed earlier in this chapter is best equipped to handle the environmental challenge? The answer is not clear. It seems certain that preserving the environment requires significant state intervention. For example, since it is unrealistic to expect industrialists to monitor and control their own pollution or to hope that all drivers will voluntarily purchase fuel-efficient cars, most analysts feel that some government regulation is needed. Consequently, the neoclassical model, which severely limits government economic intervention and depends heavily on free-market mechanisms, seems ill-suited to protect the environment (though market mechanisms, such as a cap-and-trade legislation, can be very helpful).

In theory, command economies seem particularly well suited to defend the environment because the state controls the means of production and can self-regulate. In fact, however, communist governments from the Soviet Union and Poland to China and North Korea have had very poor environmental records. For one thing, directives to managers of state enterprises usually demand that they maximize production, with little thought given to environmental consequences. At the same time, absent a free society and a free mass media, citizens are unable to organize environmental pressure groups or even to know the extent of ecological destruction.* Thus, it appears that if developing nations are to have any chance at sustainable development, they must combine an honest, effective, and responsible state with a free democratic society where green activists can mobilize popular support.

---

* The Chinese government has become far more sensitive to environmental issues and sometimes responds to grassroots pressures in that area. But, it still has a long way to go.

FINDING THE RIGHT MIX

It has often been easier to recognize what has not worked in developing countries than to identify what has. The dependency theorists' assumption that economic development was only possible if LDCs reduced their ties to the capitalist core has been shattered by the success of East Asia's export-oriented growth and the failures of protectionism in Latin America. Similarly, command economies, while often able to reduce economic inequalities, generally have had poor records of economic growth and modernization after the early stages. The abject failure of North Korea's communist economy, in stark contrast to South Korea's prosperity, demonstrates that model's failures. And, China was able to stage its breath-taking economic expansion only after it had moved away from a command economy. On the other hand, the neoclassical minimal state can hardly address the deep inequities, societal cleavages, and looming ecological nightmares plaguing so many LDCs. The challenge for Third World economies is to establish a strong and effective, but not overbearing, state—one that can promote growth, equitable income distribution, and a healthy environment, while avoiding crony capitalism, political repression, and unwarranted interference in the market.

Many Third World countries have now embraced East Asia's export-oriented industrial model. Beyond the previously mentioned problem of transferability, however, there are at least two other fundamental concerns about universalizing the East Asian experience. The first concerns the extent to which the world economy can continue to absorb mounting industrial exports. East Asia launched its EOI strategy during a period of unparalleled economic expansion in the First World. International trade was expanding rapidly, and developed countries could absorb a rising tide of industrial exports. Since the 1970s, however, First World economic growth has slowed down due, in part, to factors such as spikes in energy costs (most notably in the 1970s and the past few years), the transfer of industrial jobs to the NICs and, perhaps, the psychological and economic effects of terrorism since 9/11. Even should the Japanese and Western European economies recover their former dynamism, some analysts question whether the international market can absorb an ever-enlarging flow of industrial exports, most notably from China, the world's emerging industrial giant, or whether a protectionist backlash from the First World might place a cap on imports.[50] Supporters of EOI counter that there is no sign of a looming ceiling on industrial imports, particularly since the larger NICs have become major importers themselves. The evidence so far suggests that LDCs hoping to industrialize need to develop some type of export sector and to participate actively in the global economy. But they would be wise to also diversify their economy and to build protections against the negative aspects of globalization. During the current economic crisis, countries that are very highly dependent on the global economy for trade and foreign investment have often been badly hurt.

The Effects of Globalization on Developing Nations

Perhaps the most important and hotly debated recent economic development affecting the entire Third World is known as "globalization." The mass media and social scientists both define globalization in related, but somewhat distinct ways.

In its most fundamental sense, the term refers to the increasing interdependence of national economies throughout the world. It is characterized by rising world trade in goods and services, increasing flows of cross-national finance (including banking, stock market transactions, and corporate acquisitions), greater legal and illegal, cross-national labor migration, accelerated international transfers of advanced technologies, expansion of MNCs, and mounting influence of major, global economic institutions such as the IMF, the World Bank, and the WTO. All of these changes enhance the interdependence of national economies. In short, globalization involves the free flow of information, goods, services, and capital across national borders. Beyond that, the term is often also understood to include the spread of culture, consumer tastes, and technology from the West (particularly the United States) to the rest of the world.

Scholarly debate over globalization has centered on several questions: Is this really a new phenomenon or merely a continuation of economic trends that have existed for centuries? If it is new, when did it begin? And, most importantly for our purposes, has globalization improved or harmed Third World economies? Some scholars who claim that globalization is not a particularly new or dramatic development actually trace the first wave of economic globalization back to the Roman Empire. Some date it to the rise and spread of Western European capitalism in the sixteenth century, while others trace it to the last decades of the nineteenth century.[51] Others question whether there is anything uniquely global about the present era, arguing that the present level of economic interdependence was matched or exceeded in earlier times. Thus, for example, the level of trade as a percentage of the world economy is no higher today than it was in the early years of the twentieth century.

Still, the speed and breadth of today's IT revolution has greatly accelerated the interconnectedness of national economies. The effects of debt default in Russia very quickly spill over to Argentina and Brazil. A sharp drop in China's stock market or a French investment bank's problems with U.S. subprime mortgages each brings down prices on the New York Stock Exchange later in the same day. To be sure, skeptics point out that the volume of world trade grew only modestly from 1980 to 2000. However, as we have seen, certain regions of the developing world—Asia and, to a lesser extent, Latin America—increased their manufactured exports substantially. Furthermore, *financial* globalization escalated dramatically during that period. For example, in the last two decades of the twentieth century, direct foreign investment rose by 250 percent worldwide and by 400 percent in the LDCs.[52] The daily turnover of international currency exchanges increased more than tenfold during that same 20-year period. Moreover, other indicators of globalization—such as the volume of foreign travel, international phone calls, and cross-border use of the Internet—have exploded. As one analyst has put it, recent globalization is fundamentally different from earlier forms of international trade and commerce because "national markets are *fused* transnationally rather than [merely] linked across borders."[53]

If we accept that globalization is an important and, in some respects, recent development, particularly as it affects LDCs, when did this process begin? Some analysts trace it to the resurgence of world trade after World War II. In the 1960s, the term *globalization* acquired its present meaning. But, it was in the 1970s and 1980s, aided by the IT revolution, that the process took off and it is since then that the phenomenon has become the focus of intense scrutiny by scholars, journalists, and political leaders.

Perhaps the most contentious debate regarding globalization deals with its economic consequences for the Third World. Neoliberals and other supporters of free trade often see globalization as a panacea, able to stimulate the economies of developed and developing nations alike. They point to the benefits that export-led growth has brought to East Asia, Chile, and, now, India. By allowing for the most rational allocations of investments, labor, and natural resources across national borders, they argue, globalization creates the most efficient and productive economic outcome. The IT revolution, for example, has permitted India's educated and technologically proficient middle class to provide tech support to the world. In books such as journalist Thomas Friedman's best-seller *The World Is Flat*, the optimists see globalization as a win-win situation for the developed and the developing worlds.[54]

Critics of globalization see its impact very differently. They view it as a force that has imposed greater Western economic control and cultural dominance over the Third World. Moreover, they insist, it has widened income gaps between the First and Third Worlds—as well as *within* the LDCs— caused environmental degradation, and extended poverty. One of the most influential analyses of that kind is Joseph Stiglitz's *Globalization and Its Discontents*.[55] Unlike many critics, Stiglitz—a Nobel-Prize-winning economist, former Chair of President Bill Clinton's Council of Economic Advisers, and former chief economist for the World Bank—is the most respectable of establishment figures. Yet, his book (and other works) severely criticizes the U.S. government, the World Bank, and, especially, the IMF for pressuring Third World governments to adopt free-trade and privatization policies that have inflicted substantial pain on their populations and made their economies more vulnerable to shifts in the global economy.

While we cannot explore all aspects of this debate, we will focus on what may be the most important question: Has recent globalization deepened or alleviated Third World poverty? Much of that discussion, in turn, has centered on the issue of economic equality and inequality: Has globalization intensified or reduced the economic gaps within individual LDCs and those between LDCs and the world's wealthier nations? There seems to be general agreement that between 1945 (when the latest wave of economic integration began) and 1980, the gap between rich and poor nations widened. Evidence since the 1980s, when globalization accelerated, suggests that this economic gap may have begun to narrow.

Supporters of globalization contend that rapid industrialization in countries such as China, India, South Korea, and Brazil, and expansion of the international service industry by countries such as India have allowed the LDCs, or at least some of them, to begin catching up with the industrialized world. Further examination, however, suggests a more complex picture. Since the 1970s, the income gap between the First and Third World has, indeed, narrowed. But that was entirely the consequence of East and Southeast Asia's economic surge. On the other hand, African and Latin American incomes have fallen further behind the developed world. Advocates of globalization point out that the countries in which living standards have most improved and where poverty has most sharply declined in the past two to three decades—including China, Chile, Indonesia, and

South Korea—are precisely the nations that are most intensely integrated into the global economy.* At the same time, the poorest nations in the world and those falling furthest behind are the countries of sub-Saharan Africa, which have the least globalized economies.

If we turn to the issue of inequality *within* developing nations, the evidence is somewhat ambiguous. As countries such as Chile and China have entered the global economy more intensely, the gap between their poor and the middle and upper classes has widened. Looking more systematically at data from 65 countries from 1995 to 2001, economist Almas Heshmati found that income inequality was somewhat greater in more globalized economies. But, he also observed that globalization was but *one* of many factors contributing to inequality, explaining only about 10 percent of the difference between nations.[56] Furthermore, depending on how they analyze the data, some economists have argued that income inequality has intensified as a result of globalization in recent decades, while others argue that it has diminished.[57] But, even if there were a consensus that inequality has increased, would that mean that standards of living for the poor are declining on an absolute basis (i.e., that the poor are getting poorer)? It might, but it could also mean that *all* Third World income groups have benefited from globalization but that the upper and middle classes have gained more than the poor have.

The most serious charge leveled against globalization is that it has intensified Third World poverty. Case studies describe Nike factories that pay their workers shockingly low wages (at least by Western standards) and peasants who were pushed off their land by foreign-owned plantations and logging operations. But, while case studies often provide useful insights, we cannot know how representative they are of the general population. That is, while a careful case study may demonstrate how MNCs reduced economic opportunities in Nuevo Laredo, Mexico, or how free trade impoverished sugar plantation workers in Malaysia, we do not know whether these situations are typical of Mexico or Malaysia, much less of the entire developing world, as a whole.

If, however, we examine more systematic statistics from the United Nations and the World Bank, we find that, contrary to globalization's critics, Third World poverty has actually *declined* significantly since globalization accelerated in the early 1980s. For example, according to World Bank statistics, the percentage of the LDCs' population living in "absolute poverty"—defined as those living on less than $1 per day (PPP)—fell from 40 percent in 1980 to 19 percent in 2002 (controlling for inflation). Between 2000 and 2005 alone, the number of East Asians living in absolute poverty fell by some 100 million. Between 1980 and 2002, life expectancy in the LDCs rose from 60 to 65 years (despite the horrendous effect of AIDS on sub-Saharan Africa).

A host of factors undoubtedly helped reduce absolute poverty and increase life expectancy, and it would be an oversimplification to attribute all of that improvement to globalization. But, at the very least, the progress in recent decades does challenge allegations that rapid globalization has further impoverished the

---

* China and India rank very high on the most widely watched indicators of *economic* globalization, particularly foreign trade and investment. On the other hand, they rank low on *Foreign Policy* magazine's respected "Globalization Index," which combines economic indicators with other measures, such as international political links, Internet usage, and the extent of foreign travel.

LDCs. Furthermore, the most dramatic declines in absolute poverty have occurred in China and other parts of East Asia (where the rate fell from about 60 percent in 1981 to 13 percent in 2002), the region most intensely linked to the global economy. During that same time period, absolute poverty in sub-Saharan Africa—the least globalized region—rose slightly from under 42 to 44 percent.[58] In Latin America, a region whose level of economic globalization falls in between East Asia's and Africa's, the rate of absolute poverty has remained static since 1981.

At the same time, while *absolute* poverty fell sharply during this period, *total* poverty (which includes both those living in absolute poverty—below $1 daily—and those living on $1–2 per day) declined more gradually, from 67 to 50 percent, with most of that decline taking place in China and East Asia. Indeed, it appears that many of those who escaped absolute poverty have only advanced to a milder form of poverty (i.e., many of those who had been living on less than $1 per day now earned $1–2 per day). Furthermore, even if the effect of globalization has generally been benign, it has also produced its share of losers. Even in a wealthy nation such as the United States, many textile mill employees and other workers in manufacturing have seen their jobs disappear when their employer moved operations to Asia or Mexico. In the Third World, where workers and peasants are not protected by Western-style unemployment compensation or other safety nets, the consequences of economic dislocations are far more severe. During the Asian financial crisis in the late 1990s, an unintended consequence of globalization, millions lost their jobs, at least for a period of time. Elsewhere, reduced trade barriers in Latin America have allowed an influx of cheap foreign imports to destroy many local industries and put their employees out of work. This has led analysts such as Joseph Stiglitz to argue that, since continued globalization seems inevitable, governments must take steps to mitigate its negative consequences on the biggest losers.[59]

Opponents of globalization maintain that the current world financial crisis shows how potentially perilous it is for developing nations to link their economies to the United States and other First World nations. Beginning with the U.S. subprime-mortgage lending debacle in 2007, America's economic troubles spread to the rest of the world causing a projected 1–3 percent decline in the world economy in 2009.[60] Third World economies are suffering from several affects of the global crisis: foreign investors have withdrawn capital from the LDCs; the value of Third World commodity exports (such as aluminum and copper) and the volume of manufactured exports have fallen (e.g., Cambodia's garment exports fell in half) as First World demand has declined; remittances (money sent home to families or friends by Third World workers employed abroad) have fallen as fewer people have been able to find work overseas.[61] The World Bank estimates that total remittances to developing countries, through rarely discussed in the West, exceeded $300 billion in 2008, substantially higher than the value of all foreign aid by developed countries.* In countries such as Haiti, Lebanon, and Honduras, these remittances account for over 20 percent of the GDP, while they are also extremely important to countries such as Bangladesh, India, Mexico, and Nigeria.[62]

---

* This figure only includes formal remittances made through banks. Some experts estimate that an equal amount of funds or more are transferred informally through friends and relatives who bring the money home personally to avoid bank fees.

But, while globalization and the economic inter-connectedness which it brings undoubtedly has worsened the effects of the current financial crisis on the LDCs, it is not clear how the Third World could have avoided those consequences. Moreover, globalization's current negative effects should not obscure the benefits it brought previously (and presumably will in the future). For example, it is true that the current crisis has reduced overseas remittances. But the vast cross-national movement of Third World workers earlier in the century (a product of globalization) had caused those remittances to nearly triple from $116 billion in 2002 to $305 billion in 2008.

CONCLUSION: DEMOCRACY AND ECONOMIC DEVELOPMENT

Earlier in this chapter, we observed that in the second half of the twentieth century, the most dynamic Third World economies were often governed by authoritarian regimes, at least at the start of their economic booms. Almost all of Asia's most impressive economic performances—in, Taiwan, South Korea, Singapore, Thailand, Malaysia, Indonesia, China, and Vietnam—emerged from authoritarian or semiauthoritarian developmental states or modified command economies. Chile initiated Latin America's most successful transition from ISI to export-led growth under General Pinochet's military dictatorship. Based on such evidence, some have argued that authoritarian governments are better equipped to start economic development because they can control workers' wage demands and can impose long-term development plans on business.

On the other hand, for every authoritarian success story, there have been several economic disasters. Corrupt dictatorships throughout Africa, the Middle East, and Latin America have plundered their country's limited wealth, created inefficient private or state monopolies, and used the economy to reward themselves and their political allies. That is, for every South Korea, Chile or Singapore, there has been a Congo, Tajikistan, and Iran, all of them authoritarian regimes that experienced *negative* average annual growth rates from 1975 to 2004 (i.e., their economies lost ground). While Chile's bureaucratic authoritarian regime performed well economically, its counterparts in Argentina and Uruguay were considerably less successful. Overall, statistical analyses of Third World economic growth rates in recent decades reveal that authoritarian governments do not perform any better than democratic ones do. And one recent study indicated that dictatorships perform less well. Bruce Bueno de Mesquita et al. ranked hundreds of specific governments worldwide for the second half of the twentieth century and compared the 179 most autocratic governments with the 176 most democratic ones (over that 50-year span, every country had multiple governments; each of those governments was counted as a different case).[63] During that period, democratic administrations achieved an average real annual growth rate (adjusted for inflation) of 3.04 percent, while autocratic governments had only 1.78 percent, a substantial gap. Moreover, the authors argue convincingly that the difference in performance has a logical explanation. Governments that need to appeal to a broad coalition of voters (democracies) are more inclined to pursue policies that promote broadly based economic gains. On the other hand, governments that owe their incumbency to a small coalition of strategic allies (dictatorships) are far more likely to be corrupt and to pursue policies designed to keep themselves in power, no matter what the cost to the national economy. In recent years, India, the world's most populous democracy, has also created one of the world's fastest-growing economies. Of course, the list of democratic governments includes both strong economic performers and weak ones, as does the list of authoritarian governments. But these findings, along with many others, offer hope that democratic governments and the worldwide movement toward democracy may produce faster economic growth as well as greater political justice. The current global economic crisis threatens to undermine the stability of some Third World governments, be they democratic or authoritarian, but so far there has not been a broad retreat from democracy.

DISCUSSION QUESTIONS

1. What do you consider the major advantages and disadvantages of globalization? What measures might be implemented to alleviate those disadvantages?
2. Under what circumstances has substantial state intervention into the economy been helpful and in what cases has it had negative effects?
3. Any nation, must resolve trade-offs between economic growth and environmental losses. If you were the leader of a developing nation, what criteria might you use to determine whether or not the economic benefits of a particular development project or private-sector investment were worth the environmental costs?

NOTES

1. Joan M. Nelson, ed., *Economic Crisis and Policy Choice: The Politics of Adjustment in the Third World* (Princeton, NJ: Princeton University Press, 1990); Dharam Ghai, ed. *The IMF and the South: The Social Impact of Crisis and Adjustment* (London: Zed Books, 1991).

2. Martin Staniland, *What Is Political Economy?* (New Haven, CT: Yale University Press, 1985), 6.

3. Ibid., 12.

4. Adapted from Adam Przeworski, *Democracy and the Market* (New York: Cambridge University Press, 1991), 105, fn. 10.

5. Ed. A. Hewett, *Reforming the Soviet Economy: Equality versus Efficiency* (Washington, DC: Brookings Institution, 1988), 38.

6. Abraham Bergson, *The Real National Income of Soviet Russia Since 1928* (Cambridge, MA: Harvard University Press, 1961), 261.

7. Harry Harding, *China's Second Revolution* (Washington, DC: Brookings Institution, 1987), 30–31.

8. Stephen White, John Gardener, and George Schopflin, *Communist and Postcommunist Political Systems* (New York: St. Martin's Press, 1990), 322; Harding, *China's Second Revolution*, 30.

9. Claes Brundenius, *Revolutionary Cuba: The Challenge of Economic Growth with Equity* (Boulder, CO: Westview Press, 1984); Carmelo Mesa-Lago, *The Economy of Socialist Cuba: A Two-Decade Appraisal* (Albuquerque: University of New Mexico Press, 1981).

10. Erich Wede and Horst Tiefenbach, "Some Recent Explanations of Income Inequality," *International Studies Quarterly*, vol. 25 (June 1981), 255–282.

11. John Sheahan, *Patterns of Development in Latin America* (Princeton, NJ: Princeton University Press, 1987), 85.

12. Dale Story, *Industry, the State, and Public Policy in Mexico* (Austin: University of Texas Press, 1986), 68.

13. Ibid., 21. These statistics are extrapolated from Story's data.

14. For startling data on overstaffing and "ghost workers" in Africa, see Richard Sandbrook, *The Politics of Africa's Economic Recovery* (New York: Cambridge University Press, 1993), 43, 61.

15. *New York Times* (November 2, 1993).

16. Ibid.

17. Howard Handelman and Werner Baer, eds. *Paying the Costs of Austerity in Latin America*

(Boulder, CO: Westview Press, 1989); Stephan Haggard and Robert R. Kaufman, eds., *The Politics of Economic Adjustment* (Princeton, NJ: Princeton University Press, 1992).

18. World Bank Development Indicators, 2002

19. Extrapolated from Sinichi Ichimura and James W. Morley, "The Varieties of Asia-Pacific Experience," in *Driven by Growth*, ed. James W. Morley (Armonk, NY: M. E. Sharpe, 1992), 6; Steven Chan, *East Asian Dynamism* (Boulder, CO: Westview Press, 1990), 8; UNDP, *Human Development Report, 1997* (New York: Oxford University Press, 1997), 21–22.

20. The World Bank, *Engendering Development* (New York and London: Oxford University Press, 2001), 207.

21. Milton and Rose Friedman, *Freedom to Choose* (New York: Harcourt Brace Jovanovich, 1980), 57; David Felix, "Review of Economic Structure and Performance: Essays in Honor of Hollis B. Chenery," *Economic Development and Cultural Change*, vol. 36, no. 1 (1987), 188–194.

22. Robert Wade, *Governing the Market: Economic Theory and the Role of Government in East Asian Industrialization* (Princeton, NJ: Princeton University Press, 1990); Gary Gereffi and Donald L. Wyman, eds. *Manufacturing Miracles* (Princeton, NJ: Princeton University Press, 1990); Stephan Haggard, *Pathways from the Periphery* (Ithaca, NY: Cornell University Press, 1990); Chalmers Johnson, "Political Institutions and Economic Performance: The Government-Business Relationship in Japan, South Korea, and Taiwan," in *The Political Economy of the New Asian Industrialism*, ed. Frederic C. Deyo (Ithaca, NY: Cornell University Press, 1987).

23. Chalmers Johnson, *MITI and the Japanese Miracle* (Stanford, CA: Stanford University Press, 1982).

24. Chan, *East Asian Dynamism*, 47–48.

25. Johnson, "Political Institutions and Economic Performance."

26. Chan, *East Asian Dynamism*, 49.

27. Haggard, *Pathways from the Periphery*.

28. Robert Wade, "Industrial Policy in Asia: Does It Lead or Follow the Market?" in *Manufacturing Miracles*, 231–266; Wade, *Governing the Market*.

29. Alice H. Amsden, *Asia's Next Giant: South Korea and Late Industrialization* (New York: Oxford University Press, 1989); see also the works by Haggard, Wade, and Johnson cited earlier in this chapter.

30. Wade, *Governing the Market*.

31. *New York Times*, "Even Amid Its Wealth, India Finds, Half Its Small Children are Malnourished" (February 10, 2007); "The Myth of the New India,"

(July 6, 2006); "Low-Tech or High, Jobs are Scare in India's Boom" (May 6, 2004).

32. *New York Times*, "A Widening Gap Erodes Argentina's Egalitarian Image" (December 25, 2006).

33. Richard Albin, "Saving the Environment: The Shrinking Realm of Laissez-Faire," in *International Political Economy*, 2d ed., eds. Jeffrey A. Frieden and David A. Lake (New York: St. Martin's, 1991), 454.

34. Bela Balassa, *The Newly Industrializing Countries in the World Economy* (New York: Pergamon Press, 1981).

35. Ibid., 84.

36. Helen Shapiro and Lance Taylor, "The State and Industrial Strategy," in *The Political Economy of Development and Underdevelopment*, 5th ed., eds. Charles K. Wilber and Kenneth P. Jameson (New York: McGraw-Hill, 1992).

37. Sheahan, *Patterns of Development*, 86–87.

38. Wade, *Governing the Market*, 34, 36.

39. Barbara Stallings and Robert Kaufman, eds., *Debt and Democracy in Latin America* (Boulder, CO: Westview Press, 1989); Handelman and Baer, *Paying the Costs of Austerity*; Haggard and Kaufman, *The Politics of Economic Adjustment*.

40. Gary Gereffi, "Paths of Industrialization: An Overview," in *Manufacturing Miracles*, 15. But, Brazil's proportion grew steadily from 8 percent in 1965 to 45 percent in 1987.

41. Irma Adelman and Cynthia Taft Morris, *Economic Growth and Social Equity in Developing Countries* (Stanford, CA: Stanford University Press, 1973).

42. Richard E. Barrett and Soomi Chin, "Export-Oriented Industrializing States in the Capitalist World System: Similarities and Differences," in *The Political Economy of the New Asian Industrialism*, 28–31; Ward, *Governing the Market*, 38.

43. Robert H. Bates, "Governments and Agricultural Markets in Africa," in *Toward a Political Economy of Development*, ed. Robert H. Bates (Berkeley: University of California Press, 1988).

44. Sheahan, *Patterns of Development*; Haggard, *Pathways from the Periphery*, chap. 1.

45. U.S. Energy Information Administration (EIA), *International Petroleum Monthly*, (October 6, 2009), http://www.eia.doe.gov/ipm/.

46. "China Building More Power Plants," *BBC News* (June 19, 2007), http://news.bbc.co.uk/2/hi/asia-pacific/6769743.stm.

47. Michael Klare, "Global Warming Battlefields: How Climate Change Threatens Security,"

Current History, vol. 106 (November 2007), 357. This section of Chapter 10 draws heavily on that article.

48. Bhaskar Nath and Ilkden Talay, "Man, Science, Technology and Sustainable Development," in *Sustainable Development*, eds. Bhaskar Nath, Luc Hens, and Dimitri Devuyst (Brussels, Belgium: VUB University Press, 1996), 36.

49. Andrew Blowers and Pieter Leroy, "Environment and Society: Shaping the Future," in *Environmental Policy in an International Context: Prospects*, eds. Andrew Blowers and Pieter Glasbergen (New York: John Wiley & Sons, 1996), 262.

50. Robin Broad and John Cavanaugh, "No More NICs," *Foreign Policy*, vol. 72 (Fall 1988), 81–103.

51. Malcolm Waters, *Globalization* (New York: Routledge, 1995).

52. Mauro F. Guillén, "Is Globalization Civilizing, Destructive or Feeble?" *Annual Review of Sociology*, vol. 27 (August 2001), 235–260.

53. S. J. Kobrin, "The Architecture of Globalization," in *Governments, Globalization, and International Business*, ed. J. H. Dunning (New York: Oxford University Press, 1997), 148. Cited in Guillén, "Is Globalization Civilizing?"

54. Thomas Friedman, *The Earth is Flat*, updated ed. (New York: Farrar, Straus, and Giroux, 2006).

55. Joseph E. Stiglitz, *Globalization and Its Discontents* (New York: W. W. Norton, 2002).

56. Almas Heshmati, "The Relationship Between Income Inequality and Globalization" (Helsinki, Finland: The United Nations University, 2003).

57. G. Firebaugh and B. Goesling, in their article "Accounting for the Recent Decline in Global Income Inequality," *American Journal of Sociology*, vol. 110, no. 2 (September 2004), 283–312, argue that inequality decreased from 1980 to 2000. Robert Wade, "Is Globalization Reducing Poverty and Inequality?" *World Development*, vol. 32 no. 4, (January 2004), 567–589, challenges those findings.

58. Unless noted otherwise, all of the statistics in this section come from the "World Bank Poverty Net," http://www.worldbank.org/.

59. Joseph E. Stiglitz, *Making Globalization Work* (New York: W. W. Norton, 2006).

60. The IMF's latest forecast was for a 1.3 percent contraction, while the World Bank recently projected a 2.0 percent decline.

61. "The Global Financial Crisis and Developing Countries" (London: Overseas Development Institute, June 2009).

62. Dilip Ratha, "Remittance flows to developing countries are estimated to exceed $300 billion in 2008," *People Move: World Bank Blog* (February 18, 2009), http://blogs.worldbank.org/.

63. Bruce Buena de Mesquita et al., "Political Competition and Economic Growth," *Journal of Democracy*, vol. 12, no. 1 (2001), 58–72.

GLOSSARY

African Union (AU) An organization representing 53 African states and seeking to promote cooperation between them. It was founded in 2002 to succeed the Organization of African Unity.

Agrarian reform Distribution of farmland to needy peasants along with the government support programs such as roads, technical assistance, and lines of credit needed to make beneficiaries economically viable.

Ancien régime The old political order. The term is often used to describe a decaying regime threatened or ousted by a revolutionary movement.

Apparatchik A career bureaucrat in the Soviet government. Often used more broadly to refer to a bureaucrat whose primary interest is in protecting his or her authority and perquisites.

Arab Afghans A term used to refer to Arabs who fought as volunteers with the fundamentalist Taliban forces in Afghanistan.

Arable land Land that is suitable for cultivation of crops.

Associated-dependent development A type of Third World industrialization based on an alliance of the local, political, economic, and military elites with multinational corporations and Western governments.

Authoritarian government (regime, system) A political system that limits or prohibits opposition groups and otherwise restricts political activity and expression.

Autonomy A substantial amount of self-rule for an ethnic group or region that falls short of full independence.

BA regimes See **Bureaucratic-authoritarian regimes.**

Barrio A poor urban neighborhood in Latin America or the Philippines.

Bourgeoisie A Marxist term (also used by non-Marxist scholars) for those who own society's productive resources, most notably businesspeople.

Bureaucratic-authoritarian regimes Military dictatorships, found most often in Latin America's more developed countries, that were based on an alliance between the military, government bureaucrats, local business elites, and multinational corporations.

Capital goods (or equipment) Goods such as machinery that are used for production of other goods rather than for consumption.

Capital-intensive production Industrial or agricultural production that relies more heavily on machinery and technology than on human labor.

Caretaker government An interim government (often military) that steps in to restore order but plans to step down relatively quickly.

Caste system A rigid social hierarchy in which each person is born with a status that he or she retains regardless of their education or achievement.

Chaebols Powerful industrial conglomerates that dominate the South Korean economy.

Christian (or Ecclesial) Base Communities (CEBs) Small Catholic neighborhood groups in Latin America that discuss religious questions and community problems. Commonly located in poor neighborhoods, many CEBs were politicized or radicalized in the 1960s and 1970s.

Civic action (programs) Development programs such as road or school construction carried out by the military.

Civil society The collection of voluntary groups in society that may influence politics, but is independent of state control.

Class consciousness A measure of how much a social class (workers, peasants, or the middle class) view themselves as having common goals that are distinct from, and often opposed to, the interests of other classes.

Clientelism The dispensing of public resources by political power holders or seekers who offer them as favors in exchange for votes or other forms of public support.

Collective farming Joint farming activity involving a peasant community, state farm, or cooperative of some sort. Collective farms are created (usually by the state) by merging formerly private farms into larger units.

Collectivization The act of merging individual farms into a collective unit. Collectivization may be undertaken voluntarily (as in the Israeli Kibbutz) or may be forced by the state against the will of the affected peasant smallholders. Forced collectivization led to considerable bloodshed in countries such as the Soviet Union.

Colonization Asserting control over a previously independent region. Also used to describe the settlement of tropical forests or other previously uninhabited areas by migrating farmers or large agricultural operations.

Coloureds A South African term coined during the period of White rule to describe people of mixed racial background.

Command economy An economy in which most of the means of production are owned and managed by the state and in which prices and production decisions are determined by state planners.

Commercialization of agriculture The process whereby subsistence farmers (i.e., those raising crops largely for their own family consumption) convert, sometimes unwillingly, to farming for the commercial market.

Communal strife (violence) Conflict between ethnic communities (such as Hindus and Muslims) usually in the same country.

Comparative advantage A country's capacity to engage in a particular economic activity efficiently and cheaply relative to other nations.

Consociationalism A division of political power between formerly antagonistic groups (such as ethnicities) based on power sharing, limited autonomy, and mutual vetoes.

Consolidated democracy Democratic government that is broadly supported by all major political participants and is therefore likely to endure for the foreseeable future.

Consumer subsidies Payments made by the state that allow consumers to purchase goods at prices below their free-market value.

Core nations The richer, industrial nations of the world.

Correlation A tendency of two or more factors (variables) to change in the same direction (e.g., higher income correlates with greater education). In a *negative* correlation, two factors vary in opposite directions (e.g., as a country's educational level goes up, its crime rate tends to go down).

Coup d'état (coup) A seizure of political power by the military.

Crony capitalism A corrupt form of capitalist development in which powerful, well-connected businessmen use their government ties to accumulate vast wealth.

Cultural pluralism A diversity of ethnic groups.

Culture of poverty A sense of powerlessness and fatalism allegedly commonly found among the urban poor.

Currency exchange rates The value of a nation's currency relative to major currencies such as the dollar or euro.

Democratic consolidation The process through which democratic norms (democratic "rules of the game") become accepted by all powerful groups in society, including labor unions, business, rural landlords, the church, and the military.

Democratic transition The process of moving from an authoritarian regime to a democratic one.

Dependency theory (or approach) A theory that attributes Third World ("the periphery") underdevelopment to its economic and political dependence on the advanced industrial nations ("the core").

Dependentista An advocate of dependency theory.

Devaluation (of a nation's currency) Allowing a currency that was previously overvalued relative to the dollar and other "hard" (stable) currencies to decline in value. Devaluation is accomplished by switching from a government-imposed, artificial (currency) exchange rate to one determined by the free market. Thus, for example, whereas the government may have previously imposed an overvalued exchange rate of, say, ten pesos per dollar, the value of the peso is allowed to drop to its free-market value of 20 pesos per dollar. This is normally done to correct a negative trade balance in which the value of imports exceeds exports.

Developmental state A government system that intervenes actively in the capitalist economy in order to guide or promote its own economic development goals.

Dirty war The military's mass violation of human rights during its fight against alleged subversive groups in countries such as Argentina and Peru.

Double day The burden facing working women, who continue to perform most of the family's domestic responsibilities (such as cooking and child care) while also working outside the home.

Economic disincentives Economic policies or practices that discourage desired outcomes, such as government-enforced low food prices that discourage agricultural production.

Economies of scale Economic efficiencies achieved through large-scale operations.

Ejido Communal farm in Mexico that was given special status under the country's agrarian reform programs.

Encyclical A letter, normally from the Pope, to all churches or all churches in some area, expressing the Church's position on matters that affect its welfare.

EOI See **Export-oriented industrialization**.

Ethnicity or ethnic group A group that feels it has common traditions, beliefs, values, and history that unite it and distinguish it from other cultures.

Export-oriented industrialization (EOI) An industrialization model heavily tied to exporting manufactured goods.

Federalism A government form that divides power between the national government and smaller governing units such as states.

First World The group of wealthy advanced industrial nations that were the first countries to develop economically—Europe, North America, Australia-New Zealand, and Japan.

Formal sector The more modern sector of the economy, encompassing businesses that are registered and operate within the legal system. Typically, companies in this sector pay taxes and frequently contribute to their workers' health and retirement systems.

Four little tigers The so-called "four little tigers" (also known as the "four little dragons") are South Korea, Taiwan, Singapore, and Hong Kong—the first Asian nations, after Japan, to develop rapidly growing, export-oriented economies.

Fundamentalism A theological doctrine that seeks to preserve a religion's traditional worldview and to resist any efforts by religious liberals to reform it. It also frequently seeks to revive the role of religion in private and public life, including dress, lifestyle, and politics. Used interchangeably with "revivalism."

GDP See **Gross domestic product**.

Gender Development Index (GDI) An index measuring a country's key social indicators (literacy, income, life expectancy) for women as compared to men.

Gender Empowerment Measure (GEM) An index of women's political and economic empowerment based on their representation in parliament, average income, and their percentage of jobs in administration, management, the professions, and technical jobs relative to men.

Gender gap A systematic difference in social status or achievement between men and women (e.g., a difference in income levels).

Gender quotas A percentage of seats in an elected legislature reserved for women.

Ghost workers Employees of state enterprises and bureaucracies who were hired for political reasons. Their labor is not needed and many of them collect paychecks while rarely, if ever, showing up for work.

Globalization The tendency of today's national economies to become increasingly intertwined and interdependent, usually coupled with increased interdependence of cultures.

Green movement The political movement seeking to preserve the environment.

Greenhouse effect (greenhouse gases) Carbon gases produced by burning fossil fuels that threaten to warm the world's climate dangerously by limiting the dispersion of heat from the atmosphere.

Gross domestic product (GDP) A measure of a nation's production that excludes certain financial transfers normally included in GNP.

Gross national product (GNP) A measure of a nation's total production (see **gross domestic product**).

Gross real domestic product Gross domestic product as measured by purchasing power rather than currency exchange.

Gulags Internment camps for political prisoners. Originating in the Soviet Union, the term is also used to describe other repressive systems.

Hacienda A Latin American agricultural estate that, until recently, often included precapitalist labor relations.

Hectare Hectare, rather than acre, is the standard measurement of farmland area in most of the world. One hectare is equivalent to 2.47 acres.

HDI See **Human Development Index**.

Historical dialectic A Marxist term used to describe the ongoing tension between particular forces in history.

Honor killings Murders of women who have allegedly "dishonored" their families by engaging in sexual activity or some related lesser "offense." Honor killings are commonly committed by close male relatives of the victim.

Human Development Index (HDI) A composite measure of educational level, life expectancy, and per-capita GDP.

Import-substituting industrialization (ISI) A policy of industrial development based on manufacturing goods domestically that were previously imported.

Indigenous population The Native American (Indian) population.

Infidel One who does not believe in religion. Often used by Islamic fundamentalists to mean one who does not believe in the Islamic religion.

Informal sector The part of the economy that is unregulated by the government while similar activities are regulated and taxed. Also defined as "all unregistered (or unincorporated) enterprises below a certain size."

Infrastructure The underlying structures (including transportation, communication, and agricultural irrigation) that are needed for effective production.

Internal warfare Military action aimed at controlling guerrilla unrest or other domestic civil insurrection.

Invisible [guiding] hand The capitalist notion that the good of society is advanced most effectively when individual actors (businesspeople, workers) seek to maximize their own economic advantage.

Iron rice bowl The Chinese government's policy, now largely disregarded, of guaranteeing employment and a basic living standard to its population.

ISI See **Import-substituting industrialization**.

Islamism Islamic fundamentalism or revivalism. A movement designed to bring the Islamic faith to its fundamental, strictly interpreted beliefs and traditions. An Islamist is a believer in Islamism.

Jihad An Islamic holy war.

Jihadist A participant in a Muslim holy war.

Khmer Rouge The communist revolutionary movement in Cambodia (Kampuchea).

Koran Divinely revealed law according to the Muslim religion.

Kulaks Wealthier peasants. Originally a term used in Russia but later applied more broadly.

Kurdistan The contiguous regions within Iran, Iraq, Turkey, and Syria that many Kurdish people believe should be their independent national homeland.

Labor-intensive industry Industries that make more extensive use of human labor, as opposed to machinery and technology. The term *labor-intensive* can be applied in other contexts, as in "labor-intensive crops" (crops, like vegetables, that require more human labor and are less easily mechanized).

Laissez faire A policy of minimal state intervention in the economy.

Latifundia Large agricultural estates.

LDCs (less developed countries) The term is used synonymously with the terms *Third World* and *developing countries*.

Liberal democracy A democracy that not only has free and fair elections, but also respects civil liberties and upholds basic freedoms.

Liberalization of the economy Reducing the degree of state intervention in the economy (referring to the eighteenth-century classical liberalism of Adam Smith).

Liberated zones Areas (most notably in the countryside) controlled by the revolutionary army. Used in China and Vietnam.

Liberation theology A reformist interpretation of Catholic doctrine that stresses the emancipation of the poor.

Little tigers See **Four little tigers**.

Lost decade The decade of the 1980s during which Africa and Latin America suffered severe economic declines.

Machismo Male chauvinism (the term originated in Latin America).

Madrasa An Islamic school. The word is sometimes used to describe a school of any kind.

Macroeconomic policy Economic policies that affect society as a whole.

Marginal (groups, population) People excluded from the mainstream of the nation's political and economic life. Usually refers to the urban poor.

Market socialism A hybrid of Marxist economics and free enterprise that has been adopted by countries such as China.

Mass mobilization The process whereby large segments of the population are activated politically. Governments or revolutionary movements may choose to mobilize the population.

Mestizos Persons of mixed Indian and European cultural heritage (Latin America).

MNC See **Multinational corporations**.

Moral economy The web of economic and moral obligations that binds a social unit together. Often used in reference to peasant–landlord relations in the countryside.

Mujahideen Islamic "freedom fighters" or guerrillas in a holy war.

Mulatto A person of mixed Black and White heritage.

Mullah A Muslim cleric.

Multinational corporations Corporations with holdings and operations in a number of countries. Overwhelmingly based in the developed world, many of them exercise considerable economic power in the Third World.

Nationality A population with its own language, cultural traditions, and historical aspirations that frequently claims sovereignty over a particular territory.

Nationalization The transfer of private firms to state ownership.

Negative correlation See **Correlation**.

Neoclassical economics Economic theory that supports a free market and little state economic intervention.

Neocolonialism Economic or cultural dominance of one sovereign nation over another.

Neoliberal reforms Economic policies, now widely in favor, based on an adaptation of Adam Smith's "classical liberalism." These reforms reduce the role of the state in the economy, enhance the role of the private sector, and allow free-market forces to operate without government interference. Specific reforms have included balancing the budget, letting the market (not government regulations) determine the value of the national currency, removing barriers to free trade, and privatizing state enterprises.

New social movements Grassroots reformist movements that are free of traditional political party ties or class-based ideologies.

NGO (nongovernmental organization) An organization at the local, national, or international level that is privately funded and had no connection with the government. Most NGOs stress grassroots organization. Commonly, the support goals such as democratization, human rights, women's rights, environmental protection, housing, health care, and education.

NIC (newly industrialized country) Countries in East Asia and Latin America (such as Taiwan and Mexico) that have developed a substantial industrial base in recent decades.

Nongovernmental organization See **NGO**.

Nurturing professions Occupations such as teaching and nursing that are commonly filled by women and that involve roles commonly associated with motherhood.

Ottoman Empire Based in what is now Turkey, the empire dated to the start of the fourteenth century. At its height (the sixteenth century), it extended into much of the Middle East (including Iraq), North Africa (Egypt and parts of Libya, Morocco, Tunisia, and Algeria), and Southeastern Europe (including much of Bulgaria, Yugoslavia, Hungary, and Romania). Its governing capacity declined sharply in the nineteenth century, and it was dissolved in 1922 following its defeat in World War I.

Parastatals Semiautonomous, state-run business enterprises, such as government-owned power plants, petroleum firms, or food processing plants.

Partial democracies Governments that have some of the elements of liberal democracy, such as competitive elections, but are not totally free.

Patron–client relations Relations between more powerful figures (patrons) and less powerful ones (clients), involving a series of reciprocal obligations that benefit both sides but are more advantageous to the patron.

Periphery Third World countries, commonly seen by dependency theorists as occupying a lesser rank in the international economy.

Personalistic military regime A form of military government in which a single officer dominates. Often that regime's legitimacy is based on his charisma or his web of contacts with powerful groups.

Pirate settlement Low-income urban settlements whose members have purchased their lots but lack legal title.

Pluralist democracy A form of government that allows a wide variety of groups and viewpoints to flourish and to engage in political activity independent of government control.

Political culture The set of political beliefs and values that underlie a society's political system.

Populist parties (populism) A multiclass, reformist political movement that promises increased welfare programs for the poor and middle class but rejects a basic restructuring of the economic order. Third World populist movements are often led by a charismatic (and sometimes demagogic) political leader.

Private sector The sector of the economy that is owned by individuals or private companies.

Privatization The process of transferring to the private sector portions of the economy formerly owned by the state.

Procedural democracy Standards of democracy based on political procedures (such as free elections) rather than outcomes (such as social justice).

Professionalized military A military whose officers receive a great degree of professional training.

Progressive church The reformist and radical wings of the Catholic Church (primarily in Latin America).

Proletariat The working class (blue-collar workers).

Proportional representation A method of electing legislatures in which voters select from party lists in multimember districts and seats are allocated in proportion to the percentage of votes each party receives.

Public sector The sector of the economy belonging to the state.

Real income (wages) The true purchasing power of one's income or wages when the effects of inflation are factored in.

Reconciliation approach A more contemporary perspective of modernization theory that holds that it is possible for LDCs to simultaneously attain some development goals that were previously considered contradictory, at least in the short run (such as early economic growth and equitable income distribution).

Relative deprivation The gap between an individual's or group's expectations or desires and their actual achievement.

Reserved seats Seats in a government body such as the national parliament that are specifically set aside for an underrepresented group such as women.

Responsibility system China's policy of transferring collective farmland to peasant owners.

Reverse wave The return to authoritarianism among some of the countries that had previously democratized. To date, the reverse wave following the Third [democratic] Wave has been more limited than the reversals that occurred after the first two democratic waves.

Revivalism Attempts to revive traditional religious practices and, sometimes, to revive the role of religion in politics. See also **Fundamentalism**.

SCIRI See **Supreme Council for the Islamic Revolution in Iraq**.

Secularization The separation of church and state and, more generally, the removal of religion from politics.

Shantytown A community of poor homes or shacks built by the inhabitants. Unlike slums, they are generally in outlying urban areas rather than the central city.

SIIC Supreme Islamic Iraqi Council. See **Supreme Council for the Revolution in Iraq**.

Single-member districts (SMD) A congressional or parliamentary electoral arrangement whereby the country is divided into a relatively large number of comparable populations and only one representative (member) is elected to the legislature in each district. SMD is largely confined to English-speaking countries such as Britain, Canada, and the United States. Other democracies generally use proportional representation.

Sites-and-services Housing arrangements in which the state sells or gives each inhabitant a legal title to a plot with basic services such as electricity and water, leaving the recipient to build his or her own home.

Smallholders Peasants owning small plots of land.

SMD See **Single-member districts**.

Social mobility The ability to move from one rank or social class in society to another.

Spontaneous shelter Urban housing built independently, and without government permission, by the occupants.

Squatter settlement Communities built by the poor who illegally or semilegally occupy unused land.

Stabilization programs Government programs, often imposed by the International Monetary Fund (IMF), to cut budget and trade deficits. The purpose is to reduce inflation and stabilize the currency.

Sub-Saharan Africa Countries in Africa below the northern tier of Arab nations. Also called Black Africa.

Subsidized housing Housing provided by the state at prices below their market value.

Substantive democracy Standards of democracy that measure government policy outcomes, such as literacy and health levels or socioeconomic equality, not just democratic procedures (as distinguished from procedural democracy).

Supreme Council for the Islamic Revolution in Iraq (SCIRI) Currently the force behind the most powerful Shi'a political party and armed militia in Iraq. It was a leader of the Shi'a resistance to Saddam Hussein and has close ties to Iran. In 2007, it changed its name to the Supreme Islamic Iraqi Council (SIIC).

Supreme Islamic Iraqi Council (SIIC) See **Supreme Council for the Islamic Revolution in Iraq (SCIRI)**.

Sustainable development Economic development that "consumes resources to meet [this generation's] needs and aspirations in a way that does not compromise the ability of future generations to meet their needs."

Technocrat A government bureaucrat with a substantial degree of technical training.

Theocracy (theocratic state) Literally defined as "the rule of God." A government ruled by or subject to religious authority and in which church and state are closely linked.

Third Wave The widespread transition from authoritarian to democratic government that has taken place in the Third World and Eastern Europe since the mid-1970s.

Third World countries Less developed countries in Africa, Asia, Latin America, and the Middle East.

Traditional society Societies that adhere to long-standing values and customs that have not been extensively transformed by modernization.

Tribe Subnational groups who share a collective identity and language and who believe themselves to hold a common lineage.

Wars of national liberation Wars of independence fought against colonial powers.

Zipper-style quotas A type of quota system for electoral lists of candidates for parliament or other government bodies, in which the candidates are ranked and the group that is assigned a quota of candidates (such as women) must be given rankings comparable to the majority group on the candidate list (in this case men).

INDEX